MINDFULNESS-BASED TREATMENT APPROACHES

CLINICIAN'S GUIDE TO EVIDENCE BASE AND APPLICATIONS

EDITED BY

RUTH A. BAER
Department of Psychology
University of Kentucky
Lexington, Kentucky

ELSEVIER

AMSTERDAM • BOSTON • HEIDELBERG • LONDON
NEW YORK • OXFORD • PARIS • SAN DIEGO
SAN FRANCISCO • SINGAPORE • SYDNEY • TOKYO

Academic Press is an imprint of Elsevier

ACADEMIC
PRESS

Academic Press is an imprint of Elsevier
30 Corporate Drive, Suite 400, Burlington, MA 01803, USA
525 B Street, Suite 1900, San Diego, California 92101-4495, USA
84 Theobald's Road, London WC1X 8RR, UK

This book is printed on acid-free paper. ⊚

Library of Congress Cataloging-in-Publication Data
Application submitted

British Library Cataloguing in Publication Data
A catalogue record for this book is available from the British Library

ISBN 13: 978-0-12-088519-0
ISBN 10: 0-12-088519-0

For all information on all Elsevier Academic Press publications
visit our Web site at www.books.elsevier.com

Printed in the United States of America
05 06 07 08 09 10   9 8 7 6 5 4 3 2 1

Working together to grow
libraries in developing countries

www.elsevier.com | www.bookaid.org | www.sabre.org

ELSEVIER   BOOK AID International   Sabre Foundation

DEDICATION

To my husband, Terry Schoen, for his undying support of my journey and his love and companionship along the way.

CONTENTS

PART I

INTRODUCTION

1

OVERVIEW OF MINDFULNESS- AND ACCEPTANCE-BASED TREATMENT APPROACHES

RUTH A. BAER AND JENNIFER KRIETEMEYER

PART II
APPLICATIONS FOR PSYCHOLOGICAL
DISORDERS IN ADULTS

2

MINDFULNESS-BASED COGNITIVE THERAPY FOR
PREVENTION OF DEPRESSIVE RELAPSE

SANDRA J. COFFMAN, SONA DIMIDJIAN,
AND RUTH A. BAER

3

INCORPORATING MINDFULNESS- AND ACCEPTANCE-
BASED STRATEGIES IN THE TREATMENT
OF GENERALIZED ANXIETY DISORDER

LIZABETH ROEMER, KRISTALYN SALTERS-PEDNEAULT,
AND SUSAN M. ORSILLO

4

MINDFULNESS-BASED APPROACHES TO EATING DISORDERS

JEAN L. KRISTELLER, RUTH A. BAER, AND RUTH QUILLIAN-WOLEVER

5

ACCEPTANCE, MINDFULNESS, VALUES, AND PSYCHOSIS: APPLYING ACCEPTANCE AND COMMITMENT THERAPY (ACT) TO THE CHRONICALLY MENTALLY ILL

PATRICIA A. BACH, BRANDON GAUDIANO, JULIEANN PANKEY,
JAMES D. HERBERT, AND STEVEN C. HAYES

6

MINDFULNESS IN DIALECTICAL BEHAVIOR THERAPY (DBT) FOR BORDERLINE PERSONALITY DISORDER

STACY SHAW WELCH, SHIREEN RIZVI, AND SONA DIMIDJIAN

PART III
APPLICATIONS FOR PSYCHOLOGICAL DISORDERS IN CHILDREN, ADOLESCENTS, AND OLDER ADULTS

7
MINDFULNESS-BASED COGNITIVE THERAPY FOR CHILDREN

RANDYE J. SEMPLE, JENNIFER LEE, AND LISA F. MILLER

8
MINDFULNESS IN DIALECTICAL BEHAVIOR THERAPY (DBT) FOR ADOLESCENTS

ELIZABETH E. WAGNER, JILL H. RATHUS, AND ALEC L. MILLER

9

"LIKE WAKING UP FROM A DREAM": MINDFULNESS TRAINING FOR OLDER PEOPLE WITH ANXIETY AND DEPRESSION

ALISTAIR SMITH

10

MINDFULNESS AND DIALECTICAL BEHAVIOR THERAPY (DBT): APPLICATION WITH DEPRESSED OLDER ADULTS WITH PERSONALITY DISORDERS

THOMAS R. LYNCH AND LESLIE L. BRONNER

PART IV

APPLICATIONS WITH MEDICAL POPULATIONS

11

MINDFULNESS-BASED STRESS REDUCTION (MBSR) AS AN INTERVENTION FOR CANCER PATIENTS

MICHAEL SPECA, LINDA E. CARLSON, MICHAEL J. MACKENZIE, AND MAUREEN ANGEN

12

MINDFULNESS-BASED STRESS REDUCTION (MBSR) WITH SPANISH- AND ENGLISH-SPEAKING INNER-CITY MEDICAL PATIENTS

BETH ROTH AND LIA CALLE-MESA

13

ACCEPTANCE AND COMMITMENT THERAPY (ACT) IN THE TREATMENT OF CHRONIC PAIN

JOANNE DAHL AND TOBIAS LUNDGREN

PART V

APPLICATIONS FOR INTERPERSONAL RELATIONSHIPS

14

MINDFULNESS-BASED RELATIONSHIP ENHANCEMENT (MBRE) IN COUPLES

JAMES W. CARSON, KIMBERLY M. CARSON, KAREN M. GIL, AND DONALD H. BAUCOM

15

DIALECTICAL BEHAVIOR THERAPY (DBT): A MINDFULNESS-BASED TREATMENT FOR INTIMATE PARTNER VIOLENCE

JILL H. RATHUS, NICHOLAS CAVUOTO, AND VINCENT PASSARELLI

PART VI
APPLICATIONS FOR STRESS REDUCTION
IN THE WORKPLACE

16

MINDFULNESS-BASED STRESS REDUCTION (MBSR)
IN A WORKSITE WELLNESS PROGRAM
KIMBERLY WILLIAMS

17

ACCEPTANCE AND COMMITMENT THERAPY (ACT)
IN THE WORKPLACE
PAUL E. FLAXMAN AND FRANK W. BOND

LIST OF CONTRIBUTORS

Numbers in parentheses indicate the pages on which the authors' contributions begin.

Maureen Angen (239), Department of Psychosocial Resources, Tom Baker Cancer Centre, Alberta Cancer Board, Calgary, Alberta, Canada T2S 3C1

Patricia A. Bach (93), Institute of Psychology, Illinois Institute of Technology, Chicago, Illinois 60616

Ruth A. Baer (3, 31, 75), Department of Psychology, University of Kentucky, Lexington, Kentucky 40506

Donald H. Baucom (309), Department of Psychology, University of North Carolina, Chapel Hill, North Carolina, 27599

Frank W. Bond (377), Goldsmiths College, University of London, New Cross, London, UK SE14 6NW

Leslie L. Bronner (217), Department of Psychiatry, Duke University Medical Center, Durham, North Carolina 27710

Lia Calle-Mesa (263), Independent Consultant, Hamden, Connecticut 06514

Linda E. Carlson (239), Department of Oncology, University of Calgary, Department of Psychosocial Resources, Tom Baker Cancer Centre, Alberta Cancer Board, Calgary, Alberta, Canada T2S 3C1

James W. Carson (309), Department of Psychiatry and Behavioral Sciences, Duke University Medical Center, Durham, North Carolina 27708

Kimberley M. Carson (309), Department of Psychiatry and Behavioral Sciences, Duke University Medical Center, Durham, North Carolina, 27708

Nicholas Cavuoto (333), Long Beach Reach, Inc., Long Beach, New York, 11561

Sandra J. Coffman (31), Independent Practice, University of Washington, Seattle, Washington 98121

JoAnne Dahl (285), Department of Psychology, Uppsala University, Uppsala, Sweden 75142

Sona Dimidjian (31, 117), Department of Psychology, University of Washington, Seattle, Washington 98125

Paul E. Flaxman (377), Goldsmiths College, University of London, New Cross, London, UK SE14 6NW

Karen M. Gil (309), Department of Psychology, University of North Carolina, Chapel Hill, North Carolina, 27599

Brandon Gaudiano (93), Department of Psychiatry and Human Behavior, Brown University Medical School, Psychosocial Research Program, Butler Hospital, Providence, Rhode Island 02906

Steven C. Hayes (93), Department of Psychology, University of Nevada, Reno, Nevada 89557

James D. Herbert (93), Department of Psychology, Drexel University, Philadelphia, Pennsylvania 19102

Jennifer Krietemeyer (3), Department of Psychology, University of Kentucky, Lexington, Kentucky 40506

Jean L. Kristeller (75), Department of Psychology, Indiana State University, Terre Haute, Indiana 47809

Jennifer Lee (143), Columbia University, Teachers College, New York, New York 10027

Tobias Lundgren (285), Department of Psychology, Uppsala University, Uppsala, Sweden 75142

Thomas R. Lynch (217), Department of Psychology and Psychiatry, Duke University and Duke University Medical Center, Durham, North Carolina 27710

Michael J. MacKenzie (239), Department of Psychosocial Resources, Tom Baker Cancer Centre, Alberta Cancer Board, Calgary, Alberta, Canada T2S 3C1

Alec L. Miller (167), Department of Psychiatry and Behavioral Sciences, Montefiore Medical Center/Albert Einstein College of Medicine, Bronx, New York 10467

Lisa F. Miller (143), Columbia University, Teachers College, New York, New York 10027

Susan M. Orsillo (51), Psychology Department, Suffolk University, Boston, Massachusetts 02114

Julieann Pankey (93), Department of Psychology, University of Nevada, Reno, Nevada 89557

Vincent Passarelli (333), Department of Psychiatry, Mood and Personality Disorders Research Program, Mount Sinai School of Medicine, New York, New York 10029

Ruth Quillian-Wolever (75), Duke University School of Medicine, Durham, North Carolina 27710

Jill H. Rathus (167, 333), Department of Psychology, C.W. Post Campus/Long Island University, Brookville, New York 11548

Shireen Rizvi (117), National Center for PTSD, Boston VA Healthcare System and Boston University School of Medicine, Boston, Massachusetts 02130

Lizabeth Roemer (51), Department of Psychology, University of Massachusetts at Boston, Boston, Massachusetts 02125

Beth Roth (263), Mindfulness Meditation Consulting, New Haven, Connecticut 06511

Kristalyn Salters-Pedneault (51), National Center for PTSD, VA Boston Healthcare System, Jamaica Plain, Massachusetts 02130

Randye J. Semple (143), New York State Psychiatric Institute, Division of Clinical and Genetic Epidemiology, Department of Psychiatry, Columbia University, New York, New York 10032

Stacy Shaw Welch (117), Evidence Based Treatment Centers of Seattle, Seattle, Washington 98101

Alistair Smith (191), Psychology Service, Lancashire Care NHS Trust, Chorley, Lancashire, UK PR7 1PS

Michael Speca (239), Department of Oncology, University of Calgary, Department of Psychosocial Resources, Tom Baker Cancer Centre, Alberta Cancer Board, Calgary, Alberta, Canada T2S 3C1

Elizabeth E. Wagner (167), Department of Psychiatry and Behavioral Sciences, Montefiore Medical Center/Albert Einstein College of Medicine, Bronx, New York 10467

Kimberly Williams (361), Department of Community Medicine, West Virginia University, Morgantown, West Virginia 26506

PREFACE

For many centuries, Eastern spiritual traditions have maintained that mindfulness meditation can lead to reduced suffering and increased well-being. In recent decades, traditional mindfulness practices have been adapted for secular use in the West, and have been incorporated into several well-researched treatment approaches that are now widely available in medical, mental health, and wellness settings. These include mindfulness-based stress reduction (MBSR), mindfulness-based cognitive therapy (MBCT), dialectical behavior therapy (DBT), and acceptance and commitment therapy (ACT). The range of problems, disorders, and populations to which these interventions are applied is growing rapidly. The empirical literature shows considerable support for their efficacy, and conceptual and theoretical understanding of how they may work has greatly advanced.

This book is unique in two ways. First, it provides a comprehensive introduction to the best-researched mindfulness-based treatments in one volume. Second, it integrates theoretical and empirical rigor with detailed clinical illustration and practical utility, providing a close-up view of how these treatments are implemented, the skills required of therapists, the responses that can be expected from participants, and the issues that professionals wishing to use these treatments must consider. The book is organized by the types of populations in which these treatments are used. The introductory chapter provides a detailed overview of MBSR, MBCT, DBT, and ACT, focusing on the methods used to teach mindfulness skills. The first section describes applications for psychological disorders in adults, including anxiety, depressive relapse, eating disorders, psychosis, and borderline personality disorder. The next section describes applications for children, adolescents, and older adults. The following sections address applications for medical populations, for improving interpersonal relationships, and for stress reduction in the workplace.

Chapters were designed to include several distinctive features. Although the treatments described vary in many ways, all have a well-developed theoretical and conceptual foundation, clearly specified treatment procedures, and strong empirical support for their efficacy. All chapters were written by clinical researchers with good scientific credentials and extensive experience in the implementation of mindfulness-based treatment with their respective populations. Each chapter includes a clear explanation of the conceptual rationale for using a mindfulness-based treatment with this population and a review of the relevant evidence base. A detailed case study illustrates how the intervention is implemented with real-world people and explores the clinical and practical issues that may arise and how they can be managed.

This book should be useful for clinicians, researchers, teachers, and students at all levels of expertise. Newcomers to this area will find helpful descriptions of mindfulness, its theoretical and conceptual underpinnings, how it might work to reduce suffering, and how these interventions can be implemented with a wide range of people. Readers with more extensive knowledge of some of these interventions can expect to broaden their understanding of the wide range of mindfulness-based approaches and gain interesting insights about their commonalities and differences. All readers are likely to find themselves inspired to further exploration of this emerging area with great potential for the treatment of numerous difficult problems and the cultivation of wisdom, insight, and happiness.

Ruth A. Baer

PART I

INTRODUCTION

1

OVERVIEW OF MINDFULNESS- AND ACCEPTANCE-BASED TREATMENT APPROACHES

RUTH A. BAER

Department of Psychology, University of Kentucky, Lexington, Kentucky

JENNIFER KRIETEMEYER

Department of Psychology, University of Kentucky, Lexington, Kentucky

INTRODUCTION

Mindfulness is a way of directing attention. Originating in Eastern meditation traditions, it is increasingly discussed and practiced in Western culture. It is generally described as intentionally focusing one's attention on the experience occurring at the present moment in a nonjudgmental or accepting way (Kabat-Zinn, 1990). It has been contrasted with states of mind in which attention is focused elsewhere, such as preoccupation with memories, fantasies, plans, or worries, and with behaving automatically, without awareness of one's actions (Brown & Ryan, 2003). Kabat-Zinn (2003) notes that mindful attention includes a stance of compassion, interest, friendliness, and open-heartedness toward the experience observed in the present moment, regardless of how pleasant or aversive it may be.

The cultivation of mindfulness through the practice of meditation has a long history in Eastern spiritual traditions, primarily Buddhism (Linehan, 1993a; Kabat-Zinn, 1982). These traditions describe mindfulness meditation as a method available to anyone for reducing suffering and encouraging the development of positive qualities, such as awareness, insight, wisdom, compassion, and equanimity (Goldstein, 2002; Kabat-Zinn, 2003). In recent decades, Western mental health professionals and researchers have argued that cultivation of mindfulness may be beneficial to people who are suffering from a wide range of problems and disorders but are uninterested in adopting Buddhist terminology or traditions. By conceptualizing traditional mindfulness meditation practices as sets of skills that can be taught independently of any religious belief system, researchers and clinicians have made mindfulness training available to Western populations by incorporating it into interventions that are increasingly offered in mental health and medical settings. These interventions include mindfulness-based stress reduction (MBSR) (Kabat-Zinn, 1982; 1990), mindfulness-based cognitive therapy (MBCT) (Segal, Williams, & Teasdale, 2002), dialectical behavior therapy (DBT) (Linehan, 1993a; 1993b), and acceptance and commitment therapy (ACT) (Hayes, Strosahl, & Wilson, 1999), as well as variations on these approaches.

Mindfulness-based interventions include many methods for teaching mindful awareness. Some of these are formal meditation practices in which participants sit quietly for periods of up to 45 minutes while directing their attention in specific ways. Others are shorter or less formal exercises emphasizing mindfulness in daily life, in which participants bring mindful awareness to routine activities such as walking, bathing, eating, or driving. MBSR and MBCT include both formal meditation and informal practices, whereas DBT and ACT emphasize primarily shorter and less formal activities and exercises in which component skills of mindfulness are practiced.

In spite of these variations, several general instructions are common to many formal and informal mindfulness practices. Often, participants are encouraged to focus their attention directly on an activity, such as breathing, walking, or eating, and to observe it carefully. They are asked to notice that their attention may wander into thoughts, memories, or fantasies. When this happens, they are asked to note briefly that the mind has wandered and then gently return their attention to the target of observation. If bodily sensations or emotional states arise, participants are encouraged to observe them carefully, noticing how they feel, where in the body they are felt, and whether they are changing over time. Urges or desires to engage in behaviors, such as shifting the body's position or scratching an itch, also are observed carefully but are not necessarily acted on. Brief covert labeling of observed experience, using words or short phrases such as "aching," "sadness," "thinking," or "wanting to move," is often encouraged. Some mindfulness exercises encourage observation of environmental stimuli, such as sounds, sights, or smells. Participants are encouraged to bring an attitude of friendly curiosity, interest, and acceptance to all observed phenomena, while refraining from evaluation and self-criticism (and noticing these non-judgmentally when they occur) or attempts to eliminate or change what they observe. For example, no attempt is made to evaluate thoughts as rational or distorted, to change thoughts judged to be irrational, to get rid of unwanted thoughts, or to reduce unpleasant emotions or sensations. Rather, cognitions, sensations, and emotions are simply noted and observed as they come and go.

Mindfulness meditation differs from concentration-based meditation approaches (such as Transcendental Meditation) in that concentration methods require restricting one's attention to a single stimulus, such as a word or syllable (e.g., a mantra), sound, object, or sensation. When attention wanders, it is redirected as soon as possible to the object of attention. Wandering is considered a distraction, and no attention is paid to the nature of the stimuli to which it wanders. Instruction in mindfulness meditation often begins with concentration-based practices in which participants focus on a specific stimulus (e.g., the breath) and return their attention to this stimulus whenever they notice that it has wandered. However, mindfulness instruction then proceeds to practices involving nonjudgmental observation of the constantly changing stream of stimuli as they naturally arise in time, including thoughts, memories, fantasies, bodily sensations, perceptions, emotions, and urges. In these practices, mind wandering is simply another event to be observed. Participants learn to notice all of these events as they occur, without making judgments about their relative worth or importance. This state of nonjudgmental observation of the constantly changing stream of stimuli as they arise is often called *bare attention* or *choiceless awareness* (Kabat-Zinn, 1982).

Mindfulness-based approaches currently are being applied with a wide range of populations, from those with recognized mental disorders or medical conditions to those seeking stress reduction or enhanced well-being. This chapter describes these interventions in a general way (independent of their application to specific disorders or populations), with emphasis on the specific mindfulness and acceptance-based skills, practices, and exercises included in each. Its purpose is to provide highly descriptive accounts for clinicians, researchers, and others who may wish to learn more about these interventions. However, most experts believe that mindfulness and acceptance cannot be thoroughly understood solely by reading about them, and therefore it is important for interested persons to find ways to explore these methods in vivo through workshops, classes, or other methods of guided practice. The remaining chapters in this volume will discuss applications to specific populations, including their conceptual and theoretical foundations, empirical support for their efficacy, and practical issues in implementing these interventions.

MINDFULNESS-BASED STRESS REDUCTION

MBSR (Kabat-Zinn, 1982; 1990) was developed in a behavioral medicine setting for patients with chronic pain and stress-related conditions. It is based on intensive training in mindfulness meditation. In its standard form it is conducted as an 8-week class with weekly sessions lasting 2.5 to 3 hours. An all-day intensive mindfulness session is held during the sixth week. Extensive homework practice of mindfulness exercises is required. Classes may include up to 30 participants with a wide range of disorders and conditions. Rather than grouping participants by diagnosis or disorder, MBSR has traditionally included individuals with a wide range of problems in each group, emphasizing that all participants, regardless of disorder, experience an ongoing stream of constantly changing internal states and have the ability to cultivate moment-to-moment awareness by practicing mindfulness skills. However, in some settings, MBSR has been applied with more specific populations, such as cancer patients, women with heart disease, or couples seeking to enhance their relationship satisfaction (Carson, Carson, Gil, & Baucom, 2004; Carlson, Speca, Patel, & Goodey, 2003; Tacon, McComb, Caldera, & Randolph, 2003).

Most MBSR programs begin with an individual or small-group orientation and assessment session, in which the group leader explains the rationale and methods of the course and encourages potential participants to ask questions and to discuss their reasons for participating. The challenge presented by the program's extensive requirements for home practice of meditation exercises is discussed, and participants are encouraged to make a verbal commitment to attending all group sessions and completing daily home practice assignments (at least 45 minutes per day, 6 days per week, as described later). Many MBSR programs also include an individual post-program interview in which experiences of the program and future goals are discussed. The eight group sessions are highly experiential, with considerable time devoted to practice of mindfulness exercises and discussion of group members' experiences with them. A wide variety of mindfulness exercises is taught. Didactic information about stress is incorporated into most sessions, including topics such as stress physiology, responding to stress, and effects of appraisals on perceptions of stress.

MINDFULNESS PRACTICES IN MINDFULNESS-BASED STRESS REDUCTION

Raisin Exercise

The raisin exercise is conducted during the first session, after group members have introduced themselves, and is the group's first mindfulness meditation activity. The group leader gives everyone a few raisins and asks participants to simply look at them, with interest and curiosity, as if they have never seen such things before. Then participants are guided through a slow process of observing all aspects of the raisins and the process of eating them. First, the participants each visually examine a single raisin, paying careful attention to all aspects of its appearance. Then they notice its texture and smell and how it feels between the fingers. Next, they put it slowly into the mouth, noticing the movements of the body while doing so. This is followed by feeling the raisin in the mouth, biting it, noticing the taste and texture, and observing the sensations and movements of the mouth and throat in chewing and swallowing the raisin. If thoughts or emotions arise during the exercise, participants are asked to notice these nonjudgmentally and return attention to the raisin.

The raisin exercise provides an opportunity to engage mindfully in an activity often done on "automatic pilot," or without awareness. Many participants report that the experience of eating mindfully is very different from their typical experience of eating, in which attention is focused elsewhere and the food is not really tasted. These comments illustrate the general point that paying attention to activities that normally are done on automatic pilot can significantly change the nature of the experience. Increased awareness of experience can lead to increased freedom to make choices about what to do in a variety of situations. Participants are encouraged to eat a meal mindfully during the week following session 1.

Body Scan

Participants are asked to lie on their backs, or to sit comfortably in their chairs, with their eyes closed. They are invited to focus their attention sequentially on numerous parts of the body, often beginning with the toes of one foot and moving slowly up the leg, then slowly through the other leg, torso, arms, neck, and head. With each body part, participants are instructed to notice the sensations that are present with openness and curiosity, but without trying to change them. If no sensations are noticeable, they simply notice the absence of sensations. This exercise differs from traditional relaxation exercises in that participants are not instructed to try to relax their muscles. If any part of the body is tense, they simply notice that it is tense. If they feel an ache or pain, they are asked to observe its qualities as carefully as they can. When their minds wander, which is described as inevitable, they are asked to notice this as best they can and gently to return attention to the body scan, without self-criticism or blame. The body scan is practiced during sessions 1, 2, and 8 and is assigned for homework practice during the first 4 weeks. Participants are provided with audiotapes to guide their practice of the body scan.

The body scan provides an opportunity to practice several important mindfulness skills, including deliberately directing attention in a particular way, noticing when attention has wandered off and returning it gently to the present moment, and being open, curious, accepting, and nonjudgmental about the observed experience, regardless of how pleasant or unpleasant it is. Several common experiences can be used to make these points during the discussion that follows the body scan. For example, some participants will worry about whether they have done it "right." It is important to point out that there is no such thing as success or failure in the body scan, because there is no goal to achieve any particular outcome, such as becoming relaxed. Relaxation may occur, but if it does not, the participant simply notices that he or she is tense.

Participants may also perceive obstacles to completing the body scan, such as sleepiness or restlessness, the mind wandering, aches or pains, or emotional states. These experiences do not mean that the exercise was unsuccessful. The task is simply to notice whatever is present without judgment. Rather than telling themselves that "this is bad," or "it shouldn't be like this," or "I need to make this different," participants are encouraged to note the presence of these phenomena, including judgmental thoughts, observe them with interest and curiosity, and return attention to the body scan.

Sitting Meditation

In sitting meditation, participants sit on a chair or meditation cushion in a comfortable posture that is both alert and relaxed. Generally the back is relatively straight and aligned with the head and neck. Eyes can be closed or gazing downward. Participants first direct their attention to the sensations and movements of breathing. When the mind wanders off, which may occur frequently, participants gently return their attention to breathing. After several minutes, the focus of attention may be shifted to bodily sensations. Participants are instructed to notice these nonjudgmentally and with acceptance, bringing an attitude of interest and curiosity even to unpleasant sensations. Urges to move the body to relieve discomfort are not initially acted on. Instead, participants are encouraged to observe the discomfort with acceptance. When they decide to move, they are encouraged to do so with mindful awareness, noticing the intention to move, the act of moving, and the changed sensations resulting from having moved.

Sitting meditation also may include a period of listening mindfully to sounds in the environment. Participants are encouraged to notice the tone quality, volume, and duration of the sounds, without judging or analyzing them, and to observe periods of silence between sounds. Next, the focus of attention may shift to thoughts. Participants are instructed to observe their thoughts as events that come and go in their field of awareness and to note thought content briefly without becoming absorbed in it. A similar approach is taken to emotions that may arise. Participants observe these, briefly note the type of emotion they are experiencing (anger, sadness, desire), and notice any thoughts or sensations associated with the emotion. In later sessions, sitting meditation may end with a period of choiceless awareness in which participants notice anything that may enter their field of awareness (bodily sensations, thoughts, emotions, sounds, urges) as they naturally arise. The mountain meditation also may be used in a later session. This practice includes images of stability, strength, and stillness during all seasons and weather conditions, which are compared to the ever-changing sensations, cognitions, and emotional states of daily experience. Sitting meditation is practiced during sessions 2–7, for periods ranging from 10 to 45 minutes, and is assigned for homework most weeks. Audiotapes for guided practice are provided.

Hatha Yoga

Hatha yoga postures cultivate mindful awareness of the body while it is moving, stretching, or holding a position. The postures are very gentle and are done slowly, with moment-to-moment awareness of the sensations in the body and of breathing. Participants are encouraged to observe their bodies carefully, to be aware of their limits, to avoid forcing themselves beyond their limits, and to avoid striving to make progress or reach goals, other than moment-to-moment awareness of the body and breathing. Thus, yoga is conceptualized as a form of meditation rather than physical exercise, although strength and flexibility may gradually increase. Yoga postures provide the opportunity to practice nonjudgmental observation and awareness of the body and acceptance of the body as it is. Careful observation of the body during yoga practice tends to reveal that the body's limits are subject to change over time. Participants sometimes report that during yoga practice they are better able to maintain a state of relaxed alertness than during the body scan and sitting meditation, which may induce boredom or sleepiness. Yoga is practiced in session 3 and assigned for homework in weeks 3–6. Participants are provided with audiotapes to guide their practice.

Walking Meditation

In walking meditation, attention is deliberately focused on the sensations in the body while walking. The gaze is generally straight ahead, rather than looking down at the feet. Attention is directed to the movements, shifts of weight and balance, and sensations in the feet and legs associated with walking. As in other meditation exercises, participants are encouraged to notice when their minds wander off and gently to bring their attention back to the sensations of walking. Walking meditation often is practiced very slowly but can be done at a moderate or fast pace. Participants typically practice by walking back and forth across a room, to emphasize the absence of a goal to reach a destination. The goal is simply to be aware of walking as it happens. In the early stages, participants are encouraged to focus their attention on the sensations in their feet and legs. Over time, they may expand their attention to include sensations in the whole body while walking.

For some participants, sitting or lying still, as required by sitting meditation and the body scan, can be anxiety provoking and may feel intolerably aversive. For these individuals, walking meditation can be a valuable introduction to mindfulness practice. For all participants, walking meditation can also be incorporated into daily life, such as while running errands or walking from their cars into their worksites and vice versa. Mindful walking in daily life can help to cultivate more continuous awareness of the mind and body in the present moment.

Mindfulness in Daily Life

Participants are encouraged to apply mindful awareness to routine activities, such as washing the dishes, cleaning the house, eating, driving, and shopping. Cultivation of mindful awareness of each moment is believed to lead to increased self-awareness and the ability to make adaptive decisions about handling difficult and problematic situations as they arise, as well as increased enjoyment of pleasant moments. Awareness of pleasant moments also is cultivated during week 2 with a pleasant-events calendar, in which participants note one pleasant event per day, along with associated thoughts, emotions, and sensations. A similar exercise in which unpleasant events are monitored is assigned during week 3. Both of these exercises promote increased understanding of habitual reactions to pleasantness and unpleasantness, including thoughts, emotions, and sensations, and the relationships between these phenomena and behavior. Mindfulness of breathing in daily life also is encouraged. It complements the formal meditative awareness cultivated in sitting meditation by promoting generalization of self-awareness to the constantly fluctuating states experienced in daily life. Turning one's attention to one's breathing at any moment of the day is intended to increase self-awareness and insight and reduces habitual, automatic, maladaptive behaviors.

DISCUSSION OF MINDFULNESS PRACTICES

Much of each weekly session is devoted to discussion of in-session and home practice of mindfulness exercises. Group leaders are encouraged to refrain from advice-giving or other behavior-change strategies. Instead, they focus on detailed exploration of the participants' experiences of mindfulness practices, while modeling a curious, open, nonjudgmental, and accepting stance toward participants' and their own experiences, no matter what they are. This attitude helps to create a safe environment for participants to disclose their experiences and to adopt an attitude of curiosity and exploration. Throughout the course, group leaders utilize the discussions to clarify the characteristics of the mindful stance that is being cultivated. The central feature of this mindful stance is nonjudgmental acceptance of whatever comes up during a mindfulness practice. Even if it is unpleasant, such as an aversive sensation, emotion, or cognition, the participant brings an attitude of friendly curiosity and acceptance to the experience. Use of metaphors may help to convey this general stance. For example, participants may be encouraged to think of themselves as explorers investigating new territory and taking a strong interest in everything they discover, regardless of how pleasant or unpleasant it may feel.

Discussion of experiences that are perceived as obstacles or problems is especially important. Participants may state that they had trouble practicing because they felt sleepy or restless, they were distracted by noises in the environment (barking dogs, traffic, etc.), that their minds wandered a lot, or that they had negative thoughts about mindfulness practice being a waste of time or of no help to them. All of these experiences are accepted with openness and curiosity and are explored nonjudgmentally. Group leaders encourage participants to notice and take an interest in these experiences without trying to change them, and to return attention to the mindfulness exercise as best they can. It is important to clarify that mindful acceptance does not imply passivity or helplessness. Participants who experience pain or discomfort during meditation may choose to change their position to relieve pain, put on a sweater or open a window, or let the dog in or out to reduce barking. However, the decision to engage in any of these actions is made with mindful awareness.

THE ALL-DAY MEDITATION SESSION

During this session, usually held during week 6 of the program, participants engage in sitting and walking meditations, body scans, and yoga. Most of the day is spent in silence, except for instructions provided by the group leaders. Participants are encouraged not to speak to each other or to make eye contact. Although some participants may find the day enjoyable and relaxing, this is not the goal for the session. The goal is to be present with and accepting of whatever comes up during the day. Some participants may experience physical discomfort or pain from extended sitting meditation, whereas others may feel strong emotions that they usually attempt to avoid. Some may feel bored, anxious, or guilty about spending a day in which their usual tasks are not done. The extended period of silence encourages more intensive self-awareness and provides the opportunity to practice nonjudgmental observation of experience, without engaging in habitual avoidance strategies such as busying oneself with tasks, talking to others, reading, or watching TV. This experience can be stressful for some participants and enjoyable for others. Many will report a mix of pleasant and unpleasant experiences during the day. Participants are encouraged to let go of expectations about how the day "should" feel, or what "should" happen, but to remain mindfully aware of everything that unfolds. At the end of the day a group discussion is held, in which participants talk about their experiences.

INCORPORATION OF POETRY

As the nature of mindfulness can be difficult to convey in ordinary language, many MBSR instructors include the reading of poetry in their weekly sessions. Poems by a wide range of authors can be used to illustrate important elements of mindfulness. For example, "The Guest House," by Rumi, a thirteenth-century Sufi poet, uses simple but expressive language to describe a welcoming stance toward all internal experience. Poems or readings by Rilke, Mary Oliver, David Whyte, and others may be used to illustrate other important themes, such as awareness of moment-to-moment experience, recognition of internal wisdom, and experiencing life's difficulties within a wider perspective. MBSR instructors may choose to share other poems, readings, or stories that they find inspiring and potentially helpful to group members.

HOMEWORK

Homework generally includes 45 minutes of formal mindfulness practice, often guided by audiotapes provided by the group leaders, and 5–15 minutes of informal practice, 6 days per week. Homework is described as critically important in developing mindfulness skills and learning new ways to relate to experience. Instructors emphasize that discipline is required to practice daily, even when we do not feel like doing so. Regular mindfulness practice is described as a challenge and an adventure, rather than a chore. It may be helpful to encourage participants to suspend judgment about the value of meditation for the duration of the program and to do the homework with an attitude of exploration and experimentation, regardless of whether they like it or can perceive immediate benefits. When participants report that they have failed to do homework during a preceding week, group leaders express interest in and curiosity about their experiences surrounding the homework. Acceptance of all experiences is encouraged, including boredom, irritation, emotional reactions, and fears and uncertainties about how meditation may help. Group leaders express nonjudgmental interest in any other factors that may have interfered with their homework practice, acknowledge the difficulty of regular practice, and encourage participants to bring their own curiosity to bear on the situation so that they might find ways to engage in the homework more regularly. A punitive or critical attitude is avoided.

TEACHER QUALIFICATIONS

The Center for Mindfulness at the University of Massachusetts Medical School, where MBSR originated, provides guidelines for qualifications for MBSR instructors. Minimum qualifications include a master's degree in a mental health field; daily meditation practice; attendance at two silent, teacher-led meditation retreats of 5–10 days duration in the Theravadan or Zen traditions; 3 years experience with Hatha yoga or other body-centered disciplines; 2 years experience teaching stress reduction and yoga or other body-centered discipline in a group setting; and completion of a 5- or 7-day residential professional training program in MBSR. Required skills include translating mindfulness practice into accessible language, establishing effective and compassionate relationships with a wide range of clients, and facilitating interaction in diverse patient/client groups. In addition, several attitudinal qualities are described as central to the ability to teach MBSR effectively. These include nonjudging, patience, a beginner's mind, trust, nonstriving, acceptance, and letting go. These qualities are described as attitudes to be purposefully cultivated through mindfulness practice and an ongoing commitment to lifelong learning, rather than as prerequisites that MBSR teachers should already have mastered. In general, MBSR emphasizes continuity of experience between instructors and participants. All are expected to practice mindfulness regularly, and the experiences that may arise, such as self-critical or judgmental thoughts, negative emotion, impatience, and lack of acceptance, are seen as common to all persons, rather than specific to those seeking help. That is, instructors and group members are all participating in the same enterprise. Additional information about MBSR can be found on the website of the Center for Mindfulness at the University of Massachusetts Medical School (www.umassmed.edu/cfm).

MINDFULNESS-BASED COGNITIVE THERAPY

MBCT is based largely on MBSR and uses many of its components. The raisin exercise, body scan, sitting meditation, yoga, and walking meditation all are incorporated into MBCT, as are informal practices of mindfulness in daily life, such as mindfulness while washing the dishes, brushing one's teeth, and taking out the garbage. Poetry is incorporated into several of the sessions. Like MBSR, MBCT also includes monitoring

but the other person walks by without seeming to notice. Participants are invited to describe the thoughts, feelings, and sensations they experience when imagining this scenario. Participants' contributions to this discussion then are used to explain and illustrate the ABC model, in which a situation (A) leads to a thought or interpretation (B) that leads to a feeling or emotion (C). An important idea emerging from this discussion is that different thoughts at B can lead to different emotions at C. This leads to the important concept that thoughts are not facts. Furthermore, we are not always aware of the thoughts occurring at B, even though they may have powerful effects on our emotions. Because thoughts can have strong influence on our moods, it is important that we learn to be more aware of them. Practicing mindfulness skills will help to develop this awareness.

Discussion of Automatic Thoughts

Session 4 includes a discussion of automatic thoughts related to depression, taken from the Automatic Thoughts Questionnaire (Hollon & Kendall, 1980). Examples include "I'm no good" and "My life is a mess." The purpose of this exercise is to help participants learn to recognize the types of thoughts that are typical symptoms of depression and to see them as such rather than as true statements about themselves. Group leaders emphasize that the believability of these thoughts changes with one's mood. That is, during an episode of depression, we tend to believe that these thoughts are true. When in remission, we believe them much less. This point illustrates the importance of seeing our thoughts as mental events rather than as representations of truth or reality.

Moods, Thoughts, and Alternative Viewpoints Exercise

This exercise occurs in Session 6 and requires imagining two slightly different scenarios. First, participants imagine that they are feeling down because they've just had an argument with a colleague at work. Shortly afterward they see another colleague who rushes off quickly, saying he or she cannot stop to talk. Participants are asked to write down what they would think in this situation. Next, they imagine the scenario slightly differently: They are feeling happy because they have just been praised for good work, when they see a colleague who hurries away, saying he or she cannot stop to talk. They write down what they would think in this situation. Participants' responses usually illustrate that our thoughts are influenced by our moods. In the first scenario we may think that the colleague in a rush is avoiding or rejecting us, whereas in the second we may wonder about the colleague's well-being. This exercise also illustrates that our thoughts can have powerful influence on our feelings but that our thoughts vary so much with changing circumstances that they cannot be regarded as facts. However, our tendency to believe our thoughts is very strong. Practicing mindfulness of thoughts will help us to remember that they are not facts and to allow them to come and go.

PLEASURE AND MASTERY ACTIVITIES

This exercise occurs in session 7 and is based on the recognition that taking action can be a critical step in the prevention of depressive episodes. When mood is low, motivation to engage in activities is also low. However, as lowered activity level often worsens depression, it is important to be able to increase activity level even when we do not feel like doing so. Under these conditions, it is useful to understand two types of activities that might lift one's mood: pleasure and mastery activities. Pleasure activities are fun or enjoyable, such as watching a movie, talking with a friend, or eating a delicious dessert. Mastery activities provide a sense of accomplishment, pride, or satisfaction in having achieved something, such as paying bills, buying groceries, or completing work-related tasks. Participants are asked to generate lists of such activities that they could engage in at times when their mood is low. These lists then become useful in the development of relapse prevention action plans.

RELAPSE PREVENTION ACTION PLANS

In the final two sessions, participants work on developing relapse prevention action plans that incorporate the skills taught in the preceding sessions. Participants are encouraged to make lists of their "relapse signatures," or signs that a depressive episode might be developing. Common examples include increased irritability, decreased motivation, social withdrawal, and changes in eating and sleeping habits. Participants then generate action plans to use when they notice these signs. The first step of a relapse prevention action plan is always to take a 3-minute breathing space in order to reconnect with the present moment. The second step is to engage in one of the mindfulness activities they have learned in the group, perhaps with the guidance of an audiotape, or to review the mindfulness principles they have learned and remind themselves of the points that have been most helpful during the group. The third step is to choose actions from their lists of pleasure and mastery activities, and to engage in them, even if they do not feel like doing so. Strategies for counteracting the resistance they may experience when their mood drops are incorporated. For example, they may write at the top of their plan that it is important to do these things even if they feel unmotivated. They are encouraged to act mindfully while engaging in these activities by noticing what they are doing as it occurs (walking down the stairs, turning on the light, etc.). They are also advised to be willing to try a variety of these activities and to be open-minded and nonjudgmental about their potential effects.

TEACHER QUALIFICATIONS

The developers of MBCT have not proposed a formal set of qualifications for teachers. However, they note that training in counseling or psychotherapy, cognitive therapy, and leading groups is important. It is also essential to have one's own regular mindfulness practice, to interact effectively with patients or clients who are engaging in regular practice. The authors of MBCT use a swimming analogy to illustrate this point. An effective swimming instructor knows how to swim and probably swims regularly. Similarly, adopting a mindful, accepting stance toward the range of experience requires regular practice. More information about MBCT, including theory, methods, and an outline of each session, can be found in Segal *et al.* (2002).

MINDFULNESS SKILLS IN DIALECTICAL BEHAVIOR THERAPY

DBT is a multifaceted treatment program originally developed for borderline personality disorder (BPD), and recently adapted for use with other populations. It is based on a dialectical worldview that emphasizes the balance, integration, or synthesis of opposing ideas. The central dialectic in DBT is the integration of acceptance and change. DBT includes a variety of cognitive-behavioral strategies designed to help clients change their thoughts, emotions, and behaviors. It also includes training in mindfulness skills in order to facilitate the synthesis of acceptance and change. Linehan (1994) suggests that many clients with BPD may be unwilling to engage in the extended meditation practices of MBSR and MBCT. Thus, DBT relies instead on a large selection of shorter, less formal mindfulness exercises. Standard outpatient DBT generally includes an initial commitment to participate in therapy for one year. During this time, clients participate in weekly individual therapy and skills training group sessions. The skills training group includes four modules of skills: core mindfulness, interpersonal effectiveness, emotion regulation, and distress tolerance skills. Clients work with their individual therapists on applying skills learned in the group to their daily lives. The following paragraphs describe only the mindfulness-based elements of DBT. More detailed information about the entire treatment package can be found in Linehan (1993a; 1993b).

CORE MINDFULNESS MODULE

This module begins by providing a rationale for practicing mindfulness skills. One very important goal is to develop the ability to control one's attention. Lack of ability to direct one's attention leads to several common problems, including inability to stop thinking about the past, the future, or current difficulties, and inability to concentrate on important tasks. More generally, the goal of mindfulness skills in DBT is to develop wisdom, or the ability to see what is true and to act wisely. A useful metaphor is that life is like trying to move across a large room full of bulky furniture. It is easier to do this when our eyes are open. Developing mindfulness is like opening our eyes so that we can see what is truly there.

States of Mind

This module then continues with an overview of three states of mind. *Reasonable mind* is the rational, logical part of the mind that thinks intellectually, knows facts, makes plans, and solves problems. It can be described as the "cool" part of the mind and is a valuable asset. Without it, we could not balance checkbooks, make grocery lists, complete school work, or repair household items, nor would we have computers, skyscrapers, or medical advances.

Emotion mind is the state in which emotions control one's thoughts and behaviors. It is difficult to be reasonable or logical while in emotion mind. Perceptions of reality may be distorted to fit the ongoing emotional state. It can be described as the "hot" part of the mind and is also a valuable asset. It can motivate heroic behavior, such as risking one's safety to help others, and can facilitate creative or artistic achievements. It includes being passionate about things, which may lead to important accomplishments and contributions. An imbalance in these states of mind can cause difficulties. For example, if we allow strong feelings to propel us into behaviors we later regret, such as angry outbursts, then emotion mind is too strong. For individuals with BPD, who often have very strong emotions, this is a common occurrence. However, it is also possible to be too rational. For example, offering only logical solutions to a troubled loved one who needs empathic understanding suggests that reasonable mind is too strong.

Wise mind is described as the integration of reasonable mind and emotion mind. It balances and integrates both and thus can be seen as the synthesis of a dialectic involving emotion and reason. Wise mind can include knowledge of facts, but it also includes intuitive forms of knowing. It is sometimes described as a "centered" or "grounded" type of knowing that includes both head and heart. In DBT, wise mind is conceptualized as a universal human capability. That is, everyone has wise mind, or the capacity to develop wisdom. Practicing the mindfulness skills described next is a method for balancing reasonable and emotion mind and accessing the wise mind.

Mindfulness "What" Skills

The three "what" skills specify what one does when being mindful. They include observing, describing, and participating. *Observing* refers to noticing, sensing, or attending to the experience occurring in the present moment, without trying to change or escape it. Targets of observation can include internal experiences such as thoughts, bodily sensations, emotional states, or urges, as well as stimuli in the environment, such as sights, sounds, and smells. Participants are encouraged to notice that observing an event is distinct from the event itself. That is, observing one's thinking can be distinguished from thinking. Observing oneself feeling sad is distinct from feeling sad. Group members are encouraged to try a variety of practice exercises, such as putting one hand on the table surface and observing the sensations, or rubbing a finger across their upper lip and noticing what they feel. In another exercise, participants imagine that the mind is a conveyor belt that brings thoughts, feelings, and sensations into awareness. Each is observed as it appears. Group leaders emphasize that anything that enters awareness while practicing this exercise can be observed, including wandering of the mind and negative thoughts. Rather than interpreting these occurrences as failures to do the exercise, group members simply practice observing whatever happens.

Describing refers to labeling observed experience with words. This exercise can be applied to all observed experience and is especially useful when applied to thoughts and feelings. Labeling thoughts as thoughts encourages recognition that they are not necessarily true or important. For example, thinking "I can't do this" is not the same as being unable to do it. Recognizing the presence of such thoughts may reduce the tendency to believe them or act on them in automatic, maladaptive ways. The same principle applies to emotions and urges. For example, a group member may feel bored while practicing a mindfulness exercise and wish to stop. Covertly describing this experience in words ("I'm feeling bored and wishing to stop this") can lead to the important realization that feelings and urges do not have to control behavior. That is, one can choose to engage in specific behaviors in spite of one's feelings or urges. The conveyor belt exercise can be used to illustrate this important point. All thoughts, emotions, sensations, and urges that come along the belt are labeled ("thoughts about work," "desire to eat") but are not acted on.

Participating refers to attending completely to the activity of the present moment, becoming wholly involved with it, and acting with spontaneity and without self-consciousness. It can be practiced in group sessions by engaging in a group activity, such as singing a song or playing a brief game. Participants are encouraged to throw themselves into the activity as completely as possible. If they have thoughts ("This is silly") or emotions (embarrassment), they are asked simply to notice these briefly and return their attention to the activity. Afterward, the difference between participating fully in the activity and being distracted by thoughts or feelings can be discussed. Group members also can be encouraged to find activities in which they can practice participating outside of sessions, such as exercise, dancing, yoga, music, an art or craft, cooking, or another activity. An important goal of mindfulness practice is to develop a generalized pattern of participating with awareness in daily life. Participating without awareness, or acting mindlessly, is seen as a characteristic of impulsive and mood-dependent behavior.

Mindfulness "How" Skills

DBT includes three "how" skills: nonjudgmentally, one-mindfully, and effectively. Being nonjudgmental means taking a nonevaluative stance toward experience, in which the individual refrains from judging experiences as good or bad. Helpful or harmful consequences can be acknowledged, as can feelings of attachment and aversion, but all experiences are accepted as they are, just as a blanket spread out on the grass is equally accepting of rain, sun, leaves, and insects that land on it. It is important to note that being nonjudgmental does not mean replacing negative judgments with positive ones, nor does it imply approval of experience. It also does not mean abandoning negative reactions or dislikes. For example, disliking peanut butter is not a judgment. Rather, an aversion to peanut butter can be mindfully observed and accepted without judgment. Being nonjudgmental can be practiced in group sessions during any group activity. Participants are encouraged to notice any judgmental thoughts (e.g., "This is silly") and then to observe and describe the facts of the situation (e.g., "We are eating raisins, I am feeling aversion"). Group members are encouraged to do the same in their daily lives.

To be one-mindful is to focus undivided attention on one thing at a time. One-mindfulness may be atypical of many people's daily experiences, which often involve attempts to do two or more things at once. One-mindfulness can be practiced in group sessions with numerous activities. For example, participants can be encouraged to devote their full attention to listening to others during discussions. Food can be brought to sessions for practice of eating one-mindfully. Group members can also practice being one-mindful with numerous behaviors of daily life, such as washing dishes, bathing, petting the cat, etc.

Behaving effectively refers to doing what works or using skillful means. It includes being practical, recognizing the realities of a situation, identifying one's goals in the situation, and thinking of effective ways to achieve them, in spite of one's personal preferences or opinions about how the situation should be. It sometimes refers to being political or savvy, and includes doing this well.

Teaching Mindfulness in Dialectical Behavior Therapy

Teaching mindfulness as a DBT therapist involves several steps. Therapists must prepare by planning mindfulness exercises and practicing them in advance. Unlike MBSR and MBCT, DBT does not stipulate that therapists must have an ongoing formal mindfulness practice. However, the therapist's level of familiarity and understanding of mindfulness is important, and at a minimum, DBT therapists must have a clear understanding of the mindfulness exercises they teach. This will generally require personal experience in practicing them. Therapists then must orient the group to the mindfulness activity and lead the exercise by participating in it along with the group members. This will ensure that teaching is based on the leader's experience with the exercise. As in MBSR and MBCT, sharing and discussion of experiences occurs immediately after the exercise and provides the opportunity to address obstacles and problems that arise. In DBT, these are very similar to those described in earlier sections on MBSR and MBCT. Participants may say that they "couldn't do it" because their attention wandered, they felt unwanted sensations or emotions, or were distracted by noise. At these times, leaders point out that the fact that they noticed these experiences means that they were doing the exercise. Participants may also report frustration or discouragement if they cannot see immediate benefits from doing the exercise. Teachers must empathize with the difficulty but point out that mindfulness involves repeated practice. The paradox of letting go of goals while continuing to practice regularly is also discussed.

MINDFULNESS SKILLS IN EMOTION REGULATION AND DISTRESS TOLERANCE

The emotion regulation and distress tolerance modules of skills training also include many elements of mindfulness. In emotion regulation, identifying and labeling emotions is an essential component. This requires the application of the mindfulness skills of observing and describing. Clients are instructed in methods for observing and describing many aspects of an emotional reaction, including the event that prompted it, their interpretations of the event, their subjective experience of the emotion (including bodily sensations), action urges they felt, behaviors they engaged in, and the aftereffects of the emotion. Mindfulness of current emotions also is taught as a method for reducing the suffering associated with negative emotions. It includes experiencing emotions as they occur, without judging them or trying to suppress, change, or block them. The inevitability of negative emotions as a normal part of life is emphasized. Observing them carefully, and accepting them as they arise, functions as an exposure procedure, reducing secondary reactions to emotional experiences. Many individuals with BPD find that experiencing a negative emotion leads to secondary reactions, such as guilt, shame, panic, or anger about having the initial emotion. These secondary reactions often cause more suffering than does the initial emotion. Thus, nonjudgmental acceptance of initial emotions can be very helpful in reducing secondary reactions.

The distress tolerance module explains that pain is an unavoidable part of life, and emphasizes the importance of learning to bear pain skillfully. Several of the skills taught are direct extensions of the core mindfulness skills. These emphasize acceptance of reality, even when it is unpleasant and unwanted, and willingness to experience life as it is in each moment. The concept of radical acceptance is introduced, in which painful realities are fully acknowledged and fruitless efforts to change the unchangeable are abandoned. Distress tolerance skills are intended for situations in which painful realities or feelings cannot, at least for the moment, be changed. They allow survival of such situations without engaging in maladaptive behaviors that will create additional problems or make things worse. Skills for accepting reality as it is include several exercises involving awareness of breathing, such as counting breaths, noting in-breaths and out-breaths by silently saying "inhaling" and "exhaling" as these occur, counting breaths while walking, or following the breath while listening to music. Other skills for accepting reality include engaging in simple behaviors, such as making tea or washing dishes, slowly and with full awareness, noting every movement. These exercises are adapted from mindfulness meditations described by Hanh (1976).

MINDFULNESS AND RELATED SKILLS IN ACCEPTANCE AND COMMITMENT THERAPY

ACT is a general approach to psychotherapy that can be applied to a wide range of problems and disorders. It incorporates both behavior-change processes and mindfulness and acceptance processes. Change strategies are tailored to the needs of each client and might include psychoeducation, skills training, problem-solving, exposure, or other strategies. Mindfulness and acceptance skills facilitate the behavior changes necessary for the client to pursue a life that feels vital and meaningful.

A central concept in ACT is experiential avoidance, which is defined as unwillingness to experience negative internal phenomena, such as feelings, sensations, cognitions, or urges, and taking action to avoid, escape, or eliminate these experiences, even when doing so is harmful. ACT contends that many forms of psychopathology are related to fruitless and counter-productive efforts to avoid negative internal experiences, by engaging in behaviors such as substance abuse, dissociation, binge eating, or avoidance of people, places, and situations that elicit them. Experiential avoidance is positively correlated with psychopathology (Hayes, Wilson, Gifford, Follette, & Strosahl, 1996). In addition, laboratory studies of emotion and thought suppression have shown that the more one tries to avoid particular thoughts and feelings, the more likely one is to experience them (Gross, 2002). In place of experiential avoidance, ACT teaches psychological flexibility, which includes willingness to experience the present moment as it is and act in accordance with one's chosen values. Psychological flexibility has the following interrelated components, many of which involve mindfulness processes. Mindfulness exercises in ACT are so numerous and varied that only a few examples are described here. Others are discussed in Chapters 3, 5, 13, and 17 in this volume. More detailed information can be found in Hayes *et al.* (1999).

ACCEPTANCE AND COGNITIVE DEFUSION

Acceptance involves nonjudgmental awareness and openness to cognitions, emotions, and sensations as they occur. It includes explicit abandonment of efforts to control experiences that are not readily controllable or are subject to paradoxical increases in frequency and intensity when efforts are made to get rid of them. It promotes exposure to previously avoided experiences, such as anxiety, by focusing full attention sequentially on each of its elements (e.g., sweaty palms, rapid heart rate) and noticing the characteristics of each sensation and the possibility of experiencing it without avoidance or harm. Cognitive defusion involves teaching clients to observe their thoughts and the process of thinking without assuming that thoughts are true or important and without always behaving in accordance with their content. It reduces the behavioral impact of thoughts, as individuals come to see their thoughts as events to be noticed but not necessarily believed. It includes the idea that thoughts are not inherently harmful and can be noticed and allowed to come and go, no matter how aversive their content. In fact, harm is more likely to occur when attempts are made to control or eliminate thoughts seen as undesirable. Cognitive defusion is consistent with traditional cognitive therapy procedures that include detecting and monitoring thoughts and viewing them as hypotheses to be tested. However, cognitive defusion does not include analyzing, disputing, or changing the content of thoughts. A wide range of defusion exercises are available in ACT. Many are entirely consistent with mindfulness practices in other treatment approaches, including nonjudgmental, nonreactive observation and labeling of thoughts. For example, in the *leaves on a stream* exercise, participants are asked to close their eyes and imagine a stream with leaves floating on it. As thoughts arise, they place each one on a leaf and watch it float down the stream. The *soldiers in the parade* exercise is similar, except that thoughts are pictured on signs carried by parading soldiers. The ultimate purpose of defusion is to allow constructive behavior even in the presence of unwanted thoughts. For example, the individual who is fused with the thought, "This is going to be a disaster," when facing a challenging task is likely to believe the thought, experience related emotions (such as dread), and behave accordingly. Defusion allows the individual to notice the thought as a thought and allow it to come and go while pursuing constructive actions.

CONTACT WITH THE PRESENT MOMENT AND SELF-AS-CONTEXT

ACT uses mindfulness exercises to encourage noticing and observing whatever is present in the external and internal environments and applying descriptive labels to these experiences without excessive judgment or evaluation, regardless of how unpleasant the experiences feel. If aversion is present, it is observed and described without judgment. As experiential avoidance and cognitive fusion are the primary obstacles to this state of awareness, ACT encourages recognition of the self as the context in which cognitions, emotions, and sensations occur, rather than as synonymous with those experiences. For example, when having the thought, "I'm an idiot," clients are taught to say to themselves, "I'm having the thought that I'm an idiot." Adding this short phrase ("I'm having the thought that...") facilitates recognition that the self is separate from the thoughts and feelings that pass through awareness and reduces fusion with these experiences. This greatly reduces the potentially threatening quality of many internal experiences, as the individual recognizes that he or she is capable of having a wide range of thoughts and feelings without being harmed by them and that these experiences tend to be transient and insubstantial. The observer exercise promotes this awareness by asking the client to close her eyes, observe internal experiences (memories, body, emotions, thoughts), and then to notice the aspect of herself that does the observing (the observer-self). Many clients can readily see that the observer-self has been present throughout the client's entire life, whereas emotions, cognitions, bodily states, and other internal experiences have continually come and gone.

VALUES AND COMMITTED ACTION

ACT differs from other mindfulness-based interventions in the explicit attention it pays to clients' most deeply held values and goals in life, and to the behavior changes that may be necessary to pursue them. ACT includes exercises and discussions about clients' goals and values in areas such as career, intimate relationships, personal growth, health, and citizenship.

For example, the client may be asked what he would most like to have written on his tombstone. This may lead to identification of specific behaviors necessary to attain relevant goals, such as attending more social events, returning to school, or spending more time with his children. Clients are encouraged to make commitments to engage in the relevant behaviors. Obstacles that are preventing them from doing so are examined. Quite often these are psychological, such as anxiety, sadness, or thoughts about inability to succeed. Acceptance, defusion, being present, and self-as-context then serve as valuable tools in helping the client to overcome such obstacles. For example, the client who would like to make professional contributions in a particular field but has avoided the necessary training for fear of failure can be encouraged to defuse from failure-related thoughts, to accept the inevitable anxiety associated with pursuing challenging goals, to remain present with whatever occurs in each moment (thus increasing the likelihood of managing it well), and to remember that she is not a "failure" but rather a person who sometimes has thoughts about failure. Thus, mindfulness skills are not practiced solely for their own sakes, but rather to facilitate progress toward a life that is meaningful to the client.

CONCLUSION

Many differences between existing mindfulness and acceptance-based interventions can be noted. MBSR and MBCT emphasize lengthy meditation practices, whereas DBT and ACT emphasize shorter and less formal mindfulness exercises. ACT was originally developed as an individual therapy, whereas MBSR and MBCT are group interventions, and standard DBT includes both group and individual sessions. Duration of treatment can range from as little as a few weeks in some focused applications of ACT (e.g., Bach & Hayes, 2002) to a year or more in DBT. MBSR and MBCT emphasize primarily acceptance-based strategies, whereas DBT and ACT include many behavior-change strategies. MBSR and ACT were developed to treat a wide range of problems, whereas DBT and MBCT each were initially developed for one particular disorder (although other applications are emerging). MBSR and MBCT explicitly require that teachers/therapists have an ongoing meditation practice, whereas DBT and ACT have less specific recommendations. However, the commonalities among these treatments may be more important than their differences. All have attempted to operationalize and teach a particular way of paying attention to present-moment experience that until recent years has received very little attention in Western culture, yet may have significant potential for reducing symptoms and improving well-being in a wide range of populations. The following chapters in this volume illustrate this potential.

REFERENCES

Bach, P., & Hayes, S. C. (2002). The use of acceptance and commitment therapy to prevent the rehospitalization of psychotic patients: A randomized controlled trial. *Journal of Consulting and Clinical Psychology, 70,* 1129–1139.

Brown, K. W., & Ryan, R. M. (2003). The benefits of being present: Mindfulness and its role in psychological well-being. *Journal of Personality and Social Psychology, 84,* 822–848.

Carlson, L. E., Speca, M., Patel, K. D., & Goodey, E. (2003). Mindfulness-based stress reduction in relation to quality of life, mood, symptoms of stress, and immune parameters in breast and prostate cancer outpatients. *Psychosomatic Medicine, 65,* 571–581.

Carson, J. W., Carson, K. M., Gil, K. M., & Baucom, D. H. (2004). Mindfulness-based relationship enhancement. *Behavior Therapy, 35,* 471–494.

Goldstein, J. (2002). *One dharma: The emerging Western Buddhism.* San Francisco: HarperCollins.

Gross, J. J. (2002). Emotion regulation: Affective, cognitive, and social consequences. *Psychophysiology, 39,* 281–291.

Hanh, T. N. (1976). *The miracle of mindfulness.* Boston: Beacon Press.

Hayes, S. C., Strosahl, K., & Wilson, K. G. (1999). *Acceptance and commitment therapy.* New York: Guilford Press.

Hayes, S. C., Wilson, K. G., Gifford, E. V., Follette, V. M., & Strosahl, K. (1996). Emotional avoidance and behavioral disorders: A functional dimensional approach to diagnosis and treatment. *Journal of Consulting and Clinical Psychology, 64,* 1152–1168.

Hollon, S. D., & Kendall, P. C. (1980). Cognitive self-statements in depression: Development of an Automatic Thoughts Questionnaire. *Cognitive Therapy and Research, 4,* 383–396.

Kabat-Zinn, J. (1982). An outpatient program in behavioral medicine for chronic pain patients based on the practice of mindfulness meditation: Theoretical considerations and preliminary results. *General Hospital Psychiatry, 4,* 33–47.

——— (1990). *Full catastrophe living: Using the wisdom of your body and mind to face stress, pain, and illness.* New York: Delacorte.

——— (2000). Indra's net at work: The mainstreaming of dharma practice in society. In G. Watson & S. Batchelor (Eds.), *The psychology of awakening: Buddhism, science, and our day-to-day lives.* North Beach, ME: Weiser.

——— (2003). Mindfulness-based interventions in context: Past, present, and future. *Clinical Psychology: Science and Practice, 10,* 144–156.

Linehan, M. M. (1993a). *Cognitive-behavioral treatment of borderline personality disorder.* New York: Guilford Press.

——— (1993b). *Skills training manual for treating borderline personality disorder.* New York: Guilford Press.

——— (1994). Acceptance and change: The central dialectic in psychotherapy. In S. C. Hayes, N. S. Jacobson, V. M. Follette, & M. J. Dougher (Eds.), *Acceptance and change: Content and context in psychotherapy* (pp. 73–86). Reno, NV: Context Press.

Segal, Z. V., Williams, J. M. G., & Teasdale, J. D. (2002). *Mindfulness-based cognitive therapy for depression: A new approach to preventing relapse.* New York: Guilford.

Tacon, A. M., McComb, J., Caldera, Y., & Randolph, P. (2003). Mindfulness meditation, anxiety reduction, and heart disease: A pilot study. *Family and Community Health, 26,* 25–33.

PART II

APPLICATIONS FOR PSYCHOLOGICAL DISORDERS IN ADULTS

2

MINDFULNESS-BASED COGNITIVE THERAPY FOR PREVENTION OF DEPRESSIVE RELAPSE

SANDRA J. COFFMAN

Independent Practice, University of Washington, Seattle, Washington

SONA DIMIDJIAN

Department of Psychology, University of Washington, Seattle, Washington

RUTH A. BAER

Department of Psychology, University of Kentucky, Lexington, Kentucky

INTRODUCTION: DEPRESSION AND RELAPSE

Mindfulness-based cognitive therapy (MBCT) (Segal, Williams, & Teasdale, 2002) is an 8-week group protocol developed for the prevention of relapse of major depressive episodes. Major depressive disorder (MDD) is among the most common and severe causes of ill health and functional impairment (Murray & Lopez, 1998), with lifetime prevalence in community samples ranging from 10% to 25% for women and 5% to 12% for men (American Psychiatric Association, 2000). An important issue in the treatment of depression is the high risk of relapse or recurrence. At least 60% of individuals who experience a single episode of MDD are likely to have a second episode, and this risk increases with the number of previous episodes. Those with three previous episodes have a 90% chance of suffering

32

a fourth episode. Judd (1997) suggests that the average individual with MDD will experience four episodes during his or her lifetime.

The most common approach to relapse prevention is the continued use, after recovery, of the antidepressant medication with which the episode was treated. Unfortunately, this approach is effective only as long as the medication is continued, and noncompliance rates are reported to be about 30–40% (Basco & Rush, 1995). Some patients, such as pregnant women, should not use such medications, while others cannot tolerate the side effects or are unwilling to take them for extended periods (Segal et al., 2002). Research also suggests that cognitive behavioral therapy (CBT) is effective both for treating acute episodes of depression and for reducing risk of relapse (Blackburn, Eunson, & Bishop, 1986; Evans et al., 1992; Kovacs, Rush, Beck, & Hollon, 1981; Shea et al., 1992; Simons, Murphy, Levine, & Wetzel, 1986). However, provision of CBT or other empirically supported psychotherapies to all depressed individuals probably is not feasible, given the prevalence of depression, shortage of adequately trained clinicians, and low rates at which depressed individuals seek such treatments (Segal et al., 2002; Segal, Teasdale, & Williams, 2004). MBCT was designed to provide a cost-effective approach to relapse prevention in patients whose previous episode was successfully treated with antidepressant medication. The group format reduces the resources required for delivery of treatment, while the skills taught are designed to reduce the likelihood of relapse without reliance on extended use of medication.

THEORETICAL AND CONCEPTUAL BACKGROUND OF MINDFULNESS-BASED COGNITIVE THERAPY

MBCT is based on a theoretical model that describes factors contributing to vulnerability to relapse and recurrence of major depression and how cognitive therapy reduces this vulnerability.

VULNERABILITY TO RELAPSE OF DEPRESSION

The cognitive model of depression specifies that depressed individuals generally experience sad moods and negative thoughts regarding the self, the world, and the future. After recovery from the depressive episode, individuals' thoughts may become less negative and distorted. In fact, Haaga, Dyck, and Ernst (1991) found that levels of dysfunctional attitudes in recovered depressed patients do not differ from levels in never-depressed individuals. However, according to the model underlying MBCT, individuals who have experienced one or more depressive episodes have developed associations between sadness and negative thought patterns, and therefore they differ from never-depressed individuals in the negative patterns of thinking triggered by the ordinary sad moods that are unavoidably part of life. That is, in previously depressed individuals, these sad moods trigger patterns of thinking that are similar to those present during the previous depressive episode. During times of sad mood, these thoughts are much more negative, global, and self-critical than those reported by never-depressed individuals. This difference has been shown empirically in several studies in which previously depressed and never-depressed individuals are experimentally induced to experience a temporary sad mood (e.g., through listening to sad music). While in this sad state, their thoughts and attitudes are measured. Previously depressed individuals are much more likely to endorse global, negative self-judgments and other dysfunctional attitudes, whereas those who have never been depressed show few such changes in thinking when feeling sad (e.g., Ingram, Miranda, & Segal, 1998; Miranda & Persons, 1988; Miranda, Persons, & Byers, 1990; Segal, Gemar, & Williams, 1999; Segal & Ingram, 1994). In summary, the evidence suggests that for previously depressed individuals, small increases in sadness are associated with significant increases in depressive thought content, whereas for never-depressed individuals, such increases in negative thoughts do not occur.

In addition to increases in negative thought content, for previously depressed individuals, sadness or dysphoria also reactivates a ruminative style of thinking, which includes analyzing why they feel sad and thinking about their shortcomings and how these lead to problematic situations. Although ruminative individuals often express the belief that dwelling on their problems and trying to understand their inadequacies will yield important insights about their moods and how to improve them, empirical data suggest that ruminative thinking perpetuates depressed mood (Nolen-Hoeksema, 1991). Thus, the model underlying MBCT suggests that in previously depressed individuals, ordinary sad moods are likely to reactivate both depressive thought content and a ruminative style of thinking, leading to a vicious cycle in which sad moods escalate into episodes of depression.

HOW COGNITIVE THERAPY REDUCES RELAPSE

Early descriptions of cognitive therapy for depression suggested that vulnerability to relapse would be reduced by changes in the content of dysfunctional thoughts and attitudes. However, the empirical literature has shown that both cognitive therapy and antidepressant medication produce equally strong reductions in dysfunctional attitudes (Barber & DeRubeis, 1989; Simons, Garfield, & Murphy, 1984). Thus, it is unlikely that these changed attitudes are responsible for the superior protection against relapse afforded by cognitive therapy. More recent conceptualizations (Segal *et al.,* 2002; Segal *et al.,* 2004; Teasdale, 1999a; 1999b) suggest that cognitive therapy, in addition to changing the content of thoughts, also leads to a change in individuals' perspective about, or relationship to, their thoughts and emotions. This changed perspective, often called *distancing* or *decentering,* leads individuals to see their thoughts and feelings as mental events that come and go, that do not necessarily reflect important truths about their worth or adequacy as human beings, and that do not necessitate specific reactions or behaviors.

Traditional cognitive therapy is hypothesized to encourage this perspective by repeatedly asking participants to observe and identify their thoughts. In the past, these tasks were assumed to be important because they led to evaluation, disputing, and change of thought content. However, several researchers have suggested that decentering alone might be a central process by which cognitive therapy achieves its effects (Ingram & Hollon, 1986; Teasdale, Segal, & Williams, 1995). By allowing individuals to see their thoughts as "just thoughts," rather than as valid reflections of reality, cognitive therapy may reduce the reactivity to negative thoughts that can lead to rumination and depressive relapse.

MINDFULNESS TRAINING AND RELAPSE

Mindfulness training is directly concerned with teaching people to decenter from their thoughts and emotions without avoiding, denying, or suppressing them. It teaches close observation of these phenomena and thus discourages experiential avoidance. It also teaches nonjudgmental acceptance and nonreactivity to these phenomena. According to the MBCT model, intentionally focusing undivided attention on thoughts, emotions, and sensations in this way uses much of the individual's capacity for attentional processing, so that little capacity remains for rumination.

Segal *et al.* (2002; 2004) distinguish between *doing* and *being* modes of mind. The *doing* mode includes recognition of discrepancies between how things are and how we wish them to be. Such discrepancies trigger negative emotions, as well as thought patterns designed to find ways of reducing the discrepancy. When constructive actions can be implemented, this mode of mind is adaptive and can lead to the achievement of many important goals. However, when nothing can be done to change a problematic situation (e.g., when grieving the loss of a spouse or partner), this mode of mind can become unproductive, ruminative, and depressogenic. Much of the individual's attention will be focused on analyzing the past, reviewing what is wrong with the present, anticipating the future, and seeking solutions; however, if solutions are not found, a pervasive sense of dissatisfaction can result. Ruminating in this way, as previously noted, is likely to perpetuate negative mood states.

In contrast, Segal *et al.* (2002; 2004) describe mindfulness as a *being* mode. In MBCT the central skill learned in mindfulness practice is disengaging from *doing* mode, especially from the self-perpetuating, negative, ruminative thought patterns that are part of *doing* mode. In *being* mode the focus is on accepting and allowing whatever is present as it is, without any goal or effort to change it. In *being* mode, no efforts are made to analyze the future consequences of possible problem-solving strategies or to review past attempts to solve similar problems. Rather than thinking about problems or situations, *being* mode is characterized by direct observation and acceptance of whatever is happening in the present moment—including thoughts and feelings that urge immediate action. Instead of acting on such thoughts or feelings, the participant simply observes and notes them. No attempt is made to evaluate the rationality of observed thoughts or to dispute or change their content.

This mindful approach to thoughts and feelings slows reactivity to mood, increasing time and ability to choose new responses. It also decreases rumination and strengthens acceptance of thoughts and feelings, reducing the tendency to see them as necessarily accurate representations of the truth about the self or the world. Adopting the observant and nonjudgmental stance of *being* mode increases the likelihood that individuals will notice phenomena indicative of an approaching relapse (such as fatigue or irritability) and refrain from maladaptive attempts to suppress or ignore them. In this way, they provide themselves with much better opportunities to act skillfully and intentionally in coping with early signs of relapse and taking adaptive steps to prevent it.

The aim of MBCT, then, is to teach skills that will allow individuals, in times of sadness, to interrupt their old habitual patterns of thinking or behaving so that these moods remain mild or transient and do not escalate into more serious affective states. It is not essential, or even desirable, that the treatment aim to eliminate the experience of sadness. However, these new skills can allow the experience of sadness without automatic escalation to depression. Segal *et al.* (2002) state that a central aim of MBCT is "to help participants be able to choose the most skillful response to any unpleasant thoughts, feelings, or situations that they meet" (p. 86). MBCT is conducted with recovered depressed patients, for whom the negative, ruminative thought patterns characteristic of depressive episodes have become infrequent. However, *doing* mode is a pervasive element of most individuals' daily experience in Western culture and is likely to arise during the practice of meditation exercises used in the program (body scan, sitting meditation, yoga, walking). Thus, these exercises provide ample opportunity to practice observing and disengaging from *doing* mode. In addition, although participants are not depressed, the ordinary unpleasant emotions of daily life are welcomed as valuable opportunities for practicing this core skill.

EMPIRICAL SUPPORT

RANDOMIZED CLINICAL TRIALS

Two randomized clinical trials have provided strong empirical support for the efficacy of MBCT in reducing relapse of major depressive episodes. The first (Teasdale *et al.,* 2000) included 145 patients who had experienced two or more major depressive episodes but were currently in recovery or remission. All had been treated with antidepressant medication but had discontinued the medication at least 3 months before beginning the study and had remained in remission since that time. Patients were randomly assigned either to treatment as usual (TAU) or to TAU plus participation in MBCT. All patients then were followed for 1 year. For those with only two previous episodes, participation in MBCT had no significant effect on likelihood of relapse over the next year. However, for those with three or more previous episodes, likelihood of relapse was substantially reduced for participants in MBCT. Among patients receiving TAU, 66% relapsed, whereas only 37% of patients receiving MBCT relapsed. This difference was not related to differences in use of antidepressant medication, as the MBCT group used less medication than the TAU group.

The results of this trial were replicated by Ma and Teasdale (2004), who studied 75 formerly depressed patients. These authors also found that for participants with only two previous episodes, MBCT and TAU groups did not differ in rates of relapse. However, for those with three or more previous episodes, participation in MBCT substantially reduced the risk of relapse (78% for the TAU group versus 36% for the MBCT group). These two studies show that for patients with three or more previous depressive episodes, MBCT is likely to reduce the risk of relapse by half. Moreover, because MBCT is administered in groups of up to 12 participants, these substantial effects can be attained cost-effectively.

POPULATIONS FOR WHOM MINDFULNESS-BASED COGNITIVE THERAPY MAY NOT BE EFFECTIVE

It should be noted that MBCT does not appear to be effective for individuals with only two previous episodes of depression. Several hypotheses have been proposed to account for the lack of efficacy of MBCT among such patients. Segal *et al.* (2002) suggest that for these individuals, relapses may be triggered more often by the occurrence of major life events, such as the breakdown of relationships, rather than by reactivation of depressive thinking patterns during periods of sadness. Post (1992) has suggested that as the number of previous episodes increases, the severity of environmental stress required to provoke another episode decreases. For individuals with more previous episodes, associations between sadness and negative thinking may be stronger, so that reactivation of depressive thinking patterns occurs more readily in the face of even mild environmental stressors. The strong emphasis in MBCT on preventing the reactivation of depressogenic thinking patterns associated with sadness, and its relative lack of attention to coping with major life events, may help to explain why the treatment is efficacious only with individuals with several previous episodes.

It is also possible that different types of depression tend to have different triggers. Some may be triggered by life events, whereas others are triggered by prolonged rumination. Individuals may be more prone to one type or the other. If so, then it is important for future research to clarify ways to prevent relapse in individuals who are susceptible to relapse during stressful life events. Finally, it is possible that individuals with fewer previous episodes are less motivated to engage fully in the treatment regimen; in contrast, individuals with more previous episodes may have learned through bitter experience the importance of sustained effort to prevent future depressive relapse and therefore may be more likely to comply with treatment expectations, which include extensive meditation practice and other home-work exercises.

It is also important to note that the efficacy of MBCT has not been evaluated in patients in the midst of a depressive episode. Segal *et al.* (2004) suggest that the program may not be effective for these individuals. The intensity of negative thinking and the poor concentration typical of depressive episodes might make it difficult for currently depressed patients to participate in mindfulness exercises and to acquire the necessary atten-tional control skills. Moreover, the nature of some of the formal mindfulness practices taught in MBCT (e.g., sitting meditation) may not be consistent with efforts to activate depressed patients that are typical of cognitive and behavioral treatments for acute depression.

CASE STUDY

CONTEXT AND CLIENT BACKGROUND

The individual described in this case study was a participant in an MBCT group co-led by two of the authors (S.C. and S.D.). Participants in the group were referred primarily by psychotherapists in independent practice who work with depressed clients. Therapists were asked to refer clients who were interested in learning skills to prevent depressive relapse. Potential participants were mailed an intake packet with several assessment instruments, including the Beck Depression Inventory II (BDI-II) (Beck, 1996) and an information form that asked their primary reasons for taking the course. They were also asked to describe any current psychotherapy or pharmacotherapy and any current significant health problems. Those who completed and returned these materials along with an initial fee were invited to a brief screening interview. Applicants were assessed for current depressive severity, current Axis I psychopathology, and any interpersonal difficulties that might interfere with group learning. They were also asked to commit to daily meditation practice and other homework, and any reservations were explored. Several potential participants who appeared to be too depressed to complete the groups' substantial homework requirements were screened out at this point.

The client chosen for this case study, who we shall call Suzanne, was part of a group of seven participants. All group members had experienced previous episodes of major depression. Some were not completely recovered from their current episode of depression but had made significant progress in combating it and were judged to be able to complete the homework required by the group. Several group members also had current anxiety disorder diagnoses.

Suzanne was a 38-year-old graphic artist, referred by her previous therapist. She was eager to begin the group treatment, as she had suffered from both depression and anxiety for many years. She had experienced some relief as a result of previous psychotherapy and medication but had also suffered several relapses. A busy professional also raising a family, she feared that time to meditate and do other homework would be scarce but was motivated to enroll in the group in order to minimize the chance of future relapse.

COURSE OF TREATMENT

The group followed the MBCT manual (Segal *et al.,* 2002) with slight modifications as warranted by specific group participants. The group met for $2\frac{1}{2}$ hours per session for 8 weeks. The first week focused on the introduction to the metaphor of "automatic pilot" as a method to begin discussion of *doing* and *being* modes of mind. The first exercise in the program was mindful eating, in which participants were led through a process of eating a raisin mindfully, paying close attention to sights, sounds, texture, taste, etc. The exercise was intended to give participants a direct experience of moving from the automatic pilot of *doing* mode to *being* mode. (See Chapter 1 in this volume for more detailed discussion of the meditation exercises used in MBCT.)

Following the mindful eating practice, the instructors co-led a period of inquiry, a core component of each session. The aim of inquiry is to teach through experiential learning, modeling an open and accepting response to direct experience. Leading inquiry often requires maintaining awareness of one's own tendency to rush to fix or solve problems. Using questions, the leader instead helps participants explore their own internal experience, observing connections between thoughts, feelings, and sensations. Leaders often invite discussion and reflection with questions such as the following: How long did the experience last? Did it stay the same or did it change? Were there any other accompanying thoughts, feelings, or body sensations? What happened next? In general, inquiry begins with a focus on the practice just conducted in the group and then moves to a discussion of the weekly homework assignment.

Suzanne responded very positively to the mindful eating practice. She easily grasped the metaphor of automatic pilot and during inquiry described the multiple ways in which she felt on automatic pilot, both at work and when interacting with her husband and two sons. The early sessions of MBCT are typically both challenging and exciting for group members, and Suzanne was no exception. Although extremely busy with work, parenting, and travel, she quickly began to practice mindfulness of daily activities, concentrating on eating mindfully whenever possible. Suzanne was easily able to identify both thoughts and feelings, although several other group members struggled with this task, especially when first introduced into the second session. She commented, "After rushing home and cooking dinner with my husband, I noticed heaviness in my body when I finally sat down to eat. I felt anxious whenever I wasn't listening to the kids, even though I wanted to concentrate on my food and had explained this to them and they had agreed not to talk for the first five minutes."

The body scan also is introduced in session 1. Suzanne found this exercise meaningful and incorporated it into an evening routine with her husband, who began to practice with her as they both listened to the body scan tape. In fact, Suzanne expressed some embarrassment during the homework review in session 2, which focused on a discussion of the many barriers that participants encountered as they practiced the homework assignments from the previous week. Suzanne, by contrast, reported how pleasurable she had found the body scan to be and how few barriers she encountered in her practice.

An important task for group leaders is to create a group culture or expectation in which the full range of participant reactions to the homework can be comfortably expressed. For this reason, it was important to respond to Suzanne's positive experience with the body scan practice while, at the same time, teaching that unpleasant mindfulness practice is no "less" of a mindfulness practice. In addition, it was important to highlight the presence of judgments, including the categorizing of experiences as "pleasant" and "good," as well as "unpleasant" and "bad." Adopting a nonjudgmental stance was important for the other group members during that session and would become important to Suzanne as she worked with the following week's homework.

Session 3 introduced participants to the practice of sitting meditation, using the breath as an anchor of attention. Like several of the other group members, Suzanne found it very difficult to develop a formal sitting practice outside of the class sessions. Sometimes she found it difficult to stay awake; at other times her focus seemed to be everywhere except on her breathing, and she became discouraged. During inquiry, the group leaders normalized the experience of mind wandering as an inherent part of the practice of mindfulness for most practitioners and shared with Suzanne the common instruction, "If the mind wanders a hundred times, then simply bring it back a hundred times" (Segal *et al.*, 2002, p. 168).

In addition, the group leaders invited Suzanne to notice the judgments that arose in response to her experience of her wandering attention and to practice accepting each sitting as it was, letting go of expectation or demands. Both group leaders, as well as the other group participants, described the challenge of meeting experience nonjudgmentally, which Suzanne found helpful. She continued to work with judgmental thoughts by noticing and inviting an attitude of acceptance throughout the course; however, she frequently described feeling discouraged, wishing for more experiences of competency during her sitting practice.

By contrast, the 3-minute breathing space introduced in week 3 was easily incorporated into Suzanne's daily practice. She reported that this short exercise in breathing brought her back into the present and interrupted her tendency to ruminate, either about missed opportunities in the past or about future unknowns. She initially paired this breathing exercise with brushing her teeth for practice and later reported using it spontaneously, especially in an increasingly tense work situation.

Mindful walking and stretching were less compelling to Suzanne. She became very self-conscious and distracted as she tried to attend to carefully placing each foot on the ground. Although she tried this practice several times, she never found it useful. Group leaders responded evenly to Suzanne's reaction to mindful walking, encouraging her to experiment with the weekly assignments while observing her judgmental responses. The leaders reminded the group that one aim of the course was to introduce participants to a range of practices, with the hope that some (but perhaps not all) would be incorporated into a long-term daily routine.

Similarly, the stretching led to much self-criticism about her lack of flexibility and strength. Additionally, her children often jumped on her as she tried to stretch. Thus, while other class members found the yoga tapes and practice extremely useful, Suzanne did not. Again, there was the problem of finding time and space in her hectic life. Eventually she was able to adopt a somewhat playful attitude toward the walking and stretching practices but did not integrate either into a daily routine after the conclusion of the course, whereas she regularly practiced the body scan. Other group members, however, found that mindful walking and stretching became their primary modes of meditation practice. Interestingly, this proved true for both participants who struggled with current anxiety symptoms.

In week 4, Suzanne participated actively in the discussion of the definition of depression. She was able to describe with great detail the vegetative symptoms that felt like a profoundly heavy weight when she was depressed. She was also very moved by the mindfulness-based stress reduction (MBSR) videotape shown during this session, which shows Jon Kabat-Zinn working with chronic pain patients at the University of Massachusetts. Like others in the class, she was encouraged to see that these patients found the mindfulness practices extremely helpful in improving their quality of life. She was also touched by the kindness and empathy of Kabat-Zinn and said she would like to adopt this kind of attitude with her own struggles with depression, as opposed to the self-critical dialogue she so often repeated to herself.

The theme of week 6 (i.e., thoughts are not facts) also resonated deeply for Suzanne. In the class discussion, she was able to identify alternative viewpoints (to her typical negative thoughts) and readily saw the usefulness of the breathing space as a first step to viewing her life through a wider lens. Quickly grasping the connection between negative predictions and anxiety, she began using alternative, more accurate predictions when she thought about the future, at work and at home. She also described the negative impact on her mood and behavior of anxious thoughts about her children's welfare whenever they were apart. Instead, she now began focusing on the importance of attachment, separation, and reunion as necessary learning experiences for both parents and children.

At this point in the course of the class, Suzanne was able to interrupt the beginning of a depressive relapse. Several external events were related to this relapse. The winter holiday schedule resulted in a break of 2 weeks between mindfulness meetings, and the holidays themselves increased demands on Suzanne's time and made practicing more difficult. Moreover, these events coincided with the shortest days of the year and especially gray, dark weather. As Suzanne's mood began to slip, she responded with familiar negative self-talk, criticizing herself for not accomplishing more each day. She felt guilty about exercising and seeing her friends, and so eliminated these necessary parts of her self-care. This decrease in exercise and social contact resulted in decreased energy and a feeling that she wasn't doing anything right, accompanied by the thought that she wasn't "good enough." When her new boss demanded more attention to tasks she had previously seen as of limited importance, she interpreted this as further evidence in support of her internal self-critical thoughts.

When the class began again in the new year, Suzanne was relieved to hear that other members had also found it difficult to maintain a steady mindfulness practice. The inquiry discussion avoided any stance of blame and focused instead on the costs and benefits of a flexible relationship to practice. Other members discussed using the 3-minute breathing space and mindful walking, eating, and driving. During inquiry, Suzanne began to bring awareness to some of her patterns of negative, self-critical thought. She commented, in particular, on the frequency of all-or-nothing thinking. For instance, she discussed feeling that there was "no point" to maintaining her meditation practice, because it was not possible to do the full 40 minutes, and how she subsequently felt guilty and worthless.

During inquiry, the group leaders invited Suzanne to observe the presence of such judgments when they arose and to experiment with a more flexible and nonjudgmental approach to her practice and herself, perhaps using a briefer period of practice (e.g., 10 minutes) if a longer period was not feasible. She felt motivated by this discussion and began to practice again. Suzanne realized that her judgmental thoughts were contributing to her relapse and she began to bring awareness to such judgmental thoughts during her practice, in family life, and at work. She began to experiment with a more accepting and compassionate stance to these domains. Putting these new mindful skills into practice reversed the downward slide in her mood and prevented a full-blown relapse of depression. This increased her confidence in the model and inspired other group members to stick with their practice. Suzanne also found it helpful to create a routine for her practice. Initially she had paired practice of the 3-minute breathing space with brushing her teeth. As she added new skills, she also tied them to existing daily routines and this helped her maintain consistency in her practice.

In week 7, Suzanne struggled with the knowledge that she needed to focus on her own needs instead of caring always for others. She saw clearly that her mood improved when she and her husband had time alone, even though this was hard to schedule. Similarly, she benefited mightily from time with women friends and from time alone. Exercise and adequate sleep at times seemed like remote memories from a life before motherhood, but she acknowledged the importance of beginning to work these basics of self-care back into her life. Consequently, she included earlier bedtimes and increased exercise, pleasure, and social contact in her action plan to reduce relapse.

Because she had experienced a short relapse during the group, Suzanne was well aware of her personal relapse signature. She recognized the sadness, lethargy, and worry that often presaged a rapid decline in pleasure and mood. At this point, critical self-talk and harsh judgments about not performing well enough quickly surfaced. Subsequent irritability and withdrawal triggered more self-criticism about her mothering skills and her performance at work. Instead of asking her willing husband for help, she withdrew further and became more depressed. Identifying the steps in the relapse process, although painful, presented the opportunity for quick intervention. Attention to the basics of self-care (sleep, social contact, adequate nutrition and exercise) would help her focus on her own needs in the moment. Suzanne's use of the 3-minute breathing space remained a key component of bringing attention to the onset of her relapse signature, providing an opportunity to make different choices. In addition, regular daily practice of the body scan provided an ongoing practice of disengaging from the automatic pilot paths toward judgment and criticism. Adding yoga and sitting meditation to the body scan were also now available options. Developing alternative self-talk, in contrast to her typical critical dialogue, could help her to develop more accurate viewpoints of the present and to hold a more accepting and accurate view of herself.

Not unlike several participants, Suzanne was both sad that the group was ending after session 8 and hopeful about the future. Although she expressed some concern that she might lose her focus on the daily body scan, Suzanne was also excited to try to maintain her practice on her own and to regain an evening with her family. She was effusive in her praise of the class and the accepting stance of the leaders and materials. She was open to the idea of a future get-together or workshop but also felt hopeful about her ability to do the body scan and sitting meditation on her own. As she was more accepting of herself, she was also better able to support the other participants who had developed very different ways to bring mindfulness to their everyday activities. We were all moved by the description of how one participant, who had struggled throughout the class, now begins her day walking very mindfully to the bus and then continuing mindful awareness of each moment on the bus ride to work.

ISSUES THAT AROSE DURING TREATMENT

Like several other class members, Suzanne struggled with various forms of thinking errors common to people with depression, such as perfectionist standards and all-or-nothing thinking. Although these errors were less rigid than when Suzanne had previously experienced a full-blown depressive episode, these ways of thinking still made it a challenge for Suzanne and other class members to build skills, including the skills of acceptance and the attitude of mindfulness. For example, skill building requires making mistakes and feeling both uncomfortable and incompetent. Suzanne, a very bright and successful professional, was used to feeling quite competent in many areas of her life. Our class asked her to stretch herself, both physically and emotionally. Although the leaders and the materials modeled and encouraged the importance of simply accepting experience, this was not easy for Suzanne.

The fact that she did not easily develop a daily practice of meditation initially seemed another example of her "badness" or failing; a problem that could potentially trigger a relapse was therefore explored in our work together. Each week, this issue arose for Suzanne or for another class member, and each week we would all practice together and process the difficulty in simply being in the moment, experiencing acceptance of the present.

Addressing these thinking errors became part of the practice of mindfulness and also preparation for life problems. For example, midway through the class, Suzanne encountered conflicts and criticism with a new, difficult boss at work. The previously described relapse into depression also resulted in negative future predictions about her workplace. This, in turn, negatively affected her work performance. She became tense and irritable and had a hard time getting an accurate picture of her excellent work skills, forgetting previous positive evaluations and feedback, as well as frequent promotions.

When Suzanne returned her attention to the moment and took a 3-minute breathing space, she brought awareness to the ways in which she was increasing tension in her body (e.g., shoulders, abdomen) and in her thoughts (e.g., "I can't do this; this is impossible"). This increased awareness allowed her to shift her relationship with these experiences and to employ other strategies that would more effectively address the challenges at work. Each evening she listened to the body scan tape, and this reminded her of the power of staying focused on the moment. She also experienced increasing mastery of this skill. Mindfulness of cooking also enriched her experience of the moment and bought her new, accurate information about herself and the world.

When she was anxious, Suzanne typically tried to take control of a situation, and this tendency was also manifested in the group. Initially she was quick to say positive things about the practice and to respond to questions. As the class progressed, she was gradually able to sit with silence and let others express misgivings or difficulties. She trusted the leaders more to handle discomfort and to guide the group. Some of her old assumptions were tested, and new, more flexible ones developed about the necessity, costs, and benefits of overresponsibility. She realized how this stance increased anxiety, and she therefore began to reduce her attempts to control the future, instead accepting and enjoying the present.

Suzanne originally harbored the hope and expectation that mindfulness meditation would result, preferably immediately, in an increased state of relaxation. So she was somewhat disappointed in the hard work entailed in learning to practice mindfulness meditation and yoga stretches. As the sessions continued, Suzanne accepted the reality that relaxation might be an occasional by-product of mindfulness practice but was not the goal. This concept helped her to reduce her perfectionist strivings, bring greater awareness to her frequent judgmental thoughts, and begin to accept each imperfect moment.

OUTCOME OF SUZANNE'S TREATMENT

In the class, Suzanne developed mindfulness skills that included daily use of the body scan and mindfulness of everyday activities, such as eating and cooking. She began to use the 3-minute breathing space when she was anxious, such as in difficult interactions with her boss at work or with her children at home. She reported a heightened awareness of the present, as well as decreased rumination about the future and self-criticism about the past. She developed the skill of noticing her patterns of self-judgment and demands for very high standards for her own performance at work and as a parent. Over time, she experimented with becoming more realistic about what she could accomplish in difficult and demanding environments. She grew to appreciate her own strength and resilience and the support of her husband and family in facing challenges at work and at home, enriching her gratitude for her current life. She successfully forestalled the beginning of a depressive relapse during the group and reported confidence about the skills learned to help manage similar times in the future.

PRACTICAL ISSUES

A wide range of practical issues arises in the course of developing and leading an MBCT group. These issues generally fall within three broad categories: (1) the background and role of group leader; (2) responding to participant reactions; and (3) managing logistical and financial issues. These are addressed in the following section.

BACKGROUND AND ROLE OF GROUP LEADER(S)

MBCT requires that leaders maintain an active meditation practice (Segal et al., 2002). Clearly the therapists' ongoing meditation practice and resulting attitude of mindfulness and acceptance help set the tone for the groups and the meditation experiences within the group. Previous experience with simple yoga postures and principles is also useful. Some basic knowledge of the principles of cognitive behavioral therapy is necessary, as these principles are embedded through the treatment and made explicit in the second half of treatment. Finally, clinical experience with mood disorders, specifically depression and anxiety, is useful. Experience with leading groups may also prove helpful.

Having a co-leader, while not required or even discussed in the manual, provides a depth of experience and attention that, in our experience, enriches the group for both leaders and participants. It is also easier to learn new skills without the pressure of leading each session alone. The co-leaders met and talked each week before and after each group session. Planning before sessions and debriefing afterward strengthened their confidence in the presentations and allowed for coordination and division of labor. Subsequent groups required briefer planning, but debriefing continued in order to adapt the teaching to each particular group and to adapt to the specific needs of each participant. Assisting an experienced group leader is another way to gain skill in leading MBCT groups and is a format commonly used in centers providing MBCT.

An important aspect of the role of group leader is to tie mindfulness practices and inquiry to the prevention of depressive relapse. The aim of the course is not to teach mindfulness for the sake of mindfulness; there is an explicit mental health agenda, in contrast to the teaching of similar practices in retreat settings. Group leaders can use their expertise in treating depression and providing CBT techniques to provide psychoeducation about the symptoms of depression and anxiety and how mindfulness skills can help to both strengthen nondepressed states and alert the class members to early signs of relapse. For example, mindfulness of mood and feelings of minor sadness may provide early warning signs of relapse. Attentiveness to and acceptance of the moment can also increase awareness of positive and neutral mood, further opening the previously negative lens of depression and so strengthening awareness of small pleasures and gratitude in living.

In addition, it is important for group leaders to maintain a balance between teaching through experiential exercises and imparting information. This balance requires clinical experience and a willingness to dance with the tension of differing needs of different classes and class members. MBCT demands a subtle ability to weave information into the class while maintaining the overall emphasis on experiential learning. Moreover, as in good CBT, the agenda is adjusted to meet the needs of the group. For example, the 3-minute breathing space can be used in any session if the focus is becoming overly didactic or leading away from experiential learning and knowing. Similarly, as a leader, one needs to move constantly back and forth from *doing* mode to *being* mode. Examples of this back and forth movement include leading inquiry and mindfulness practices, a dance that emerges in each session. Beginning leaders may at times refer to the treatment manual, or preferably preparation notes, to keep on task. However, the intention of the treatment is to teach and guide from one's own moment-to-moment experience; therefore, excessive reliance on the manual is strongly discouraged. Planning in advance the time allowed for each task may prove helpful, especially initially. With experience, it becomes more possible to lead from one's immediate experience, while monitoring time constraints and attending to class members' needs. This is an enriching and increasingly elegant experience, enhanced by the leaders' mindfulness practice and clinical expertise and sensitivity.

Finally, it is of paramount importance that leaders protect time and space for adequate preparation for group. Experience teaches that it does not work to run in from a hectic day and lead the group. Instead, leaders need time to access *being* mode in order to function well as leaders.

Ideally, leaders would arrive early enough to meditate in the room before the class begins.

RESPONDING TO PARTICIPANT REACTIONS

A number of common reactions or difficulties frequently arise during treatment. The following discussion outlines some guidelines for group leaders for responding to such reactions:

1. In general, it is often helpful to maintain the intention to provide corrective feedback in a manner consistent with the model; this includes staying present in the moment, not shying away from participants' misconceptions or misuse of strategies, and maintaining openness and curiosity. For example, class members often confuse the intent of the 3-minute breathing space and may use it as a distraction or way of tuning out. A mindful response will often include questioning and inviting reflection as a way of giving feedback.

2. Leaders should be prepared for participants to voice strong negative reactions to practices. It is common to hear the following: "I hate the body scan," "I can't stand the physical discomfort or pain from sitting," or "I always fall asleep when I meditate or listen to the tapes." In response to such experiences, it is often helpful to model a calm, accepting stance that provides a mindful, curious response while also conveying the importance of continuing to practice and accept the experience that arises.

3. It is important to maintain a nonjudgmental stance when responding to confusion about what mindfulness practice is and/or hopelessness and discouragement about one's practice (e.g., "I can't do this; my mind keeps wandering"). Be prepared to keep making the point that bringing back your attention *is* the practice.

4. It is helpful for leaders to be thoughtful in responding to participants not completing homework and/or not sharing openly about homework. It can be hard to assess homework compliance in MBCT classes. The leader does not want to create a "school" environment but does need to emphasize the importance of doing the work and practice. There are no formal mechanisms for checking on practice other than providing a weekly time for reporting back to the group. It is particularly important to model acceptance and also to encourage increased effort, an ongoing dialectic.

5. Leaders should be prepared to respond thoughtfully to participants changing the homework practices based on personal preference, either because they did not like the assigned practice or because they prefer to do their "own" practice (especially for people with meditation experience).

MANAGING LOGISTICAL AND FINANCIAL ISSUES

The MBCT manual sets an ambitious course for each 2-hour group session. At times, it can be challenging to give adequate attention to each agenda item in each session; this is particularly the case in week 3. Possible remedies include extending sessions to 2.5 hours (as we did) or extending the course to 9 weeks. Another practical solution would be to decrease the time allowed for the opening mindfulness practice (e.g., reducing a 45-minute meditation to 30 minutes). However, given the emphasis on learning through direct and immediate experience, this option may be problematic.

Finding an adequate space can also present challenges for therapists providing MBCT outside of a research trial or institutional setting. A room with available table and chairs is helpful for the initial sessions (and for clients who prefer chairs for the mindfulness practices); however, the room also needs large open space, preferably carpeted, for yoga, body scan, and sitting meditation. Windows are ideal for seeing meditation and general comfort, yet privacy is also ideal for confidentiality. A space of beauty may also add to the spirit of mindfulness and invite group attentiveness and cohesiveness. In our experience, many of these features can be hard to find in traditional independent practice settings. Although a strong leader and motivated participants would likely be successful in an unheated, dark basement, it is often worthwhile to seek an environment that is sufficiently inviting and spacious.

In independent practice settings, it is often important to consider how to work with managed care and insurance reimbursement. Because the treatment is described as a class, and not as group psychotherapy, in our experience insurance payments were not possible. However, practitioners and/or clients in other settings may find it advantageous to advocate with insurance companies to cover this service. Since insurance reimbursement was not possible for our clients, we maintained a few sliding scale spots if payment would have precluded individuals from attending the group.

SUMMARY

MBCT is an 8-week group treatment that combines mindfulness strategies with traditional cognitive behavioral strategies. It is designed to help patients with histories of depression develop core skills that will help to prevent the relapse and recurrence of depression in the future. This chapter has reviewed the rationale and background of the model, as well as relevant research. A case illustration has been presented to provide additional detail about the use of common treatment strategies and client responses, describing the experience of one client who benefited tremendously from the treatment. In our experience, leading these classes presents both challenges and opportunities for the instructors: Staying mindfully in the moment while also running a group and teaching new approaches to experience blends many clinical and personal skills.

As described in other chapters in this volume, current efforts to apply this model to a range of other disorders are under way. In the group described herein, participants also reported that the skills were of assistance in managing anxiety. We eagerly await ongoing clinical reports and research investigations to increase the applicability and future directions of mindfulness-based therapies.

ACKNOWLEDGMENTS

The authors thank Zindel Segal for very helpful supervision and encouragement during the MBCT group described in this chapter.

REFERENCES

American Psychiatric Association (2000). *Diagnostic and statistical manual of mental disorders* (4th ed., text revision). Washington, DC: Author.

Barber, J. P., & DeRubeis, R. J. (1989). On second thought: Where the action is in cognitive therapy for depression. *Cognitive Therapy and Research, 13*, 441–457.

Basco, M. R., & Rush, A. J. (1995). Compliance with pharmacology in mood disorders. *Psychiatric Annals, 25*, 269–275.

Beck, A. T. (1996). *Beck Depression Inventory–II manual.* San Antonio, TX: The Psychological Corporation.

Blackburn, I. M., Eunson, K. M., & Bishop, S. (1986). A two-year naturalistic follow-up of depressed patients treated with cognitive therapy, pharmacotherapy, and a combination of both. *Journal of Affective Disorders, 10*, 67–75.

Evans, M. D., Hollon, S. D., DeRubeis, R. J., Piasecki, J. M., Groe, W. M., Garvey, M. J., et al. (1992). Differential relapse following cognitive therapy and pharmacotherapy for depression. *Archives of General Psychiatry, 49*, 802–808.

Haaga, D. A. F., Dyck, M. J., & Ernst, D. (1991). Empirical status of cognitive theory of depression. *Psychological Bulletin, 110*, 215–236.

Ingram, R. E., & Hollon, S. D. (1986). Cognitive therapy for depression from an information processing perspective. In R. E. Ingram (Ed.), *Information processing approaches to clinical psychology* (pp. 261–284). Orlando, FL: Academic Press.

Ingram, R. E., Miranda, J., & Segal, Z. V. (1998). *Cognitive vulnerability to depression.* New York: Guilford Press.

Judd, L. J. (1997). The clinical course of unipolar major depressive disorders. *Archives of General Psychiatry, 54*, 989–991.

Kovacs, M., Rush, A. J., Beck, A. T., & Hollon, S. D. (1981). Depressed outpatients treated with cognitive therapy or pharmacotherapy: A one-year follow-up. *Archives of General Psychiatry, 38*, 33–39.

Ma, S. H., & Teasdale, J. D. (2004). Mindfulness-based cognitive therapy for depression: Replication and exploration of differential relapse prevention effects. *Journal of Consulting and Clinical Psychology, 72*, 31–40.

Miranda, J., & Persons, J. B. (1988). Dysfunctional attitudes are mood state dependent. *Journal of Abnormal Psychology, 97*, 76–79.

Miranda, J., Persons, J. B., & Byers, C. (1990). Endorsement of dysfunctional beliefs depends on current mood state. *Journal of Abnormal Psychology, 99*, 237–241.

Murray, C. J. L., & Lopez, A. D. (1998). *The global burden of disease: A comprehensive assessment of mortality, injuries, and risk factors in 1990 and projected to 2000.* Cambridge, MA: Harvard School of Public Health and the World Health Organization.

Nolen-Hoeksema, S. (1991). Responses to depression and their effects on the duration of depressive episodes. *Journal of Abnormal Psychology, 100*, 569–582.

Post, R. M. (1992). Transduction of psychosocial stress into the neurobiology of recurrent affective disorder. *American Journal of Psychiatry, 149*, 999–1010.

Segal, Z. V., Gemar, M. C., & Williams, S. (1999). Differential cognitive response to a mood challenge following successful cognitive therapy or pharmacotherapy for unipolar depression. *Journal of Abnormal Psychology, 108*, 3–10.

Segal, Z. V., & Ingram, R. E. (1994). Mood priming and construct activation in tests of cognitive vulnerability to unipolar depression. *Clinical Psychology Review, 14*, 663–695.

Segal, Z. V., Teasdale, J. D., & Williams, J. M. G. (2004). Mindfulness-based cognitive therapy: Theoretical rationale and empirical status. In S. C. Hayes, V. M. Follette, & M. M. Linehan, (Eds.), *Mindfulness and acceptance: Expanding the cognitive-behavioral tradition.* New York: Guilford Press.

Segal, Z. V., Williams, J. M. G., & Teasdale, J. D. (2002). *Mindfulness-based cognitive therapy for depression: A new approach to preventing relapse.* New York: Guilford Press.

Shea, M. T., Elkin, I., Imber, S. D., Sotsky, F. M., Watkins, J. T., Collins, J. F., et al. (1992). Course of depressive symptoms over follow-up: Findings from the NIMH Treatment of Depression Collaborative Research Program. *Archives of General Psychiatry, 49*, 782–787.

Simons, A., Garfield, S. L., & Murphy, G. E. (1984). The process of change in cognitive therapy and pharmacotherapy for depression. *Archives of General Psychiatry, 41*, 45–51.

Simons, A. D., Murphy, G. E., Levine, J. L., & Wetzel, R. D. (1986). Cognitive therapy and pharmacotherapy for depression: Sustained improvement over one year. *Archives of General Psychiatry, 43*, 43–50.

Teasdale, J. D. (1999a). Emotional processing, three modes of mind and the prevention of relapse in depression. *Behaviour Research and Therapy, 37*, S53–S78.

——— (1999b). Metacognition, mindfulness, and the modification of mood disorders. *Clinical Psychology and Psychotherapy, 6*, 146–155.

Teasdale, J. D., Segal, Z. V., & Williams, J. M. G. (1995). How does cognitive therapy prevent depressive relapse and why should attentional control (mindfulness) training help? *Behaviour Research and Therapy, 33*, 25–39.

Teasdale, J. D., Segal, Z. V., Williams, J. M. G., Ridgeway, V. A., Soulsby, J. M., & Lau, M. A. (2000). Prevention of relapse-recurrence in major depression by mindfulness-based cognitive therapy. *Journal of Consulting and Clinical Psychology, 68*, 615–623.

3

INCORPORATING MINDFULNESS- AND ACCEPTANCE-BASED STRATEGIES IN THE TREATMENT OF GENERALIZED ANXIETY DISORDER

LIZABETH ROEMER

*Department of Psychology, University of Massachusetts at Boston,
Boston, Massachusetts*

KRISTALYN SALTERS-PEDNEAULT

*National Center for PTSD, VA Boston Healthcare System,
Jamaica Plain, Massachusetts*

SUSAN M. ORSILLO

Psychology Department, Suffolk University, Boston, Massachusetts

In our work developing a new integrative treatment for generalized anxiety disorder (GAD), we have incorporated elements of mindfulness-based cognitive therapy (MBCT) (Segal, Williams, & Teasdale, 2002), acceptance and commitment therapy (ACT) (Hayes, Strosahl, & Wilson, 1999), and dialectical behavior therapy (DBT) (Linehan, 1993a) into existing cognitive behavioral treatments (CBT) for this disorder (e.g., Borkovec, Newman, Lytle, & Pincus, 2002; see Chapter 1 in this volume for overviews of MBCT, ACT, and DBT). In this chapter, we present the theoretical rationale for our approach, describe how we integrate these interventions to specifically target the clinical presentation of GAD, and present a case study as an example of how our treatment unfolds and what specific considerations may arise. We then review the preliminary empirical support for this new treatment and discuss some practical considerations in our approach. Readers interested in a more extensive review of GAD are directed to Roemer, Orsillo, and Barlow (2002), while those interested in a more extensive discussion of our model can read Roemer and Orsillo (2002).

BRIEF DESCRIPTION OF GENERALIZED ANXIETY DISORDER

GAD is a chronic anxiety disorder centrally defined by pervasive, excessive worry that is difficult to control (American Psychiatric Association, 1994). Individuals diagnosed with GAD also report several associated symptoms such as chronic muscle tension, being easily tired, feeling irritable or on edge, and difficulty sleeping. Epidemiological studies reveal a lifetime prevalence of 5.1% for GAD and an association with significant psychosocial impairment (Wittchen, Zhao, Kessler, & Eaton, 1994). GAD commonly co-occurs with other psychological disorders (most often social phobia and major depression) and is often associated with somatic complaints, both of which lead to greater functional impairment (see Roemer et al., 2002, for a review).

Cognitive behavioral interventions have demonstrated efficacy for GAD (Borkovec & Ruscio, 2001). Common treatment packages include applied relaxation, cognitive therapy, and some form of exposure/desensitization (e.g., Borkovec et al., 2002). Nonetheless, GAD remains one of the least successfully treated of the anxiety disorders, with fewer than 60% of participants meeting criteria for high end-state functioning at 12-month follow-up in even the most successful trials (e.g., Borkovec & Costello, 1993; Ladouceur et al., 2000). Further, the effect of these treatments on quality of life or other broad measures of functioning has yet to be explored. Several recent developments in understanding worry and GAD suggest the potential utility of mindfulness and acceptance-based elements in treating GAD.

THEORETICAL AND CONCEPTUAL RATIONALE FOR A MINDFULNESS AND ACCEPTANCE-BASED APPROACH TO TREATING GENERALIZED ANXIETY DISORDER

THE FUNCTION OF WORRY

Tom Borkovec's seminal work in understanding and treating GAD (cf. Borkovec, Alcaine, & Behar, 2004; Borkovec & Sharpless, 2004) has focused on identifying the function of worry, GAD's central defining feature, which is characterized by continual verbal-linguistic activity focused on potential threats in the future. Although worry is experienced as distressing by individuals with GAD, it is associated with restrictions in autonomic arousal (Borkovec & Hu, 1990) and is perceived as a distraction from more emotionally distressing topics (e.g., Borkovec & Roemer, 1995). Thus, continually thinking about potential catastrophes in the future seems to serve the function of avoiding more intense distress (possibly about the present). This avoidant function of worry coincides with Hayes and colleagues' (1999) construct of experiential avoidance in that worry appears to reduce distressing internal experiences in the short term, although it likely prolongs them over time by interfering with emotional processing (recovery), as well as preventing recognition of the adaptive information provided by emotional states (Roemer & Orsillo, 2002). If experiential avoidance is a central problem in GAD, then experiential acceptance, which mindfulness practice promotes, may be the solution.

EXPERIENCING INTERNAL EVENTS AS THREATENING

Mennin and colleagues (Mennin, Heimberg, Turk, & Fresco, 2005) have noted that habitual worry may arise to reduce emotional distress among individuals who have intense, poorly understood emotional responses that they react negatively to and have difficulty regulating. Wells (1995) has also noted that individuals with GAD may come to experience their own worry (another internal experience) as threatening, which may exacerbate anxiety and perpetuate the cycle of worry. Research has confirmed that individuals with GAD experience both their emotions and worries as threatening and undesirable (Mennin et al., 2005; Roemer, Salters, Raffa, & Orsillo, 2005; Wells & Carter, 1999). This reaction to one's own internal experience may prompt efforts at avoidance that paradoxically increase distress (Hayes, Wilson, Gifford, Follette, & Strosahl, 1996; Wegner, 1994) and also decrease clarity of emotional experience. Emphasis on the function of emotions (i.e., their utility in giving us information about our environment and ourselves, communicating with others, and enriching our lives), coupled with practice in noticing and compassionately accepting one's internal state, while simultaneously being aware that it is transient and separate from one's sense of self, may counteract this problematic response to one's internal experience.

CHARACTERISTICS OF WORRY, AVOIDANCE, AND REACTIVITY TO EMOTIONS IN GENERALIZED ANXIETY DISORDER

Narrowed Awareness and Focus on the Future

Individuals with GAD have narrowed attention that is focused on the detection of potential upcoming threats. They thus are less in contact with experiences as they unfold in the present moment. Further, any present-moment awareness they do have is again focused on potential threat. This habitual way of attending likely limits their ability to respond adaptively to contingencies in the present moment and also diminishes their awareness of the complexities of their own emotional responses. It is not that these individuals are unaware of their internal experiences; in fact, our clients often report that they are painfully in touch with their internal distress. However, this awareness is narrowed, focused on anxiety and distress rather than the full range of their experience. Mindfulness practice may be beneficial for these individuals because it promotes an expanded awareness of both internal and external cues in the present moment, allowing for more clarity and flexible adaptation that takes into account the constantly changing current internal and external context.

Amplification of Internal Experiences

Reactivity to one's internal experiences, along with efforts to suppress or avoid these thoughts and feelings, likely leads to an amplification of these experiences. This may account for the intensity of emotional responses that characterizes individuals with GAD (Mennin et al., 2005). This amplification also decreases clarity of emotions: As thoughts and feelings are intensified through negative reactions to and judgments of them and efforts to avoid them, the original responses become less clear, or muddied (similar to the ACT concept of "dirty" emotions [Hayes et al., 1999]). Thus, our clients often report feeling "stressed" or "upset" but have difficulty more specifically identifying their emotional state. This lack of clarity inhibits the ability to use one's emotional responses adaptively and also adds to the experience of one's internal state as undesirable and negative, perpetuating the cycle. While an acceptance (as opposed to judgmental or reactive) response to one's internal state will not necessarily reduce the initial (or primary) (Greenberg & Safran, 1987) emotional response, it can reduce the amplification that results from judgment, reactivity, and efforts at control. Therefore, strategies (such as mindfulness practice) that foster acceptance form a centerpiece of our treatment.

Rigid, Habitual, and Ineffective Behavior Driven by Avoidance

The chronic anxiety, focus on the future, and experiential avoidance that characterize GAD result in habitual responses that limit both cognitive and behavioral flexibility. Extant treatments of GAD have typically not emphasized in vivo exposure because GAD is not characterized by focal behavioral avoidance like the other anxiety disorders. However, individuals with GAD often make behavioral choices aimed at minimizing distress or discomfort. Our clients often describe feeling "frozen" as they anticipate multiple potential negative outcomes and have difficulty choosing a course of action. Other clients describe themselves as constantly busy with activities but not feeling "present" in their actions because they are preoccupied with thoughts about what may come next. These behavioral patterns likely contribute to the functional impairment associated with GAD.

In order to target this ineffective pattern of behavior, our treatment focuses on increasing clients' awareness of what matters to them in their lives (values from ACT) (Hayes *et al.*, 1999), helping them determine potential obstacles between their values and their actions, and helping them set intentions to engage in and explore the potential consequences of a different way of being. This action-oriented element differs from the explicit focus of many mindfulness-based interventions and draws heavily from ACT and other behavior therapies. Nonetheless, it is consistent with the concept of mindful or intended action. In order to capture both the acceptance focus of our intervention and its behavioral focus, we consider it an acceptance-based behavior therapy.

BRIEF OVERVIEW OF THE TREATMENT

Our treatment consists of 16 weekly individual sessions, with the last two sessions taking place every other week in order to allow for tapering. Each session begins with a mindfulness exercise. The first seven sessions involve instruction in relevant concepts, in addition to relevant experiential exercises, whereas the last nine sessions are focused on reviewing clients' efforts to engage in valued, mindful action, obstacles encountered, and plans for future actions. Relapse prevention is also addressed in the final sessions.

As noted previously, our treatment combines elements from Borkovec's CBT treatment for GAD (Borkovec *et al.*, 2002) with acceptance and mindfulness-based interventions discussed in this volume (ACT, MBCT, DBT). Interested readers should read the original sources for more details about each approach. Here we will focus primarily on the integration of these treatments and novel aspects to our intervention. We divide our discussion into the three major components of our treatment, all of which are addressed throughout its course, although some are emphasized more at certain phases.

PRESENTATION OF OUR MODEL

In the beginning of treatment, emphasis is placed on presenting our model of GAD and developing with the client a shared conceptualization of his or her difficulties and a related treatment plan. Consistent with CBT (e.g., Borkovec & Roemer, 1994), the anxiety response is conceptualized as adaptive, and the human ability to imagine past or future events is presented as an unavoidable source of the universal experience of worry. We present the avoidance model of worry, underscoring how worry takes one out of present-moment internal (emotional) experiences but also interferes with engagement in life, leaving one feeling like a "spectator." In addition, time is spent on the function of emotions (using material from DBT), as well as problems arising from efforts at experiential control and the potential benefits associated with exercising control behaviorally rather than experientially (using principles from ACT). All concepts are presented in multiple ways: through direct psychoeducation involving handouts, description, and discussion with clients regarding applicability to their lives, through experiential exercises (described in the following section) that allow clients to directly experience the concepts, and through homework assignments in which clients monitor their own responses in light of these concepts in order to see how well they apply.

Clients often present with the goal of improving control over their internal experiences, so it is important to directly address this desire and gently introduce the possibility that fully controlling internal experiences may not be possible. An early session is spent exploring the role that emotions, even negative ones, play in our lives (preparation for action, communication to self and others, enhancing experience). We also explore the clients' experience with attempts to control their internal experience, typically receiving confirmation that these efforts often amplify distress rather than minimize it. While clients often quickly conclude that control efforts worsen their distress, they are often unwilling to turn toward accepting internal experiences that seem dangerously potent, diffuse, and unrelenting. We validate this experience through our exploration of how emotional responses to events in the moment can become intensified and muddied by a number of internal processes such as imagining future events and outcomes, ruminating over past events, and judging and attempting to control experiences. We propose that while a compassionate, present-moment focus will not eliminate distress, it may clarify internal experiences so that they can be normalized, tolerated, and potentially used more adaptively.

Early in treatment, we explicitly shift the focus to addressing the way clients are living their lives. Clients engage in writing assignments that explore the ways that worry and anxiety interfere in central domains in their lives (interpersonal, occupational/educational, and personal, including self-care, spiritual, and physical well-being), as well as how they would like to be living in each of these domains if there were no obstacles. Collaboratively, we set a goal of addressing these domains throughout the course of treatment. In this way, acceptance is framed as in service of fully engaging in a meaningful life, rather than as in service of altering one's internal experience.

ACCEPTANCE AND MINDFULNESS-BASED STRATEGIES

A central component of treatment involves teaching clients how to practice the accepting, nonjudgmental stance of mindfulness in a range of contexts. Many exercises come from MBCT/MBSR and ACT, although we also include diaphragmatic breathing and progressive muscle relaxation from CBT (for these, we emphasize awareness of sensations, rather than efforts to alter these sensations). We emphasize that mindfulness is a process that involves redirecting one's attention again and again, gently, rather than achieving a static state of awareness.

We introduce clients to both formal and informal mindfulness practices, which they continue throughout the course of treatment in and between sessions. Formal practices include breathing, progressive muscle relaxation, sensory exercises (e.g., mindfulness of sounds), imagery exercises (e.g., the "thoughts-on-leaves" exercise from ACT; the mountain meditation from MBSR) (Kabat-Zinn, 1994), and emotion-focused exercises (mindfulness of emotions). In the first half of therapy, these exercises follow a set progression from awareness of body sensations to beginner's mind exercises (e.g., raisin exercise) to the challenge of thoughts and emotions (e.g., thoughts on leaves) to compassion (using the poem "Wild Geese" by Mary Oliver, as cited in Segal et al., 2002) to the development of a transcendent, observer self (e.g., mountain meditation), with clients addressing more challenging aspects of mindfulness after simpler ones have been practiced. Later, clients and therapists collaboratively choose exercises that highlight elements of mindfulness and acceptance that remain particularly challenging (this often involves compassion or the development of a transcendent, observer self). This can include developing idiosyncratic exercises to highlight specific concerns (such as mindfulness of pain among clients with specific health concerns).

These formal practices are complemented by informal practice in which clients bring mindfulness to various daily activities, such as eating, washing dishes, showering, etc. (Nhat Hanh, 1992). These exercises also become progressively more challenging, including practice being mindful in valued life activities such as interpersonal interactions. Clients (and therapists) are encouraged to bring mindfulness to painful and challenging emotions and experiences that arise in session. As a result of this practice, clients often report finding that their emotions evolve or become more differentiated and more easily tolerated.

One element of mindful awareness that we have found to be particularly important, and challenging, for our clients is nonjudgmental, compassionate awareness. In addition to repeated mindfulness practice, we promote compassion through modeling and the therapeutic relationship. Often, clients express the belief that a harsh internal stance is necessary to keep undesirable thoughts, feelings, and behavior in check. Rather than accepting this rule as fact, we encourage clients to test out and more closely examine what sort of vital and fulfilling changes are possible under a compassionate, as compared with a judging, stance.

We also incorporate exercises from ACT that emphasize the limits of language and the importance of experiential learning, in order to promote acceptance and provide additional ways that clients can separate themselves from their thoughts. For example, we have clients try to describe how they walk, swim, or play tennis to illustrate the limits of language in describing our experiential knowledge. We also have clients repeat a word (such as "milk") to see how it initially has numerous associations (e.g., "white," "cold," etc.) but with repetition becomes just sounds. We find that particularly helpful practices include changing "but" to "and" (e.g., "I'm feeling anxious AND I'm planning to go to the party") and using, for example, "I'm having the thought that I'm incompetent" (rather than "I'm incompetent") to describe one's thoughts.

BEHAVIORAL CHANGE

The final component of our treatment focuses on helping clients to engage more fully in their lives and to act in ways that are consistent with what matters to them. Here, we draw heavily from ACT's approach to valued action. From this perspective, values imply a way of being in the present moment and a direction or a process that unfolds over time that is distinct from goals or future-oriented, static outcomes. For instance, being emotionally intimate is viewed as a value, while finding a committed partner is classified as a goal. Values can be worked on continuously by taking small and large actions in everyday living (such as opening up in a therapy session, engaging in a conversation with someone at work).

In early sessions we help clients identify their values in the interpersonal, occupational/educational, and personal domains. Often, clients will be living more consistently with their values in one or the other of these domains; we emphasize the importance of attending to all three domains in order to live a balanced, fulfilling life (although it is likely that this will include fluctuations in which one domain is attended to more than the others).

Once clients identify their core values, they begin to monitor daily activities to see how consistent their actions are with these values. Often, clients discover that their worry is distracting them from fully participating in valued activities (such as a mother who is distracted while interacting with her child) and that attempts to control and avoid certain internal experiences may result in a missed opportunity to engage in a valued action (e.g., a client who values emotional intimacy may pass up a dating opportunity because it brings up feelings of uncertainty and discomfort). Once clients gain mindfulness and acceptance skills and increase their awareness of the importance of valued action in their lives, they are encouraged to begin to make specific behavioral commitments to valued actions each week.

In the last several sessions, progress is reviewed and future areas for continued growth and practice are identified. Relapse prevention is aimed at emphasizing that these practices are lifelong, as life continues to present stressors and challenges, and using the skills that have been acquired will help clients remain on their chosen path as painful thoughts and emotions inevitably arise. Lapses in accepting internal experience and pursuing valued actions are predicted, and plans for addressing them are formed, including ideas for keeping mindfulness practice and valued action present, such as attending meditation or yoga classes and placing reminders around the clients' homes, including the binder of therapy materials, mindfulness books, and symbols of mindfulness.

CASE STUDY

CLIENT BACKGROUND AND PRESENTING COMPLAINTS

Thomas was a 36-year-old married white man who presented to the clinic with complaints of excessive worry and pervasive anxiety. He described himself as someone who had always been a "worrywart," and remembered being told by his parents that he had been an anxious child. Thomas reported that his anxiety had increased somewhat after finishing graduate school 10 years earlier, and he described an acute exacerbation of worry and anxiety symptoms (involving a suicide attempt and subsequent hospitalization) 6 months prior to contacting our clinic due to increased marital tension and other life stressors. After his hospitalization, Thomas began interpersonal/psychodynamic psychotherapy with a provider outside the clinic and began Celexa (40 mg daily) to treat depression. He contacted our clinic to pursue "treatment focused on the anxiety." He also reported that he had begun to read some self-help books that used traditional cognitive behavioral methods to manage anxiety and had found these to be somewhat helpful.

Upon intake, Thomas described excessive, subjectively uncontrollable worry and anxiety about a wide range of topics, including the health and safety of his family, social and interpersonal interactions, being on-time for meetings and appointments, and work performance. He reported worrying about 70% of the day and also experiencing restlessness, fatigue, difficulty concentrating, irritability, muscle tension, and difficulty sleeping.

Thomas reported that the worry and anxiety interfered significantly with his functioning and satisfaction in multiple domains, including relationships and career. Based on an assessment by an independent reliable rater using the Anxiety Disorders Interview Schedule (ADIS-IV) of the *Diagnostic and Statistical Manual of Mental Disorders,* 4th ed. (DSM-IV) (Brown, DiNardo, & Barlow, 1994), he was assigned a principal diagnosis of GAD with a severity rating of 5 (of 8), and an additional diagnosis of social phobia (severity 4). Additionally, he reported symptoms that were below clinical threshold for major depressive disorder (MDD) (severity 2) and post-traumatic stress disorder (severity 3; related to a severe trauma he experienced in his adolescence). He was given a pretreatment global assessment of functioning (GAF) score of 65. Thomas was referred to a research study exploring the efficacy of this new treatment, and he consented to the conditions of the protocol.

PSYCHOEDUCATION, CONCEPTUALIZATION, AND MONITORING

The first several weeks of therapy focused on presentation of the model and development of a shared conceptualization. While Thomas was quickly able to identify ways that his anxiety reactions often occurred in response to imagined future threat, rather than threats actually present in the current environment, he initially had some difficulties with the idea that efforts to control worry and anxiety may be problematic. Thomas had specifically sought out the clinic because he was aware of the focus on cognitive behavioral treatments of anxiety, and his experiences with CBT in the past had focused on strategies intended to facilitate control of internal experiences. The therapist and Thomas worked together to foster an understanding of the ways in which efforts at control (through both worry and other attempts to suppress emotional experiences and/or avoid emotional situations) may have negative consequences. For example, Thomas came to realize that his decision to pursue a program of graduate study that he was not necessarily interested in but that minimized financial risks was motivated by efforts to reduce financial anxiety, resulting in his feeling unfulfilled in his work. He also began to notice that when he attempted to push away emotions, his attempts were often unsuccessful. For example, when Thomas attempted to suppress his anger in an interaction with his wife to minimize conflict, this attempt actually left him feeling angrier longer and likely contributed to a bigger conflict arising later in the day. Thomas' examination of his own experiences with emotional control facilitated his understanding of how control attempts can maintain or amplify internal experiences, can interfere with the recognition of pertinent information, and can inhibit taking actions that may address the source of the emotion. His weekly monitoring of anxiety and worry also increased his awareness of these patterns, as well as his willingness to be in contact with his emotional experience.

Concurrently, the therapist normalized and validated Thomas' attempts to control and avoid. The learning environments that foster avoidance, including the cultural messages that emotions are "bad," and the apparent short-term success of these attempts, were addressed. In addition, Thomas' significant early trauma history was incorporated into a conceptualization of his attempts at avoidance. Thomas had experienced an interpersonal trauma during adolescence, and the therapist noted that one of the salient "rules" he might have learned through that experience was "emotions are dangerous both in you and in others." Thomas began to accept that the paradoxical consequences of these natural attempts to avoid and suppress emotional experiences may have led to his difficulties with anxiety.

SKILLS TRAINING IN MINDFULNESS

Mindfulness skills training proceeded according to the guidelines described previously. For example, an initial exercise involving diaphragmatic breathing was taught in the first session. However, while traditional diaphragmatic breathing practice focuses on a change agenda (i.e., relaxation), this exercise was taught as an example of attending to more concrete internal experiences such as breathing; Thomas was encouraged to first simply practice awareness of his breath, and to then deepen his breathing with continued attention to internal experiences. Progressive muscle relaxation was also introduced, although this exercise was conceptualized as a way to practice awareness of tension and of the sensation of "release." Thomas observed that these exercises were relaxing to him; he noted that these were good ways to "block out" anxiety. He was encouraged to attend to the awareness of the exercise in the present moment, to notice how these exercises were different each time he practiced them, and to use these exercises to "let go" of the desire to reduce anxiety.

As therapy progressed, Thomas began practicing informal mindfulness exercises, as described previously. He also began to do sitting meditation for brief periods (less than 5 minutes) almost daily, based on his own interest in this form of practice. Again, Thomas reported that sitting meditation often produced a relaxation response, and he indicated that he often practiced with this outcome of relaxation in mind (and would then judge that he had done the practice "wrong" if it did not produce the desired effect). The therapist normalized attachment to the relaxation Thomas associated with mindfulness, and also noted that this may be indicative of attempts to use this new skill as another form of avoidance. The importance of awareness of both pleasant and aversive aspects of experience was emphasized, and Thomas was asked to attend to all aspects of his experience during his practice, while also acknowledging and accepting his natural desire to approach relaxation and avoid distress.

Therapy then focused on mindfulness of thoughts and feelings using incidents from Thomas' life for practice. For example, Thomas recalled that during the previous week he encountered his father-in-law doing something Thomas felt was unsafe, had asked him to stop, and became angry when the father-in-law refused. Thomas was asked to imagine this situation in vivid detail and to allow awareness and acceptance of the thoughts and emotions that came up, while at the same time practicing acceptance of his natural attempts to push away these experiences. In session, Thomas was able to be aware of the thoughts he had during the situation (e.g., "My father-in-law is an idiot") but had more difficulty experiencing emotions.

Clients commonly find awareness of a particular domain more salient than that of other domains; for Thomas it was easiest to access cognition but more difficult to notice and have contact with emotional experiences. Access to emotional experience can be particularly difficult in clients with GAD, because often the affect has been pervasively and chronically avoided. Thomas and the therapist discussed his tendency to rely on cognitive activity, in the form of both worry and intellectual analysis, as a coping strategy, making access to this internal experience likely easier because reliance on this experience was more habitual. Mindfulness as a process, with an emphasis on intention to accept and allow, was emphasized as a potential method of increasing Thomas' access to his emotions, and Thomas was asked to continue practicing exercises that included emotional awareness components, despite his frustration with these exercises. The therapist normalized the difficulty in this process and suggested continued practice of mindfulness of emotions, with a focus on *allowing,* rather than forcing, experiences to arise. As Thomas' mindfulness practice progressed, he did begin to experience greater openness to and awareness of his emotional experiences. This became particularly clear in his mindfulness of emotions during interpersonal interactions. In his initial monitoring, Thomas described predominantly anxious feelings during interactions with others. However, as he practiced mindful interacting, Thomas began to describe more complexity in his emotional experience, with increased awareness of guilt, anger, sadness, and loneliness. As he experienced a fuller range of emotion, Thomas also reported having "clearer" emotional experiences and reported that these clear emotions, while painful, felt less aversive than the undifferentiated anxiety he had experienced previously. While Thomas still sometimes practiced mindfulness with the goal of relaxation, he also made progress in accepting and allowing distress.

Thomas struggled with thoughts that mindfulness may actually exacerbate his difficulties, given his subjective experience that he was quite hypervigilant. For example, he stated, "I am concerned that increased awareness might make my GAD worse because I seem to pay too much attention and inflate the importance of everything." The therapist encouraged Thomas to reflect on how his keen attention was narrowed to threatening information and how mindfulness may be seen as a way to cultivate a more expansive awareness. During his homework practice, Thomas did notice that, particularly in interpersonal situations, his attention was drawn to others' reactions, particularly when he was having thoughts that the other person was negatively evaluating him. Thomas was encouraged to use mindfulness practice to expand his awareness to notice all aspects of the situation.

Thomas also reported that he was becoming "more self-conscious" during mindfulness practice, and he asked his therapist about the similarities between mindful and self-conscious awareness. Upon further examination, it became clear that Thomas was experiencing more awareness of a variety of internal experiences and was judging himself for having those experiences. Thomas' difficulty with self-judgment illustrates another common process seen in clients in their initial mindfulness practice; clients become more open and accepting of their internal experiences but often require additional practice to become accepting of *themselves* as individuals who have these experiences. Thomas was introduced to the idea of "compassionate" or "kindly" awareness as an aspect of the nonjudgmental stance in mindfulness.

The process of cultivating compassion can be a difficult one for both the therapist and the client, because the process suggests access to emotional or cognitive control (e.g., "I should feel better about myself"). Thus, compassion is approached as an intention, rather than a way of thinking or feeling. Thomas was encouraged to imagine that he could observe his experience in the same way that a supportive friend would. In session, exercises were utilized to promote a compassionate stance. For example, the mountain meditation (Kabat-Zinn, 1994) was used to facilitate connection with the unchanging, core sense of self, which, like a mountain, may "simply be what it is" despite changing thoughts and emotion. Throughout therapy, Thomas became more aware of his self-judgments and of the very high standards he often set for himself. Mindful awareness enabled Thomas to begin to practice more flexibility in these standards and apply more compassion for himself when he did not meet them. Thomas began to regard distressing internal experiences as normal and essential aspects of the human experience, and he reported that he was more often able to "laugh with himself."

IDENTIFYING VALUES AND INTRODUCTION TO VALUED ACTION

Thomas was introduced to an additional application of mindfulness: awareness and attention to personal values when making choices about behavior. Through treatment he had become aware that he often made choices in his life based on managing his emotions and avoiding anxiety rather than on what was important to him. Through practice of more "mindful action," Thomas was encouraged to take values-directed intentional action even when taking such actions may have been painful, frightening, and anxiety provoking. Mindfulness skills were described as a way to facilitate valued action, by:

- encouraging awareness of values in choice moments,
- promoting awareness of internal obstacles to action as they arise (e.g., thoughts and feelings),
- enhancing engagement with and participation in the valued behavior as it occurs, and
- enhancing acceptance and nonjudgment of the emotions that may result from valued action.

Thomas completed the values writing assignments described previously and monitored action in valued domains along with obstacles that arose. Initially, Thomas reported mainly external barriers to participation (e.g., "Too many things to do today"). However, after identifying "being a supportive father" as one of his values, he also became aware that even when he did find time to spend with his daughter, he often felt detached from her because his attention tended to be narrowed to potentially dangerous stimuli in her environment. Thomas began to shift his schedule so that he found more time to spend with his daughter and applied mindfulness skills during the time he spent so as to better engage with the present moment. Using this combination of mindfulness and valued action, Thomas made progress in several valued domains. For example, over the course of treatment Thomas observed that he often remained passive in interpersonal relationships in order to avoid upsetting others. Through mindful attention to this process he was able to take a more willing stance in his interactions, making the intentional choice to sometimes assert his own needs and accept the possibility that this may cause himself or the other person some distress. By the end of treatment he had made some significant changes in his relationships with his wife, family, and coworkers and was increasingly willing both to assert himself and to support others. He had also made progress in the domain of self-care; he was spending time each week focusing on activities that he considered nourishing and fun and was more accepting and compassionate toward himself and his own needs.

PROGRESS REVIEW, RELAPSE PREVENTION, AND TERMINATION

The last several sessions were used to process these experiences, problem-solve, clarify treatment components, and provide support. In addition, ways to prevent relapse were reviewed in session. Thomas was encouraged both to expect and to plan for normal fluctuations in practice. Thomas scheduled regular weekly "check-in" appointments with himself to replace the structure of therapy. He also chose several books on mindfulness in order to keep these concepts fresh. Thomas also chose some items related to his daughter (for example, a photograph of her on his desk, and a particular toy that was kept in the home's family room), and other items related to his self-care needs (for example, a fishing fly he had tied) to serve as cues of mindfulness and valued actions. Thomas practiced using these items to cultivate awareness of the present moment when he saw them. For example, as Thomas practiced being engaged in play with his daughter, his mind would frequently wander to worries about her safety. The toy reminded him to return to the present moment with her, and he found that by using this cue he was better able to return to mindfulness even in this particularly difficult context.

By the end of treatment Thomas was practicing mindfulness both in long formal meditation sessions and informally in his daily interactions. He became better at noticing internal events such as thoughts and feelings as they arose and noticing the urge to judge, avoid, or suppress emotional responses. Thomas reported that he was living his life in a way that felt more meaningful after making these changes. He felt that the mindfulness component of the treatment had been particularly helpful and planned to expand his practice by visiting a local meditation center.

CLIENT'S STATUS POSTTREATMENT AND AT FOLLOW-UP

When assessed by an independent rater following his final treatment session, Thomas reported significantly lower levels of generalized worry and anxiety, as well as lower anxiety related to social situations. He was not given any principal DSM-IV diagnoses; he was judged to have GAD in partial remission (severity 2 of 8), social phobia in partial remission (severity 2), and a GAF score of 78. Just after the last session of therapy, Thomas' wife gave birth to a baby girl; Thomas reported that despite this significant new stressor in his environment, his worry and anxiety remained low. Thomas also reported that he coped with anxiety very differently than he had prior to treatment. He stated that he managed anxiety by "being in the moment, letting go, meditating." When Thomas was assessed 9 months posttreatment, he again received no principal diagnosis (GAD and social phobia in partial remission) and was assigned a GAF score of 83. He reported continued regular formal and informal mindfulness practice several times a week, and reported that he was more aware of his personal values and regularly used this awareness when choosing action.

EMPIRICAL SUPPORT TO DATE

We are just finishing a treatment development grant in which we conducted an open trial of this treatment, followed by a small randomized controlled trial (comparing it with a waitlist condition). At this early stage of empirical study, preliminary findings are promising.

Sixteen clients completed the treatment in the open trial. Five of these clients were treated by the developers of the treatment (L.R. and S.O.) and the other 11 were treated by graduate and postdoctoral-level clinicians supervised by the developers of the treatment. The sample of completers was 56.3% female, with 87.5% identified as white, one client identifying as Latina, and one as white/Southeast Asian, and they had an average age of 36.44 years $(SD = 12.34)$. Their average clinical severity rating for GAD was 5.93 (on a scale of 0 to 8, with 4 as a clinical cutoff; $SD = 0.93$). Two clients presented with comorbid principal diagnoses of depression (a population typically omitted from GAD clinical trials), and the overall sample presented with an average of 1.31 additional diagnoses (ranging from 0 to 3). These clients demonstrated significant reductions in clinician ratings of severity of GAD and in self-report measures of anxiety, worry, and depressive symptoms. Further, clients demonstrated significant increases in self-reported quality of life, an outcome that has not been investigated in previous investigations of GAD. Clients also demonstrated significant decreases in measures of proposed mechanisms of change (experiential avoidance and fear of emotional responses), suggesting the treatment may be effectively targeting intended psychological processes. All of these were large effects; large effects were also revealed on measures at the 3-month follow-up.

To date, 17 clients have completed the randomized controlled trial (10 randomly assigned to treatment). These clients presented with an average GAD severity of 5.66 $(SD = .61)$ and an average of .88 $(SD = .86)$ in additional diagnoses. Two clients presented with comorbid principal diagnoses of MDD and one client presented with a comorbid principal diagnosis of dysthymia (other comorbid conditions included social phobia, specific phobia, and obsessive-compulsive disorder). Clients were an average of 31.81 years old $(SD = 9.06)$. The majority of clients identified themselves as white, with one Latino and one Asian American client. There were nine women in the sample. The treatment and waitlist group did not differ significantly in demographic variables or pretreatment levels of any of the outcome and process variables. In analyses controlling for pretreatment levels of each variable, the treatment group demonstrated significantly better outcomes in GAD clinician severity rating, number of additional diagnoses, anxiety, worry, and depressive symptoms, and quality of life. Significantly lower levels of experiential avoidance, fear of emotions, and emotion dysregulation were also revealed for the treatment group. Among those clients who have completed a posttreatment assessment, 62% meet criteria for high end-state functioning using criteria similar to those in other trials (Borkovec & Costello, 1993; Ladouceur *et al.*, 2000), suggesting comparable or slightly improved outcomes to previous trials, although such comparisons should be considered extremely preliminary at this point. As data collection is still under way, long-term follow-up data are not yet available. It remains to be seen whether this intervention is more efficacious than an alternative credible treatment. We are planning a study to test this next. Thus, while current findings are promising, more research is needed to determine whether the novel elements of this intervention increase efficacy in treating GAD.

PRACTICAL CONSIDERATIONS

COMPLEX CLINICAL PRESENTATIONS: PSYCHOTROPIC MEDICATIONS, COMORBIDITY, AND ADDITIONAL TREATMENTS

Individuals with GAD commonly present with other disorders and problem areas. They are often taking psychotropic medications for anxiety, depression, or both. In our clinic (Center for Anxiety and Related Disorders, Boston University), clients are often in additional therapies for other problems in their life and are seeking more targeted treatment of their anxiety disorder from us.

Although the conceptualization presented previously is tailored specifically for GAD, there are many elements of it that we consider to be much broader. An experiential avoidance conceptualization can explain multiple presenting problems (e.g., Hayes *et al.*, 1996; Hayes *et al.*, 1999), and we suspect that the numerous difficulties our clients present with are often joined in their experientially avoidant function. Thus, with each client, we work to develop a conceptualization that captures his or her full diagnostic and clinical picture, rather than focusing solely on GAD, although for the purposes of research, GAD is the specified target of treatment. We have found that comorbid disorders and depressive symptoms are both targeted successfully in our treatment. However, outside of a research protocol, we incorporate treatment elements from empirically supported interventions for comorbid problems, provided they are consistent with our conceptualization. Thus, interoceptive exposure might be emphasized for a client with comorbid panic disorder, although the emphasis would be on noticing interoceptive cues, rather than trying to reduce them through exposure (experimental research suggests that an acceptance rationale may, in fact, reduce the distress associated with physical symptoms in panickers; Levitt, Brown, Orsillo, & Barlow, 2004). Similarly, we might emphasize action (similar to behavioral activation; Martell, Addis, & Jacobson, 2001) earlier among individuals with comorbid depressive symptoms, with a similar rationale of living a valued life, rather than reducing depressive symptoms. In our research trial, we rule out clients with substance dependence, bipolar disorder, or psychotic disorders, because these problems need to be directly targeted. Although none of these problems preclude a mindfulness-based intervention, other elements of treatment would need to be incorporated.

Medication status has not predicted outcome in our trials to date (although our data on this issue are preliminary), suggesting that our treatment seems to work equally well when coupled with pharmacotherapy. However, when clients are concurrently taking medication, it is important that therapists work closely with medication providers to ensure that levels of medication are not raised as clients become less experientially avoidant and therefore experience phasic increases in emotional distress. Similar considerations apply when combining medications with exposure therapies. It is our impression that medications may be helpful in some cases because they bring levels of distress to more tolerable levels, allowing clients to practice mindfulness and acceptance and develop those skills. We have worked with several clients to taper their medications successfully following development of mindfulness skills and increases in valued action.

For practical reasons, in our research we have allowed individuals to be in adjunctive therapies if these therapies do not target anxiety in any way. However, it is our preference clinically that clients do not engage in multiple therapies concurrently. Clients and other treatment providers often view cognitive behavioral therapies as narrowly targeting certain problems, leading to a practice of pursuing a more general treatment in addition to a specific CBT treatment. However, with our focus on living a valued life and our attention to a range of emotional experiences, we do not consider this to be a focal treatment. Often other treatments, particularly if they subtly encourage experiential avoidance, can conflict with our treatment. Minimally, this treatment requires substantial time and effort, and therefore we feel clients will fare better if they are not splitting their focus by engaging in additional therapy.

TYPE AND NATURE OF MINDFULNESS PRACTICE

One aspect of our treatment that is different from many mindfulness-based interventions is the absence of required extensive sitting practice and the flexibility in types of practice clients engage in. In order to maximize the acceptability of our intervention, and to promote behavioral flexibility, we allow clients to choose which practices they will do regularly. Some clients find progressive muscle relaxation particularly beneficial and use it regularly; others practice it for a few weeks and then stop using it. Some clients, like Thomas, begin their own formal sitting practice and go on to pursue other contexts for meditation practice. Some clients use yoga as a regular practice. Other clients develop their own idiosyncratic practices such as mindfully riding the subway every day or mindfully spending time in a church. We try to strike a balance between allowing clients to choose what works best for them and gently encouraging them to at least try those practices they find less appealing, because there may be something to be learned from them. However, we feel that allowing clients to gravitate toward the practice that seems most helpful to them makes it more likely that they will maintain their practice. In addition, we emphasize informal practice, as this may also be one of the ways that practice more effectively stays with a person. It remains an empirical question how much and what forms of mindfulness practice are optimal.

QUALIFICATION AND TRAINING OF THERAPISTS

We have not yet systematically studied the optimal form of training for therapists using our treatment. We encourage our therapists to read multiple sources about mindfulness and acceptance-based treatments and to engage in a range of mindfulness practices, although we do not require that they have a formal practice (as some mindfulness-based interventions do). We believe that therapists need to have their own experiences with the practice of mindfulness and valued action in order to better understand their clients' struggles. We use the "two mountain" metaphor from ACT to describe the relationship we see between the therapist and the client: The therapist is not above the client on a mountain, telling him or her where to go on a path already traveled. Instead, the therapist is on his or her own mountain, facing his or her own challenges, but with a clearer view of some of the obstacles in the client's path because of the unique perspective. We encourage our therapists to be mindful of their own path and their own learning as they help clients navigate theirs. We also suggest that therapists engage in some form of mindful practice prior to and within sessions in order to engage optimally with their clients.

In addition to reading our extensive manual, our therapists read several of the sources it draws from. We also have new therapists listen to therapy tapes in order to provide a model of how the therapy is carried out. We then work extensively with therapists as they see their cases to help them develop and refine an acceptance-based conceptualization of their clients and a corresponding treatment plan. We consider this level of consistent reflection to be an essential component of successfully carrying out the treatment and have found that supervision is important, particularly during early stages of training.

RELAPSE PREVENTION

As noted previously, relapse prevention is an integral part of our treatment. During our open trial, clients displayed some reductions in treatment gains at follow-up, although they remained significantly improved. Since then we have devoted more time to making sure that clients leave treatment with a clear conceptualization of what elements of treatment were beneficial to them, how they can continue their practice on their own, and how to proceed when inevitable lapses occur. We have tried to incorporate outside structures in these relapse prevention efforts when they fit well with the client, such as meditation centers and yoga studios that can provide a context for sustaining mindfulness practice. We have also had clients identify cues (e.g., pictures of mountains to remind them of the mountain mediation, stones or figures that remind them of mindfulness, posted notes that say "breathe") that they can include in various environments to keep their practice alive. We provide lists of books that we have found helpful in promoting our own practices and encourage clients to locate their own resources (in fact, some of the books on our list have been suggested by previous clients). Clients also develop lists of values within each domain or important lessons learned from valued action in order to help them remember to live intentionally a life that matters to them.

CHALLENGES OF MINDFULNESS

Much has been written about the numerous challenges inherent in mindfulness practice. Here we highlight particularly salient areas in our work with individuals with GAD.

Mindfulness as a Way to Avoid Distress

As noted in the case description of Thomas, it is easy for anxious clients to find mindfulness practice relaxing and to begin engaging in it as another way to reduce distress. It is important to notice and discuss this process, both validating the inevitability of enjoying that consequence and highlighting the cost of clinging to that outcome. We encourage clients to be present to whatever emerges from their practice, to notice when they begin to judge an outcome as more or less desirable, and to gently let go of that judgment and return to the experience itself. If clients are repeatedly experiencing mindfulness practice as pleasant, we will invite them to practice mindfulness in more distressing contexts in order to ensure that they also have experiences during the course of therapy in which mindfulness is difficult or challenging, rather than having these experiences emerge as obstacles following termination.

Mindfulness as a Waste of Time

As individuals with GAD often lead very busy lives, it can be a significant challenge to get them to set aside time for mindfulness practice, particularly when it is not clear to them how this practice will help. In order to increase initial compliance with mindfulness practice, we are careful to develop a shared conceptualization of GAD and a shared treatment plan that delineates the potential benefits of practice. While we validate the doubts a client might have about the potential utility of mindfulness, we ask for willingness to commit to trying some of the prescribed exercises and watching to see whether or not they seem beneficial. In our experience, even early, brief mindfulness practices increase many clients' awareness of how rarely they attend to the present and how they may be missing out on living their lives as a result. Further, clients often have at least some experience of mindfulness deepening their experience of life after some degree of practice, so a commitment to practice for a few weeks is usually enough to engage them in more consistent and sustained mindfulness practice.

Mindfulness in Action

In our treatment we are constantly addressing the dialectic between acceptance and change (Linehan, 1993b). On the one hand, we encourage clients to be aware and accepting of whatever is, in this moment. On the other hand, we encourage them to look at their lives and take intentional action to change the way things are. However, in these actions, we focus on the process, the intention, and the action itself, rather than a desired internal or external outcome. In other words, a client who valued honest communication in relationships would focus on clearly stating his or her needs to a loved one, rather than the desired outcome of those needs being met or a reduction in his or her distress. This emphasis is similar to bringing awareness to the breath and focusing on this action, rather than the desired consequences of doing it (such as wanting to feel more calm). Thus, the elements of mindfulness and action are consistent with one another, although it has been less common for behavioral change to be explicitly emphasized in mindfulness-based treatments. The action element of our treatment is heavily influenced by ACT, as well as other writings that emphasize engaged mindfulness (Nhat Hanh, 1992) and intentional, mindful action without attachment to the consequences (e.g., Chodron, 2001; Salzberg, 2002).

Despite this congruence between mindfulness and action, we find that often clients either confuse acceptance and mindfulness with complacency or begin to use valued action as yet another thing they need to be doing to achieve happiness and reduce distress. Therefore, we emphasize that mindfulness is not in opposition to action, and also emphasize that when acting, our focus is awareness, intention, repeated practice, and nonattachment to the desired internal and external consequences of actions. (However, we also note that it is inevitable that one will desire certain outcomes and feel disappointed if they do not occur, all of which is something else to notice with compassion). We find that with experience, clients begin to cultivate and ultimately own the value of living intentionally and experience it as quite different from their typical patterns of acting.

DIRECTIONS FOR FUTURE RESEARCH

While preliminary findings are encouraging, significant research is still needed on acceptance-based behavior therapy for GAD. In addition to randomized controlled trials that determine efficacy compared with credible alternative treatments, dismantling studies exploring the efficacy of specific elements of the treatment are needed to determine their additive effects. In addition, longitudinal research exploring mechanisms of change will help us determine whether the treatment works through the proposed mechanisms. It will also be important to explore the stability of observed effects, as well as the breadth of these effects by including broader assessments of functioning and valued living. Finally, we need to explore whether the treatment is equally efficacious with clients who vary across demographic and other variables (e.g., race, ethnicity, age, gender, comorbid diagnoses, Axis II diagnoses) or whether adjustments need to be made for specific groups of clients.

A host of other questions remain, such as optimal amount and type of mindfulness practice, optimal amount and type of therapist training required, optimal parameters of treatment, role of outside resources, etc. In addition, controlled experimental research is needed on the phenomena of experiential avoidance, acceptance, and aspects of mindfulness in order to determine whether the proposed consequences of these strategies are accurate and what the conditions are under which they are most likely to occur.

We are excited about this new incarnation of interest in the extremely old construct of mindfulness and look forward to learning more about its utility through clinical innovation and careful empirical study in the years to come.

ACKNOWLEDGMENTS

Preparation of this chapter was supported in part by National Institute of Mental Health Grant MH63208 to the first and last authors. The authors thank Dave Barlow for his support of this research. We also thank the therapists and clients involved in the grant, whose wisdom greatly enhances this treatment.

REFERENCES

American Psychiatric Association. (1994). *Diagnostic and statistical manual of mental disorders* (4th ed.). Washington, DC: Author.

Borkovec, T. D., Alcaine, O. M., & Behar, E. (2004). Avoidance theory of worry and generalized anxiety disorder. In R. G. Heimberg, C. L. Turk, & D. S. Mennin (Eds.), *Generalized anxiety disorders: Advances in research and practice* (pp. 77–108). New York: Guilford.

Borkovec, T. D., & Costello, E. (1993). Efficacy of applied relaxation and cognitive-behavioral therapy in the treatment of generalized anxiety disorder. *Journal of Consulting and Clinical Psychology, 61*, 611–619.

Borkovec, T. D., & Hu, S. (1990). The effect of worry on cardiovascular response to phobic imagery. *Behaviour Research and Therapy, 28*, 69–73.

Borkovec, T. D., Newman, M. G., Lytle, R., & Pincus, A. (2002). A component analysis of cognitive behavioral therapy for generalized anxiety disorder and the role of interpersonal problems. *Journal of Consulting and Clinical Psychology, 70*, 288–298.

Borkovec, T. D., & Roemer, L. (1994). Generalized anxiety disorder. In R. T. Ammerman & M. Hersen (Eds.), *Handbook of prescriptive treatments for adults* (pp. 261–281). New York: Plenum.

——— (1995). Perceived functions of worry among generalized anxiety disorder subjects: Distraction from more emotionally distressing topics? *Journal of Behavior Therapy and Experimental Psychiatry, 26*, 25–30.

Borkovec, T. D., & Ruscio, A. M. (2001). Psychotherapy for generalized anxiety disorder. *Journal of Clinical Psychiatry, 62*, 37–45.

Borkovec, T. D., & Sharpless, B. (2004). Generalized anxiety disorder: Bringing cognitive-behavioral therapy into the valued present. In S. C. Hayes, V. M. Follette, & M. M. Linehan (Eds.), *Mindfulness and acceptance: Expanding the cognitive-behavioral tradition* (pp. 209–242). New York: Guilford.

Brown, T. A., DiNardo, P. A., & Barlow, D. H. (1994). *Anxiety Disorders Interview Schedule for DSM-IV*. Albany, NY: Graywind Publications.

Chodron, P. (2001). *The places that scare you: A guide to fearlessness in difficult times*. Boston: Shambhala.

Greenberg, L. S., & Safran, J. D. (1987). *Emotions in psychotherapy*. New York: Guilford.

Hayes, S. C., Strosahl, K. D., & Wilson, K. G. (1999). *Acceptance and commitment therapy: An experiential approach to behavior change*. New York: Guilford Press.

Hayes, S. C., Wilson, K. G., Gifford, E. V., Follette, V. M., & Strosahl, K. (1996). Experiential avoidance and behavioral disorders: A functional dimensional approach to diagnosis and treatment. *Journal of Consulting and Clinical Psychology, 64*, 1152–1168.

Kabat-Zinn, J. (1994). *Wherever you go there you are: Mindfulness meditation in everyday life*. New York: Hyperion.

Ladouceur, R., Dugas, M. J., Freeston, M. H., Leger, E., Gagnon, F., & Thibodeau, N. (2000). Efficacy of a new cognitive-behavioral treatment for generalized anxiety disorder: Evaluation in a controlled clinical trial. *Journal of Consulting and Clinical Psychology, 68*, 957–964.

Levitt, J. T., Brown, T. A., Orsillo, S. M., & Barlow, D. H. (2004). The effects of acceptance versus suppression of emotion on subjective and psychophysiological response to carbon dioxide challenge in patients with panic disorder. *Behavior Therapy, 35*, 747–766.

Linehan, M. M. (1993a). *Skills training manual for cognitive behavioral treatment of borderline personality disorder*. New York: Guilford.

——— (1993b). *Cognitive-behavioral treatment of borderline personality disorder*. New York: Guilford.

Martell, C. R., Addis, M. E., & Jacobson, N. S. (2001). *Depression in context: Strategies for guided action*. New York: Guilford.

Mennin, D. S., Heimberg, R. G., Turk, C. L., & Fresco, D. M. (2005). Preliminary evidence for an emotion dysregulation model of generalized anxiety disorder. *Behaviour Research and Therapy, 43*, 1281–1310.

Nhat Hanh, T. (1992). *Peace is every step: The path of mindfulness in everyday life.* New York: Bantam Books.

Roemer, L., & Orsillo, S. M. (2002). Expanding our conceptualization of and treatment for generalized anxiety disorder: Integrating mindfulness/acceptance-based approaches with existing cognitive-behavioral models. *Clinical Psychology: Science and Practice, 9*, 54–68.

Roemer, L., Orsillo, S. M., & Barlow, D. H. (2002). Generalized anxiety disorder. In D. H. Barlow (Ed.), *Anxiety and its disorders: The nature and treatment of anxiety and panic* (2nd ed.). New York: Guilford Press.

Roemer, L., Salters, K., Raffa, S., & Orsillo, S. M. (2005). Fear and avoidance of internal experiences in GAD: Preliminary tests of a conceptual model. *Cognitive Therapy and Research, 29*, 79–88.

Salzberg, S. (2002). *Faith: Trusting your own deepest experience.* New York: Riverhead Books.

Segal, Z. V., Williams, J. M., & Teasdale, J. D. (2002). *Mindfulness-based cognitive therapy for depression: A new approach to preventing relapse.* New York: Guilford.

Wegner, D. M. (1994). Ironic processes of mental control. *Psychological Review, 101*, 34–52.

Wells, A. (1995). Meta-cognition and worry: A cognitive model of generalized anxiety disorder. *Behavioural and Cognitive Psychotherapy, 23*, 301–320.

Wells, A., & Carter, K. (1999). Preliminary tests of a cognitive model of generalized anxiety disorder. *Behaviour Research and Therapy, 37*, 585–594.

Wittchen, H.-U., Zhao, S., Kessler, R. C., & Eaton, W. W. (1994). DSM-III-R generalized anxiety disorder in the National Comorbidity Survey. *Archives of General Psychiatry, 51*, 355–364.

4

MINDFULNESS-BASED APPROACHES TO EATING DISORDERS

JEAN L. KRISTELLER

Department of Psychology, Indiana State University, Terre Haute, Indiana

RUTH A. BAER

Department of Psychology, University of Kentucky, Lexington, Kentucky

RUTH QUILLIAN-WOLEVER

Duke University School of Medicine, Durham, North Carolina

INTRODUCTION: CHARACTERISTICS AND PREVALENCE OF EATING DISORDERS

The *Diagnostic and Statistical Manual of Mental Disorders*, 4th ed. (DSM-IV-TR) (American Psychiatric Association, 2000), recognizes two primary eating disorders: anorexia nervosa (AN) and bulimia nervosa (BN). It also includes a category for eating disorders not otherwise specified (EDNOS), which includes binge eating disorder (BED), subthreshold versions of AN and BN, and other disordered eating patterns. The primary features of AN include refusal to maintain a minimally normal body weight, intense fear of weight gain, disturbances in how body shape and weight are experienced and evaluated, and amenorrhea. Primary features of BN include frequent binge-eating episodes and the use of compensatory behaviors to prevent weight gain, such as self-induced vomiting, misuse of laxatives, fasting, or excessive exercise. In both AN and BN, self-evaluation is unduly influenced by body shape and weight. BED includes frequent binge eating but without the compensatory behaviors typical of BN. Whereas individuals with AN are severely underweight, those with bulimia or BED tend to be normal weight to obese.

In females, the lifetime prevalence of AN is approximately 0.5%. For BN, lifetime prevalence rates of 1% to 3% are commonly reported. Both are much more common in women than in men. EDNOS may be more common than either AN or BN (Ricca *et al.*, 2001). Millar (1998) reported that 47% of referrals to an eating disorder service met criteria for EDNOS, whereas 40% had BN and 13% had AN. Herzog, Keller, Lavori, & Sacks (1991) reported prevalence rates for all eating disorders combined of 5% to 15% when subthreshold cases were included. King (1989; 1991) also combined subthreshold with clear cases and found prevalence rates for eating disturbances of 3.9% for women and 0.5% for men.

Among obese persons, Spitzer *et al.* (1993) found prevalence rates of BED of about 30% for those in weight control programs, and 5% for those in community samples. BED is 1.5 times more common in women attending weight loss programs than in men, and is at least as common in whites and African Americans (Spitzer *et al.*, 1993; Sptizer *et al.*, 1992; Striegel-Moore, Wilfley, Pike, Dohn, & Fairburn, 2000). While the evidence is mixed, some studies have found that the prevalence and severity of binge eating increases with increasing adiposity (Bruce & Agras, 1992; Lowe & Capputo, 1991; Marcus & Lamparski, 1985; Spitzer *et al.*, 1993; Telch & Rossiter, 1988). For both obese and BED patients, caloric intake tends to increase as the individual's obesity increases. Additionally, BED patients tend to experience larger and more frequent weight fluctuations (Walsh & Devlin, 1998). These issues suggest that binge eating places obese individuals among those at highest risk for the medical complications of obesity. Some studies suggest that obese binge eaters are less successful in weight management programs, being more likely to drop out of treatment and to regain weight more rapidly (Gormally, Rardin, & Black, 1980; Keefe, Wyshogrod, Weinberger, & Agras, 1984; Marcus, Wing, & Hopkins, 1988; Sherwood, Jeffrey, & Wing, 1999). Those who achieve abstinence from binge eating may be more successful in weight loss and maintenance (Eldredge *et al.*, 1997), suggesting a need for treatment of the eating disorder prior to weight loss therapies.

All of the eating disorders are associated with significant distress and/or dysfunction, including mood disturbance, anxiety symptoms, substance abuse, and physical complications. Subthreshold cases also appear to have significant levels of distress or impairment. For example, Striegel-Moore, Dohm, *et al.* (2000) found that a community sample of women with subthreshold BED did not differ from those meeting full criteria on measures of shape and weight concern, dietary restraint, or psychiatric distress. Overall, the evidence suggests that a wide range of eating disturbances cause significant distress and dysfunction in the general population. These problems are more common in women than in men.

MINDFULNESS-BASED TREATMENTS FOR EATING DISORDERS

The most widely researched treatments for eating disorders are based on cognitive-behavioral procedures and have focused largely on BN and BED. Treatment of AN has received less research attention (Roth & Fonagy, 2005). For BN, the literature suggests that cognitive-behavioral therapy (CBT) eliminates binge eating and purging in about 50% of participants, and reduces it in many others, and that maladaptive dieting and distorted body image also are substantially improved (Wilson, 2004). CBT for BED also has strong empirical support (Apple & Agras, 1997; Fairburn, Marcus, & Wilson, 1993), as does interpersonal therapy (IPT) (Klerman, Weissman, Rounsaville, & Chevron, 1984) for both BN and BED. However, as many participants show incomplete response to treatment, additional work seems necessary to find more broadly effective interventions. Wilson (1996) has suggested that acceptance-based methods for treating eating disorders deserve increased attention, and several interventions that incorporate mindfulness training and acceptance-related procedures recently have been introduced. Some of these are adaptations of previously developed interventions. For example, dialectical behavior therapy (DBT) (Linehan, 1993) has been adapted for BED and BN; mindfulness-based cognitive therapy (MBCT) (Segal, Williams, & Teasdale, 2002) has been adapted for BED; and acceptance and commitment therapy (ACT) (Hayes, Strosahl, & Wilson, 1999) has been applied to AN. In addition, mindfulness-based eating awareness training (MB-EAT) (Kristeller & Hallett, 1999) was developed specifically for BED. These interventions are summarized in the following sections. As DBT, MBCT, and ACT are described in more detail in several other chapters in this volume, the current chapter summarizes these briefly and devotes more comprehensive attention to MB-EAT.

DIALECTICAL BEHAVIOR THERAPY

The recent adaptation of DBT for eating disorders consists of 20 weekly sessions and has been applied in both group and individual formats (Safer, Telch, & Agras, 2000; 2001; Telch, Agras, & Linehan, 2000; 2001). The rationale for this approach is based on an affect regulation model of binge eating, which states that eating binges function to reduce unpleasant emotional states in individuals who lack more adaptive emotion regulation skills (Wiser & Telch, 1999). Negative emotions may be triggered in a variety of ways, such as through comparison of one's body with images found in fashion magazines, by unpleasant interactions with others, or by other undesirable circumstances. Once negative emotion has been triggered, the individual fears that it will escalate and searches for a means of reducing it. By distracting attention from the negative affect, binge eating temporarily relieves this distress and thus is negatively reinforced.

This version of DBT is designed to improve participants' ability to manage negative affect adaptively and includes training in three of the four skills modules included in standard DBT: mindfulness, emotion regulation, and distress tolerance. It also includes training in behavioral chain analysis, which is applied to binge eating episodes. The mindfulness skills are taught to counteract the tendency to use binge eating to avoid emotional awareness. These skills emphasize nonjudgmental and sustained awareness of emotional states as they are occurring in the present moment, without reacting to them behaviorally. Thus, participants learn to watch their emotions as if they were clouds moving across the sky, without efforts to change them and without self-criticism for having these experiences. Participants also practice mindful eating by engaging in the raisin exercise (see Chapter 1 in this volume for a more detailed description). Mindfulness skills are a critical foundation for the emotion regulation and distress tolerance skills that also are taught, as they enable participants to recognize and acknowledge their emotional states without engaging in automatic, impulsive behaviors. While in a state of mindful awareness, the individual is better able to make adaptive choices about emotion regulation and distress tolerance skills that could be used in place of binge eating.

MINDFULNESS-BASED COGNITIVE THERAPY

An adaptation of MBCT for BED has been explored by Baer, Fischer, and Huss (2005; in press). Although MBCT was developed to prevent depressive relapse, most MBCT strategies are not specific to depression, and the adaptation for BED adheres very closely to the MBCT manual (Segal et al., 2002; see Chapter 1 in this volume for a detailed description), with only a few changes. For example, the number of sessions was expanded from 8 to 10, and material specific to binge eating was substituted for material related to depression. Baer et al. (2005; in press) note that several recent theoretical formulations of binge eating imply that mindfulness skills might be useful in treating this problem. For example, Heatherton and Baumeister (1991) argue that binge eating is motivated by a desire to escape from self-awareness. Setting high personal standards leads to negative thoughts and unpleasant emotions when these standards are not met. This aversive internal state leads to a narrowing of attention and reduces inhibitions against eating. A model of emotional schemas proposed by Leahy (2002) suggests that individuals who label their emotions as pathological may attempt to reduce awareness of their emotional states through substance use, dissociation, or binge eating. In addition, Lowe (1993) and Craighead and Allen (1995) note that individuals who binge eat often have extensive histories of unsuccessful dieting and weight cycling, which may lead to impaired sensitivity to hunger and satiety cues. MBCT includes a variety of mindfulness practices designed to cultivate nonjudgmental and nonreactive observation and acceptance of bodily sensations, perceptions, cognitions, and emotions. Thus, participation in MBCT should encourage increased ability to observe hunger and satiety cues, increased willingness to experience negative affect that previously has triggered binge eating, decreased believability of negative thoughts common in binge eating individuals, and increased ability to choose adaptive behaviors in stressful circumstances.

ACCEPTANCE AND COMMITMENT THERAPY

ACT is based on an experiential avoidance model that suggests that many forms of disordered behavior are related to attempts to avoid or escape aversive internal experiences, including sensations, cognitions, emotions, and urges (Hayes, Wilson, Gifford, Follette, & Strosahl, 1996). ACT emphasizes nonjudgmental acceptance of thoughts and feelings while changing overt behavior to work toward valued goals and life directions (Hayes *et al.,* 1999). The application of ACT to anorexia nervosa has been described in a recent clinical case study (Heffner, Sperry, Eifert, & Detweiler, 2002) and a recently published self-help manual (Heffner & Eifert, 2004). The intervention includes several mindfulness and acceptance-based strategies directed toward fat-related thoughts, images, and fears. For example, the *thought parade* is a mindfulness exercise in which the participant imagines that her thoughts are written on cards carried by marchers in the parade. Her task is to observe the parade of thoughts, such as "I'm a whale" and "My stomach is gross" (Heffner *et al.,* 2002, p. 234) as they come and go, without becoming absorbed in them or necessarily believing or acting on them. This exercise promotes the ability to observe cognitions nonjudgmentally and with acceptance, rather than engaging in anorexic behaviors in reaction to such thoughts. Similarly, the *bus driver* exercise asks the participant to imagine that she is the driver of a bus, which represents her movement toward valued life goals. Fat-related thoughts are conceptualized as passengers on the bus, who demand that she change direction and drive the bus "down the anorexia road" (Heffner *et al.,* 2002, p. 235). This exercise encourages the ability to allow negative thoughts to be present without acting in accordance with them and while maintaining movement in valued directions. Good nutrition generally is required to maintain the energy to move in valued directions (i.e., to be a good friend, family member, or citizen, or to do good work). Thus, an important feature of the intervention is the clarification of the patient's most valued goals and directions.

MINDFULNESS-BASED EATING AWARENESS TRAINING

MB-EAT (Kristeller & Hallett, 1999) was developed by integrating elements from MBSR and CBT with guided eating meditations. The program draws on traditional mindfulness meditation techniques, as well as guided meditation, to address specific issues pertaining to shape, weight, and eating-related self-regulatory processes such as appetite and both gastric and taste-specific satiety. The meditative process is integrated into daily activity related to food craving and eating. It is informed by our current knowledge of processes in food intake regulation, including the role of hunger and satiety cues, and places primary attention on underlying eating patterns, relative to the other models outlined previously. Patterns of overeating, particularly binge eating, can be viewed as symptomatic of a prototypical dysregulation syndrome involving disturbances of affect regulation, cognitive and behavioral dysregulation, and physiological dysregulation. Mindfulness meditation is conceptualized as a way of training attention to help individuals first to increase awareness of automatic patterns and then to disengage undesirable reactivity. It is also viewed as a way to heighten awareness of potentially more healthy aspects of functioning, in this case physiologically based hunger and satiety cues, and to use such awareness to more "wisely" inform behavior and experience (Kristeller, 2003).

As is outlined in Table 4.1, each session incorporates meditation practice. General sitting meditation is similar to practices used in MBSR and MBCT. "Mini-meditations" also are taught, in which participants learn to stop for a few moments at key times during daily activities, particularly meal and snack times, to practice nonjudgmental awareness of thoughts and feelings. Several eating-related guided meditations are included, in which participants focus nonjudgmental attention on sensations, thoughts, and emotions related to hunger, satiety, and binge triggers. A number of the eating-related meditations use food, beginning with the raisin meditation and moving toward more complex and challenging foods, culminating with making food choices mindfully, first between just two foods and then at a buffet. Several sessions also incorporate mindful body work, moving from a body scan to self-soothing touch to mindful walking. The intervention then transitions to a forgiveness meditation related to one's own body and self, and a wisdom meditation, to emphasize that the wisdom to make better choices lies within.

Interventions that incorporate mindfulness meditation, with a goal of increasing general psychological and physiological self-regulation, are particularly well suited to the complexity of behavioral, emotional, and

TABLE 4.1   Outline of Sessions for MB-EAT Group

Session 1: Introduction to self-regulation model; Raisin exercise; Introduction to mindfulness meditation with practice in group. Assignment: Meditate with tape (continues all sessions).

Session 2: Brief meditation (continues all sessions); Mindful eating exercise (cheese and crackers); Concept of mindful eating; body scan. Assignment: Eat 1 snack or meal per day mindfully (continues all sessions with increasing number of meals/snacks).

Session 3: THEME: Binge triggers. Binge trigger meditation; Mindful eating exercise (sweet, high-fat food). Assignment: Mini-meditation before meals.

Session 4: THEME: Hunger cues—physiological vs. emotional. Hunger meditation; Eating exercise: Food choices—cookies vs. chips; healing self-touch. Assignment: Eat when physically hungry.

Session 5: THEME: Taste satiety cues—type and level of cues; Taste satiety meditation; Seated yoga. Assignment: Attend to taste and satisfaction/enjoyment.

Session 6: THEME: Stomach satiety cues—type and level of cues. Satiety meditation; Pot luck meal. Assignment: Stop eating when moderately full; Eat at a buffet.

Session 7: THEME: Forgiveness. Forgiveness meditation. Assignment: Eat all meals and snacks mindfully.

Session 8: THEME: Inner wisdom. Wisdom meditation; Walking meditation. Assignment: Eat all meals and snacks mindfully.

Session 9: THEME: Have others noticed? Where do you go from here? Relapse prevention; Celebratory pot luck meal.

Follow-up Sessions: Meditation practice; Review of progress; other weight management approaches.

cognitive dysregulation observed in eating disorders. This model is consistent with other perspectives on dysfunctional eating patterns: the chronic dieting model (e.g., Herman & Polivy, 1980), affect regulation models (e.g., Wilson, 1984), and the escape model (Heatherton & Baumeister, 1991).

The dysregulation model, which forms the theoretical basis of MB-EAT, synthesizes key aspects of the aforementioned models into a comprehensive explanation of a binge cycle. This model posits that the chronic dieting that many binge eaters engage in makes them susceptible to binge triggers that include physical stimuli, distorted cognitions, and negative affect. While it is informed by the affect regulation model, it gives more attention to introducing skills and awareness-related processes to food intake per se. Chronic dieting, patterns of binge eating, and use of food for nonnutritive reasons (i.e., emotional eating) are not only symptoms of underlying dysfunction but actively contribute to it. Emotionally, dieting may lead to frustration and deprivation, as well as dysphoria due to negative self-awareness. Once a dietary rule is violated (such as by eating a "forbidden" food or eating at an inappropriate time), the individual may give up control altogether, judging that she has "blown it," and binge, in a pattern consistent with the abstinence violation effect (AVE) (Marlatt & Gordon, 1985). This is further compounded by a lack of physiological awareness of satiety (Hetherington & Rolls, 1988) that also leaves one vulnerable to binge eating in that normal cues to stop eating are ignored or not experienced. The binge may bring some immediate physical and emotional gratification but is likely to be followed by physical discomfort and guilt. This then leads to continued negative self-evaluation and a reinstatement of dietary restraint. The binge cycle may vary by person, and some may not experience all of these components.

While CBT approaches address some aspects of this model, such as the distorted thinking of the AVE and the use of behavioral substitutions for emotional eating, the MB-EAT program may attenuate or interrupt more aspects of this cycle, and do so in a way that is more effective in internalizing and maintaining change. In comparison with the DBT approach, it is also more focused on the regulation of experiences of eating *per se*, but could be combined with DBT or CBT in an extended and more comprehensive program.

EMPIRICAL SUPPORT FOR MINDFULNESS-BASED APPROACHES TO EATING DISORDERS

Several clinical trials have provided strong support for the efficacy of DBT as adapted for the treatment of BN and BED. Telch *et al.* (2000) describe an uncontrolled trial with 11 women diagnosed with BED who participated in the group form of this treatment, with 20 weekly 2-hour sessions. Results showed that 9 of the 11 women had completely stopped binge eating by the end of treatment and no longer met criteria for BED. Substantial reductions in the urge to eat when feeling negative affect were observed, as were increases in self-reported ability to regulate negative moods. These findings suggest that the treatment was successful in teaching affect regulation skills, and that participants' ability to use these skills when experiencing negative affect improved. At 6-month follow-up, seven of the women remained abstinent from binge eating, and those who had binged did not meet the frequency criterion for BED diagnosis.

These authors followed this paper with a randomized trial in which DBT for BED was compared with a wait-list control condition (Telch *et al.,* 2001). At the end of treatment, 89% of participants in DBT had stopped binge eating, whereas only 12.5% of the control group had stopped. DBT participants also showed reduced urges to eat when feeling angry and reduced concerns about weight, shape, and eating patterns. At the 6-month follow-up, 56% of the DBT participants were abstinent from binge eating.

Findings did not support the hypothesis that increased ability to regulate affect was responsible for the observed improvements, as no differences between groups in negative affect or in mood regulation were noted. However, it is possible that the treatment reduces urges to eat in the presence of negative affect, rather than reducing the affect itself or increasing confidence in ability to regulate it.

Safer *et al.* (2001) report an additional randomized controlled trial (RCT) in which DBT was applied to bulimia nervosa. Treatment involved 20 weekly individual sessions. At posttreatment, binge eating and purging had stopped for 29% of treatment participants and had been greatly reduced for an additional 36% of participants. The others remained symptomatic. There were no dropouts from the treatment group. Substantial decreases in the tendency to eat when feeling negative affect also were observed.

Empirical support for MBCT applied to BED is preliminary but encouraging. In a recent case study, Baer *et al.* (2005) reported a complete cessation of eating binges and large reductions in eating, shape, and weight concerns, as well as increases in mindfulness. In a subsequent uncontrolled pilot study with six participants, Baer *et al.* (in press) reported large reductions in binge eating, eating concern, and the expectancy that eating leads to feeling out of control. Increases in mindfulness also were noted. To date, the use of ACT for treating anorexia has been reported only in a single case study (Heffner *et al.*, 2002). However, given that anorexia can be life-threatening and is widely regarded as difficult to treat, these findings are encouraging and suggest that additional studies could yield valuable information.

The evidence for MB-EAT to date is based on a nonrandomized, extended baseline/follow-up study (Kristeller & Hallett, 1999) and a recently completed randomized clinical trial (Kristeller, Quillian-Wolever, & Sheets, in preparation). Eighteen women completed the original study, out of 20 initial participants; their average age was 46.5 and mean weight was 238 lbs (body mass index: 40). None had previous experience with meditation, and all met DSM-IV criteria for BED with obesity. They participated in a manualized seven-session group treatment program lasting over 6 weeks, with 3 weeks of weekly assessment prior to, and following, treatment. Binges per week dropped from slightly over 4 to about 1.5, with only 4 participants still meeting criteria for BED at follow-up; the binges that remained decreased substantially in magnitude, another useful measure. Scores on the Binge Eating Scale (Gormally, Black, Daston, & Rardin, 1982) fell from the "severe" range to a level just higher than having "little or no problem" with binge eating (scores lower than 14). Measures of depression and anxiety also decreased from clinical to subclinical levels. There were no significant weight changes related to treatment.

The strongest predictor of improvement in eating control was the amount of time participants reported engaging in eating-related meditation, rather than general meditation. Improvement in awareness of satiety cues was significantly correlated with a reduction in the number of binges reported, but change in awareness of hunger cues was not.

While the results could not be attributed unequivocally to the meditation effects, the pattern suggested that engagement in the meditation practice contributed to the changes in mood and behavior. The magnitude of change was also consistent with those from treatments drawing on more traditional methods including CBT (Agras *et al.*, 1995), suggesting that they did not simply reflect nonspecific effects. Furthermore, results suggest that mindfulness and increased awareness of satiety cues may be particularly important as mediating variables. While awareness of hunger cues also improved, BED is inherently more a dysfunction of failure to terminate eating than one of initiating eating too frequently (though both may occur). Therefore, becoming more sensitive to satiety signals may be particularly useful for increasing control of binge eating.

The recently completed RCT (Kristeller *et al.*, in preparation) included a larger sample (total $N = 85$ completed), with similar characteristics to the first study but also including 15% men, who were randomized to the MB-EAT condition, a psychoeducational (PE) treatment or a wait-list control condition, with follow-up at 1 and 4 months. The MB-EAT treatment components were somewhat revised and expanded (see Table 4.1) to nine sessions. In particular, mindfulness of satiety experience was separated into two sessions: taste awareness (sensory-specific satiety) and fullness awareness. A session was added that included a wisdom meditation. Again, the focus was on decreasing binge eating, rather than weight loss. The PE treatment drew on education materials used in the nationally known obesity treatment program at the Duke Diet and Fitness Center. As has been reported in other studies comparing specific interventions with psychoeducation, the MB-EAT and the PE groups showed somewhat comparable improvements in behavior and on the Binge Eating Scale. However, the MB-EAT group improved significantly more on the Disinhibition Scale of the Stunkard and Messick (1985) Eating Inventory, indicative of greater internalization of change. Again, while there was no overall average weight loss, improvement on this scale was highly correlated with weight loss. Measures of practice suggested that it was the use of eating-related meditations and mini-meditations that predicted greater improvement on other indicators of improved self-regulation.

CASE STUDY

The individual described here was a participant in our RCT on MB-EAT. She completed the protocol described previously and outlined in Table 4.1, as part of a group intervention.

CLIENT BACKGROUND

Paige was a 56-year-old, remarried African American female with well-treated high blood pressure, high cholesterol, impaired glucose tolerance, and binge eating disorder. She entered the MB-EAT program to obtain control of her eating and to gain "more control over life."

At 5′ 7″, Paige weighed 267 pounds. She reported that she had fluctuated around this weight for about a year, after having gained significant weight over the previous 6–7 years, despite multiple diets; in the past year alone she had dieted six times. Paige often skipped meals, restricted calories and fats, and attempted fad diets. The result: her binge eating continued at about four times per week, "often interfered" with her work and daily activities, and "always interfered" with her thoughts and feelings about herself and her personal relationships. In addition, she noted that even if not binge eating, she overate at least twice per day.

Paige lived with her husband of 10 years and her disabled teenage son. In addition to caring for her son, she had used her college education to develop a children's ministry in her neighborhood, where she sheltered a number of at-risk children. Paige noted that her eating disorder had affected her relationships with the children. She found herself hiding eating from them due to feelings of embarrassment. At intake, she was moderately distressed with her overall life and mildly depressed. Specifically, she was concerned about her marriage (a "mistake") and her tendency to please others, even at her own expense.

RESPONSE TO TREATMENT

From the first experiential exercise, Paige immediately understood the concept of mindful eating. She reported during the second week that when she sat down to a chicken meal, she noticed she was feeling excited. She looked at the food carefully and then said to herself, "Why are you so excited? That is nothing but a dead bird." Her delightful sense of humor brought laughter to the group and also demonstrated her ability to use awareness to recognize emotional reactivity and thoughts. Furthermore, she was able to apply these concepts without judgment in order to undermine her previous attachment to food.

Paige was fascinated by the process of meditation and immediately found it soothing. Though she had several children with her most of the time, she established a routine in which all of them took 30 minutes of "quiet time" so that she could practice her meditation. She instituted the practice to improve her health and was excited about passing on a skill to help the children self-soothe as well.

Paige's binge eating and her overall intake dropped steadily over the course of treatment and follow-up. Number of binges decreased from about 16 per month to 9 per month by the fifth week of treatment, and then declined to 2 binges per month by the end of 9 weeks. Binge eating completely subsided during the month following treatment, and remained this way at last measurement, 6 months posttreatment. Interestingly, Paige's weight remained stable at 260 lbs. throughout treatment but began to drop in the 6 months following treatment. Significant overeating episodes, as measured by the Eating Disorders Examination (EDE) (Fairburn & Cooper, 1993), dropped from twice daily at baseline to twice per month one month posttreatment, to once per month at the 6 month follow-up. Paige had lost 10 pounds (to 249.6) and 4.5 cm from her waist by continuing to practice the principles learned in the MB-EAT program; she pointed out that she eats only what she wants and stops eating when she is full. Over the course of treatment, while she continued to enjoy eating, food regained an ordinary rather than powerful place in her world.

Paige's level of depression steadily improved as well. Her scores on the Beck Depression Inventory (BDI-II) (Beck, Steer, & Brown, 1996) dropped from 15 at baseline, to 10 at week 5, to 9 at week 9, and to a score of 3 at 6 months posttreatment. Improvements in mood were paralleled by improvements in self-care. Paige increased her walking regimen from 25 minutes three times per week to daily walks. She became more concerned about cleaning up her surroundings and improving her living environment. Most importantly, she began to set boundaries with family members and friends who were used to taking advantage of her. Her enhanced confidence and self-care was so noticeable that her husband asked her if she was having an affair. She laughed and then explained, "What has happened is that I used to be a little tiny tree that would blow whichever way his wind blew me. Now I am a strong tree with a thick trunk. I don't just bend to his or anyone else's wind."

PRACTICAL AND CONCEPTUAL ISSUES IN USING MINDFULNESS-BASED INTERVENTIONS IN EATING DISORDERED POPULATIONS

Engaging individuals in a mindfulness approach to eating issues presents several challenges. Patients typically have a history of trying multiple diets and have a difficult time conceiving of an approach that does not promise yet another "quick fix." Yet this same experience can be used as a framework for presenting the need for a more permanent, enduring approach that involves an alternative to dieting. Initially, most individuals who have difficulty with binge eating are so distrustful of their own judgment in regard to food that they may not be convinced that such a goal is possible. Two issues are most salient: presenting the value of a mindfulness rather than a dieting approach, and the challenge of how to introduce meditation components to the client.

As in many applications of mindfulness and related meditation techniques, there is some value in framing it within a relaxation or stress management context. This is salient in relation to eating problems, because stress and negative emotions are common triggers for compulsive over-eating. However, eating problems particularly lend themselves to the concept of cultivating a "wise" mind, to the idea of going off automatic pilot, and to the value of cultivating awareness of internal cues. In that dieting itself entails a disengagement from the use of internal cues of hunger and satiety (substituting rules about foods and calories), a framework of becoming more attuned or mindful of such experiences is often appealing. Furthermore, the idea of becoming more mindful of the enjoyment and satisfaction that can be obtained from the quality of food—rather than the quantity—is appealing and is built into mindful eating exercises, whether simple ones like eating a raisin mindfully, or the more challenging ones we use in the MB-EAT program, in which "challenging" (i.e., potential binge) foods and entire meals are eaten mindfully.

Another issue is how to present meditation practice in a way that is nonthreatening, without raising concerns about religious identity. In the MB-EAT program, we found that it was valuable to address this issue in an individual orientation meeting, both in our Midwest community and in the south, when we run the program at Durham, North Carolina. Doing so virtually eliminated dropouts in the first or second session. We ask people what they know about meditation and if they have any concerns about sharing their participation in the program with family, friends, or church members. We raise the issue that some Christian religious teachings view meditation as inappropriate because it is associated with Buddhism or Hinduism, an attitude we have found to be common in our areas. We then point out that virtually all known religions, including Christianity, have meditative traditions, because it is a way to quiet the mind and access inner wisdom. This seems to help many participants be more comfortable with their involvement. These issues could also be raised in the first meeting of a group, but it is somewhat harder to predict the time needed to allow for this, or for individuals to raise questions of concern during a first meeting with strangers.

Motivating people to practice meditation is often a challenge. Although virtually everyone will acknowledge that engaging in meditation feels relaxing, practicing daily can feel like an effort or chore. Practice can be presented in several supportive ways: as a way to give yourself a "break," as a time to practice mindfulness so that it is easier to do under more stressful circumstances, as inherently challenging. Acknowledging "racing thoughts" as normal and to be expected is particularly helpful, as is the challenge of being disciplined enough to do nothing! It is invaluable to put materials onto audiotapes or CDs to provide more support and structure, but it is also important to try to "wean" people off a dependency on the tapes as active treatment moves toward completion. While using a tape may feel more supportive, it is important for individuals to experience being able to do sitting meditation without one. Instead of a tape, using a digital timer can be helpful. Although somewhat controversial, it mimics the timekeeping that a group leader would provide in more formal retreat settings and decreases preoccupation with time during an individual sitting.

While some of our data support the clinical value of the eating-focused meditations—both longer ones and the "mini-meditations"—over the general mindfulness practice in regulating eating behavior and experience, practice in general mindfulness meditation lays the groundwork. Unfortunately, virtually no empirical evidence exists about the comparative effects of different approaches to meditative practice. Problem-focused meditations can be particularly powerful, as these help support and integrate general sitting meditation with application of mindfulness practice to issues of most concern. Of note, a number of our participants in the MB-EAT program had had previous experience with the MBSR program. Despite the exposure to the concept of mindful eating by using the raisin meditation, this had not been sufficient to allow them to change the ingrained and serious eating problems with which they were struggling.

Appropriate or recommended training and qualifications for therapists is an issue in providing mindfulness-based interventions, as with many focused therapeutic approaches. Traditionally, meditation has been taught as part of a complex heritage of practice; therapeutic training is also embedded in certain expectations of comprehensive coursework and experience. Despite the apparent simplicity of meditation practice in some respects, it is generally strongly advised that therapists using these approaches with individuals with eating disorders have the appropriate background, which entails not only the appreciation for the underlying behavioral and psychological processes, but also a personal practice in mindfulness meditation. Such personal practice and training in the MBSR or DBT certification programs is also desirable. At the same time, to the extent that the structure of the interventions and materials are available in manuals and the guided or focused meditations are available on audiotapes, relatively less training may be required. For example, we require a personal practice of the co-leaders of the MB-EAT program of at least 3 months. Given that, and use of the structured manual materials, clinical outcome appears to be comparable between graduate student clinicians and those with more meditation and therapy background.

CONCLUDING COMMENTS

Mindfulness-based interventions appear particularly well suited to address disordered eating behaviors. We have reviewed several approaches that vary in the degree to which meditation practice is a core element and to which focus on underlying eating issues is central to treatment. Regardless, each of the approaches provides individuals with a heightened ability to simply observe feelings, behaviors, and experiences, to disengage automatic and often dysfunctional reactivity, and then to allow themselves to work with and develop wiser and more balanced relationships with their selves, their eating, and their bodies. Because making choices around food is such an ever-present part of daily life, yet is tangible (in contrast to a private experience of pain and emotion), understanding the role of these approaches in relation to eating regulation may not only serve to improve treatment for eating disorders and obesity, but it may also serve to inform the fuller potential of mindfulness-based interventions in other areas of treatment.

REFERENCES

American Psychiatric Association (2000). *Diagnostic and statistical manual of mental disorders* (4th ed., text revision). Washington, DC: Author.

Apple, R. A., & Agras, W. S. (1997). Overcoming eating disorders: A cognitive-behavioral treatment for bulimia and binge-eating disorder. New York: Psychological Corporation.

Baer, R. A., Fischer, S., & Huss, D. B. (2005). Mindfulness-based cognitive therapy applied to binge eating: A case study. *Cognitive and Behavioral Practice, 12*, 351–358.

———— (in press). Mindfulness and acceptance in the treatment of disordered eating. *Journal of Rational Emotive and Cognitive Behavioral Therapy.*

Beck, A. T., Steer, R. A., & Brown, G. K. (1996). *Beck Depression Inventory–II manual.* San Antonio, TX: The Psychological Corporation.

Bruce, B., & Agras, W. (1992). Binge-eating in females: A population-based investigation. *International Journal of Eating Disorders, 12*, 365–373.

Craighead, L. W., & Allen, H. N. (1995). Appetite awareness training: A cognitive behavioral intervention for binge eating. *Cognitive and Behavioral Practice, 2*, 249–270.

Eldredge, K. L., Agras, W. S., Arnow, B., Telch, C. F., Bell, S., Castonguay, L., *et al.* (1997). The effects of extending cognitive-behavioral therapy for binge eating disorder among initial treatment nonresponders. *International Journal of Eating Disorders, 21*, 347–352.

Fairburn, C. G., & Cooper, Z. (1993). The Eating Disorder Examination (12th ed.). In C. G. Fairburn & G. T. Wilson (Eds.), *Binge eating: Nature, assessment, and treatment* (pp. 317–332). New York: Guilford Press.

Fairburn, C. G., Marcus, M. D., & Wilson, G. T. (1993). Cognitive-behavioral therapy for binge eating and bulimia nervosa: A comprehensive treatment manual. In C. G. Fairburn and G. T. Wilson (Eds.), *Binge eating: Nature, assessment, and treatment.* New York: Guilford Press.

Gormally, J., Black, S., Daston, S., Rardin, D. (1982). The assessment of binge eating severity among obese persons. *Addictive Behaviors, 7*, 47–55.

Gormally, J., Rardin, D., & Black, S. (1980). Correlates of successful response to a behavioral control clinic. *Journal of Consulting and Clinical Psychology, 27*, 179–191.

Hayes, S. C., Strosahl, K. D., & Wilson, K. G. (1999). *Acceptance and commitment therapy: An experiential approach to behavior change.* New York: Guilford Press.

Hayes, S. C., Wilson, K. G., Gifford, E. V., Follette, V. M., & Strosahl, K D. (1996). Emotional avoidance and behavioral disorders: A functional dimensional approach to diagnosis and treatment. *Journal of Consulting and Clinical Psychology, 64*, 1152–1168.

Heatherton, T. F., & Baumeister, R. F. (1991). Binge eating as escape from self-awareness. *Psychological Bulletin, 110*, 86–108.

Heffner, M., & Eifert, G. H. (2004). *The anorexia workbook: How to accept yourself, heal your suffering, and reclaim your life.* Oakland, CA: New Harbinger.

Heffner, M., Sperry, J., Eifert, G. H., & Detweiler, M. (2002). Acceptance and commitment therapy in the treatment of an adolescent female with anorexia nervosa: A case example. *Cognitive and Behavioral Practice, 9*, 232–236.

Herman, C., & Polivy, J. (1980). Restrained eating. In A. Stunkard (Ed.), *Obesity.* Philadelphia: Saunders.

Herzog, D. B., Keller, M. B., Lavori, P. W., & Sacks, N. R. (1991). The course and outcome of bulimia nervosa. *Journal of Clinical Psychiatry, 52*(Suppl. 10), 4–8.

Hetherington, M., & Rolls, B. (1988). Sensory-specific satiety and food intake in eating disorders. In B. Walsh (Ed.), *Eating behaviors in eating disorders.* Washington, DC: American Psychiatric Press.

Keefe, P., Wyshogrod, D., Weinberger, E., & Agras, W. (1984). Binge eating and outcome of behavioral treatment of obesity: A preliminary report. *Behavior Research and Therapy, 22*, 319–321.

King, M. B. (1989). Eating disorders in a general practice population: Prevalence, characteristics, and follow-up at 12 to 18 months. *Psychological Medicine, 22*, 951–959.

——— (1991). The natural history of eating pathology in attenders to primary care. *International Journal of Eating Disorders, 10*, 379–387.

Klerman, G. L., Weissman, M. M., Rounsaville, B. J., & Chevron, E. S. (1984). *Interpersonal psychotherapy of depression.* New York: Basic Books.

Kristeller, J. L. (2003) Mindfulness, wisdom and eating: Applying a multi-domain model of meditation effects. *Journal of Constructivism in the Human Sciences, 8*, 107–118.

Kristeller, J. L., & Hallett, C. B. (1999). An exploratory study of a meditation-based intervention for binge eating disorder. *Journal of Health Psychology, 4*, 357–363.

Kristeller, J. L., Quillian-Wolever, R., & Sheets, V. (in preparation). *Mindfulness-based eating awareness therapy (MB-EAT): A randomized trial with binge eating disorder.* Manuscript in preparation.

Leahy, R. L. (2002). A model of emotional schemas. *Cognitive and Behavioral Practice, 9*, 177–190.

Linehan, M. M. (1993). *Cognitive-behavioral treatment of borderline personality disorder.* New York: Guilford Press.

Lowe, M. R. (1993). The effects of dieting on eating behavior: A three-factor model. *Psychological Bulletin, 114*, 100–121.

Lowe, M. R., & Capputo, G. (1991). Binge eating in obesity: Toward the specification of predictors. *International Journal of Eating Disorders, 10*, 49–55.

Marcus, D., & Lamparski, D. (1985). Binge eating and dietary restraint in obese patients. *Addictive Behaviors, 19*, 163–168.

Marcus, D., Wing, R., & Hopkins, J. (1988). Obese binge eaters: Affect, cognitions, and response to behavioral weight control. *Journal of Consulting and Clinical Psychology, 56*, 433–439.

Marlatt, G. A., & Gordon, J. (1985). *Determinants of relapse: Implications for the maintenance of behavior change.* New York: Brunner Mazel.

Millar, H. R. (1998). New eating disorder service. *Psychiatric Bulletin, 22*, 751–754.

Ricca, V., Mannucci, E., Mezzani, B., DiBernardo, M., Zucchi, T., Paionni, A., *et al.* (2001). Psychopathological and clinical features of outpatients with an eating disorder not otherwise specified. *Eating and Weight Disorders, 6*, 157–165.

Roth, A., & Fonagy, P. (2005). *What works for whom? A critical review of psychotherapy research* (2nd ed.). New York: Guilford Press.

Safer, D. L., Telch, C. F., & Agras, W. S. (2000). Dialectical behavior therapy adapted for bulimia: A case report. *International Journal of Eating Disorders, 30*, 101–106.

——— (2001). Dialectical behavior therapy for bulimia nervosa. *American Journal of Psychiatry, 158*, 632–634.

Segal, Z. V., Williams, J. M. G., & Teasdale, J. D. (2002). *Mindfulness-based cognitive therapy for depression: A new approach to preventing relapse.* New York: Guilford.

Sherwood, N., Jeffrey, R., & Wing, R. (1999). Binge status as a predictor of weight loss treatment outcome. *International Journal of Obesity, 23*, 485–493.

Spitzer, R., Devlin, M., Walsh, B., Hasin, D., Wing, R., Marcus, M., *et al.* (1992). Binge eating disorder: A multisite field trial of the diagnostic criteria. *International Journal of Eating Disorders, 11*, 191–203.

Spitzer, R., Yanovski, S., Wadden, T., Wing, R., Marcus, M., Stunkard, A., *et al.* (1993). Binge-eating disorder: Its further validation in a multisite study. *International Journal of Eating Disorders, 13*, 137–153.

Striegel-Moore, R. H., Dohm, F. A., Solomon, E. E., Fairburn, C. G., Pike, K. M., & Wilfley, D. E. (2000). Subthreshold binge eating disorder. *International Journal of Eating Disorders, 27*, 270–278.

Striegel-Moore, R., Wilfley, D., Pike, K., Dohm, F., & Fairburn, C. (2000). Recurrent binge eating in Black American women. *Archives of Family Medicine, 9*, 83–87.

Stunkard, A. J., & Messick, S. (1985). The three-factor eating questionnaire to measure dietary restraint, disinhibition and hunger. *Journal of Psychosomatic Research, 29*, 71–83.

Telch, C. F., Agras, W. S., & Linehan, M. M. (2000). Group dialectical behavior therapy for binge-eating disorder: A preliminary, uncontrolled trial. *Behavior Therapy, 31*, 569–582.

——— (2001). Dialectical behavior therapy for binge eating disorder. *Journal of Consulting and Clinical Psychology, 69*, 1061–1065.

Telch, C. F., & Rossiter, E. (1988). Binge eating increases with increasing adiposity. *International Journal of Eating Disorders, 7*, 115–119.

Walsh, T. B., & Devlin, M. J. (1998). Eating disorders: Progress and problems. *Science, 280*, 1–8.

Wilson, G. T. (1984). Toward the understanding and treatment of binge eating. In R. Hawkins, W. Gremouw, & P. Clement (Eds.), *The binge–purge syndrome.* New York: Springer.

——— (1996). Acceptance and change in the treatment of eating disorders and obesity. *Behavior Therapy, 27*, 417–439.

——— (2004). Acceptance and change in the treatment of eating disorders: The evolution of manual-based cognitive-behavioral therapy. In S. C. Hayes, V. M. Follette, & M. M. Linehan (Eds.), *Mindfulness and acceptance: Expanding the cognitive-behavioral tradition.* New York: Guilford Press.

Wiser, S., & Telch, C. F. (1999). Dialectical behavior therapy for binge eating disorder. *Journal of Clinical Psychology, 55*, 755–768.

5

ACCEPTANCE, MINDFULNESS, VALUES, AND PSYCHOSIS: APPLYING ACCEPTANCE AND COMMITMENT THERAPY (ACT) TO THE CHRONICALLY MENTALLY ILL

PATRICIA A. BACH

Institute of Psychology, Illinois Institute of Technology, Chicago, Illinois

BRANDON GAUDIANO

Department of Psychiatry and Human Behavior, Brown University Medical School, Psychosocial Research Program, Butler Hospital, Providence, Rhode Island

JULIEANN PANKEY

Department of Psychology, University of Nevada, Reno, Nevada

JAMES D. HERBERT

Department of Psychology, Drexel University, Philadelphia, Pennsylvania

STEVEN C. HAYES

Department of Psychology, University of Nevada, Reno, Nevada

THEORETICAL AND CONCEPTUAL RATIONALE

PSYCHOTIC SYMPTOMS: PREVALENCE AND RELAPSE

Disorders that include psychotic symptoms, such as delusions and hallucinations, have generally been regarded as difficult to treat. Schizophrenia, the most common of the chronic psychotic disorders, occurs in approximately 1% of the population (American Psychiatric Association, 2000) and can be severely debilitating (Bellack, Morrison, & Mueser, 1992). Other psychotic disorders that may be severe and chronic include schizoaffective disorder, mood disorder with psychotic features, and delusional disorder. While antipsychotic medications reduce negative, as well as positive, symptoms of psychosis, their impact on psychosocial outcomes is mixed (Corrigan, Reinke, Landsberger, Charate, & Toombs, 2003). Medication typically reduces but does not completely eliminate symptoms of psychosis (Breier, Schreiber, Dyer, & Pickar, 1991), and relapse rates are high among those receiving pharmacotherapy alone and those receiving both medication and psychosocial interventions (Gorman, 1996). For example, according to Wieden and Olfson (1995), the relapse rate is as high as 4% *per month* among persons with schizophrenia who adhere to treatment and are initially responsive to medication.

ESTABLISHED TREATMENTS FOR PSYCHOTIC SYMPTOMS

Psychiatric Rehabilitation

Current thinking suggests that the disability that often accompanies serious mental illness is a result of a combination of factors, including biological events, the impact of symptoms, and skill deficits that are often secondary to the impact of symptoms and to long periods of institutionalization. A psychiatric rehabilitation approach emphasizes the need for comprehensive treatment, including skills training, problem solving, token economies, medication management, vocational rehabilitation, environmental and social supports, and, when applicable, family interventions (Kuipers, 2000). These psychosocial interventions have not targeted symptoms of the illness directly so much as they have addressed treatment adherence and skills deficits associated with serious mental illness.

Cognitive Behavior Therapy for Psychotic Symptoms

In recent years psychotherapies, especially cognitive behavioral approaches, have been developed for the treatment of delusions and hallucinations (Haddock *et al.,* 1998). Cognitive behavior therapy (CBT), which includes strategies such as verbal challenges to beliefs and planned reality testing, has been shown in several randomized controlled trials to be efficacious for the treatment of psychosis. A recent meta-analysis demonstrates that CBT produces large effect size reductions on both positive and negative symptom measures compared with control groups, and with effects maintained through follow-up periods (Gould, Mueser, Bolton, Mays, & Goff, 2001).

ACCEPTANCE AND COMMITMENT THERAPY FOR PSYCHOSIS

Acceptance and commitment therapy (ACT; pronounced as a single word, not initials) (Hayes, Strosahl, & Wilson, 1999) is one of a number of new, "third wave" treatments (Hayes, 2004) that have arisen within the behavioral and cognitive therapies. Emphasizing issues typically not associated with the behavior therapy tradition, these treatments include such technologies as dialectical behavior therapy (DBT) (Linehan, 1993), functional analytic psychotherapy (FAP) (Kohlenberg & Tsai, 1991), integrative behavioral couple therapy (IBCT) (Jacobson & Christensen, 1996), and mindfulness-based cognitive therapy (MBCT) (Segal, Williams, & Teasdale, 2002). No single factor unites these new methods, but all have ventured into areas traditionally reserved for the less empirical wings of clinical intervention and analysis, emphasizing such issues as acceptance, mindfulness, cognitive defusion, dialectics, values, spirituality, and the therapeutic relationship. Their methods are often more experiential than didactic; their underlying philosophies are more contextualistic than mechanistic.

Although ACT emerged from the CBT tradition, broadly defined, and ACT shares some similarities with traditional CBT, they differ in important theoretical and technical ways, particularly in the area of psychosis (Gaudiano, 2005). Like all forms of behavioral and cognitive therapy, ACT is an empirically focused approach (Hayes, Masuda, Bissett, Luoma, & Guerrero, 2004). In contrast to psychodynamically oriented therapies, both CBT and ACT are structured, time-limited, and goal-oriented psychosocial treatments that aim to improve patients' coping with psychotic symptoms and related problems. Moreover, both CBT and ACT are rooted in traditional behavior therapy and therefore reject the idea that symptoms are mere manifestations of mysterious underlying psychic processes. However, ACT and traditional CBT differ in their theoretical stance toward the patient and his/her symptoms. The primary goal of CBT is to reduce symptoms and distress in order to improve the individual's quality of life. CBT utilizes gentle disputation (e.g., cognitive restructuring) and formal reality testing techniques (e.g., behavioral experiments) in an effort to reduce hallucinations and correct false beliefs. In contrast, ACT focuses on altering the context within which the person experiences negative private events, including hallucinations and delusional beliefs, in order to promote movement toward valued life goals, thereby enhancing overall functioning and quality of life. ACT incorporates mindfulness and acceptance-based interventions to alter the process through which patients interact with their psychotic symptoms. More philosophically and strategically, ACT is based on relational frame theory (RFT), a contextual approach linked to an active basic research program in language and cognition (Hayes, Barnes-Holmes, & Roche, 2001) that emphasizes the function of thoughts over their form or frequency. As a result, ACT encourages increased willingness to experience thoughts and feelings in the moment—as they are and not as what they say they are—while simultaneously fostering action toward valued goals. This does not imply that patients undergoing ACT do not obtain symptom relief or a reduction in distress. In fact, this often is an associated effect of successful treatment in ACT. However, ACT is less concerned with the presence of symptoms that will fluctuate naturally over time, and more focused on changing the context in which psychotic symptoms are associated with nonfunctional forms of behavior. In other words, the focus is on strengthening workable coping for dealing with any symptoms that are present in a given moment.

ACT may be uniquely suited to the treatment of psychotic symptoms, as it addresses both the impact of symptoms and the motivation to set goals and adhere to treatment regimens, and is likely to have utility in multi-disciplinary inpatient treatment settings. ACT does not take a stand on the source of psychotic symptoms per se. But the clinical issue is less a matter of symptoms than of symptom impact. According to the ACT model, language processes lead naturally to processes of evaluation and prediction, which in turn support experiential avoidance. Experiential avoidance is the tendency to attempt to avoid or alter the form, frequency, or situational sensitivity of private events, even when attempts to do so cause behavioral harm. For example, a person experiencing hallucinations may try to argue them away, deny their occurrence, avoid situations in which they might occur, scan for their presence, and so on. As this happens, the internal cognitive focus increases and paradoxical processes may lead to even greater frequencies of hallucinations (through the rebound produced by thought suppression; due to greater sensitivity to anomalous cognitions, increased stress, and so on). In an ACT model, patients are instead taught to

- accept their feelings, as feelings,
- notice their own thoughts but take them less literally,
- contact the present moment as conscious people,
- focus on their values, and
- act in accordance with their values.

Most of the features of psychotic behavior seem amenable to such a model. Delusions, for example, are viewed not so much as a *target* of avoidance but as a *means* of avoidance. This is consistent with Bentall (2001), who hypothesized that delusions function as a defense against low self-esteem. That is, delusions may function to place the blame for personal failures outside of the individual. ACT teaches clients reporting delusions to notice their thoughts mindfully (i.e., in the present moment, without attachment or struggle to make them true or false) and then to redirect behavior toward attaining desired goals instead of toward acting in relation to delusional beliefs (Bach, 2005).

One rationale for this approach is that the real impact of psychosis in patients' lives and level of functioning comes not from psychotic symptoms per se, but from behavior related to these symptoms. In fact, symptoms themselves are poor predictors of outcomes important to the individual, such as employment success (Rogers, Anthony, Toole, & Brown, 1991). For example, persons experiencing command hallucinations are not hospitalized because they are hearing voices, but because they act on the content of the hallucinations, and persons with delusional beliefs are not hospitalized for bizarre thoughts per se, but instead because they act in relation to delusional beliefs, such as by causing a public disturbance in confronting persons they believe wish to cause them harm, or by repeatedly calling law enforcement agencies.

Negative symptoms can be just as problematic; for example, negative symptoms of schizophrenia, including flat affect and lack of motivation, tend to be more resistant to treatment than positive symptoms. Many persons with schizophrenia are unemployed, have unstable living arrangements, and have few meaningful social contacts. The emphasis in ACT on behavior activation through exploring values, goals, and choices and examining barriers to changing behavior can be a starting point for increasing opportunities for reinforcement and can be easily combined and integrated with psychiatric rehabilitation programming that tends to emphasize individual choice, goal setting, and empowerment. In addition, the application of acceptance, mindfulness, and defusion methods tends to undermine the chronic experiential and overt avoidance that can lead to negative psychotic symptoms such as social withdrawal or avolition and anhedonia.

It is worth noting that although the systematic use of CBT interventions in the treatment of psychotic disorders is relatively new, the practice is amassing a body of empirical support in the literature. Nevertheless, a significant proportion of patients still do not respond to these interventions, and even those who do are by no means symptom free. Therefore, clinical researchers are attempting to augment the effectiveness of CBT for this population through the inclusion of acceptance and mindfulness-based strategies into cognitive behavioral protocols (Gaudiano, 2005). Also, experts in CBT for psychosis warn that a strong therapeutic alliance should be developed over time prior to using disputational methods, which are then to be done only in a gentle and nonconfrontational fashion (Kingdon & Turkington, 1994). Some evidence supports the wisdom of this practice, as confrontational styles are associated with poor outcomes with this population (see Milton, Patwa, & Hafner, 1978). These two changes are fundamentally consistent with ACT principles, as the treatment emphasizes acceptance rather than disputation, and targets symptoms indirectly by altering the context within which they are experienced rather than their frequency and believability per se. Further, the stance of the therapist that both therapist and client are in the same human predicament can foster rapid alliance building.

CASE STUDY

Inpatient treatment is often characterized by very brief hospital stays in which the client may receive only three or four sessions, or sometimes even a single session of psychotherapy. The case study presented here illustrates work with a client who was hospitalized for several weeks and participated in more than a dozen therapy sessions. However, treatment consisting of as little as a single session can be beneficial. Therefore, the lengthier case study, which is included to present multiple ACT treatment components, is followed by a table and description of ACT techniques that can "stand alone" in a single session to illustrate how the therapist might use ACT even when the patient has a very brief inpatient stay.

PATIENT BACKGROUND AND COURSE OF TREATMENT

Jay, a 28-year-old Mexican American male with a diagnosis of schizoaffective disorder, was hospitalized for the tenth time since age 20, reporting symptoms of depression and paranoid beliefs. Jay had been living with his parents prior to being hospitalized, and his father reported that in the 2–3 weeks prior to hospitalization, Jay had become convinced that his coworkers were laughing at him because of his mental illness. He appeared to have been avoiding work by leaving early with the excuse of vague medical complaints. His father also suspected that Jay had not been taking his antipsychotic and antidepressant medication for at least a week prior to being hospitalized. Jay's father also reported that Jay had been angrily confronting him, expressing his conviction that his father did not approve of him and that he would never live up to his father's expectation that he become a restaurant manager like his father had been at the same restaurant where Jay was employed as a busboy.

In the first therapy session a day after he was hospitalized, Jay was hostile toward the therapist and agreed to participate in the therapy session only "to get my 25 points" (in the inpatient unit token economy). He denied having a mental illness and complained that his primary problem was that others wrongly believed that he was "a psycho" and made life difficult for him because of their mistaken beliefs about his mental health status. When the therapist asked Jay about his own beliefs about his mental health, he abruptly terminated the session.

A second session was held 2 days later, and Jay was more receptive; at this time he had been taking medication as prescribed for 3 days. He continued to deny mental illness and to insist that others were trying to "make things hard for me." Jay stated his belief that his hospitalization was unnecessary and was, in fact, preventing him from returning to work. The therapist spent the remainder of the session and the next session exploring Jay's goals, which included a desire to get out of the hospital, to work full-time at the restaurant and eventually become a manager, to live independently in his own apartment, to have more friends and dating experiences, to "make my family proud," and in the long term to marry and have children. After Jay articulated these goals, the therapist explored values with Jay to help him identify and clarify his values in life domains, including relationships, career, recreation, spirituality, citizenship, and health. Some time was spent on the psychoeducational task of defining values—which in ACT are defined as "verbally construed global desired life outcomes" (Hayes et al., 1999, p. 206); the relationships between goals and values; and the distinction between feelings and actions as related to values. The therapist used the metaphor of values as points on a compass that point one in a direction in which to move (Hayes et al., 1999, p. 209). The argyle socks exercise (Hayes et al., 1999, p. 211) was used to illustrate the distinction between feelings and actions, and that we can continue to move in valued directions even when we do not feel like it. (This exercise points out that one could work hard to bring argyle socks back into fashion even without any personal beliefs or feelings about the desirability of argyle socks.) The therapist also began completion of the values assessment form (Hayes et al., 1999, pp. 224–228) with Jay to make sure he understood it, and asked Jay to complete the form to bring to the next session. On this form, participants note their valued directions and goals in areas such as relationships, work, and health. During this phase of treatment a therapeutic alliance was firmly established as Jay began to view the therapist as an ally in his pursuit of valued goals. Jay identified several values and linked his specific goals to these values. For example, he identified his goal of being employed full-time with the value of being self-supporting. The focus of therapy then shifted to identifying barriers to attaining desired goals and toward approaching the topic of "creative hopelessness." In ACT, creative hopelessness occurs when the client realizes that habitual behaviors have not worked effectively for attaining desired outcomes or for avoiding unwanted private events. This condition is "hopeless" in that the client's change agenda is unworkable, and creative in that it serves as a foundation for willingness to try something different (Hayes et al., 1999). As a springboard for exploring creative hopelessness, the therapist revisited Jay's early comments that he was hospitalized because others were trying to make life difficult for him. Jay described a series of hospitalizations that always followed periods when he felt especially successful in his work or social life.

Jay described how in the weeks prior to his current hospitalization he had increased his work hours at the restaurant and befriended a waitress whom he hoped to date. Jay described the pain he felt upon overhearing a coworker disclose his mental illness to others and laughingly describe Jay as a "psycho." Jay said he stopped taking his medication soon after because he had been feeling well, and taking medication made him *seem* mentally ill; his reasoning was that if he did not take medication, it would prove that he did not have a mental illness. Soon after, Jay noticed that "all of them were laughing at me, and even the customers were talking about me." Jay then began arguing with some of his coworkers and asking them to stop laughing at him, and soon after began making excuses to leave work. The therapist turned discussion to "workability"—whether Jay's efforts to attain his occupational and social outcomes were working. The "Chinese handcuffs" metaphor (Hayes *et al.*, 1999, p. 104) was presented to illustrate the sense of increasing "stuckness" one experiences in using a change strategy that is not only unworkable but makes the problem worse. (A Chinese handcuff is a woven straw tube about five inches long and one-half-inch wide, into which the index fingers are inserted. Attempting to pull the fingers out causes the tube to tighten and the fingers to become trapped. They can only be removed by first pushing them in, which feels counter-intuitive but loosens the tube.) Jay acknowledged that whenever he stopped taking medication, he was hospitalized a short time later. He also acknowledged that he tended to have paranoid thoughts when not taking medication (it is not uncommon for clients who experience symptoms of psychosis to have insight into the delusional nature of their thoughts when not acutely psychotic). The therapist disclosed her own experience of mistakenly believing others were saying something negative about her, which led to discussion of a continuum of "normal" and "paranoid" thoughts.

Eventually Jay recognized that his strategy for "acting normal" by not taking medication increased the chances that he would behave in a manner likely to be perceived as abnormal. From that session on Jay and the therapist began using the expression "acting normal" in a light-hearted, irreverent way to refer to Jay's unworkable attempts to succeed; for example, "Is that Jay talking right now, or are you acting normal?" or "What would you do if you were trying to act normal?" "Acting like Jay" became an expression to refer to acting according to his values. The final phase of therapy focused on cognitive defusion and increasing mindfulness.

Though Jay was able to distance himself enough from the idea of his being "abnormal" to talk about it openly and with humor, he still feared he would always be seen as "a loser" within his family and that he would never have friends or a girlfriend because others believed he was "crazy" and because of his self-perceived inability to attain social and occupational achievements equal to those of his parents and siblings. As Jay had difficulty using words to describe his feelings, the *physicalizing exercise* (Hayes *et al.*,

1999, pp. 170–171) was used, in which the client, with eyes closed, visualizes thoughts and feelings and ascribes to them color, texture, shape, movement, etc., in order to contact them nonverbally. Jay contacted feelings of disappointment and many negative self-evaluations. When presented with the idea that these were thoughts that he could choose to believe or not to believe, he was at first skeptical. Use of metaphors and the *taking your mind for a walk* exercise (Hayes *et al.,* 1999, pp. 162–163) were employed to facilitate the experience of distancing himself from thoughts. In this exercise, participants practice listening to thoughts without acting in accordance with them. In between sessions Jay had a visit from his father and had a discussion with him about some of what he had been talking about in therapy. Jay was surprised by his father's admission that he sometimes felt protective of Jay because he was concerned about the discrimination Jay might face. Jay had perceived his father's behavior as being motivated by the belief that Jay was "a loser," and Jay was able to see his father's behavior as a means his father used to cope with his own pain over Jay being made fun of. Jay was able to use some of his cognitive defusion strategies to also defuse from the verbal behavior of others.

Mindfulness work commenced with a return to the theme of "being Jay" versus "acting normal," where "acting normal" was seen as a part of self-as-content. Self-as-content is the sense of self based on verbal statements about the self and self-evaluations, and in Jay's case it was centered around the belief that there was something fundamentally wrong with him. Ongoing self-awareness is the verbal sense of self that is connected to the present moment and allows one to be verbally aware of what one is thinking, feeling, or doing. In Jay's treatment this was identified as the self who noticed his negative self-judgments and reacted to events occurring in the moment. Finally, Jay contacted self-as-*context,* which is also sometimes identified as the "observing self" and is described as the sense of self one experiences when one notices not only what one is thinking and feeling, but also that there is a self that can see that one is seeing or notice that one is noticing. From this perspective of self-as-context, contacted through experiential exercises (e.g., see Hayes *et al.,* 1999, pp, 158–162 and 192–196), Jay might notice that he was having the thought that he should "act normal" and notice it as an evaluation and not a description of reality.

Therapy concluded with linking this work to Jay's values and goals. He identified stopping his medication as a barrier to attaining his goals and committed himself to participating in treatment, including taking medication as prescribed. He also made a decision to approach potential friendships differently. Instead of focusing on "acting normal," he wanted to "be Jay" and make choices about pursuing a potential friendship on the basis of how others responded to him rather than trying to adjust his behavior to please others. He had the opportunity to practice some of these behaviors in the hospital, and the therapist informed other members of the interdisciplinary treatment team of these goals so they could monitor, prompt, and reinforce Jay's behavior during the last 2 weeks before he was discharged.

ADAPTATIONS FOR SHORTER INPATIENT STAYS

While many inpatients who are like Jay, and especially those in state psychiatric facilities, have hospital stays long enough for several therapy sessions, many more patients have very brief hospitalizations. Further, many chronically psychotic patients do not follow through consistently with outpatient psychotherapy following discharge. This raises the possibility that short-term interventions delivered while the patient is hospitalized might be useful. The short and variable lengths of inpatient stays raises unique problems in delivering a comprehensive intervention like ACT, particularly in a group format in which the composition of each group varies as patients are admitted and discharged to the unit on an ongoing basis. One approach is to develop a protocol in which each session represents a microcosm of the overall model. Gaudiano and Herbert (2004) recently developed just such a protocol, permitting patients to participate in treatment as their inpatient status dictates. During each of these "stand alone" ACT sessions, all essential elements of the treatment are presented briefly, including the basic ACT rationale, interventions to enhance a mindful stance toward private events in general and hallucinations and delusions in particular, and work in clarification of values and goals. Each 1-hour session contains a core set of components, which are then rotated over subsequent sessions. For example, regarding the presentation of the ACT rationale, the first session focuses on examining unsuccessful past attempts to cope with symptoms and introduces the concepts of acceptance and willingness as alternatives to control strategies. Future sessions briefly review the topics of previous sessions and introduce new concepts consistent with the ACT rationale, such as workability as a guide to coping, and the concept of an observer-self that is distinct from one's transient private experiences. Each session is designed to stand on its own, so that patients can participate in treatment as their stay dictates. This format also entails ongoing review of core ACT concepts, which we have found to be particularly helpful with this population. Table 5.1 contains a sample session outline.

REVIEW OF EMPIRICAL SUPPORT

STUDIES OF ACT WITH PSYCHOSIS

There is growing empirical support for the efficacy of ACT in the treatment of serious mental illness. Bach and Hayes (2002) found that a

TABLE 5.1   Sample "Stand Alone" ACT for Psychosis Session Outline

Components	Description
Homework review *(if applicable from previous session)*	Encourage **practice** but refrain from adopting a punitive stance if nonadherent.
	Stress **behavioral consistency** and commitment toward values.
	Reinforce the process as "success" regardless of outcome.
	Emphasize increasing **behavioral flexibility** in response to psychological distress
ACT model	Explore unsuccessful past coping attempts that relate to avoidance or struggle with psychotic symptoms (i.e., foster "**creative hopelessness**").
	Describe **Polygraph Metaphor** (pp. 123–124).
	Introduce **willingness** as an alternative stance toward symptoms.
Mindfulness/ acceptance exercise	Describe and practice the **Soldiers in the Parade meditation** (pp. 159–160).
	Focus on the **process** of doing the exercise in contrast to any expected outcome to be achieved.
	Discuss the exercise in the larger context of willingness.
Vales/goals clarification	Describe the **Skiing Metaphor** (pp. 220–221), which emphasizes making the process the goal.
	Discuss the difference between values and goals.
	Elicit personal **values** in several areas (e.g., intimate relationships, family relations, work, education, recreation, spirituality).
	Discuss **perceived obstacles** to goal attainment.
	Elicit **goals** in the form of specific behavioral steps that can be taken in the present moment to work toward values.
Session review	Be sensitive to possible cognitive limitations.
	Review the **"take home" messages** from session.
Homework practice	Emphasize homework as a form of **committed action** one chooses in order to work toward personal values (e.g., mental/physical health).
	Ask the patient to practice the **Soldiers in the Parade meditation** 15–30 min daily. Provide handout containing brief description of exercise and self-monitoring form.
	Emphasize that "success" is defined as simply practicing the exercise, regardless of the outcome.

Note: Page numbers refer to the text by Hayes *et al.* (1999).

four-session ACT intervention plus treatment as usual (TAU) with inpatients reporting hallucinations or delusional beliefs was associated with decreased probability of rehospitalization at follow-up as compared with the rehospitalization rates of patients receiving only TAU.

ACT subjects reported decreased symptom-associated distress and decreased believability of symptom content and reported increased symptom frequency as compared with TAU control subjects. Bach and Hayes (2002) posit that this seemingly paradoxical outcome of increased symptom frequency and decreased distress and believability is related to acceptance of symptoms. That is, patients who do not accept their symptoms may deny them, while patients who accept symptoms are likely to accurately report their occurrence.

Gaudiano and Herbert (in press) recently replicated and extended the Bach and Hayes (2002) study on ACT in the treatment of psychosis using an adapted protocol in a sample of hospitalized patients with psychotic symptoms and comorbid conditions. Patients were randomly assigned to enhanced treatment as usual (ETAU), or ETAU plus ACT. ACT sessions (averaging three sessions over 1 week) were delivered in an individual format as substitutes for other milieu therapy provided to patients in the ETAU condition. This design helped to control for the potential confound of additional treatment in the Bach and Hayes (2002) study. Analyses for treatment completers revealed that patients receiving ACT showed greater improvements in clinician-rated mood symptoms, self-reported distress about hallucinations, and impairment in social functioning, and clinically significant symptom change in overall psychiatric symptoms at discharge relative to the ETAU group at discharge. Although raters were not blind to treatment condition, different assessment methods (clinician vs. patient ratings) yielded similar results favoring the ACT group. The conditions did not differ in frequency of self-reported hallucinations, with both groups showing significant decreases pretreatment to posttreatment. However, only the ACT group demonstrated decreases in believability of hallucinations over time. At 4-month follow-up, the ACT group showed a trend toward reduced rehospitalization compared with the ETAU group.

Although both ACT and CBT attempt to improve coping behaviors to achieve similar goals (i.e., reduction in distress and improvement in quality of life), their unique theoretical underpinnings lead to differences in processes, in addition to any differences in outcomes. For example, Bond and Bunce (2000) examined mediators of change in ACT and a problem-focused behavioral intervention for reducing worker stress. ACT was significantly more effective in producing long-term improvement in mental health and stress and was similarly effective in producing changes in work-related variables, but only improvement in the ACT condition was mediated by acceptance of private events. Similar results have been shown in several other studies (e.g., Hayes, Masuda, et al., 2004).

Emerging evidence suggests that theoretically consistent change processes may be operating in ACT for psychosis as well. Bach & Hayes (2002) showed particularly strong outcomes for patients who did not deny symptoms and showed decreases in their believability. Gaudiano and Herbert (in press) found that current believability of hallucinations mediated the relationship between symptom frequency over the past month and future distress in a sample of psychiatric inpatients. Furthermore, hallucination believability significantly decreased in patients randomly assigned to ACT, but not in those receiving enhanced treatment as usual. Pretreatment to posttreatment change in believability of hallucinations predicted change in associated distress after controlling for change in frequency of hallucinations. Future research is needed to identify whether similar results would be obtainable using traditional CBT for psychosis or whether this mechanism of change is specific to ACT. However, other studies have shown that these effects seem to be especially strong in ACT as compared with CBT (e.g., Zettle & Hayes, 1986).

STUDIES OF RELATED TOPICS

With the exception of uncontrolled case studies (e.g., Garcia & Perez, 2001; Garcia & Perez, in press), there remains a paucity of research examining mindfulness-based interventions for psychosis other than the studies by Bach and Hayes (2002) and Gaudiano and Herbert (in press). However, since psychosis is treated similarly to other common psychiatric symptoms within an ACT model of psychopathology, the relevant data available may be more extensive. According to RFT, verbally mediated private events (e.g., cognitions, emotions, memories, body sensations) do not directly influence behavior through their content or frequency, but instead through the context in which they occur. In other words, the theory proposes that similar processes may account for the pernicious effects of both milder forms of dysfunctional thinking, such as negative automatic thoughts, and externally experienced perceptual abnormalities, such as auditory hallucinations. The research of Verdoux and van Os (2002) on "psychotic" symptoms in normal populations offers further support for this perspective in suggesting that these symptoms are best conceptualized as representing a continuum of severity, rather than a categorical distinction between normal and abnormal thinking. For example, Garcia and Perez (2001) present a case study describing the successful treatment of a 17-year-old boy with schizophrenia using ACT. They argue that common patient approaches to coping with psychotic symptoms can be understood as problems resulting from experiential avoidance. In this case, using ACT to treat psychosis can be seen as a logical extension of its more common use in treating other conditions characterized by experiential avoidance, such as anxiety disorders (see Orsillo, Roemer, Block, LeJeuner, & Herbert, in press, for a review). These same authors have recently provided some evidence that it can extend as well to negative symptoms in schizophrenia (Garcia & Perez, in press).

More generally, evidence suggests that mindfulness-based interventions may be particularly helpful in preventing relapse. For example, recent research has shown that MBCT (Segal et al., 2002), a variant of traditional cognitive therapy that emphasizes mindfulness, is more effective than TAU in reducing relapse rates in recovered depressed patients (Ma & Teasdale, 2004; Teasdale et al., 2000). However, this benefit was only demonstrated for individuals with three or more past depressive episodes, suggesting that mindfulness-based interventions are particularly helpful for treating chronic psychiatric conditions. As mentioned, Bach and Hayes (2002) found that ACT resulted in a 40% reduction in rehospitalization rates in patients with psychotic disorders. Gaudiano and Herbert (in press) found similarly encouraging trends for those in the ACT group.

The mindful act of noticing internal experiences without trying to control them generates a powerful mechanism whereby the individual can stop expending effort to change thoughts, feelings, and urges, and instead focus on his relationships with or reactions to these phenomena. Ironically, lessening the active attempts to control odd cognitions lowers susceptibility to them. For example, research on psychotic individuals has demonstrated that *interpretation* of hallucinations, and not their content per se, determines the distress associated with them (Morrison & Baker, 2000).

Although results have been promising, the literature on mindfulness interventions suffers from a need to broaden the scope of populations investigated, and from methodological weaknesses. Notably, although the effects of mindfulness-based interventions have been investigated across a broad range of clinical problems, many of the studies conducted to date have been uncontrolled (Dimidjian & Linehan, 2003). The two most pertinent barriers to empirical research in the area of mindfulness appear to be a lack of clear operational definitions of concepts and procedures and the identification of clearly delineated mechanisms of change (Baer, 2003). Further examination of mindfulness-based interventions with psychotic clients is merited given the promise of the few existing studies.

Overall, available outcome studies support the efficacy of mindfulness-based approaches generally and of ACT specifically in the treatment of serious mental illness. Given that clients with a diagnosis of a psychotic disorder often present with multiple problems, consideration of important practical issues is also important in conducting effective ACT with clients with serious mental illness. These issues are considered next.

PRACTICAL ISSUES

There are several practical issues to consider when working with inpatients, especially those who are involuntarily enrolled and are diagnosed with serious mental illness. Some considerations include:

- the unpredictable and usually brief duration of inpatient hospitalization,
- examining one's own beliefs about persons with serious mental illness,
- working with involuntary clients, dually diagnosed clients, and consumers with moderate to severe cognitive deficits, and
- working in an interdisciplinary setting where other health care providers may be unfamiliar with ACT.

ADAPTATION OF ACT FOR INPATIENT SETTINGS

ACT for psychosis is proving to be a flexible treatment option for patients who typically would not be able to participate in traditional psychotherapy. One situation in which this often is a factor is inpatient hospitalization settings. Formal psychotherapy is rarely attempted with inpatients experiencing psychotic disorders, because of short and unpredictable lengths of stay. However, adaptations of ACT have been made to treat patients with psychotic disorders who are unable to complete a predetermined number of therapy sessions. As discussed previously, Gaudiano and Herbert (2004b) adapted ACT so that the treatment could be delivered in stand-alone sessions for patients who are unable to complete a prescribed number of sessions. In this way, ACT can be adapted for various inpatient lengths of stay, whether the patient is treated for 1 day or 1 month.

Other psychotherapies for psychosis, such as traditional CBT, may be more difficult to adapt to current inpatient environments. Most CBT protocols developed to treat people with schizophrenia have consisted of multicomponent packages that are delivered over a longer period, typically to outpatients. Minimal work has been done adapting CBT for inpatients. For example, Dury, Birchwood, Cochrane, and MacMillan (1996) conducted one of the only randomized controlled trials of CBT exclusively for inpatients. Even in this study, CBT was provided over a longer period— 12 weeks of individual and group CBT (approximately 8 hours per week)— which limits its usefulness in the current climate of much shorter inpatient stays.

Practitioners of CBT for psychosis stress the importance of building a strong therapeutic alliance prior to initiating the characteristic features of the treatment, such as dysfunctional belief modification techniques.

However, ACT may prove more useful in settings in which it is difficult or even impossible to build a strong alliance before engaging the patient in new approaches to coping with symptoms, due to time considerations. In contrast to CBT, ACT focuses on modifying patients' relationships to their thoughts, but not the thoughts themselves. Therefore, patients may be less defensive to such approaches in general and more willing to discuss and consider alternative strategies for dealing with psychotic symptoms. Our clinical experience and results from the study by Gaudiano and Herbert (in press), in particular, support the hypothesis that patients with psychosis can be engaged quickly and effectively using ACT.

THERAPISTS' BELIEFS ABOUT SERIOUS MENTAL ILLNESS

Therapists' thoughts, feelings, and beliefs about their clients may weigh more heavily in the treatment of persons with serious mental illness. Stigma and prejudice about persons with serious mental illness are rampant among mental health professionals, as well as among members of lay society (Caldwell & Jorm, 2001; Hugo, 2001). Clients themselves may believe that they are somehow defective and unable to achieve, and this belief is often supported by mental health treatment providers, as well as by members of the population at large.

Symptoms of serious mental illness are not legitimate reasons for not pursuing valued goals. Stigma on the part of the therapist may go in one of two directions; either to suggest that the client ought to limit his or her choices and remain in a restricted setting, or to criticize the client who prefers a restricted over a more independent living arrangement. It is important to maintain a consistent stance of empowering consumers to pursue their values. ACT is helpful in this regard, since its principles are known not just to help clients but also to undermine the believability of stigmatizing thoughts and the behavioral impact of uncomfortable feelings in therapists themselves (Hayes, Bissett, *et al.,* 2004).

WORKING WITH INVOLUNTARY CLIENTS

Clients seen in inpatient settings are often on an involuntary status and may or may not have a long history of mental health treatment. When doing ACT it is important to examine the client's beliefs and attitudes about treatment. The involuntary and therapy-wise client is more likely to benefit from participation in ACT if it is clearly different from past approaches and begins with an examination of goals and values rather than with why the client has been hospitalized. This population may, in fact, be especially motivated to participate in ACT as opposed to traditional therapies that focus on symptom elimination.

Clients in this population may also tend to underreport and minimize symptoms, because all too often a client who acknowledges symptoms such as hallucinations or suicidal ideation is kept in the hospital, while the client who denies such symptoms is discharged. Unfortunately, many psychiatric hospital policies collude in maintaining the stance that the symptom is the problem, despite growing evidence that this is not true. Even very reluctant clients can be hooked into treatment when they see the possibility of attaining goals, even if the symptom never remits.

Whether voluntary or involuntary, some clients will find that their symptoms quickly remit upon beginning a course of treatment. This may occasion early termination of therapy, but the processes targeted by ACT may help prevent relapse after the acute phase is completed (Bach & Hayes, 2002). Quickly engaging the client around symptoms in a larger context, and especially symptoms that tend not to remit quickly and/or permanently, can help to focus clients on the issue of relapse rather than the issue of "getting out of the hospital."

DUAL DIAGNOSIS

Dually diagnosed individuals are a challenging population at all levels of service delivery. Approximately 50% of persons with serious mental illness are also diagnosed with a substance use disorder (Mueser, Bennett, & Kushner, 1995). Because these patients are highly resistant to change, they often bear the brunt of stigmatization even within the very mental health care industry that stands to serve them. In the absence of treatment, dually diagnosed individuals are doomed to a poor quality of life, housing instability, and repeated relapses and hospitalizations, with society paying the high economic costs (Mueser, Bellack, & Blanchard, 1992).

Several treatment issues are related to the dually diagnosed population. Mental health and substance abuse treatment have historically involved different providers, different treatment models, and different treatment funding sources. As a result, the dually diagnosed tend to receive either mental health services or substance abuse services, but not both (Drake, Mercer-McFaddin, Mueser, McHugo, & Bond, 1998). Notably, substance abuse counselors and mental health treatment providers may disagree about policies related to abstinence and reasons for discharge, and may have divergent views about treatment approaches (Grella, 2003).

Dually diagnosed individuals often present as poor candidates for psychotherapy. These individuals often manifest high levels of aggression and violence (Soyka, 2000), significant levels of medication noncompliance (Swartz et al., 1998), and clinically significant depression (Margolese, Malchy, Negrete, Tempier, & Gill, 2004). Problems with medication may also arise, in that individuals may experience symptom persistence even with pharmacological intervention (Breier et al., 1991), which brings into question the effectiveness of antipsychotic medication (Pilling *et al.,* 2002), especially for those manifesting with negative symptoms.

The dually diagnosed population presents unique demands on clinical personnel. Health care providers may be unwilling to take dually diagnosed cases, as these individuals typically present with low levels of functioning, difficulty making long-term behavioral changes, and a tendency to "manipulate" program staff and others (Grella, 2003). Additionally, it may be difficult for clinicians to parse the symptom picture, particularly when the individual presents for therapy after self-medicating with drugs or alcohol. For example, the client may be at once floridly psychotic and high on cocaine, which creates a challenge for behavior management and for providing enough orientation to reality for the individual to participate in therapy.

From an ACT perspective, the psychotic individual's entanglement with odd cognitions and the substance user's engagement with substances often differ more topographically than functionally. Both the psychotic individual who shows opposition to attempting a therapeutic or pharmacological means to "reality" and the addict who continues to use drugs are resistant to altering their forms of avoidance. On the level of principle, unwillingness to alter or change the experience of psychotic cognitions and the attachment to the urge to use drugs both manifest as avoidance mechanisms meant to remove the individual from contacting negative private experiences. Both populations experience the need to actively change or modify the form or content of their private experience.

In the dually diagnosed population, these mechanisms are compounded, in that a psychotic individual may be resistant to traditional antipsychotic medication because it increases engagement in the "real world" and therefore increases anxiety related to psychotic intrusions and dissonance in perception, yet they may be dysregulated enough by the odd cognitions that they seek to alter their reality through other methods, such as engaging in drug and alcohol use. In a sense, this type of avoidance is almost a *meta* avoidance, in that these individuals are seeking to avoid the very cognitions that function as avoidance in the first place. Given the complexity of the avoidance strategies in the dually diagnosed population, health care practitioners may feel unable to intervene in a meaningful way.

Mindfulness techniques offer a paradoxical strategy for the dually diagnosed client struggling with avoidance. Traditional CBT is employed both with persons with symptoms of psychosis and with substance abusers, focusing on targeting faulty thoughts and behavior patterns. Standard elements of the CBT model include logical reasoning, examining evidence for and against distressing beliefs, reality testing, and generating alternative explanations (Kingdon & Turkington, 1994). CBT targets reduction in distress; however, evidence from the thought suppression literature implies that active attempts to eliminate or control thoughts may paradoxically increase them (Wegner & Zanakos, 1994). The chronic tendency to suppress thoughts may be an important component of emotional avoidance. The phenomenon of thought suppression is paradoxical in that individuals are unable to avoid the very thoughts they are struggling to suppress. This phenomenon is explained by Wegner's ironic process theory (Wegner, Erber, & Zanakos, 1993), which suggests that cognition includes both intentional and ironic operating processes. Thought suppression may paradoxically lead to increases in the time spent thinking unwanted thoughts and may sharpen emotional reactions to those thoughts and provide the beginnings of ruminative symptoms (Gold & Wegner, 1995).

Mindfulness strategies differ in that mindfulness training does not include the evaluation of thoughts as rational or distorted and does not target change or modification of thoughts or emotions as a goal (Baer, 2003). Because individuals with dual diagnoses present with seemingly intractable thought and behavior patterns that are made more complex by the comorbidity of a substance abuse problem, the evidence cited previously suggests that mindfulness may be a useful alternative to active control techniques that may inadvertently increase rumination about odd cognitions. The utility of mindfulness-based techniques lies at the intersection between distress about the content of an odd cognition or urge to use substances and how the individual interacts with this distress. The dually diagnosed population may benefit from strategies that turn the focus from the content of the thought or urge to the relationship the individual has with the thought or urge. Instead of turning down a path of control-based strategies that may paradoxically increase negative content, individuals who employ mindfulness strategies learn to notice their experience, distance themselves from the content of the thought, and turn away from judging the thought and themselves for having it. Thus, ACT may be utilized with only minimal modification both with persons with serious mental illness and with clients dually diagnosed with a serious mental illness and a substance use disorder.

The empirical evidence for the efficacy of ACT specifically and for mindfulness-based interventions generally with dually diagnosed clients is limited. There are encouraging early indications, however. ACT and other mindfulness-based treatments have been shown to be useful with substance abuse problems (e.g., Linehan et al., 1999), as well as many other clinical problems (see Baer, 2003, for a recent meta-analysis of selected mindfulness-based interventions). ACT has been shown to have a significant impact on severe polysubstance abuse (Hayes, Masuda, et al., 2004) above and beyond methadone maintenance and 12-step facilitation. It has also been shown to have an impact on smoking (Gifford et al., 2004) beyond nicotine replacement therapy. With the dually diagnosed, Bach and Hayes (2002) demonstrated that individuals experiencing odd cognitions and substance abuse could experience lower symptom believability and lower rates of rehospitalization than TAU subjects after participating in an ACT protocol designed to assist them in simply noticing odd cognitions and urges to use rather than actively attempting to change, modify, eliminate, or control thoughts or behavior.

COGNITIVE DEFICITS

Serious mental illness is associated with cognitive deficits, and schizophrenia in particular is associated with deficits in abstract thinking and social cue recognition (Penn, Combs, & Mohamed, 2001). As a result, the abstract nature of mindfulness-based therapies can be challenging for this population. However, metaphors and stories can be adapted for persons with cognitive deficits and will be particularly useful if they are simple, concrete, personally relevant, and specifically related to important clinical issues. One way to "concretize" metaphors is to use physical props. Some common ACT metaphors described by Hayes *et al.* (1999) already include props, but where they do not the therapist may be able to innovate. For instance, instead of merely describing *Chinese handcuffs* (Hayes *et al.,* 1999, p. 104) or the *bad cup* metaphor (Hayes *et al.,* 1999, pp. 168–169), the therapist might have Chinese handcuffs and a coffee cup on hand while presenting these metaphors. When referring to social settings and situations and to life experiences, it is important that the therapist use examples relevant to the client's social history and functioning. For example, while many clients relate to the metaphor of a person inviting *Joe the bum* (Hayes *et al.,* 1999, pp. 239–240) to a party, a client who is homeless or has lived in an institution much of his life may be confused by the metaphor, having no experience with hosting parties, or even relating more to "Joe the bum" than to the party host. When in doubt, the therapist can always get feedback about the client's understanding in the moment and review and provide clarification when necessary.

WORKING IN AN INTERDISCIPLINARY SETTING

Interdisciplinary treatment is the norm in inpatient settings. Communication among treatment providers from different disciplines is useful in practicing ACT in an interdisciplinary setting, where incorporating ACT principles and interventions into other treatment modes will likely be necessary. In inpatient settings therapy may consist of only a few sessions, given that average hospital stays are brief. However, many ACT concepts can be introduced and/or reinforced in multiple treatment modalities; for example, identifying goals and values and opportunities to practice skills, addressing barriers to participation in other treatment components, and monitoring progress. Milieu therapy may be the primary setting in which the client has opportunities to practice defusing from thoughts and feelings.

Communicating with other staff and educating them about ACT conventions, such as saying, "I'm having the thought that..." or asking a client, "Are you going to buy that thought?" can reinforce what is learned in therapy sessions if ACT concepts are repeated by other staff.

In inpatient (or outpatient) psychosocial rehabilitation programs ACT can be effectively done in a group therapy setting with persons with serious mental illness. Group meeting time should be kept relatively brief, around 45 minutes. Alternately, ACT principles and exercises can be incorporated into existing groups. For example, it can be effective to introduce cognitive defusion, acceptance, and mindfulness practices into a symptom management group, or willingness and values into medication management and goal setting groups.

Finally, other treatment providers may believe that the client's symptoms should completely remit before they are discharged from the hospital. Many clients have learned that denying symptoms means that they are more likely to be discharged, while acknowledging symptoms means they are more likely to remain hospitalized. If longer hospitalization seems indicated, the therapist can work with the client on goals and values other than discharge and explore how remaining in the hospital might increase opportunities to learn more skills and put the client in a better position to attain valued goals. Alternately, if discharge is indicated in spite of ongoing symptoms, the therapist might act as an advocate on the treatment team and point out positive changes in the client's behavior in spite of ongoing symptoms, and if applicable, educate staff about ACT.

CONCLUSIONS

ACT appears to be a promising approach to the treatment of psychotic symptoms that is characterized by radical acceptance and validation. Medications have traditionally been the treatment of choice for persons with symptoms of psychosis, and though they are helpful with these patients, they are frequently not nearly enough. ACT can be integrated or used adjunctively with the interdisciplinary treatment modes commonly used in inpatient settings. Although most participants in ACT continue to acknowledge experiencing hallucinations and/or delusions, the believability of their symptoms is greatly reduced, and this change appears to contribute to lower rates of relapse and rehospitalization and to decreases in subjective distress associated with symptoms. The emphasis on moving toward chosen values while accepting or allowing the inevitable occurrence of psychotic symptoms appears to enhance participants' motivation to adhere to treatment regimens (such as medication) while working on goals consistent with their values, rather than acting in accordance with their symptoms, or wasting energy trying to avoid or escape them.

REFERENCES

American Psychiatric Association (2000). *Diagnostic and statistical manual of mental disorders* (4th ed., text revision). Washington, DC: Author.

Bach, P. A. (2005). ACT with the seriously mentally ill. In S. C. Hayes & K. D. Strosahl (Eds.), *A practical guide to acceptance and commitment therapy*. New York: Springer.

Bach, P., & Hayes, S. C. (2002). The use of acceptance and commitment therapy to prevent the rehospitalization of psychotic patients: A randomized controlled trial. *Journal of Consulting and Clinical Psychology, 70,* 1129–1139.

Baer, R. A. (2003). Mindfulness training as a clinical intervention: A conceptual and empirical review. *Clinical Psychology: Science and Practice, 10,* 125–143.

Bellack, A. S., Morrison, R. L., & Mueser, K. T. (1992). Behavioral interventions in schizophrenia. In S. M. Turner, K. S. Calhoun, & H. E. Adams (Eds.), *Handbook of clinical behavior therapy* (2nd ed., pp. 135–154). New York: John Wiley & Sons.

Bentall, R. P. (2001). Social cognition and delusional beliefs. In P. W. Corrigan & D. L. Penn (Eds.), *Social cognition and schizophrenia* (pp. 123–148). Washington, DC: American Psychological Association.

Bond, F. W., & Bunce, D. (2000). Mediators of change in emotion-focused and problem-focused worksite stress management interventions. *Journal of Occupational Health Psychology, 5,* 156–163.

Breier, A., Schreiber, J. G., Dyer, J., & Pickar, D. (1991). National Institute of Mental Health longitudinal study of chronic schizophrenia: Prognosis and predictors of outcome. *Archives of General Psychiatry, 48,* 239–246.

Caldwell, T. M., & Jorm, A. F. (2001). Mental health nurses' beliefs about the likely outcomes for people with schizophrenia or depression: A comparison with the public and other healthcare professions. *Australian and New Zealand Journal of Mental Health Nursing, 10,* 42–54.

Corrigan, P. W., Reinke, R. R., Landsberger, S. A., Charate, A., & Toombs, G. A. (2002). The effects of atypical antipsychotic medications on psychosocial outcomes. *Schizophrenia Research, 63,* 97–101.

Dimidjian, S., & Linehan, M. (2003). Mindfulness practice. In W. O'Donohue, J. E. Fisher, & S. C. Hayes (Eds.), *Cognitive behavior therapy: Applying empirically supported techniques in your practice.* (pp. 229–237). Hoboken, NJ: John Wiley and Sons.

Drake, R. E., Mercer-McFaddin, C. M., Mueser, K. T., McHugo, G. J., & Bond, G. R. (1998). A review of integrated mental health and substance abuse treatment for patients with dual disorders. *Schizophrenia Bulletin, 24,* 589–608.

Dury, V., Birchwood, M., Cochrane, R., & MacMillan, F. (1996). Cognitive therapy and recovery from acute psychosis: A controlled trial. I. Impact on psychotic symptoms. *British Journal of Psychiatry, 169,* 593–601.

Garcia, J. M., & Perez, M. (2001). ACT as a treatment of psychotic symptoms. The case of auditory hallucinations [in Spanish]. *Analisis y Modificacion de Conducta, 27,* 455–472.

——— (in press). Exposition in existential terms of a case of "negative schizophrenia" approached by means of acceptance and commitment therapy. *International Journal of Existential Psychology & Psychotherapy.*

Gaudiano, B. A. (2005). Cognitive behavior therapies for psychotic disorders: Current empirical support and future directions. *Clinical Psychology: Science and Practice, 12,* 33–50.

Gaudiano, B. A., & Herbert, J. D. (in press). *Acceptance and commitment therapy for psychiatric inpatients with psychotic symptoms.*

——— (2004). *The treatment of psychotic disorders with acceptance and commitment therapy in an inpatient setting.* Unpublished manuscript, Drexel University, Philadelphia.

Gifford, E. V., Kohlenberg, B. S., Hayes, S. C., Antonuccio, D. O., Piasecki, M. M., Rasmussen-Hall, M. L., *et al.* (2004). Applying a functional acceptance based model to smoking cessation: An initial trial of acceptance and commitment therapy. *Behavior Therapy, 35*, 689–705.

Gold, D. B., & Wegner, D. M. (1995). Origins of ruminative thought: Trauma, incompleteness, nondisclosure, and suppression. *Journal of Applied Social Psychology, 25*, 1245–1261.

Gorman, J. M. (1996). *The new psychiatry.* New York: St. Martin's Press.

Gould, R. A., Mueser, K. T., Bolton, E., Mays, V., & Goff, D. (2001). Cognitive therapy for psychosis in schizophrenia: An effect size analysis. *Schizophrenia Research, 48*, 335–342.

Grella, C. E. (2003). Contrasting views of substance misuse and mental health treatment providers on treating the dually diagnosed. *Substance Use and Abuse, 38*, 1433–1446.

Haddock, G., Tarrier, N., Spaulding, W., Yusupoff, L., Kinney, C., & McCarthy, E. (1998). Individual cognitive-behaviour therapy in the treatment of hallucinations and delusions. *Clinical Psychology Review, 18*, 821–838.

Hayes, S. C. (2004). Acceptance and commitment therapy, relational frame theory, and the third wave of behavior therapy. *Behavior Therapy, 35*, 639–665.

Hayes, S. C., Barnes-Holmes, D., & Roche, B. (Eds.) (2001). *Relational frame theory: A post-Skinnerian account of human language and cognition.* New York: Plenum Press.

Hayes, S. C., Bissett, R., Roget, N., Padilla, M., Kohlenberg, B. S., Fisher, G., *et al.* (2004). The impact of acceptance and commitment training and multicultural training on the stigmatizing attitudes and professional burnout of substance abuse counselors. *Behavior Therapy, 35*, 821–835.

Hayes, S. C., Masuda, A., Bissett, R., Luoma, J., & Guerrero, L. F. (2004). DBT, FAP, and ACT: How empirically oriented are the new behavior therapy technologies? *Behavior Therapy, 35*, 35–54.

Hayes, S. C., Strosahl, K., & Wilson, K. G. (1999). *Acceptance and commitment therapy: An experiential approach to behavior change.* New York: Guilford Press.

Hayes, S. C., Wilson, K. G., Gifford, E. V., Bissett, R., Piasecki, M., Batten, S. V., *et al.* (2004). A randomized controlled trial of twelve-step facilitation and acceptance and commitment therapy with polysubstance abusing methadone maintained opiate addicts. *Behavior Therapy, 35*, 667–688.

Hugo, M. (2001). Mental health professionals' attitudes towards people who have experienced a mental health disorder. *Journal of Psychiatric and Mental Health Nursing, 8*, 419–425.

Jacobson, N. S., & Christensen, A. (1996). *Integrative couple therapy: Promoting acceptance and change.* New York: Norton.

Kingdon, D. G., & Turkington, D. (1994). *Cognitive-behavioral therapy of schizophrenia.* New York: Guilford.

Kohlenberg, R. J., & Tsai, M. (1991). *Functional analytic psychotherapy: Creating intense and curative therapeutic relationships.* New York: Plenum.

Kuipers, E. (2000). Psychological treatments for psychosis: Evidence based but unavailable? *Psychiatric Rehabilitation Skills, 4*, 249–258.

Linehan, M. M. (1993). *Cognitive-behavioral treatment of borderline personality disorder.* New York: Guilford.

Linehan, M. M., Schmidt, H., Dimeff, L. A., Craft, J. C., Kanter, J., & Comtois, K. (1999). Dialectical behavior therapy for patients with borderline personality disorder and drug dependence. *American Journal on Addiction, 8*, 279–292.

Ma, M. S., & Teasdale, J. D. (2004). Mindfulness-based cognitive therapy for depression: Replication and exploration of differential relapse prevention effects. *Journal of Consulting and Clinical Psychology, 7*, 31–40.

Margolese, H. C., Malchy, L., Negrete, J. C., Tempier, R., & Gill, K. (2004). Drug and alcohol use among patients with schizophrenia and related psychoses: Levels and consequences. *Schizophrenia Research, 67*, 157–166.

Milton, F., Patwa, V. K., & Hafner, R. J. (1978). Confrontation vs. belief modification in persistently deluded patients. *British Journal of Medical Psychology, 51,* 127–130.

Morrison, A. P., & Baker, C. A. (2000). Intrusive thoughts and auditory hallucinations: A comparative study of intrusions in psychosis. *Behaviour Research and Therapy, 38,* 1097–1106.

Mueser, K. T., Bellack, A. S., & Blanchard, J. J. (1992). Comorbidity of schizophrenia and substance abuse: Implications for treatment. *Journal of Consulting and Clinical Psychology, 60,* 845–856.

Mueser, K. T., Bennett, M., & Kushner, M. G. (1995). Epidemiology of substance use disorders among persons with chronic mental illness. In L. B. Dixon & A. F. Lehman (Eds.), *Double jeopardy: Chronic mental illness and substance use disorders* (pp. 9–25). Langhorne, PA: Harwood Academic Publishers.

Orsillo, S., Roemer, L., Block, J., LeJeuner, C., & Herbert, J. D. (in press). ACT with anxiety disorders. In S. Hayes and K. Strosahl (Eds.), *Acceptance and commitment therapy: A clinician's guide.* New York: Guilford.

Penn, D. L., Combs, D., & Mohamed, S. (2001). Social cognition and social functioning in schizophrenia. In P. W. Corrigan & D. L. Penn (Eds.), *Social cognition and schizophrenia* (pp. 97–122). Washington, DC: American Psychological Association.

Pilling, S., Bebbington, P., Juipers, E., Garaety, P., Geddes, J., Orbach, G., et al. (2002). Psychological treatments in schizophrenia: Meta-analysis of family intervention and cognitive-behavioral therapy. *Psychological Medicine, 32,* 763–782.

Rogers, E. S., Anthony, W. A., Toole, J., & Brown, M. A. (1991). Vocational outcomes following psychosocial rehabilitation: A longitudinal study of three programs. *Journal of Vocational Rehabilitation, 1,* 21–29.

Segal, Z. V., Williams, J. M. G., & Teasdale, J. D. (2002). *Mindfulness-based cognitive therapy for depression: A new approach to preventing relapse.* New York: Guilford Press.

Soyka, M. (2000). Substance misuse, psychiatric disorder and violent and disturbed behavior. *British Journal of Psychiatry, 176,* 345–350.

Swartz, M. S., Swanson, J. W., Hiday, V. A., Borum, R., Wagner, H. R., & Burns, B. J. (1998). Violence and severe mental illness: The effects of substance abuse and nonadherence to medication. *American Journal of Psychiatry, 155,* 226–231.

Teasdale, J. D., Segal, Z. V., Williams, J. M. G., Ridgeway, V. A., Soulsby, J. M., & Lau, M. A. (2000). Prevention of relapse/recurrence in major depression by mindfulness-based cognitive therapy. *Journal of Consulting and Clinical Psychology, 68,* 615–623.

Verdoux, H., & van Os, J. (2002). Psychotic symptoms in non-clinical populations and the continuum of psychosis. *Schizophrenia Research, 54,* 59–65.

Wegner, D. M., Erber, R., & Zanakos, S. (1993). Ironic processes in the mental control of mood and mood-related thought. *Journal of Personality and Social Psychology 65,* 1093–1104.

Wegner, D. M., & Zanakos, S. (1994). Chronic thought suppression. *Journal of Personality, 62,* 615–640.

Wieden, P. J., & Olfsen, M. (1995). Cost of relapse in schizophrenia. *Schizophrenia Bulletin, 21,* 415–429.

Zettle, R. D., & Hayes, S. C. (1986). Dysfunctional control by client verbal behavior: The context of reason giving. *Analysis of Verbal Behavior, 4,* 30–38.

6

MINDFULNESS IN DIALECTICAL BEHAVIOR THERAPY (DBT) FOR BORDERLINE PERSONALITY DISORDER

STACY SHAW WELCH

Evidence Based Treatment Centers of Seattle, Seattle, Washington

SHIREEN RIZVI

*National Center for PTSD, Boston VA Healthcare System,
Boston University School of Medicine, Boston, Massachusetts*

SONA DIMIDJIAN

Department of Psychology, University of Washington, Seattle, Washington

INTRODUCTION

Dialectical behavior therapy (DBT) is a comprehensive psychosocial treatment that was first developed for suicidal individuals with a diagnosis of borderline personality disorder (BPD) (Linehan, 1993a, 1993b). A number of randomized controlled trials have documented the efficacy of DBT for BPD (see Koerner & Dimeff, 2000, and Rizvi & Linehan, 2001, for reviews of empirical research on DBT). Although there is clearly a need for more

117

research on DBT for specific populations, and compared with more rigorous control conditions, data are promising enough to warrant enthusiasm for DBT as an effective treatment for BPD. After providing a brief overview of DBT, this chapter will focus on the use of mindfulness strategies in the treatment, the rationale for their use with clients with BPD, how they differ from other mindfulness-based treatments, and possible mechanisms of efficacy. A case example will be presented to demonstrate how DBT mindfulness skills are incorporated into individual therapy. Finally, practical issues and common questions that occur when teaching mindfulness skills to clients with BPD will be addressed.

OVERVIEW OF DIALECTICAL BEHAVIOR THERAPY

DBT blends change strategies from traditional cognitive-behavioral therapies with acceptance strategies adapted from Eastern (Zen) teaching and practice. The primary dialectic facing the DBT therapist is between complete acceptance of the client as he or she is in the current moment and an unwavering dedication to behavioral change and building a life worth living. The change procedures consist of systematic and repeated behavioral analyses of dysfunctional response chains, training in behavioral skills, contingency management in order to weaken or suppress disordered responses and to strengthen skillful responses, and cognitive restructuring. Exposure-based strategies are also used, aimed at blocking avoidance and reducing maladaptive emotional responses. The acceptance procedures consist of mindfulness skills and a variety of validation and stylistic strategies.

In its standard form the treatment is provided in once-weekly individual psychotherapy and group skills training sessions, skills coaching phone calls with the primary therapist (when needed), and adjunct pharmacotherapy when indicated. DBT has a strong team emphasis and requires weekly team meetings of all DBT therapists. This "therapy for the therapists" is aimed at reducing burnout and increasing therapists' adherence to the treatment model and competence in treating these clients. Individual sessions are based on clearly prioritized targets and focus on reducing maladaptive response patterns (life-threatening behaviors, behavioral patterns that interfere with or threaten therapy, severe Axis I disorders, and patterns that preclude a reasonable quality of life) and enhancing motivation for skillful behaviors. The foci of specific sessions are determined by the client's behavior and problems since the previous session, which are recorded on a diary card that the client completes each day and brings to each session.

The function of skills training in DBT is to teach the client specific behavioral skills that he or she presumably lacks and that are viewed, at least theoretically, as important for the amelioration of dysfunctional behavioral patterns and the resolution of the disorder. The treatment manual for DBT skills training (Linehan, 1993b) is extremely structured and provides session-by-session guidelines regarding content, organization, methods of presentation, and practice exercises. DBT skills training is didactically focused, with a heavy emphasis on skill training procedures, including modeling, instructions, behavioral rehearsal, feedback, and coaching, as well as homework assignments. There are four skills training modules targeting

1. interpersonal effectiveness,
2. emotion regulation,
3. distress tolerance, and
4. mindfulness, which is taught first and is the only skills set that is formally repeated throughout the skills group.

The reader is referred to Linehan (1993b) for a discussion of the first three skills modules.

OVERVIEW OF DBT MINDFULNESS SKILLS

DBT was one of the first psychosocial treatments to incorporate mindfulness as a core component. Originally, Linehan (2001) experimented with asking suicidal clients with BPD to engage in formal meditation tasks, such as extended sitting and walking meditation. This proved to be highly unsuccessful for two reasons. First, clients felt that they were unable to engage in this practice due to considerable distress or behavioral dyscontrol. Second, clients were unsure of the rationale for such lengthy practices. As a result, they often refused to engage in the meditation tasks at all. Linehan then began a process of distilling the essential components of mindfulness practice and developing methods for teaching that would be more accessible and user-friendly (Linehan, 1993a; 1993b).

Mindfulness in DBT is conceptualized as the experience of entering fully into the present moment at the level of direct and immediate experience. The practice of mindfulness in DBT is operationalized as a set of seven skills. The first is *wise mind*. Wise mind is an abstract idea: It represents the integration of two other states of mind, identified as *emotion mind* and *reasonable mind*. Emotion mind is what most clients with BPD feel that they are in all the time—it is the state in which emotions are experienced as having control over thoughts and behaviors. In reasonable mind the individual is controlled by logic in a cool and calculated manner. Wise mind is the combination of these two states; it is the integrated, intuitive sense of knowing something deep within. Knowing that you love someone or that you would run into a burning building to save a child might be examples of wise mind. The concept of wise mind assumes that every person has this capacity for wisdom and can learn to recognize and access it through practice.

The other six mindfulness skills are organized into two categories: *what* skills and *how* skills. The three *what* skills refer to the actions that one does to practice mindfulness: *observing*, *describing*, and *participating*. Observing refers to direct perception of experiences, independent of concepts and categories. The practice of observing can include attending to various senses: hearing, touch, taste, sight, and smell. Frequently when learning this skill, clients report moving quickly and without awareness from direct observation to conceptual description—and often to judgmental evaluation. For instance, a client might observe a tightening sensation in her abdomen, make an interpretation (e.g., "I'm afraid"), and move quickly to extreme statements (e.g., "I can't stand this," "This is unbearable") and/or judgment (e.g., "I am stupid for being afraid," "I am weak"). Practice with the observing skill helps clients to return to the level of direct sensation, including those judged to be unpleasant. Describing is the addition of a label to what is observed. For instance, in the previous example the client might practice noticing "thinking" or "judging" or "a thought went through my mind" as she experiences the thought "I can't stand this." The skill of describing is extremely important for helping clients experience thoughts as mental events, as opposed to literal, objective truths. Both observing and describing can also have the effect of adding some distance, or perspective, between the client and the experience. In this sense, the practice of stepping back, noticing thoughts, and verbally describing them without necessarily acting on them can help to break a pattern of impulsive responding or behavioral dyscontrol.

The skill of participating is the practice of fully and completely engaging in an experience, such that there is no separation between self and activity. This is a very difficult task for anyone who is highly self-conscious, as is commonly true of BPD clients, who worry constantly about how they are perceived by others. This worry frequently intrudes upon their ability to "let themselves go" and truly be one with any activity. It can also be difficult (but essential) for those who are highly sensation seeking or quick to judge certain activities as mundane/boring. Thus, participating becomes a way in which one can live fully and entirely in each moment, without intrusions or judgments. These *what* skills can be practiced only one at a time; for example, it is not possible to observe and describe or to describe and participate in the same moment.

The three *how* skills refer to the way in which one practices the *what* skills; and, in contrast to the *what* skills, they can be practiced simultaneously. The *how* skills are *nonjudgmentally*, *one-mindfully*, and *effectively*. *Nonjudgmentally* is often introduced as the most radical skill in the entire treatment because it entails dropping all judgments, both good and bad. Most people have a strong reaction to this, in part because they have a misunderstanding about what being nonjudgmental involves. Therefore, it is important to emphasize that being nonjudgmental is not the same as approving of something as "good" or "okay," nor does it mean giving up working toward change. Being nonjudgmental is also not the same as adopting a passive, callous, or unfeeling stance toward tragedy and pain. Instead, being non-judgmental emphasizes observable facts (e.g., who, what, when, and where) and describing consequences, as opposed to evaluations and interpretations.

One-mindfully refers to the quality of attending to one thing at a time. This means giving up on multitasking and the tendency to do one thing while thinking about another. Thus, practicing one-mindfully increases attentional control and interrupts the tendency of ruminative processes to compound emotional distress.

Effectively refers to the emphasis on doing what works in a given situation to maximize achieving desired goals. The often-cited maxim when teaching this skill is "Don't cut off your nose to spite your face." This is sometimes difficult to teach, because being effective is often at odds with proving that one is "right." Clients, and therapists, often have to learn to let go of being right in some situations in order to have a more skillful outcome. An extreme example is what a person would do when being held at gunpoint by a dangerous and violent thief. The effective, and skillful, behavior is to give over whatever this thief demands, even though you might be morally opposed to doing so. Clients with BPD often have to learn to be more effective with everyone in their lives, including treatment providers and family members. In this way, being effective is incorporated throughout treatment, and the question, *What is the effective thing to do in this situation?* is one that will remind clients to "keep their eyes on the prize."

RATIONALE FOR THE USE OF MINDFULNESS SKILLS IN DBT

DBT is based on a biosocial model that views the central area of dysfunction in BPD as emotion regulation. Through a combination of biology and an invalidating environment (for more detail, see Linehan, 1993a), these clients are thought to develop a heightened sensitivity to emotional cues, greater emotional reactivity, and a slower return to baseline. The mindfulness skills included in DBT are therefore intended to target the kinds of problems that accompany chronic difficulties with emotion regulation, such as difficulty learning, attending, and problem-solving under highly aroused states, learned self-invalidation, and impulsive, often dysfunctional behaviors that serve as desperate attempts to decrease emotional suffering.

Therapy for individuals with BPD is, at times, an excruciatingly difficult experience that puts them in direct contact with many of the cues they try to avoid. This is quite problematic, as highly dysregulated states impair cognitive processes, attention, and new learning. The first important function of mindfulness skills in DBT, then, is its critical role as the foundation for the acquisition of all the other skills. Mindfulness essentially targets attention by emphasizing full participation in each moment. It provides the building blocks for clients to practice experiencing and attending to their own emotions without acting to eliminate them. These skills are drawn upon again and again as the client learns the emotion regulation, interpersonal, and distress tolerance skills. Secondly, the mindfulness skills help clients to increase awareness of their private experience. Since the foundation of DBT, as well as cognitive-behavioral treatments generally, is accurate and comprehensive behavioral assessment, full awareness allows for a more complete assessment of problems and the mechanisms that maintain them. This, in turn, leads to better solution generation and implementation.

Third, mindfulness targets the self-invalidating behaviors so common to clients with BPD. These clients have often grown up in environments where their thoughts and emotions were consistently invalidated; they have learned, in turn, to invalidate themselves. Therapists who treat BPD frequently attest to the stunning rate at which clients tell themselves that they shouldn't think what they think, feel what they feel, or be who they are. Clinical lore often speaks to the high rate of judgments and anger BPD clients unleash upon others, but this phenomenon is probably far outweighed by the amount of judgments they direct toward themselves. Unfortunately, a large body of research on thought suppression and avoidance demonstrates that these strategies have the unintended consequence of increasing the very thoughts and feelings one was trying to decrease (Gross & John, 2003). Mindfulness directly targets the tendency to self-invalidate and judge, helping clients take a more gentle, accepting stance toward themselves and others. By emphasizing an open stance to anything that the moment brings, including thoughts or emotions they might be tempted to invalidate, mindfulness also decreases the vicious cycle brought about by emotion and thought suppression.

Finally, mindfulness skills can help decrease impulsive action to reduce painful negative emotions. DBT therapists conceptualize efforts to escape pain as the primary goal of the destructive behaviors characteristic of BPD. Whether the cause is the extent of their pain, the effectiveness of destructive behaviors such as parasuicide, their lack of other skillful behaviors, or the fact that accepting and tolerating pain is a concept not typically taught in Western culture, BPD clients often believe that they cannot survive the suffering of a moment without trying to alter it. Mindfulness skills teach clients to approach pain differently, focusing on decreasing their suffering by, paradoxically, accepting and tolerating their pain. Additionally, mindfulness may function as an exposure procedure in which clients learn that they can tolerate emotional pain and that feared outcomes do not occur. It may also help BPD clients distinguish thoughts and emotions from literal "truth"; the fact that they have the thought that everything is hopeless, for instance, does not necessarily mean that it is true. Mindfulness can be invaluable in teaching these difficult lessons.

COMPARISON WITH OTHER MINDFULNESS-BASED APPROACHES

The conceptualization and use of mindfulness in DBT is unique in a number of ways. Most notably, mindfulness is operationalized as a set of skills independent of a particular form of practice. Therefore, there is no requirement or expectation that clients or therapists engage in any formal type of mindfulness practice, such as sitting meditation. In this way, DBT differs significantly from other mindfulness-based treatments, such as mindfulness-based cognitive therapy (MBCT) (Segal, Williams, and Teasdale, 2002) and mindfulness-based stress reduction (MBSR) (Kabat-Zinn, 1990), which prescribe formal, specific meditation practices for both clients and therapists. In fact, Linehan (1994) states explicitly that extended meditation practice is contraindicated for many clients with severe psychopathology; without some basic skills it is simply a setup for failure, and shaping principles are indicated. Thus, the use of the specific behavioral mindfulness skills and/or the use of highly abbreviated periods of formal practice (e.g., a few minutes) are highlighted.

Furthermore, although DBT does not require that therapists maintain a regular meditation practice, it should be noted that DBT does require therapists to regularly practice some mindfulness activities. Linehan (2001) has suggested that the most important element of a therapist's training may be having a mindfulness teacher (either in person or through reading) and/or being a member of a community of mindfulness practitioners. Toward this end, consultation team meetings, which are a required part of standard DBT, begin with a formal mindfulness practice led each week by one of the team members. These practices may include traditional mindfulness of breathing exercises and/or practices that are taught as part of the skills training groups. Therapists are also required to practice the skills and exercises that they assign to clients for homework and in-session practice; such practice is essential for developing effective metaphors and personal examples that are frequently necessary to teach the skills. Moreover, such practice adds weight and credibility to therapists' repeated assertions that mindfulness requires ongoing and repeated practice for most people, as opposed to something that is easily mastered. In this light, the therapist's experience of mindfulness practice can be used to model the process of learning these skills.

Finally, DBT strongly emphasizes the importance of the therapist conducting treatment mindfully. Similar to recent discussions of the importance of the mindful practice of medicine (Epstein, 2001), competent and effective DBT therapists model the behaviors that they are teaching to clients, including fully participating in the therapy session and being nonjudgmental. Wholehearted participation in the session also allows for the discovery of important clinical information that might otherwise be easily overlooked. This is easier said than done, especially in the face of extreme emotional affect, intense suffering, and/or anger directed at the therapist (even with all our good intentions and excellent training!). It is our experience that the ability to be mindful and open to each moment as it comes, without judgment, is absolutely crucial to the successful treatment of these clients.

EMPIRICAL SUPPORT FOR THE EFFICACY OF MINDFULNESS IN DBT

Numerous studies have documented the efficacy of DBT across multiple client populations; however, DBT, like other mindfulness-based approaches, is a multifaceted treatment that includes a wide range of other cognitive and behavioral interventions. To date, no studies have specifically evaluated the independent role of mindfulness strategies. Nonetheless, a number of related lines of research provide emerging support for the role of mindfulness interventions in DBT.

Most importantly, investigators have recently begun to examine the role of the avoidance and suppression of thoughts and emotions in BPD. Accumulating evidence suggests that this style of relating to private stimuli might be among the core mechanisms leading to the expression of BPD-criterion behavior. A large literature documents the negative mental and physical health outcomes of emotion and thought suppression (Purdon, 1999; Wenzlaff & Wegner, 2000). For instance, Gross (2002) and Gross and John (2003) have reported numerous studies comparing the consequences of two emotion regulation strategies, reappraisal and suppression. Reappraisal (cognitively altering the meaning of a situation to regulate emotion) is consistently documented to be more advantageous than suppression, which is ineffective in regulating emotional experience and has negative consequences for memory and physiological functioning.

Recently, investigators have begun to extend the study of thought and emotion suppression to the specific examination of BPD symptomatology. For instance, Rosenthal, Cheavens, Lejuez, and Lynch (in press) found that thought suppression was a significant mediator of negative affect intensity and reactivity in BPD symptomatology, even after controlling for other factors commonly associated with the disorder (e.g., childhood sexual abuse). This research parallels findings about the frequency of behavioral avoidance/escape as a strategy for coping with stressful situations among individuals with BPD symptomatology (Bijttebier and Vertommen, 1999; Kruedelbach, McCormick, Schulz, and Grueneich, 1993). Finally, a number of BPD researchers have suggested that targeting experiential avoidance and thought suppression phenomena through nonreinforced exposure to internal experiences (e.g., thoughts, feelings, bodily sensations) may be one of the primary ways in which DBT mindfulness skills yield positive change (Linehan, 1993a; 1993b; Lynch, Chapman, Rosenthal, Kuo, & Linehan, in press).

The evidence of specific mechanisms of change in other mindfulness-based treatments also bears relevance for patients with BPD receiving DBT. For instance, Davidson et al. (2003) found that patients receiving an 8-week MBSR course evidenced significant increases in neural activation associated with positive affect and increased immune functioning, as compared with a control condition. Given the high levels of negative affect that characterize the experiences of individuals with BPD, these data provide empirical evidence for the role of mindfulness practice in enhancing the types of emotional experience so often lacking in the lives of patients with BPD.

Teasdale and colleagues (2001; 2002) additionally suggest that mindfulness interventions can lead to significant increases in metacognitive awareness. The development of metacognitive awareness involves learning to observe thoughts as mental events, as opposed to objective reflections of reality, and parallels the practice of the observing skill in DBT. Teasdale et al. (2002) suggest that MBCT specifically increases metacognitive awareness in patients for whom depressive relapse is prevented. Teasdale et al. (2001) suggest that MBCT is useful, in large part, because it "systematically trains patients to operate in an intentional rather than automatic cognitive mode, to be more aware of unwanted thoughts and feelings, and to relate to them as 'events in the mind' without necessarily attempting to modify their content" (p. 355). It is likely that the DBT observing and describing skills achieve similar ends with respect to the development of metacognitive awareness.

Finally, evidence suggests that mindfulness skills are among the most highly rated in importance by clients receiving DBT. Miller et al. (2000) reported that suicidal adolescents receiving DBT reported that mindfulness and acceptance skills were the most helpful skills taught.

These studies provide an emerging empirical foundation for the specific role of mindfulness strategies within DBT. However, the importance of dismantling designs investigating the specific role of mindfulness strategies cannot be underestimated. Future research is needed to determine the degree to which mindfulness strategies are a critical component of DBT in the treatment of BPD.

CASE EXAMPLE

The following example is based primarily on a case treated by the first author; however, details from another case have been added to protect confidentiality. Transcripts presented in the following sections are compilations from session notes. Hannah was a 35-year-old woman with BPD who presented for treatment reporting serious difficulties with anger dyscontrol. Her previous therapist had referred her to our clinic, after deciding that she could no longer treat Hannah following a session in which Hannah threw a heavy tape dispenser in her direction. Hannah had recently been on short-term disability for depression and wanted her new therapist to help her arrange more long-term disability. While she thought therapy might be helpful for managing her anger more effectively, she was convinced that her depression was a "biological disease" from which she would never recover. Prior to going on disability in the past year, she had worked as an administrator in her local parish. She had two teenage daughters (Anna and Sophie) and an infant son (Nate), and had been married for 4 years to her second husband, whom she met in Narcotics Anonymous (NA). Hannah had a prior history of cocaine dependence, but she had been clean and sober since she met her husband. He, on the other hand, had experienced a relapse recently that was of great concern to her. After a fight in which she had verbally "torn him apart," he had left the home for several days and used drugs. As he worked as a drug counselor for a local church-sponsored program, he was now in danger of losing his job, and Hannah blamed this on herself.

Both Hannah and her husband were very religious and had been quite involved with their church since they met. However, Hannah said that she had a great deal of trouble relating to others in her church, which provided her primary source of social contact. For instance, she would have women over for a prayer circle, but felt so uncomfortable discussing "real issues" that she made things up for them to pray about for her and did not reveal anything genuine herself (she called this her "Stepford wife" act). Afterward, she would be furious at them and herself and engage in activities such as throwing objects around the house, intentional self-injury (often cutting on her thighs or stomach with a razor blade), or writing "hate letters" to herself or to the women. Most of Hannah's overt anger, however, was directed at her husband. She stated that she thought he was on the verge of leaving her because of her angry behavior, which included verbal attacks approximately three times a week and physical assaults (e.g., slapping, hitting, throwing objects at him) approximately once a week. She said that she occasionally yelled at her children in a way that felt out of control to her, although she did not feel she was verbally abusive and had never been physically violent with them.

CASE FORMULATION

As previously mentioned, mindfulness is taught to all clients in DBT skills groups and is considered to be the basis for many other skills. The degree to which mindfulness is emphasized by the individual DBT therapist depends on the client's goals, therapy targets, and case formulation. In Hannah's case, the therapist began to conceptualize mindfulness skills as key during the first few sessions, as they worked together to formulate Hannah's goals. While she wanted to decrease her angry behavior in order to have a better quality of family life, she was also intensely bothered by the sense that she was "a blank, a nothing" and saw this as the root of many other problems. She described the feeling as, "being lost all the time, like I don't know who I am ... or what I want to do ... or what is okay and what isn't ... and I just feel like other people have these souls and I just have this blank, it's like white space inside me ... it's like I can't even tell what I'll do, one moment to the next. ... What kind of a person is that? That's not a person, it's just a body full of emptiness."

A thorough behavioral assessment revealed a consistent pattern. Hannah invalidated herself internally to such an extreme degree that whenever an unwelcome thought or emotion would arise (e.g., "I'm inferior to these women, and if they knew about my real life, they'd reject me"), she would immediately try to dismiss it or suppress it, feeling that these thoughts were "bad" and "shameful." This resulted in the emotion becoming even stronger, and at this point her behavior would appear similarly out of control. She would act impulsively, despite her best intentions. Self-invalidation permeated Hannah's behavior in other ways as well. As is common with clients with BPD, Hannah also looked to others for cues as to what constituted appropriate behavior. It appeared that over time, any experience of herself had become aversive, and she avoided being alone without activity or distractions. Given all this, it is not surprising that her sense of having a "self" had eroded. Mindfulness was conceptualized as helpful to increase her ability to observe her private experiences without judgment, self-invalidation, or avoidance, so that she could (1) increase her understanding of how her behavior was influenced by environmental cues, (2) more mindfully choose a response (thereby decreasing impulsive, destructive behavior), and (3) increase her sense of "self" by observing her likes, dislikes, patterns, etc.

The focus on mindfulness was achieved primarily by emphasizing the seven mindfulness skills in individual therapy. This was not done in a formal protocol, but in response to the problems and issues Hannah brought up each week in treatment. Practicing the skills in the treatment session was a priority, as the skills were novel and difficult for Hannah.

Simply describing them and assigning them for homework would have set her up for failure. Examples of how the skills were incorporated into the treatment session are given later.

WISE MIND

As described previously, DBT skills groups introduce the concept of mindfulness with a review of two major states of mind—reasonable mind and emotion mind. Hannah, like almost all clients with BPD, immediately identified herself as someone who "lives in emotion mind...That reasonable mind is one forest I don't walk through very often!" When encouraged to access her wise mind to make a decision, she expressed serious doubts about her capacity for internal wisdom. She was also extremely concerned that practicing wise mind might be a substitute for listening to the voice of God and therefore violate her religious beliefs. The following excerpt is an illustration of a typical interaction over this kind of issue and an example of practicing wise mind with clients.

Hannah: So what should I do?

Therapist: Well I could tell you what I might do based on my own wise mind, but I'm a lot more interested in what your wise mind is telling you. Listen, you have this really hard decision to make, something anyone in your shoes would find difficult. And you're asking everyone you can think of what you should do, which isn't a bad idea. The thing that concerns me about it is that if you never really go inside, and ask yourself what YOU think, you'll keep having this sense of yourself as empty or void, and I simply don't think that's true. What if you just take a few minutes right now, and go into wise mind about it?

H: I'm not doing that wise mind thing. It's against my religion.

T: What do you mean?

C: It's like New Age woo-woo stuff and my priest says it's wrong. I mean, isn't the whole thing like saying that you don't need God, that you are your own god or something? I don't want to do something that my church is going to consider a sin ...

T: Oh, very excellent point. Well, the idea is that you have the capacity for wisdom inside you, where you intuitively have knowledge, or wisdom—it's the place that combines the reasonable and the emotional. Do you believe that God gives that to people?

H: Well, maybe I could look at it as the Holy Spirit. Like the voice of Christ within me or that still small voice that I am supposed to listen to.

T: Yes, you can think of it that way, certainly—but do you think you would always be listening for God to speak to you, or do you think that God might have also given you a sense of wisdom that is you? Kind of like in your soul?

H: I guess that doesn't violate my faith...I guess I believe that, since God made everyone in his image...

T: Okay, great. So think of it that way. But you said that you were having a hard time experiencing it in group?

H: Yeah, we did this ridiculous exercise in group where we were supposed to imagine ourselves like a pebble floating to the bottom of a lake ... [This imagery is sometimes used as an exercise to help clients experience wise mind; see the DBT skills book for more detail.]

T: And for you ...

H: I just was laughing to myself. I didn't feel anything!

T: Okay, well, maybe that imagery isn't going to be as helpful for you as it is for some. That's fine, we just have to find what does work for you. What about just going within yourself and just listening?

H: Uhhhhh...

T: Like with what we were just talking about. You have this really tough issue where your mom has offered to pay for your daughter to get therapy, and you could really use the financial help. On the other hand, you feel like your mother undermines you as a parent a lot of the time, and you don't want to feel beholden to her, especially over something like this. And you've felt like you should do both things at different times, and you've talked to a bunch of people about it and tried to reason it all out a million times and yet you're still not sure what to do.

H: Right.

T: So how about right now, just trying to go into wise mind and see what comes?

H: How?

T: Well, let's just breathe together for a moment and focus, so just focus on your breath for the next few minutes... [moments pass] Okay, now just ask yourself this question, and then just wait and listen and see what you get. What should I do? Should I take this money?... Don't force anything, just observe and see what happens...

H: [looks up, tearful] Oh ...

T: What did you notice?

H: I have to let her help, this isn't about me.

T: That's what you got?

H: Yes...

T: Do you think that it was your wise mind?

H: I still don't know if it's listening to the Holy Spirit or to wise mind or whatever, but I see what you're talking about. It's the strangest thing, I guess I just felt like I knew...

In this example, Hannah experienced her wise mind almost immediately; at other times, it takes practice, and clients should be encouraged to keep at it and experiment with different methods. After this session, the therapist suggested that Hannah begin to practice going into wise mind often when making decisions, even those that were seemingly mundane. For instance, Hannah would practice going into wise mind when deciding which chores to do first at home, whether to exercise, etc. At times, she reported that this was helpful, at times she said she felt nothing, and at times she reported that her wise mind had informed her that it did not matter! She also began to practice doing one pleasant event daily. During and after the practice, she would go into wise mind and ask herself whether she found the event pleasurable. If so, she incorporated the activity more often into her daily routine and practiced doing it one-mindfully. Regardless of the outcome, the practice of mindfully observing her own thoughts, desires, logic, and emotion began to help Hannah observe herself. Over time, this helped her develop a sense of self.

OBSERVE AND DESCRIBE

Observing and describing skills were the main vehicle of treatment for Hannah's angry behavior. In DBT, the therapist conducts a detailed chain analysis whenever a client has engaged in a dysfunctional target behavior. For Hannah, this was usually either parasuicide or a verbal/physical assault on her husband. Chain analyses quickly revealed that avoidance of the experience of sadness was almost always behind Hannah's experience of intense anger; whenever she felt deeply hurt or sad, she would quickly move to anger, usually without realizing it. A typical pattern was feeling sad or ashamed about an event in her life (usually, problems with her daughters or disagreements with her husband), which would set off judgmental thoughts about herself and whomever else was involved. She would then begin to ruminate on the judgments, experience intense surges of anger and urges to lash out physically or verbally, engage in some form of anger expression, and then feel extremely ashamed afterward. She often coped with the shame by cutting her thighs or stomach with razor blades, after which she felt a sense of relief and exhaustion. As she began to recognize the recurrence of this pattern in therapy, she began referring to it as her "wounded dog" behavior, referring to the way animals sometimes attack when hurt or threatened.

Observing and describing were used to help Hannah begin to experience intense negative affect without necessarily doing anything to change it, and to mindfully choose her responses instead of reacting impulsively. At first, the therapist began asking Hannah to observe and describe her emotions whenever they escalated in session (which was quite frequent!). Instead of "becoming" her emotion, Hannah began to step back and observe the thoughts, physiological sensations, and urges she was having. She also began asking "Can I tolerate this moment?" or "Can I tolerate this for the next 5 minutes?" She would then use the describing skills to either describe to herself what was happening ("I feel like smashing something. The thought that I would be better off single keeps coming into my head. Images of me throwing things against the wall keep flitting in my mind. I feel hot all over. Breathing is short and shallow"). She also began asking herself, "Is there anything I am sad about?" or "Where is the threat to me?" and focusing on those emotions and thoughts instead of anger. The difficulty of this task for Hannah (and many clients with BPD) cannot be overstated, as illustrated by the following phone call, when she paged the therapist for skills coaching.

Therapist: Hi, Hannah, what's going on? I got your page.

Hannah: [sobbing hysterically] Oh god, oh god, I'm doing what you told me and I can't stand it, I can't get out, you have to help me, please. I've got to cut, I can't take it. Please...

T: Oh my goodness! Hannah, what on earth has happened to get you this upset?

H: It's Sophie! She's in trouble again, it's so awful, and I started to get the anger so I asked myself if there was sadness, and then I observed the tightness in my chest and the lump in my throat, and then I just started crying, and I keep just trying to greet the sadness like in the book you gave me [Thich Nhat Hanh's *Miracle of Mindfulness*]...

T: This is great, you're doing a great job!

H: Yeah, so I haven't yelled at anyone or hit anyone, but now it's like the darkness is swallowing me whole... I'm so sad and I can't get out, it's like it's never going to end! [sobbing]

T: The sadness is incredibly painful.

H: Yes, and the only way to make it go away is to cut or burn. I can't take it, I'm telling you, I don't want to let you down, but you have to help me or I can't take it... and [starts yelling] *if it wasn't for that asshole I married this never would have happened!*

T: [cutting her off] Okay, I'm so glad you called so I can coach you, because this sounds incredibly difficult. Don't go to anger, just put it on the shelf for a moment. Now, have you cut yourself yet?

H: No.

T: Okay, fabulous. So first I just want you to breathe on the phone for a minute with me, okay? Just observe your breath and I'll do it with you for a minute, right here on the phone. Okay, good, I can hear you breathing. Just observe the breath, and notice anything that distracts you from it and let that go, and then return to your breath... [lets a minute go by] You're doing great, what are you noticing?

H: That it's too hard...

T: So, that thought went through your mind?

H: Yes, it's just too hard, I can't stand it . . .

T: Okay, so just notice that that is a thought that went through your mind. Just a thought like any other one . . . Do you remember how we were talking about that in the session today?

H: Yes, right.

T: Okay, good. So now focus just on this one moment, not all the future moments, but just this one. Right here and now. Tell me what you notice in your body.

H: Pain.

T: Where?

H: My eyes hurt, my chest is tight, lump in my throat, anger surging up and down.

T: Oh, you're doing such a great job. And what thoughts are you noticing?

H: That I'm a terrible mother, that she is going to have a life of pain, that I don't know what to do . . . failure . . .

T: Okay, are you noticing them and letting them pass through?

H: It's so hard.

T: I know, Hannah, I know. Just hang in there with me, okay? I think one of the things that's happening is that this moment is incredibly painful, and it should be painful, because what happened is painful. And I think you can tolerate it in one moment, but not for the rest of your life, which is maybe what your brain is telling you. Do you think you could tolerate being this sad for the next minute? Just observing those physical sensations and those thoughts?

H: I guess so.

T: Okay, so keep breathing, focus on what you're experiencing in the moment, and I'll just stay here on the phone with you for the next minute, okay?

H: Okay . . . [a minute passes]

T: Okay, it's been about a minute. What did you notice?

H: It was hard, and I noticed these awful images of her going to jail or being dead and me crying. And then the strangest thing happened, I thought, I need to go grocery shopping . . . and that was a little bit funny to me and I noticed that.

T: Oh, too good, so you really were observing the thoughts, you really had the Teflon mind there. ["Teflon mind" is language often used in skills groups to illustrate the concept of observing stimuli without attachment]

H: But its still so hard.

T: Yes, but you are tolerating being incredibly sad and noticing that it ebbs and flows, that it's totally intense one moment and then lifts, and then back, like waves. That's how emotions are, and so its like riding the waves, noticing them all the time and just sitting with them. And they don't last forever, even when it feels like that. And notice that you are tolerating it without doing anything that will mess up your life, like cutting.

H: What am I going to do?

T: You mean about your daughter?

H: Yes.

T: How about spending some time mindfully considering it, like going into wise mind about it. Then we'll talk more about it in our session.

The intense fear of being in "the abyss," as Linehan (1993a) has called it, and never being able to get out is a common one with BPD clients. While practicing mindfulness of their emotions can help them experience pain and decrease suffering, it is also true that their pain is extraordinary. Over time, Hannah became increasingly comfortable with "just feeling sad," and reported that the more she did it, the more she realized that it would not last forever. Although she experienced a mild increase in depression during the next few months, her anger episodes and parasuicidal behavior completely ceased. Interestingly, so did her feeling of not having a self, or being "blank." After noticing that she had not brought up the issue in several weeks, the therapist questioned her about it. Hannah replied that by doing the daily pleasant events with mindfulness, she felt that she had "rediscovered herself" and had a sense of what she did and did not enjoy. She also thought that by doing all the "unbelievable mountain of recording you do around here" (referring to the diary cards, chain analysis homework sheets, and various research instruments), she had begun to understand how she responded to her environment in a way that gave her a sense of having a more cohesive self. She also said "You know, when you don't have any control over yourself, like you don't understand chains of events or how to use the skills and all of that, you can't feel like a real person when you never know what you're going to do or how you're going to feel from one moment to the next. I think the mindfulness skills sort of gave me my self back, or maybe helped me observe my self."

OTHER MINDFULNESS SKILLS

Often, the other mindfulness skills were also incorporated into the treatment; space precludes detailed transcripts of each. Working on decreasing judgments was a frequent topic in treatment. While Hannah agreed with the concept that being less judgmental would be a good thing, she found it difficult to put into practice. The first hurdle was simply to notice her judgmental thoughts. In therapy, the following type of interaction occurred numerous times:

> Hannah: God, I can't believe I'm such a damned idiot.
>
> Therapist: Could you please say that again and lose all the judgments?
>
> H: I can't believe I did something ... so stupid!
>
> T: Again please! Describe it. "Stupid" doesn't really give me any information.
>
> H: I can't believe ...
>
> T: You mean you notice the feeling of surprise arising within you.
>
> H: Right, I notice surprise—well, no, it's more like I notice shame at the thought that I yelled at my husband again.
>
> T: Well, that was marvelous! Now I actually know what is going on here.

The key to interactions such as the one described previously is delivery in a light, nonjudgmental (even gently teasing or irreverent) tone, and coaching where needed. Often, Hannah was asked to reframe judgments or say things in a less judgmental tone. She also took a lap counter one day and clicked it each time she noticed a judgment (including judgments of how many judgments she had counted!). Once she had learned to recognize and "catch" them, she worked on reframing them, just noticing them and letting them go, or building empathy for whomever she was judging—most often, herself. This practice was also helpful in decreasing her subjective experience of anger. For instance, she began noticing judgments of other drivers on the road and hypothesizing reasons for their driving habits (she often used the line, "Maybe they're rushing to the hospital and aren't focused on driving"). Once, on her way to the hospital herself (to visit her daughter, who had been placed in an inpatient eating disorders unit), Hannah used this strategy—only to find that the car she had been judging had indeed pulled into the hospital parking lot!

Hannah also began saying phrases to herself intended to remind her to practice being effective. She wrote a few down on notecards and would read them when she was becoming angry or had urges to cut herself. These included things like "Be effective, do what works," "Forget about if it's right or not, focus on if it's effective," and lists of why certain behaviors were and were not effective.

Hannah incorporated the participation skill into two main areas. First was listening to her husband when they were having tense conversations; she would practice intensely listening to what he was saying before formulating her own responses. Second, she began participating in routine household tasks, such as washing dishes, doing laundry, etc.

Over the course of treatment, Hannah showed remarkable improvement. By the end of treatment, she no longer met criteria for stage I (see Linehan, 1993, for more details of client stages), as she was in excellent behavioral control. It appeared to both the therapist and Hannah that the mindfulness skills had been of paramount importance to her. The most striking example was her use of the observing and describing skills; once Hannah learned that she could tolerate emotional pain and that it would not last forever without her doing anything about it, avoidance behaviors such as anger expression and parasuicide decreased dramatically. It also appeared that the practice of these skills, along with participating and wise mind, resulted in her increased sense of self. The practice of the nonjudgmental and effective skills was also very helpful to her in increasing her behavioral control.

COMMON REACTIONS AND PROBLEMS

Although mindfulness is becoming more and more widely known in the general community, it is very likely that the DBT mindfulness skills will still be foreign concepts to most clients with BPD (and perhaps to treatment providers as well!). What follows are some common reactions to the introduction of mindfulness skills and some practical guidance for how to deal with these reactions.

"HOW WILL THIS HELP ME?"

Individuals with BPD often feel that their lives, as they are currently being led, are completely unbearable. They may react to their first experience of mindfulness practice with something akin to shock that they are being asked to be more aware of this current suffering. They are often looking for "quick fixes" to their lifelong problems (as are most people!). Thus, it is important to provide a thorough and convincing rationale for why the practice of the mindfulness skills will ultimately benefit them. There are several elements of this rationale that we have used over time. Although the rationale for using DBT mindfulness skills was presented earlier, here it is presented in a "user-friendly" manner that can be easily disseminated to clients. First, most clients with BPD have learned, over time, that escape from the moment (through avoidance, dissociation, substance use, and/or parasucidal behavior, for example) has very powerful short-term benefits. However, these behaviors are self-damaging and prevent them from achieving long-term goals. Thus, they have to learn to tolerate the moment as it is without avoiding or escaping. Second, most clients with BPD would agree that they feel like they suffer a great deal. However, a close examination of suffering reveals that it is usually linked to thoughts about past events or worries about future ones. The idea is that mindfulness will help remove a large part of suffering by allowing a client to experience only this one moment, be it painful or joyous. Third, the capacity to experience joy and happiness can be found in the present moment. The experience of happiness requires practice, like anything else, yet often individuals will "spoil" a moment of happiness by worrying about when it will end or being distracted by thoughts or memories of past events. Through full participation in the present moment, clients will learn that all emotions, both positive and negative, come and go and they do not have to be controlled by them.

"I DON'T LIKE MINDFULNESS," "MINDFULNESS IS STUPID"

The DBT mindfulness skills, in practice, force a person to examine the here and now in its entirety. Again, rationale is crucial, as is a very real understanding of what the client may have to lose by practicing mindfulness. Asking people to give up heavily reinforced behaviors, such as substance use or parasuicide, and replace them with nonjudgmental observing and describing is not an easy sell. One approach to this problem is to try to convince clients to practice, even if they do not like it. This is also a skill that most people have to master in order to function well in society. Another approach is to find ways to make mindfulness fun. Experimenting with different types of practice exercises is good for showing that mindfulness practice is flexible and obtainable. Finally, the use of self-disclosure can be incredibly valuable here. If the therapist has personal examples of how he or she did not initially like mindfulness but then grew to like it due to achieved benefits, it is often helpful to share this with clients.

"I TRY, BUT I JUST CAN'T DO IT"

With this complaint, two areas of exploration are very important. First, what are clients actually doing when they say that they are trying? Second, what outcome are they expecting when they practice? With regard to the first point, it is very important to get a sense of how the client is practicing. This helps clear up misconceptions about what mindfulness is and further differentiates among avoidance, dissociation, and mindfulness. With regard to the second point, in truth, the practice of mindfulness is *doing it*; there is nothing more than the practice. This cannot be overemphasized. It is likely that even the biggest novices to DBT skills have moments of mindfulness practice already in their lives. One of the things we like to do first when teaching a skill like participation is ask clients what activities they have in their lives that they already actively participate in with awareness. It is often the case that they have some. You can then use these examples to highlight that they are already practicing mindfulness. What is now needed is to expand the time that they are practicing or the types of activities during which they can practice.

"MY WISE MIND IS TELLING ME TO KILL MYSELF"

Unfortunately, this is not a rare statement heard among suicidal clients learning these skills. It represents a complete conviction in the moment that they deserve to die and that it would be "wise" to do so. It is a misunderstanding of the notion of wise mind and is at odds with the therapist's own wise mind (we hope!). It is also our experience that this is not a belief that can go away overnight or with one lesson in the skill. Often, when teaching this skill to new learners, we emphasize that it is easy to confuse wise mind with emotion mind, and we make a list of how to differentiate the two. Often, the first item on the list is to delay action until intense emotion has ceased. A "wise mind decision" is one that will hold up over time, with and without the presence of a strong emotion. Ask clients to give themselves 6 months (6 weeks, 6 days, or even 6 hours to get through an immediate crisis) to really determine whether it is indeed a wise mind decision. They can always kill themselves, of course, but it is not their best move to risk making a mistake that they cannot take back—so waiting a few days is a smart thing to do. Pointing out specific examples of how killing themselves might result in negative consequences can also be helpful (for instance, maybe death will not really lead to an end to all pain, or perhaps their suicide would irreparably damage those they care for). There is, of course, a dialectic here. While a DBT therapist would never agree with a client's decision to suicide, this dilemma of the client's and therapist's wise minds diverging sometimes appears in less extreme forms. Humility and a true respect for the client's ability to be wise is essential.

"IS MINDFULNESS ALWAYS THE ANSWER?"

One of the authors was presented with the following scenario by a client who was struggling with the application of mindfulness in his life: What if you are at the dentist, having a painful drilling in your tooth with no Novocain? Would you practice being in the present moment then? This is not an uncommon question for any practitioner of mindfulness, especially among clients with BPD whose every moment in life feels filled with such pain. The reply to this client was that when you are actually in really difficult, painful moments, how much are you adding to the pain with your thoughts or your avoidance? Are you thinking about how awful this is, how it is just going to get worse, how you are not sure you will survive it, how this is the worst thing you have ever experienced? That is not being mindful and, in fact, usually serves to "fuel the fire" and make things worse. When you are truly aware of only this one moment, it usually is not as bad as you think or fear. Pain is often in the future or in the past and not in the current moment. Of course, there are truly awful moments in life, and at these times one may often choose to distract. Adaptive, short-term distraction is also a DBT skill in the Distress Tolerance Module. The important lesson to teach clients is that they have an option and should try something different from distraction at least a few times to see what happens. In practice, it is difficult to conceive of a situation in which mindfulness would not be helpful, but this is something that clients have to learn experientially for themselves.

CONCLUDING COMMENTS

DBT was one of the first psychosocial treatments to incorporate mindfulness as a core component. Linehan made a major contribution to the field by adapting traditional forms of mindfulness practice into discrete skills that can be practiced in everyday life, by individuals with varying levels of behavioral control. While the data on the overall efficacy of DBT are promising, the degree to which mindfulness is an important mechanism remains an important area of empirical inquiry. We have reviewed here the rationale for use of mindfulness with clients who meet criteria for borderline personality disorder, and we believe that the extant data on how mindfulness has been helpful with other problems, combined with clinical experience, makes a strong case for mindfulness as a crucial element in the successful treatment of BPD. It is our hope that research efforts will increasingly focus on testing this hypothesis.

REFERENCES

Bijttebier, P., & Vertommen, H. (1999). Coping strategies in relation to personality disorders. *Personality and Individual Differences, 26,* 847–856.
Davidson, R. J., Kabat-Zinn, J., Schumacher, J., Rosenkranz, M., Muller, D., Santorelli, S. F., et al. (2003). Alterations in brain and immune functioning produced by mindfulness meditation. *Psychosomatic Medicine, 65,* 564–570.
Epstein, R. M. (2001, November). Mindful practice in medicine. In S. Dimidjian & L. Dimeff (Co-chairs), *The clinical application of mindfulness practice.* Panel discussion conducted at the Association for the Advancement of Behavior Therapy 35th Annual Convention, Philadelphia.
Gross, J. J. (2002). Emotion regulation: Affective, cognitive, and social consequences. *Psychophysiology, 39,* 281–291.
Gross, J. J., & John, O. P. (2003). Individual differences in two emotion regulation processes: Implications for affect, relationship, and well-being. *Journal of Personality and Social Psychology, 85,* 348–362.
Kabat-Zinn, J. (1990). *Full catastrophe living: Using the wisdom of your body and mind to face stress, pain, and illness.* New York: Dell Publishing.

Katz, L. Y., Cox, B. J., Gunasekara, S., & Miller, A. L. (2004). Feasibility of dialectical behavior therapy for suicidal adolescent inpatients. *Journal of the American Academy of Child Psychiatry*, 43(3), 276–282.

Koerner, K., & Dimeff, L. A. (2000). Further data on dialectical behavior therapy. *Clinical Psychology: Science and Practice*, 7, 104–112.

Kruedelbach, N., McCormick, R. A., Schulz, S. C., & Grueneich, R. (1993). Impulsivity, coping styles, and triggers for craving in substance abusers with borderline personality disorder. *Journal of Personality Disorders, 7*, 214–222.

Linehan, M. M. (1993a). *Cognitive-behavioral treatment of borderline personality disorder.* New York: Guilford Press.

———— (1993b). *Skill training manual for treating borderline personality disorder.* New York: Guilford Press.

———— (1994). Acceptance and change: The central dialectic in psychotherapy. In S. C. Hayes, N. C. Jacobson, V. M. Follette, & M. J. Dougher (Eds.), *Acceptance and change: Content and context in psychotherapy* (pp. 73–86). Reno, NV: Context Press.

———— (2001, November). Mindful practice in behavior therapy. In S. Dimidjian & L. Dimeff (Co-chairs), *The clinical application of mindfulness practice.* Panel discussion conducted at the Association for the Advancement of Behavior Therapy 35th Annual Convention, Philadelphia.

Lynch, T. R., Chapman, A. L., Rosenthal, M. Z., Kuo, J. R., & Linehan, M. M. (in press). Mechanisms of change in dialectical behavior therapy: Theoretical observations. *Journal of Clinical Psychology.*

Miller, A., Wyman, S. E., & Huppert, J. D (2000). Analysis of behavioral skills utilized by suicidal adolescents receiving dialectical behavior therapy. *Cognitive and Behavioral Practice, 7*, 183–187.

Purdon, C. (1999). Thought suppression and psychopathology. *Behaviour Research and Therapy, 37*, 1029–1054.

Rosenthal, M. Z., Cheavens, J. S., Lejuez, C. W., & Lynch, T. R. (in press). Thought suppression mediates the relationship between negative affect and borderline personality disorder symptoms. *Behaviour Research and Therapy.*

Rizvi, S. L., & Linehan, M. M. (2001). Dialectical behavior therapy for personality disorders. *Current Psychiatry Reports, 3*, 64–69.

Segal, Z. V., Williams, M. G.,& Teasdale, J. D. (2002). *Mindfulness-based cognitive therapy for depression: A new approach to preventing relapse.* New York: Guilford Press.

Teasdale, J. D., Moore, R. G., Hayhurst, H., Pope, M., Williams, S., & Segal, Z. V. (2002). Metacognitive awareness and prevention of relapse in depression: Empirical evidence. *Journal of Consulting and Clinical Psychology, 70*, 275–287.

Teasdale, J. D., Scott, J., Moore, R. G., Hayhurst, H., Pope, M., & Paykel, E. S. (2001). How does cognitive therapy prevent relapse in residual depression? Evidence from a controlled trial. *Journal of Consulting and Clinical Psychology, 69*, 347–357.

Wenzlaff, R. M., & Wegner, D. M. (2000). Thought suppression. *Annual Review of Psychology, 51*, 59–91.

PART III

Applications for Psychological Disorders in Children, Adolescents, and Older Adults

7

MINDFULNESS-BASED COGNITIVE THERAPY FOR CHILDREN

RANDYE J. SEMPLE

New York State Psychiatric Institute, Division of Clinical and Genetic Epidemiology, Department of Psychiatry, Columbia University, New York, New York

JENNIFER LEE AND LISA F. MILLER

Columbia University, Teachers College, New York, New York

INTRODUCTION TO MINDFULNESS-BASED COGNITIVE THERAPY FOR CHILDREN

After several years of working with children and mindfulness techniques, we have discovered some important differences between conducting adult mindfulness groups and conducting groups with children. We found that adults rarely (if ever) use their meditation mats to construct forts, and in our experience, never experiment to see how many meditation cushions they can balance on their heads. As is often stated, children are not just small adults; therefore, mindfulness practices for children must address developmental differences in attentional and cognitive capabilities and interpersonal functioning. For many practical reasons, children are also more embedded in their supportive environmental systems than is typical for adults. When using mindfulness approaches with children, effective theory and clinical applications must address some key developmental differences as they apply to conducting psychotherapy with symptomatic children.

Mindfulness-based cognitive therapy for children (MBCT-C) differs from the structured adult MBCT program described in the first chapter of this book in three important ways. First, children typically have less developed memory and attentional capacities than do adults (Posner & Petersen, 1990; Siegler, 1991), which suggests that they may benefit from shorter and more repetitious therapy sessions. The manualized MBCT for adults was designed as an 8-week program, with each weekly session lasting 2 hours (Segal, Williams, & Teasdale, 2003). In response to our clients' less developed attentional capacities, MBCT-C is a 12-week program consisting of weekly, 90-minute sessions. In addition, children typically find it challenging to stay engaged in a single activity for long periods. Consequently, we replaced the 20- to 40-minute seated breath meditations traditionally used in adult mindfulness programs with more frequent meditations, which are practiced throughout each session in 3- to 5-minute blocks.

Second, adult psychotherapies depend largely on clients' abilities to identify and verbalize their affective experiences by using abstract thinking and logical analysis. Because latency-age children have limited verbal fluency, abstract reasoning, and conceptualization, they may more effectively engage in psychotherapy when games, activities, and stories are integrated into the treatment protocols (Gaines, 1997; Stark, Rouse, & Kurowski, 1994). Educational programs using a variety of multisensory approaches and learning-style theories have been shown to improve student achievement in elementary school settings (Moustafa, 1999; Thornton, 1983; Wislock, 1993). The primacy of sensory experience in childhood may make the moment-to-moment practice of being mindful particularly accessible to children. MBCT-C experiential learning exercises rely primarily on enhancing mindfulness by more fully experiencing one's internal and external environments via specific sensory modes (sight, sound, touch, taste, smell, and kinesthetics). Some of the sensory exercises also address children's needs for physical activity. Exercises are varied over the course of a session, alternating among sensory activities, sitting meditations, body scans, visualization practices, and drawing or writing.

Finally, because children are more integrated within their family and school environments than are adult clients, family involvement in treatment can enhance outcomes (Kaslow & Racusin, 1994). The MBCT-C program is designed so that the parents of the young clients are an integral part of the program. Parents are encouraged to support their child by participating in the home practice exercises and by promoting mindful speech, behaviors, and intentions at home and at school. Parents participate in the program with their children in three different ways. First, we invite all the parents to attend therapist-conducted mindfulness sessions. The orientation session, an introduction to mindfulness, is held before the children's 12-week program begins. During this time, therapists lead the parents through several mindfulness exercises (i.e., breathing and eating a raisin). Parents are actively recruited to be co-participants in the home practice exercises that support their children's efforts. Parents are encouraged to ask questions during this initial session and to dialogue with the therapists throughout the program. Second, to facilitate parental participation, the children each receive supportive materials to take home in their "travel folders" (folders that they bring to and from class) at the end of each session. These include written session summaries, home practice instruction sheets, and daily practice recording sheets. Reviewing written session materials informs a systematic understanding of each session and allows parents to better participate in the home practice exercises with their child. We also encourage clients' parents to share these home practice exercises with the child's sibling(s). Third, a parental "review and dialogue" session is held at the conclusion of the program. At this review session, parents have opportunities to share their experience of the MBCT-C program and to discuss ways in which they can continue to cultivate and support their child's mindfulness practices at home.

Thus, three key developmental differences (i.e., attentional capacity, abstract reasoning, and family embeddedness) inform our adaptation of MBCT for children. Other tenets prompted by developmental characteristics of childhood include:

- *Repetition enhances learning.* Mindful learning is bolstered by a high degree of repetitiveness built into the structure of the sessions. For example, each session begins with a review and group discussion of the prior week's session, followed by a group discussion of the children's experiences of their home practice exercises.
- *Variety increases children's interest.* Each mindfulness exercise is shorter than is common with adult programs, and we introduce several different exercises within each session.
- *Most of the exercises require active participation.* Examples include drawing pictures, listening to or making music, touching a variety of objects, tasting different foods, and smelling various scents.

Similar to MBCT, group discussions after each exercise are an integral element of the MBCT-C program. By sharing their sometimes radically different viewpoints, children learn to appreciate how much their individual past experiences, present cognitive or affective states, and expectations of outcomes influence their direct apperceptions and interpretations of present-moment experiences.

Practical adaptations that we have developed for mindfulness work with children include the following:

- The adult MBCT program typically employs a ratio of 12 participants per instructor. In the MBCT-C program, two co-therapists facilitate groups of 6 to 8 children, which provides each child with greater individualized attention.

- We create an environment distinctly different from the typical school setting. Children and therapists sit in an inward-facing circle on floor cushions rather than in chairs. We invite the children to remove their shoes when entering the therapy room. Yoga mats are used during guided imagery, body scan, and mindful movement exercises. This environment helps the children differentiate MBCT-C from school lessons in two ways. First, MBCT-C embraces guided experiential learning rather than a didactic method of teaching. Second, the environment informs the children that the co-therapists are integrated participants in the program and are present to support a process of self-discovery rather than "teaching" certain truths or imparting information. In this manner, the therapists become equal players in the children's worlds. For example, therapists' names are included on the attendance board and they earn a sticker for "being present" each week. Therapists actively participate in class activities, complete home practice exercises each week, and share their personal experiences of mindfulness with the group.

Similar to the adult program, MBCT-C places strong emphasis on creating a cohesive, safe, and confidential environment—particularly during the initial sessions. In response to children's increased need for structure, five "Rules for Mindful Behavior" are written down, discussed, and made explicit in a way that is not typically necessary when working with adults. These rules are:

1. Act and speak to group members with care and kindness.
2. Do not talk when another person is talking.
3. Raise your hand to share your ideas with the group.
4. Do not talk during mindfulness exercises.
5. If you do not want to take part in an activity, one person at a time may sit in *My Quiet Space* (a designated chair placed in one corner of the room).

Children earn rewards (cartoon stickers) for session attendance and for completing their home practice exercises. Each child receives a notebook, with which to collect attendance stickers, session summaries, practice exercise worksheets, drawings, writings, poems, and stories. At the beginning and end of the program, the children decorate the front and back covers, respectively, of their notebooks with pictures, colors, or words that represent what mindfulness means to them. They take their notebooks home at the end of the program.

THEORY AND CONCEPTS

CHILDHOOD ANXIETY AND DEPRESSION

We generally recognize that when children face the inevitable stressors and challenges of daily life, they frequently feel apprehension, develop fears and worries, and experience physiological responses that they interpret as anxiety (i.e., the fight, flight, or freeze responses). Experiences of loss and feelings of inadequacy or helplessness can contribute to dysphoric or irritable mood states. Across many theoretical models, acute major stressors and chronic minor stressors are believed to contribute to depression and anxiety spectrum disorders (for examples, see Chethik, 2000; Kendall, 2000; Klerman, Weissman, Rounsaville, & Chevron, 1995). Throughout our lives, stressors are indeed inevitable. To help manage these vicissitudes of life, MBCT-C integrates a cognitive-behavioral paradigm of identifying and restructuring maladaptive thoughts with mindfulness and acceptance exercises derived from Buddhist meditation practices.

COGNITIVE THEORIES OF ANXIETY AND DEPRESSION

Cognitive theory suggests that once an individual has experienced the negative thinking associated with anxiety and depression, there is an increased risk that he or she will develop maladaptive cognitive schemas, which, with repetition, can become entrenched (Beck, 1995). For many clients, a small amount of nervousness or disappointed expectations can trigger a rush of negative cognitions (e.g., "Terrible things will happen," "I am a failure," "I feel overwhelmed," "I can't control my life"). You may watch your depressed client ruminating: "What has gone wrong?" "Why is this happening to me?" "This is all my fault," or "Where will it all end?" During an episode of anxiety, worried mood typically accompanies negative futuristic thinking, while depressive thinking is characterized by a back-ward-looking orientation. What anxious and depressed thinking have in common is that, in both, the individual is not fully engaged in the present moment. Body sensations associated with anxiety include muscular tension, heart palpitations, gastrointestinal distress, shallow breathing or hyper-ventilation, and hyperarousal. Mild sadness or dysphoric moods may precipitate body sensations of fatigue, apathy, hypoarousal, or unexplained pains. The negative thoughts and the physiological reactions are often far out of proportion to the environmental or situational triggers. When the episode is past, and the mood has returned to normal, the anxious or depressive cognitions and body sensations fade away. However, they have not really disappeared. The brain has learned associations among these cognitive, affective, and physiological states. Reactivation of anxious or depressive schemas and physiological responses becomes automatic and fosters inaccurate perceptions of the threat level of the present situation. This automaticity suggests that, essentially, the mind "has a mind of its own." Therefore, when an undesirable event reactivates a mildly anxious or dysphoric mood, the mood state can then trigger these now automatic responses. When this happens, old habits of anxious or depressed thinking begin again. Consequently, cognitive, affective, or physiological reactions to present-moment events may prove to be maladaptive or inappropriate responses to the situation. Negative thinking falls into the same rut, and a full-blown episode of anxiety or depression may result. The discovery that even when a client's mood is euthymic, the habituated link between negative moods and negative thoughts remains ready to be reactivated is of enormous importance. It means that self-management of anxiety and depression may depend on learning how to keep mild states of dysphoria or apprehension from spiraling out of control.

ATTENTIONAL SELF-MANAGEMENT

In both children and adults, self-management of attention appears to be a necessary prerequisite for learning to occur (Ehrenreich & Gross, 2002; Lam & Beale, 1991; Shiffrin & Schneider, 1977). Children spend many of their waking hours engaged in formal and informal learning processes. They must acquire a vast amount of knowledge if developmental growth is to progress at an appropriate pace (Taublieb, 1996). Anxiety and depression typically disrupt attention and concentration, which then impedes learning abilities beyond that associated with dysphoric or anxious mood states. In addition, chronic learning difficulties can become associated with feelings of personal inadequacy or low self-esteem, exacerbating tendencies toward anxiety or depression.

Attention is a fascinating and complex phenomenon. What are we actually doing when we pay attention to something external to ourselves? Where are we when we become "lost in thought" and unaware of otherwise intrusive stimuli? When our attention is focused inward, who or what is attending to whom? Deikman (1982) distinguished among the thinking self, the emotional self, the functional self, and the observing self. He considered the latter, the observing self, to be markedly different from the other three. The observing self is the domain that is aware. The observing self precedes and experiences thoughts, emotions, and behaviors:

> No matter what takes place, no matter what we experience, nothing is as central as the self that observes. In the face of this phenomenon, Descarte's starting point, "I think; therefore I am," must yield to the more basic position, "I am aware, therefore I am." (Deikman, 1982, p. 94)

Deikman (1996) suggested that practices of mindfulness meditation raise awareness of our ability to consciously respond to everyday experiences.

The observing self is constant throughout life. It is featureless and makes no value judgments. When our observing selves are manifest, we experience a greater range of conscious choices and we become less emotionally reactive to our experiences.

When practicing mindfulness, we strengthen the observing self. Ordinary daily experiences, stressful or otherwise, provide the raw materials for this attention enhancement process. Experiential and conceptual information presented in a particular way provides repeated learning experiences for the mindfulness practitioner. When mindfulness is taught, thoughts, emotions, and sensations are interpreted as interesting phenomena to *observe* rather than to *judge* (including observing the experience of judging) and as events to be *noted* rather than *changed*. By experiencing thoughts, emotions, and sensations as independent of external events, a practitioner of mindfulness can more easily "decenter" from anxious, previously conditioned, internal experiences. Through repeated personal experiences, we begin to perceive our thoughts, emotions, and sensations as transient, continually shifting events in the mind rather than evidence of objective truths. Within this framework, mindfulness practice can be interpreted as a form of exposure with response prevention—a commonly used behavioral technique in the treatment of anxiety disorders (Foa & Kozak, 1986). These repeated quasi-exposure experiences can produce an adaptive perceptual shift in the mental representations that shape individuals' relationships to their own anxious or depressive thoughts, feelings, and body sensations (Segal, Williams, & Teasdale, 2002; Teasdale, 1999; Teasdale, Segal, & Williams, 1995). The goal of decentering is to engage fully in the affective experience, rather than to change it.

De-automatization and decentering are *not* akin to desensitization or dissociation of affect. Sustained mindfulness exercises commonly result in subjectively enhanced sensory perceptions and increased present-focused awareness (Walsh, 1977; 1978). Brown (1977) and Goleman (1984) have described case reports of heightened awareness of internal events: thoughts, emotions, and body sensations.

To be mindful is to cultivate attention and therefore enhance our moment-to-moment awareness. We assume that stressful situations are inevitable for everyone. Habituated, often maladaptive reactivity is not. Modifying or retraining habituated, reactive patterns requires us to pay meticulous attention to the present situation to identify clearly how it differs from previous situations, and then consciously select a response with awareness and personal choice. Mindful awareness allows our clients and ourselves to perceive more adaptively many challenging situations by experiencing them with clarity, and then responding in a skillful way (attentively and nonjudgmentally). The purpose is not to dissociate from, repress, or change the experiences, but to move beyond them. This is accomplished by enhancing attention and awareness to our cognitions, emotions, and sensory perceptions "in the moment." With repeated practice, we develop a capacity for nonjudgmental observation and clarity. Consequently, mindless *reactivity* and mindful *responsivity* to one's internal and external environments become incompatible states of being. Increasing mindfulness is therefore associated with decreases in the automaticity of maladaptive thoughts, emotions, and behaviors.

EMPIRICAL SUPPORT FOR MINDFULNESS AS A CLINICAL APPROACH

REVIEW OF RESEARCH

At present, there is very little published research about the clinical effects of mindfulness practices with children. Two controlled studies have reported significant improvements in academic performance by college students practicing mindfulness techniques (Fiebert & Mead, 1981; Hall, 1999). However, these studies are in need of replication with youth samples. Linden (1973) studied the effects of meditation training on aspects of the cognitive and affective functioning of third-grade children. After 18 weeks of meditation practice, participants became less anxious about test taking. Linden hypothesized that meditation practice may help children learn to concentrate and volitionally alter feeling states by shifting their attention.

In a 6-week, open clinical trial with 7- and 8-year-old children, Semple, Reid, and Miller (2005) and Reid, Semple, and Miller (in press) found preliminary support for the feasibility and acceptability of treating childhood anxiety with cognitively based, group mindfulness techniques. This feasibility study was followed by a randomized controlled trial (RCT) of the manualized 12-week MBCT-C psychotherapy protocol with children aged 9–12 years (Semple, Lee, & Miller, 2004). That study found significantly reduced attention problems, as reported on the attention subscale of the Child Behavior Checklist, Parent Report Form (Achenbach, 1991). Although not statistically significant, consistent trends were found toward fewer symptoms of anxiety and depression for participants who completed the program. Sixty-one percent of the parents reported their child having fewer conduct or anger management problems following participation in the program. The small number of participants ($N = 25$) reduced the power of these analyses and is likely to have limited the opportunities to achieve statistically significant outcomes.

The experimenters' observations suggested that nearly all children in this study easily grasped the core concepts of mindfulness, readily engaged in exploring mindfulness using the various senses, and were creative in finding ways to integrate mindfulness into their daily experiences. Parent ratings and anecdotal reports were overwhelmingly favorable and suggested that some of the children achieved notable improvements in academic functioning and were better able to manage a variety of chronic problematic behaviors. Our clinical observations supported these indications that mindfulness training holds promise as a treatment component for anxious or depressed children.

Research teams at the University of Pennsylvania (A. Jha, personal communication, July 27, 2004) and the authors at Columbia University, Teachers College, are presently exploring the use of mindfulness techniques with children. Other researchers are developing adolescent mindfulness research programs (W. Britton and A. M. West, personal communications, July 27, 2004). Numerous clinical case reports suggest that meditation techniques can be useful in treating anxiety symptoms in school-aged children (Chang & Hiebert, 1989; Dacey & Fiore, 2000; Fish, 1988; Fontana & Slack, 1997; Humphrey, 1988; Murdock, 1978; 1987; Rozman, 1976; Smith & Womack, 1987).

APPLICATION TO SPECIFIC DISORDERS

Mindfulness meditation involves the observation of internal and external stimuli as they arise and change (Baer, 2003). Thus, mindfulness-based approaches may be appropriate interventions for childhood disorders that involve misperceptions or avoidance of internal and external cues, such as anxiety or depression, and conduct disorders, respectively. Initially, we did not expect the MBCT-C program to be effective for children with attention deficit/hyperactivity disorder (ADHD), because a minimal level of attentional control and self-management seemed to be necessary to practice mindfulness. Clinical observations of two participants with ADHD in our research were inconclusive. One child with ADHD strongly resisted participating in the program and showed no gains, whereas the other easily engaged with the program and, according to self-report and parental report, found mindfulness to be beneficial. This child strongly agreed that mindfulness helped him to be more patient and to control his anger. His mother reported that the program helped her son by improving the manner in which he interacted with others. Further research on this population is required to determine whether a minimal level of attentional control or behavioral self-management is required for ADHD children to gain from MBCT-C. The acceptability and effectiveness of MBCT-C for children with more severe mental disorders such as schizophrenia, autism, and other pervasive developmental disorders or mental retardation are unknown.   —

THE TWELVE-SESSION PROGRAM

SPECIFIC GOALS, STRATEGIES, AND TECHNIQUES

One core goal of the MBCT-C program is to help children become more aware of their cognitions (thoughts), emotions (feelings), and body sensations as discrete entities. Through experiential exercises, children begin to develop a language that describes, without judging, their internal cognitive and affective states and somatic experiences. These exercises also encourage the childrens' understanding of how thoughts, feelings, and body sensations are separate but interrelated phenomena, and how these interact to influence their perceptions of day-to-day experiences. This theme is consistently reinforced throughout the course of the program.

The following is an illustration of how internal cognitive, affective, and physiological states influence interpretations of experience. During an in-class exercise in session 3, we read the following passage to the children:

> You are walking down the street, and on the other side of the street you see somebody you know. You smile and wave. The person just doesn't seem to notice and walks by.

The children are invited to imagine this scene as vividly as they can, carefully observing their thoughts, feelings, and sensations, and then record their responses in their notebooks. After observing and recording their responses, the children are encouraged to share their imaginal experiences with the rest of the class. One child expressed the thought, "She didn't want to say hello to me," reported feeling embarrassed, and experienced a sensation of her "face getting warm." Another child offered the thought, "He was mad at me and tried to ignore me" with an accompanying feeling of "anger." Sensations of "chest getting tighter" and "heart beating faster" were associated with the anger. After the children had opportunities to share their diverse imaginal experiences with one another, the therapists facilitated a discussion of the individualized experiences. We asked, "How is it that you all had such different responses to the exact same event?" Through group sharing, the children became aware of their own "filters" and how their own past- and future-oriented thoughts, their present emotional state, and associated sensations color and change their experiences in the world.

Mindful listening exercises are used to begin differentiating thoughts, feelings, and sensations. In one mindful listening exercise, children lie down on yoga mats and are invited to listen mindfully to a 30-second segment of music. They are invited to experience the music, observe any thoughts (or images), feelings, and sensations that may arise while listening to the music, and then write down their observations in their notebooks. This is repeated for 15 to 20 minutes with a variety of styles and genres of musical segments. In subsequent group discussion, the children share their individual responses to the music. One child noted that one song reminded her of a wedding (thought or image). She felt joyful (feeling) and noticed that her toes were tapping to the rhythm of the music (body sensation). Another child shared that the same song evoked thoughts of a funeral. He felt somewhat sad and noted a heavy feeling in his body. The children help each other identify each element of their experience as a thought, feeling, or body sensation. As noted earlier, through repeated observations about the children's varying reactions to the same piece of music, they experientially learn that their idiosyncratic interpretations have powerful influences on how they think, feel, and experience their worlds.

Another core goal in MBCT-C is to help children develop the ability to experience a person, event, object, or sensation "in the moment" without falling into a (very common) habitual and automatic tendency to evaluate and judge the experience. When we judge a person, experience, or object as "good" or "positive," we typically feel a desire to hold on to it, have more of it, or not want it to go away. When we judge the same person, event, or object as "bad" or "negative," we feel a desire to have less of it, or we feel an aversion and wish to move away from the object. We make use of several different exercises that focus on learning to differentiate "judging" or "labeling" versus "noting" or "describing." For example, instead of seeing a flower and then judging the flower as "pretty" or "ugly," the children practice seeing *a particular* flower as an interesting and unique constellation of colors, shapes, textures, scents, and movements. When (inevitably) judging thoughts arise, we encourage the children merely to note the judgment as best as they can and then bring their attention back to describing what they are experiencing. The first goal is to observe the myriad judgments that we habitually invoke (accurate to the situation or not) to make sense of our experiences. The second goal is to observe how strongly these automatic, but not necessarily accurate, judgments influence our perceptions of each experience.

The theme of distinguishing between "judging" and "describing" is further reinforced through mindful touching. In this exercise, one child is blindfolded and an object is placed in the palm of his or her hands. The child explores the object with his or her sense of touch and then is invited to "describe" the object without "labeling" or "judging" it. If the child responds, "It feels gross" or "I don't like the touch of it," the rest of the class provides feedback on whether the statement is a descriptive observation or a personal judgment. The observers can ask questions to gather more information from the child who is holding the object. For example, "Is it soft or hard? Rough or smooth? Cold or hot? Big or small?" These types of interactive exchanges reinforce the abstract concepts taught in class and provide experiential applications to generalize this skill into everyday life. The children also have opportunities to demonstrate their competency by acting as mini-instructors to their peers, thereby increasing their sense of empowerment and personal motivation to participate in the class. At the end of the exercise, we facilitate further group exploration of how describing, rather than judging, might be applied to everyday situations, and how this practice might influence anxious or sad moods.

When children stop automatically judging something as "good" or "bad," they learn to be more fully present with what they are experiencing. Similarly, when feelings of anxiety, fear, anger, or sadness arise, they can simply observe what is happening without mindlessly reacting to their own emotions as being "bad" or "negative." Through these types of exercises, children discover that "negative" thoughts, feelings, and body sensations are not experiential facts or fundamental aspects of the self, but rather are ways in which they have learned to interpret and respond to their experiences. Children can understand thoughts as passing events in the mind and simply accept them as "just thoughts" and not necessarily accurate reflections of reality. Mindful awareness replaces a tendency to react out of "automatic pilot mode," with an increased awareness of how they may choose to respond to personal hardships and challenges. By developing this very different relationship to all of their experiences, children begin to adopt an attitude of acceptance and nonidentification with their own thoughts, feelings, and body sensations. Through repeated practice, the children decenter from the content of their thoughts, which allows them to respond to events with conscious and mindful awareness, rather than react with habituated, often inappropriate, automaticity.

The MBCT-C program also seeks to help children identify past, present, and future thinking. Depressive-oriented thoughts tend to be associated with regret, remorse, guilt, and other past-oriented emotional states, while anxiety-oriented thoughts tend to engender anticipation, worry, fear, and other future-focused feelings. Enhancing awareness of this present moment helps children who are habituated to depressive or anxious thinking notice their tendency to fall into past- or future-oriented thinking, and then make a conscious choice to redirect their attention back to the present experience. Through simple, repetitive exercises (e.g., focusing on the breath moving in and out of the body), children enhance their ability to stay present in this moment and begin to retrain the habit of becoming "lost in thought." We introduce basic breathing exercises at the beginning of the program, and each session begins and ends with a short breath meditation. The children learn that their breath is always with them and they can "tune into it" at any moment during their day. The breath is represented as being much like an anchor, which can bring stability to their bodies and minds once they become aware of it and choose to make use of it. "All" they need do is mindfully observe, note, and experience each breath. One breath at a time. Breath by breath. A simple, but challenging exercise.

An abbreviated guided "body scan" exercise (see Kabat-Zinn, 1990) promotes awareness of body sensations, develops attentional self-management, and helps children enhance their moment-by-moment awareness. We invite the children to observe and note minute sensations in each part of their body, the moment-to-moment changes, and any desire or urge to change position or wish for a sensation to be different than it actually is. For both the breath meditations and the body scan exercises, the children are instructed that when their minds wander, they are just to note that their minds wandered and then gently bring their attention back to the task at hand.

In addition to identification of emotions, cognitive exercises, and more traditional mindfulness meditations, we also use a variety of movement exercises to enhance the child's sense of body awareness. Normally active children have difficulties sitting for long periods, so physical movement exercises help sustain their interest and attention during the sessions. The therapists offer brief instruction in a few basic yoga postures, and the children are invited to become mindfully aware of discrete body sensations generated with each small movement. Hatha yoga exercises performed very slowly also offer the additional benefit of promoting relaxed physiological and emotional states.

Mindfulness is also incorporated into the more mundane activities such as putting away the meditation cushions, yoga mats, and art supplies at the end of each session. We practice taking off and putting on our shoes and coats mindfully. We practice mindfully walking into the room, and we practice mindfully sitting down. In the context of MBCT-C, the children are frequently encouraged to be present and aware of whatever they are doing in each and every moment. To enhance this present-focus, the "bell of mindfulness" is sounded at the beginning and end of each exercise and at other, nonregular intervals to remind us to be present in this moment. Each child may choose to ring the bells whenever he or she wants a reminder to be mindful. The sound soon becomes a delightful symbol of mindfulness for the children.

THE IMPORTANCE OF HOMEWORK

As in the MBCT program for adults, homework is an integral part of MBCT-C. Homework assignments focus on experiential learning, so that children learn from experience rather than from theory. Sessions 2 through 12 begin with a review of the home practice exercises from the previous week. Time is allotted at the end of each session to discuss the designated exercises for the coming week. In sessions 2 and 3, we offer opportunities for the children to explore their own obstacles to daily home practice and brainstorm ideas to help themselves and the other children who are generally struggling with similar issues. We encourage the children to record their daily practice in written form on the home practice records that are distributed at the end of each session.

Segal *et al.* (2002) emphasize the importance of the "everydayness" of practice. Incorporating the practice of mindfulness into the children's daily lives builds continuity and sustains motivation and momentum. Through consistency and daily practice with a variety of exercises, children learn to integrate mindfulness into their everyday lives. In essence, the children are developing a package of skills that can be used to help themselves more effectively manage their own feelings of anger, fear, anxiety, or sadness.

The home practice assignments for each week consist of three to four short exercises that can be completed in about 15 minutes per day, for 6 days during the week. In session 1, we introduce the exercise *mindful smiling while waking up*. Children first color and decorate a small picture of a smiley face during the session. They are instructed to take the picture home. They are told, "Hang up your picture on the ceiling or wall of your bedroom so that you can see it right away when you open your eyes in the morning. This picture is your reminder to watch your breath before you get out of bed. Inhale and exhale three breaths while keeping a half smile on your face, and follow your breaths mindfully." One child reported doing this exercise every morning and commented, "It was easier to start my day, especially when I woke up grumpy. It helped me when I get [*sic*] on the train, when people pushed into me. If I didn't do it, I would still be grumpy."

Every home practice exercise is first introduced and practiced in session. The exercise *mindfulness while lying down* is also assigned for home practice. In this exercise, the children are instructed to lie down on a flat surface, keeping their arms loosely by their sides and their legs stretched out straight and slightly apart. While maintaining a half smile on their face, they are encouraged to relax, let go of any muscle tension, and feel how the floor supports their body. Then, they begin gently breathing in and out, counting 15 slow breaths, while keeping their attention focused on the sensations of their breathing and their half-smile.

Another exercise that the children practice at home is *mindfulness in everyday activities*. They receive the following directions: "Choose one daily activity and bring moment-to-moment awareness to that activity. You could use brushing your teeth, getting dressed, eating, making your bed, walking to school, or anything that you do every day. Simply be aware of what you are doing as you actually do it." One child shared his experience of mindfully taking out the garbage. He described his surprise at learning that being more "in the moment" with this chore resulted in his being less angry at having to do a task that he previously considered quite unpleasant.

The children are encouraged to find a quiet space and a consistent time for their practice. We acknowledge and discuss how difficult it may be to find time in their busy lives but emphasize that the development of mindfulness is directly related to their own practice of mindfulness between sessions. The development of observational skills manifests in small increments.

We describe this process as being somewhat like gardening—we have to prepare the ground, plant the seeds, water and feed the sprouts, and then wait patiently for the results. In the same way, we invite the children to participate in the session and home practice exercises with patience, being mindful of this moment, and being aware that the fruits of their efforts may not show up immediately.

SESSION-BY-SESSION FORMAT AND GOALS

The aims of the early sessions are to provide an orientation to mindfulness and establish parameters for the program. Establishing a safe and trusting environment within which group members can individually explore their mindfulness is essential. Core themes such as identifying thoughts, feelings, and body sensations and differentiating between judging and describing are repeated throughout subsequent sessions using multisensory exercises. As mindfulness skills develop, session goals focus on integrating and generalizing mindfulness into everyday life. What follows is a précis of the main theme, mode of working, and primary mindfulness exercise for each session.

Session 1: Developing community; defining expectations; emphasizing the importance of homework; orientation to mindfulness; *mindful smiling while waking up* exercise.

Session 2: Dealing with barriers to practice; introduction to *mindfulness of the breath*; *eating a raisin* exercise.

Session 3: Practice differentiating among thoughts, feelings, and body sensations; introduction to *mindful body movements.*

Session 4: Mindful hearing; *receptive listening* exercise to identify thoughts, feelings, and body sensations; introduction to *body scan* exercise.

Session 5: Mindful hearing (continued); *creating expressive sounds* exercise; introduction to *3-minute breathing space* exercise.

Session 6: Mindful seeing; practice differentiating between *judging* and *describing*; *guided imagery* exercise.

Session 7: Mindful seeing (continued); practice directing attention; *seeing optical illusions* exercise.

Session 8: Mindful touch; learning how to "stay present" with what is here right now.

Session 9: Mindful smell; continue practice differentiating between *judging* and *describing*.

Session 10: Mindful taste; *thoughts are not facts* exercise.

Session 11: Mindfulness in everyday life; review of previous sessions; integrating acceptance of our experiences through mindfulness.

Session 12: Generalizing mindfulness to everyday life; exploring and sharing personal experiences of the program; brief graduation ceremony.

CASE STUDY: NATHAN

When he participated in the MBCT-C program, Nathan was a 12-year-old Hispanic boy who lived in a low-income, inner-city environment. His parents were divorced and Nathan was being raised by his mother. He had one brother who was 4 years younger. Nathan's mother was interested in enrolling him in the program to "help him concentrate more" and "be more aware of his surroundings." She reported that he often received detention at school for being overly talkative and argumentative with the teachers, and she hoped that the program could ultimately help improve his school behaviors and academic performance.

Initially, Nathan explicitly expressed his low expectations about the helpfulness of mindfulness. He initially thought that the program was "boring," and he frequently commented that the exercises gave him headaches. Nonetheless, he kept coming each week. Nathan participated in all the class activities and, with his mother's active encouragement and support, completed the daily home practice exercises.

Nathan was an outgoing, intelligent, inquisitive, and assertive child. He was very curious about making new discoveries during exercises and initiated many class discussions by asking insightful questions. In the exercise *mindfully eating a raisin*, Nathan carefully explored his raisin with all of his senses and discovered that his raisin "made a noise" when he attended to his sense of hearing. He found that his raisin made a subtle clicking sound when he gently rolled it between his fingers. Many people might easily concur that you cannot hear a raisin, but Nathan discovered that by listening mindfully, he could. He did this by disengaging from his habitual ways of experiencing the world and letting go of the preconceived assumption that raisins do not make sounds. Nathan began to express his delight in discovering new information about many everyday experiences and objects of which he was not previously aware.

Nathan's mother was deeply involved with her son's mindfulness practice. She made sure that Nathan attended every session and accompanied him to and from them. At home, she reviewed the contents of his travel folder and allocated time each day to practice the mindfulness exercises with him. During session 1, the children were given the home practice assignment of *mindful smiling while waking up*. At home, Nathan and his mother spent an evening creating and decorating two large smiley faces made of construction paper. Nathan posted one smiley face in his bedroom, and his mother did the same in hers. They also placed a small smiley face in the bathroom, as a reminder for him to be mindful while brushing his teeth. Nathan diligently completed his home practice exercises each week and came to sessions eager to share his experiences of mindfulness with the group.

Nathan's favorite exercise was the *3-minute breathing space,* which he used in school whenever he started to feel angry. If he felt he was on the verge of starting an argument with one of his teachers, he would pause for a moment and observe the feelings of irritation growing within him. Then he would ask to be excused so that he could go to the hallway (which he had self-designated as "my breathing space") to do his *3-minute breathing space* exercise. By mindfully choosing to remove himself from the class and spend a few moments being present with his breath, Nathan regained his composure. He then returned to his classroom with a greater sense of calmness and self-efficacy. His automatic mode of reacting transformed into a more conscious and adaptive way of responding. When he used his breath to decenter from his thoughts and feelings, he became less defensive and confrontational with his teachers. During the semester that followed his completing the MBCT-C program, Nathan did not receive a single school detention.

Nathan's mother reported that he was responding to challenging events in a more "positive and mature way." She told the therapists, "He has changed in a dramatic way. For instance, when other kids bother him or they say certain things, instead of Nathan getting angry towards them—or he could easily curse or say something that is not nice and he could easily get into a fight—he learns how to think and ignore it." In essence, Nathan "decentered" from his negative thoughts by creating a mindful "space" between his initial emotional reaction and his subsequent inappropriate behavioral response. He gradually developed a different relationship with his anger by observing the associated cognitions and body sensations "from a distance." He consequently enjoyed having the freedom to choose to respond with mindful awareness.

During the 12-week program, Nathan grew to embrace mindfulness and integrate it into his daily life. He informed the group that his headaches went away once he became accustomed to the exercises. At the end of the program, he spoke eloquently of his personal experience of mindfulness:

> Mindfulness means being more aware of my actions, and knowing when I am angry so I can stop it from getting too far. I don't talk back at my teachers or get mad as much as I did in the past. The knowledge I gained is to stop getting so angry. When I do get angry I would realize it and do the breath in and breath out technique.

AFFECTIVE AND BEHAVIORAL OUTCOMES

Nathan's MBCT-C group was composed of children from varying backgrounds, who brought to the program their different life experiences and circumstances. The therapists helped the children to develop mindfulness practices that were uniquely theirs. For children like Nathan, mindfulness helped with anger management. For other children, mindfulness techniques helped manage long-standing feelings of sadness. Christopher shared, "When my daddy is angry at me, he argues with me because I'm not doing what he tells me to do. ... He yells at me and that scares me so much that it makes me cry. When I am sad, I always need to breathe ten times each day." Several children, who were particularly anxious about their performance in school, discovered that they could also use the breathing exercises to alleviate tension before an exam. Patricia shared, "Mindfulness means to learn how to calm down when you're mad, or stressed, or worried. Before I take a test, I breathe three minutes or more."

A number of children indicated that the program helped them become more emotionally expressive. Elsie said, "I think it has helped me a lot at home. It has helped me [to be] more calm in the way I react. Now I like to express my feelings to my mom or sister. It made my life easier." We underscore the importance of active participation from each member in the group discussions. Children are encouraged to share their own experience of mindfulness with their peers, and this type of affective sharing is continually reinforced throughout the program. Laura shared a similar experience, "I learned that I could participate with the others ... because I used to be shy, but now I know how to share my ideas without being shy." Samara also observed, "It has made me have more confidence in myself." For Samara, the capacity to be expressive and assertive had a positive influence on her self-esteem.

Some children felt that the program helped them feel less isolated and lonely. During one group discussion, several children openly shared family circumstances that had engendered feelings of grief, sorrow, and fear. Jamie's mother was single-handedly raising two children, while Jamie's father was serving time in prison. Her uncle, the other significant male figure in her life, had recently died in a car accident. Jamie was under a great deal of stress, worrying about her parents' future and mourning the loss of her uncle. Eleven-year-old Caleb empathized with Jamie and shared his own experience of losing his mother to a terminal illness 2 years earlier. Painful memories of his mother chronically filled him with an overwhelming sense of grief. He often felt alone and insecure, terrified that his father would be taken away from him just as his mother had been. Jamie and Caleb expressed their feelings about their personal losses and were comforted knowing that someone else empathized with what they were experiencing. Jamie expressed, "I felt happy that I can share my thoughts with people like my real friends. I know that I'm not the only one that goes through difficulties in life." The rest of the group listened mindfully and then collectively explored ways to help Jamie and Caleb process their grief. We also learned that children can be very good psychotherapists.

PRACTICAL ISSUES IN WORKING WITH CHILDREN

TRAINING THE THERAPISTS

Facilitating the development of mindfulness in others seems to be best accomplished by demonstrating mindfulness in oneself (Fontana & Slack, 1997; Goleman, 1981; Kabat-Zinn, 1990; Segal *et al.,* 2003; Walsh, 1989). If you have read this far, it should now be clear that to be effective with clients, psychotherapists must have a sound *experiential* understanding of the mindfulness model of therapy and be able to nonjudgmentally observe their own cognitions, emotions, physiological responses, and behaviors. Responses to client inquiries must never be theoretical or technical, but rather emerge from the therapists' own personal experiences of mindfulness. When a master violinist teaches a student, the teacher's experiential skills, developed from his or her own personal practice over a long time, is the essential foundation that supports the teacher's theoretical knowledge of how to play a violin. Without that experiential knowing on the part of both the master and the student, knowledge of all the theory in the world is unlikely to produce a competent violinist. We believe that the moment-to-moment challenges of maintaining a mindful attitude cannot be truly understood unless experienced. Personal efforts to develop a consistent practice in the midst of our often-hectic lives will enhance our empathic understanding of our clients and inform all our responses to their inquiries. This may not be good news for some busy clinicians, because developing a mindfulness practice requires dedicating 30 to 45 minutes every day to mindfulness exercises—just as we demand of our adult clients in mindfulness-based stress reduction and MBCT programs. The need to make this personal commitment may (honorably) preclude some clinicians from working with mindfulness-based psychotherapy models.

Without continuous daily self-observing, some psychotherapists may find it easy to fall into a "mindless" or automatic habit of teaching a didactic model of mindfulness. This is, in fact, the antithesis of mindfulness and may inadvertently convey a therapist's misunderstanding that changes in thoughts and feelings are desirable therapy outcomes. Goals of *change* rather than nonjudgmental *acceptance,* even delivered as unconscious messages, may well undermine the effectiveness of mindfulness-based treatment approaches. This is why we have a 20- to 30-minute personal practice session for the co-therapists before beginning each MBCT-C session. The authors strongly recommend that clinicians develop their own mindfulness practice before attempting to use this model in psychotherapy. We also recommend participating in some of the many available mindfulness-based therapist-training programs. Mindfulness-based stress reduction, mindfulness-based cognitive therapy, dialectical behavior therapy, and acceptance and commitment therapy are all models that bring mindfulness perspectives to clinical practice.

EFFECTIVENESS OF GROUP VERSUS INDIVIDUAL TRAINING

In addition to the obvious advantages of cost and time efficiency, group training in mindfulness is preferred over individual training for various reasons. Group discussions are an integral part of the MBCT-C program and help facilitate learning around a central theme. A fundamental aim of the program is to explore how everyday events are colored by intrapsychic factors, for example, core beliefs or expectations, automatic thoughts, existing cognitive or affective schemas, current affective state, and interpretation of physical sensations. Group discussions allow the children to explore "how and why" they have different reactions to the same event. They become more aware of their own idiosyncratic styles of interpreting situations and gain clarity as to where their perspectives may differ from those of their peers.

Through group discussions, children learn from each other, teach each other, and help each other learn. They offer encouragement and feedback to other group members. During sessions 2 and 3, we discuss obstacles to completing the home practice assignments. As a group, the children brainstorm and share ideas about finding the time and remembering to do the exercises. One child suggested posting the home practice record in a place where it would be visible every day, such as on the refrigerator door. Another child shared with the group that she found it helpful to put her mindfulness exercises with her school assignments. She discovered that if she treated her mindfulness "homework" like her schoolwork, she could remember to do it every day.

We carefully attend to the emotional tone of the group from the beginning of the program. Expectations are made explicit, not implied. All of the children are expected to honor the Rules for Mindful Behavior, particularly expressing respect and kindness toward others. It is important for each child to experience the group environment as a safe, comfortable, and trusting one. For Nathan, the group provided him with a newfound sense of belonging:

> I liked hanging around them because you could just act like yourself, and you didn't have to act like nobody else. Because the people that were here just accept you for who you was [sic], so I was just myself.

For other children, the group becomes a supportive network, helping them manage common but stressful life events. For example, children shared their anxieties about the upcoming citywide exams. During group discussions, feelings of anxiety and fearfulness were normalized as specific reactions to demanding events. The group as a whole then explored different ways in which mindfulness techniques might help manage their anxieties during the exams. At the end of the program, most of the children chose to continue identifying as a group by exchanging addresses and telephone numbers.

ENGAGING FAMILIES IN MINDFULNESS PRACTICES

Establishing an effective working alliance with the parents is always the first step in clinical work with children. Younger children need their parents to bring them to sessions every week. They are also emotionally dependent on their parents, needing assistance, support, and guidance with everyday activities. For many reasons, we recognize that we cannot be completely effective therapists without successfully enlisting parental participation and involvement in the treatment. The MBCT-C program strongly emphasizes engaging family members in the daily mindfulness practice. Parents are initially oriented to mindfulness practices during the introductory session, in which parents learn about the program, have an opportunity to ask questions, and experience mindfulness through sensory exercises. Experiential learning is intended to stimulate the parent's interest and involvement in their child's practice. The role of the parent is also established and made explicit during the orientation session. We advise parents that they are expected to review session handouts with their children and help them with the home practice exercises each week.

Our clinical observations suggest that the more parents are engaged in the program, the greater the observed development of mindfulness in the child. As with any other skill, learning is greatly enhanced through reinforcement in the home environment. Mrs. Ahmed enrolled her son in the program because she believed it could help improve his concentration at school. She attended the orientation session with scant knowledge of mindfulness but was enthusiastic to learn how mindfulness techniques could benefit her son. When we led the parents through the *mindfully eating a raisin* exercise, we observed that Mrs. Ahmed was completely absorbed in the activity. During the discussion period, she enthusiastically proclaimed, "It was as if I never tasted a raisin before." She quickly discovered that she too could benefit from mindfulness exercises.

While her son developed his mindfulness practice within the program, Mrs. Ahmed was cultivating her own mindfulness practice at home. Every evening, she led her family in the practice of mindfully eating dinner together. She reminded them to be aware of the different tastes, textures, and smells of the various foods. She encouraged them to savor each bite and to be present with the experience of eating. Mrs. Ahmed shared with us that her family not only enjoyed the mindfulness exercise but also began to lose weight because they ate more slowly and were more aware of their hunger and satiety cues. This vignette shows how family members can have a direct and lasting influence on children's abilities to generalize mindfulness into everyday life and underscores the importance of engaging families in the practice of mindfulness.

IN CLOSING

Our clinical and research experience with children supports that of other clinical practitioners who have worked with mindfulness-based practices or with cognitive-behavioral therapies for children. These early indicators suggest that MBCT-C is an acceptable and feasible group psychotherapy for children who are experiencing anxious and depressive symptoms. It is important to remember, however, that empirical research on the efficacy and effectiveness of mindfulness paradigms as a treatment for major depressive disorders or anxiety spectrum disorders has barely begun. We are experiencing a promising beginning; nonetheless, there is significantly more research to conduct before we are ready to evaluate MBCT-C as an empirically supported treatment. At present, it is an evolving program. Although the development of this model as a manualized treatment is in progress, the spirit of mindfulness requires that the therapist meet the children where they are right now—in the present moment. True mindfulness allows us to use whatever arises in this moment as appropriate material for mindfulness instruction.

For psychotherapy practitioners who are interested in integrating mindfulness approaches into their clinical practices, we would like again to emphasize the importance of therapists developing and maintaining their own personal mindfulness practices before beginning to guide others in the cultivation of mindfulness. This model of psychotherapy is not likely to be suitable for every clinical practitioner. To teach the essence of mindfulness, we submit that you must have experienced the multitude of challenges inherent in developing this rigorous daily discipline. You must have personally experienced the benefits of mindfulness and the consequences of lapses of mindfulness within yourself; and you must act and speak with mindfulness to those who wish to learn this most challenging and most rewarding of human phenomena. For ourselves and for our clients, mindfulness practices offer opportunities to experience the totality of our lives, moment by moment, in the only moment we actually have—the present one.

REFERENCES

Achenbach, T. M. (1991). *Manual for the Child Behavior Checklist: Ages 4–18 and 1991 profile.* University of Vermont, Department of Psychiatry, Burlington.

Baer, R. A. (2003). Mindfulness training as a clinical intervention. *Clinical Psychology: Science and Practice, 10,* 125–143.

Beck, J. S. (1995). *Cognitive therapy: Basics and beyond.* New York: Guilford Press.

Brown, D. P. (1977). A model for the levels of concentrative meditation. *International Journal of Clinical and Experimental Hypnosis, 25,* 236–273.

Chang, J., & Hiebert, B. (1989). Relaxation procedures with children: A review. *Medical Psychotherapy: An International Journal, 2,* 163–176.

Chethik, M. (2000). *Techniques of child therapy: Psychodynamic strategies* (2nd ed.). New York: Guilford Press.

Dacey, J. S., & Fiore, L. B. (2000). *Your anxious child.* San Francisco: Jossey-Bass.

Deikman, A. J. (1982). *The observing self: Mysticism and psychotherapy.* Boston: Beacon Press.

——— (1996). Intention, self, and spiritual experience: A functional model of consciousness. In S. R. Hameroff, A. W. Kaszniak, & A. C. Scott (Eds.), *Toward a science of consciousness: The first Tucson discussions and debates* (pp. 695–706). Cambridge, MA: MIT Press.

Ehrenreich, J. T., & Gross, A. M. (2002). Biased attentional behavior in childhood anxiety: A review of theory and current empirical investigation. *Clinical Psychology Review, 22,* 991–1008.

Fiebert, M. S., & Mead, T. M. (1981). Meditation and academic performance. *Perceptual and Motor Skills, 53,* 447–450.

Fish, M. C. (1988). Relaxation training for childhood disorders. In C. E. Schaefer (Ed.), *Innovative interventions in child and adolescent therapy* (pp. 160–192). New York: Wiley.

Foa, E. B., & Kozak, M. J. (1986). Emotional processing of fear: Exposure to corrective information. *Psychological Bulletin, 99,* 20–35.

Fontana, D., & Slack, I. (1997). *Teaching meditation to children.* Shaftesbury, UK: Element Books.

Gaines, R. (1997). Key issues in the interpersonal treatment of children. *The Review of Interpersonal Psychoanalysis, 2,* 1–5.

Goleman, D. (1981). Buddhist and Western psychology: Some commonalities and differences. *Journal of Transpersonal Psychology, 13,* 125–136.

——— (1984). The Buddha on meditation and states of consciousness. In D. H. Shapiro, Jr., & R. N. Walsh (Eds.), *Meditation: Classical and contemporary perspectives* (pp. 317–360). Hawthorne, NY: Aldine.

Hall, P. D. (1999). The effect of meditation on the academic performance of African American college students. *Journal of Black Studies, 29,* 408–415.

Humphrey, J. H. (1988). *Teaching children to relax.* Springfield, IL: Charles C. Thomas.

Kabat-Zinn, J. (1990). *Full catastrophe living.* New York: Bantam Doubleday Dell.

Kaslow, N. J., & Racusin, G. R. (1994). Family therapy for depression in young people. In W. M. Reynolds & H. F. Johnston (Eds.), *Handbook of depression in children and adolescents: Issues in clinical child psychology* (pp. 345–363). New York: Plenum Press.

Kendall, P. C. (Ed.). (2000). *Child and adolescent therapy: Cognitive-behavioral procedures* (2nd ed.). New York: Guilford Press.

Klerman, G. L., Weissman, M. M., Rounsaville, B., & Chevron, E. S. (1995). Interpersonal psychotherapy for depression. *Journal of Psychotherapy Practice and Research, 4,* 342–351.

Lam, C. M., & Beale, I. L. (1991). Relations among sustained attention, reading performance, and teachers' ratings of behavior problems. *Remedial and Special Education, 12,* 40–47.

Linden, W. (1973). Practicing of meditation by school children and their levels of field dependence-independence, test anxiety, and reading achievement. *Journal of Consulting and Clinical Psychology, 41,* 139–143.

Moustafa, B. M. (1999). *Multisensory approaches and learning styles theory in the elementary school* (Descriptive Report).

Murdock, M. H. (1978). Meditation with young children. *Journal of Transpersonal Psychology, 10*, 29–44.

——— (1987). *Spinning inward: Using guided imagery with children for learning, creativity, and relaxation.* Boston: Shambhala Publications.

Posner, M. I., & Petersen, S. E. (1990). The attention system of the human brain. *Annual Review of Neuroscience, 13*, 25–42.

Reid, E. F. G., Semple, R. J., & Miller, L. F. (in press). Accessing mindfulness in young children: Exploring the five senses. *Journal of Infant, Child, and Adolescent Psychotherapy.*

Rozman, D. (1976). *Meditating with children: A workbook on new age educational methods using meditation* (rev. ed.). Boulder Creek, CA: U Trees Press.

Segal, Z. V., Williams, J., & Teasdale, J. D. (2003). Mindfulness-based cognitive therapy for depression: A new approach to preventing relapse. *Psychotherapy Research, 13*, 123–125.

——— (2002). *Mindfulness-based cognitive therapy for depression.* New York: Guilford Press.

Semple, R. J., Lee, J., & Miller, L. F. (2004). *Mindfulness-based cognitive therapy for children: A treatment model for childhood anxiety and depression.* Manuscript in preparation.

Semple, R. J., Reid, E. F. G., & Miller, L. F. (2005). Treating anxiety with mindfulness: An open trial of mindfulness training for anxious children. *Journal of Cognitive Psychotherapy, 19*, 387–400.

Shiffrin, R. M., & Schneider, W. (1977). Controlled and automatic human information processing: II. Perceptual learning, automatic attending and a general theory. *Psychological Review, 84*, 127–190.

Siegler, R. S. (1991). *Children's thinking* (2nd ed.). Upper Saddle River, NJ: Prentice Hall.

Smith, M. S., & Womack, W. M. (1987). Stress management techniques in childhood and adolescence: Relaxation training, meditation, hypnosis, and biofeedback: Appropriate clinical applications. *Clinical Pediatrics, 26*, 581–585.

Stark, K. D., Rouse, L. W., & Kurowski, C. (1994). Psychological treatment approaches for depression in children. In W. M. Reynolds & H. F. Johnston (Eds.), *Handbook of depression in children and adolescents: Issues in clinical child psychology* (pp. 275–307). New York: Plenum Press.

Taublieb, A. B. (1996). *The psychopathology of childhood and adolescence.* New York: Addison-Wesley.

Teasdale, J. D. (1999). Metacognition, mindfulness and the modification of mood disorders. *Clinical Psychology and Psychotherapy, 6*, 146–155.

Teasdale, J. D., Segal, Z., & Williams, J. M. G. (1995). How does cognitive therapy prevent depressive relapse and why should attentional control (mindfulness) training help? *Behaviour Research and Therapy, 33*, 25–39.

Thornton, C. A. (1983). A multisensory approach to thinking strategies for remedial instruction in basic addition facts. *Journal for Research in Mathematics Education, 14*, 198–203.

Walsh, R. N. (1977). Initial meditative experiences: Part I. *Journal of Transpersonal Psychology, 9*, 151–192.

——— (1978). Initial meditative experiences: Part II. *Journal of Transpersonal Psychology, 10*, 1–28.

——— (1989). Toward a synthesis of Eastern and Western psychologies. In A. A. Sheikh & K. S. Sheikh (Eds.), *Eastern and Western approaches to healing: Ancient wisdom and modern knowledge* (pp. 542–555). New York: Wiley.

Wislock, R. F. (1993). What are perceptual modalities and how do they contribute to learning? *New Directions for Adult and Continuing Education, 59*, 5–13.

8

MINDFULNESS IN DIALECTICAL BEHAVIOR THERAPY (DBT) FOR ADOLESCENTS

ELIZABETH E. WAGNER

Department of Psychiatry and Behavioral Sciences, Montefiore Medical Center/Albert Einstein College of Medicine, Bronx, New York

JILL H. RATHUS

Department of Psychology, C.W. Post Campus/Long Island University, Brookville, New York

ALEC L. MILLER

Department of Psychiatry and Behavioral Sciences, Montefiore Medical Center/Albert Einstein College of Medicine, Bronx, New York

INTRODUCTION

The present chapter explores the use of mindfulness in our clinical adaptation of dialectical behavior therapy (DBT) for suicidal and self-injurious adolescents who have borderline features or who meet formal criteria for borderline personality disorder (BPD) (Miller, Rathus, Linehan, Wetzler, & Leigh, 1997; Rathus & Miller, 2002). DBT is a comprehensive treatment program developed originally for chronically suicidal adults diagnosed with BPD. Miller *et al.* (1997) adapted DBT for a multiproblem, suicidal, adolescent population in response to the lack of empirically

167

supported psychosocial treatments available for these at-risk teens. The modifications involved in DBT for adolescents include:

1. reducing treatment length,
2. reducing the number of skills taught and simplifying language used in handouts and skills training lectures,
3. including family members in the skills training group and providing intersession skills coaching,
4. adding family therapy sessions as needed,
5. creating additional skills training handouts that pertain to family issues and to parenting, and
6. adding an optional follow-up patient consultation group (known as "graduate group").

The purpose of this chapter is to examine the use of mindfulness within DBT adapted for suicidal adolescents.

MINDFULNESS IN ADOLESCENT DBT: LAYING THE FOUNDATION

Understanding the nature of adolescent suicidal behavior, the requisite changes and challenges adolescents confront during normal development, and how these normal changes and challenges can go awry and exacerbate emerging psychiatric difficulties lays the foundation for understanding how mindfulness skills are likely to be helpful to our target population of adolescents. In this section we provide a brief overview of adolescent development and its relation to emerging psychiatric difficulties and suicidal behavior.

SUICIDAL BEHAVIOR IN ADOLESCENTS

Suicide is the third leading cause of adolescent death in the United States, preceded only by accidents and homicide (Anderson, 2002). Although the base rate of adolescent suicide is relatively low, approximately 13.8 per 100,000 (Anderson, 2002), the rates of completed suicide for adolescents between the ages of 15 and 19 have increased 245% over the past four decades (Peters, Kochanek, & Murphy, 1998). Between 31% and 50% of adolescent suicide attempters reattempt suicide, many within 3 months of their first attempt (Shaffer & Piacentini, 1994).

Suicidal ideation is a strong predictor, if not the best predictor, of suicide attempts (Andrews & Lewinsohn, 1992; Kienhorst, De Wilde, Van den Bout, Diekstra, & Wolters, 1990). Specifically, as suicidal ideation becomes more frequent and intense, the risk of suicide attempts increases (Lewinsohn, Rohde, & Seeley, 1996). Distal risk factors for adolescent suicidal behavior include psychopathology, chronic family dysfunction, and homosexual or bisexual orientation (Adcock, Nagy, & Simpson, 1991; Lewinsohn *et al.*, 1996). Internationally, three classes of Axis I disorders characterize most attempted and completed suicides among adolescents: mood disorders, substance use disorders, and conduct disorders (Andrews & Lewinsohn, 1992; Brent *et al.*, 1993; Fergusson & Lynskey, 1995; Marttunen, Aro, Henriksson, & Lonnqvist, 1991; Shaffer *et al.*, 1996). The relationship between suicidal behavior and BPD in adolescents has been recognized for more than two decades (Brent *et al.*, 1994; Clarkin, Friedman, Hurt, Corn, & Aronoff, 1984; Crumley, 1979). In addition, the comorbidity of BPD with major depression and substance use among suicidal adolescents heightens the suicide risk. Proximal risk factors include numerous arguments or fights, a history of leaving home or moving away, an arrest or legal trouble, a breakup with a girlfriend or boyfriend, and a relative or friend who (a) tried to commit suicide, (b) had problems with drugs or alcohol, (c) remarried or started living with someone else, or (d) died. Physical diseases and injuries resulting in physical impairment have also been found to increase risk of suicide in adolescents (Lewinsohn *et al.*, 1996). Interpersonal conflicts and separations are considered the most common precipitants of adolescent suicidal behavior (Marttunen *et al.*, 1995).

Although many risk factors have been identified for suicidal and nonsuicidal self-injurious behavior, currently there are few empirically validated treatments available for these adolescents. Moreover, many randomized clinical trials of adolescent depression exclude teens who have histories of, or who present currently with, significant suicidal ideation or behavior (e.g., Clarke *et al.*, 1995). During the past few years, two studies have begun to evaluate treatments that have shown reductions in deliberate self-harm (Wood, Trainor, Rothwell, Moore, & Harrington, 2001) and suicide attempts (Huey *et al.*, 2004). We highlight the nature of suicidal behavior in adolescents because our adaptation of DBT was developed specifically for adolescents who are struggling with suicidal behaviors and who have borderline personality features. The mindfulness skills used in our adaptation appear both to target some of the conditions that contribute to their suicidal behaviors and to build resiliency, as will be explicated later.

NORMAL ADOLESCENT DEVELOPMENT

Adolescence is a time of growth in physical, cognitive, social, and emotional domains, each with characteristic challenges and changes. Adolescence marks the period of puberty, during which dramatic biological changes occur, including the development of primary and secondary sex characteristics, which can create myriad psychological concerns. Adolescents' sexual maturation often serves as a stimulus for behavior changes, including increased autonomy from parents and various levels of sexual behavior. Early sexual activity in adolescence is associated with poor school functioning, limited educational goals, parental divorce, or a lack of parental support and monitoring. By age 14, more than half of adolescents have smoked cigarettes, four-fifths have tried alcohol, and two-fifths have tried at least one illicit drug such as marijuana. Adolescents who rely on substances to cope with psychological distress do not master healthier and more effective problem-solving and distress tolerance skills. Further, adolescents show both increased impulsiveness and increased sensation seeking, resulting in more risk-taking behavior, and consequently, more accidents involving motor vehicles, firearms, and athletics. Thus, puberty brings myriad physical and behavioral changes that can threaten the adolescent's safety and well-being.

In terms of cognitive development, adolescents are embarking on Piaget's *formal operations* stage, in which the ability to engage in abstract and hypothetical reasoning emerges. Thus, they show improved capacity for cognitive self-regulation, which involves monitoring progress and continually redirecting efforts toward their goals. At this time, adolescents acquire an understanding of metaphors, irony, and sarcasm. Egocentrism also characterizes adolescent thinking. There may be a subjective sense of being continually "on stage" and the focus of others' attention. Overall, adolescents' new cognitive abilities can be helpful in managing increasingly difficult cognitive tasks. Their expanded capacities also allow for self-knowledge, self-correction, and self-reflection—all of which can support a teen in keeping himself or herself on a healthy course. However, their new cognitive abilities can leave adolescents feeling paralyzed as they consider all the information available for processing. This can place adolescents at risk for making poor decisions, as they attempt to take on more adult roles but with a dearth of experience with their new intellectual abilities.

In terms of social and emotional development, adolescents face the task of identity development. Identity versus identity diffusion is the major psychological conflict of adolescence (Erikson, 1968). Those with identity diffusion have a poor sense of themselves, their values, and their goals. During adolescence, self-esteem becomes informed by a broader range of areas, including romantic and peer relationships, as well as academic and job success. Many adolescents experience an increase in self-esteem; however, those experiencing school failure, drug use, poor relationships with parents, and poor economic conditions are at risk for lowered self-esteem. Adolescents, as compared with younger children or adults, report more negative moods, greater extremes of mood, and more mood lability. Adolescence also brings increased parent/adolescent conflict. Adolescent friendships become increasingly important and can promote the development of social skills and identity formation. Adolescents spend more time with their peers than their families and are focused on peer acceptance and vulnerable to peer pressure. Positive peer relationships can foster perspective-taking and self-esteem, providing a buffer for stress.

PROBLEMS IN ADOLESCENT DEVELOPMENT

Interestingly, many *typical* adolescent behaviors actually overlap with diagnostic criteria for BPD in the *Diagnostic and Statistical Manual of Mental Disorders* (DSM), 4th edition. These include report of increased negative mood states, more affective dysregulation compared with younger children and adults, an underdeveloped identity, increased argumentativeness and familial conflicts, and increased impulsiveness and risk-taking behaviors (e.g., risky sexual behavior and experimentation with drugs and alcohol). These features are within the range of normal adolescent development and do not necessarily indicate dysfunction or the presence of BPD. However, central areas of adolescent development may go off course—for example, identity development, emotion regulation, impulse control, interpersonal relationships—and features of BPD may emerge. A substantial research literature indicates that adolescent risk behaviors tend to cluster. Adolescents having trouble in one area (e.g., polydrug use) are likely to have trouble in others (e.g., pregnancy risk, school absenteeism), with problems compounding over time in the absence of prevention or intervention efforts. Consequently, researchers are identifying clusters of risk behaviors and looking for common underlying causes for the syndrome of problem behaviors. These underlying causes are assumed to be multiply determined, involving interactions among high-risk communities (e.g., drug-filled and crime-ridden neighborhoods and schools), high-risk families (e.g., unemployment, substance abuse, physical or sexual abuse), negative peer influences, and individual characteristics.

Adolescent resiliency factors in the face of these vulnerabilities include self-regulation skills, a nurturing environment (even if only one caring relationship with an adult), social support outside the family, high intelligence, charm or other personal assets, problem-solving skills, and a smaller family size with wider spacing between siblings. Note that while some of these factors are intrinsic, others can be taught. Mindfulness skills and other DBT skills can help to build these competencies.

CORE MINDFULNESS SKILLS IN ADOLESCENT DBT

DBT for adolescents includes a cognitive-behavioral version of an Eastern meditative practice used for thousands of years that is user-friendly for Westerners, and more specifically, for suicidal adolescents with features of borderline personality disorder. The mindfulness taught in DBT for adolescents is denuded of any religious meaning and is consistent with most forms of Eastern meditative or Western contemplative practice. Note that adolescents' emerging cognitive capacities for abstract and critical thinking allow them to be proficient at understanding and applying mindfulness. Following is an overview of DBT's three states of mind and the core mindfulness "what" and "how" skills. (See Chapter 1 in this volume for a more detailed description of mindfulness in standard DBT.)

THREE STATES OF MIND

DBT presents three states of mind: emotion mind, reasonable mind, and wise mind. In *emotion mind,* one's emotional state controls thinking and behavior, reasonable or logical thinking becomes difficult or impossible, facts may be distorted to be consistent with the current emotion, and behavior may be impulsive. *Reasonable mind* is one's logical, rational, "cool" mind. Examples of being in reasonable mind include doing easy homework or making a shopping list. While logical, rational thinking is important, it is not always a good idea to make decisions purely in reasonable mind. For example, in deciding whether or where to go to college, or whether to break up with your boyfriend or girlfriend, feelings provide important information. *Wise mind* is a balance between emotion mind and reasonable mind that includes intuitive knowing. In a state of wise mind, one can slow down, step back, and act after considering one's own thoughts and feelings. Clients are coached to get into wise mind whenever they become aware of moving toward acting purely out of emotion mind, especially when the behavior can lead to destructive consequences. Clients develop their own understanding of wise mind, and some come to consider it their "gut feeling," "intuition," or "wisdom."

Core mindfulness is the vehicle DBT teaches for moving from emotional dysregulation to emotional regulation, or from emotion mind to wise mind. Yet suicidal adolescents with features of BPD can be easily overwhelmed when dealing with their emotions or with emotionally charged material. Therefore, we introduce mindfulness to clients in a way that breaks down and concretizes the skills it requires. Just as a piano instructor breaks down a difficult concerto into individual scales or chords for targeted practice, so DBT does for mindfulness practice. By concretely defining individual core mindfulness skills, the therapist can more readily highlight discrete skills that may need additional practice. The core mindfulness skills are not intended to be a deconstruction of, or a reductionistic approach to, mindfulness. Instead, using concrete, objective language, they provide the client with "things to do" to begin learning about mindfulness. These skills are divided into two groups: the "what" skills and the "how" skills.

"WHAT" AND "HOW" SKILLS

The mindfulness "what" skills include observing, describing, and participating. Observing means attending to events—both external to oneself, as well as one's own thoughts, emotions, and behaviors—without trying to change, prolong, or terminate the experience in any way. It is described as "wordless watching." Examples might include observing one's stomach muscles tighten when peers start teasing, or observing one's urge to ignore curfew and stay out an extra hour. Describing also involves attending to and experiencing the moment but includes putting verbal labels on the observed events without judging or adding interpretations. Naming things can help to organize thoughts and make sense of the environment, as in, "My stomach muscles tightened when they started teasing me" or "My heart started racing when my closest friend started pushing me to take a drink." Observing and describing one's thoughts and emotions can support learning not to take them literally or as factual reflections of the environment. Adolescents who are considered borderline often take their thoughts and emotions as facts, equating "I think I am stupid" with "I am stupid," or "I feel furious at her" with "She has done something horrible to me that merits this level of anger." Finally, participating involves throwing oneself completely into the activity of the present moment without self-consciousness. An example of mindful participation is a musician who is alert to the present moment, responding flexibly without self-consciousness.

The mindfulness "how" skills, as relabeled for teens (Miller, Rathus, & Linehan, in press), include: Don't Judge, Stay Focused, and Do What Works. "Don't Judge" means noticing but not evaluating something as "good" or "bad." The focus, instead, is on observing the consequences of behavior. One can acknowledge the harmful and the helpful without judgment. For example, "You're a jerk" can be replaced with "I feel mad when you do that." A nonjudgmental approach suggests that it would make sense to change behaviors that lead to painful or destructive consequences, but it does not label those behaviors as "bad." As many adolescents with borderline features judge themselves and others in extremely positive or negative terms, letting go of judgment is an important skill. The "Stay Focused" skill consists of doing one thing at a time, letting go of distractions, and concentrating one's mind without splitting attention between the current task and previous or upcoming tasks and without ruminating about painful or pleasant past or expected emotions. This can be extremely difficult for suicidal adolescents with borderline features, who often struggle with chronic suicidal ideation. The "Do What Works" skill consists of being effective, acting skillfully, or "playing by the rules," rather than trying to prove that one is right. It is doing what is needed to achieve one's goals in the current situation and not letting one's emotions, particularly negative emotions that can control one's behavior (e.g., vengeance, anger), make the situation worse.

The explicit identification of individual mindfulness skills is unique to DBT and has several advantages. An adolescent who has difficulty with one of these skills can engage in targeted practice of that skill. For example, nonjudging can be practiced while watching a movie, listening to the parent's choice of music, or sitting in class. Practicing the individual skills of core mindfulness can sharpen one's awareness, strengthen the ability to engage, and provide the opportunity for an "experiential taste" of that particular skill, thus allowing the client to experience the naturally reinforcing consequences of skillful behavior and increasing the probability of future skillful behavior.

APPLICABILITY OF MINDFULNESS TO SUICIDAL ADOLESCENTS WITH BORDERLINE FEATURES

The core mindfulness skills are interwoven throughout DBT. In fact, it is almost impossible to overstate the importance of mindfulness in adolescent DBT. Mindfulness informs a treatment milieu and interaction style (therapist to client, as well as therapist to therapist) of awareness, acceptance, not judging, and doing what works. Core mindfulness skills are present in all modalities of treatment: Formal mindfulness practice begins the multifamily skills group (MFSG), the therapists' consultation group, and the graduate group (explained later); mindfulness skills are used as needed in individual therapy, family therapy, and phone coaching; mindfulness is taught formally in MFSG (by co-leaders to clients), in consultation group (by staff to staff), and in graduate group (by clients to clients). Across modalities, adolescents and their family members are explicitly coached to be mindful of the transaction between the adolescents' emotional vulnerabilities and their often invalidating environments, a transaction theorized to be the core etiology of BPD. Mindfulness skills target each part of this transaction: Mindfulness is the primary skill targeting the borderline adolescent's pervasive emotional dysregulation. Further, family members are taught to remain mindful of the often invalidating nature of their interactions and of self- and other-validation.

Biosocial Theory of Borderline Personality Disorder

DBT is based on Linehan's (1993) biosocial theory, in which BPD is viewed primarily as a dysfunction of the emotion regulation system. According to the theory, the etiology of this dysfunction lies in the transaction between a biologically vulnerable individual and an environment that is a poor fit with this vulnerability (i.e., is invalidating). The biosocial theory is useful for understanding the central role of mindfulness in DBT. First, it highlights the relationship between emotional dysregulation and borderline behavior patterns, specifically that most dysfunctional behavior patterns in individuals with BPD can be viewed either as a direct consequence of emotional dysregulation or as a means of re-regulation. For example, an emotionally dysregulated patient in the midst of feeling abandoned might lash out physically against his or her parent (a direct consequence of emotional dysregulation) or might ingest substances to try to ease his or her panic and sadness (a means of re-regulating). Thus, parasuicidal or other dysfunctional behaviors are considered maladaptive attempts at problem solving, where the problem to be solved is generally the presence of painful affective states. DBT identifies mindfulness as the skill that directly targets the adolescent borderline client's central difficulty of emotion dysregulation and that, furthermore, provides the foundation for the skills in the remaining skill modules. Mindfulness targets emotional dysregulation essentially by teaching adolescents to observe and label their feelings and to notice, rather than act on, the associated action urges.

Mindfulness Skills as Foundation for Other Skills

DBT's structured modules provide the skills to cope with many of the stressors posing problems for teenage youth. Mindfulness skills are taught in the core mindfulness module and provide the foundation for many other important skills. Core mindfulness skills involve nonjudgmental awareness of the present moment and of aspects of the self and environment. Specifically, the adolescent may have difficulty experiencing or identifying what he or she feels or identifying a stable sense of self. Moreover, the adolescent may report a pervasive sense of emptiness and have problems maintaining his or her feelings, opinions, or decisions around others. For suicidal and self-injurious teens, nonjudgmentally observing and describing their feelings and thoughts in the moment may be one of the most difficult, but also the most critical, skills to learn. The mindfulness skills target troubled identity development with mind-focusing and observation skills that can ultimately enhance self-knowledge and self-awareness while preparing one to take needed actions to skillfully reach goals. Overall, mindfulness skills can enable adolescents paralyzed by indecision to focus and make decisions with both rational and emotional input.

Distress tolerance skills address the impulsivity inherent in high-risk sexual, substance-related, self-injurious, and other dangerous behaviors. Distress tolerance skills help overwhelmed adolescents to resist impulsive decisions, as well as those impulsive actions brought on by an egocentric sense of invulnerability. These skills address impulsivity by teaching adolescents how to distract and soothe themselves while considering the pros and cons of their actions. Distress tolerance skills build directly on mindfulness skills. They include nonjudgmental acceptance of both oneself and one's current situation. That is, the individual experiences and observes his or her thoughts, emotions, behaviors, and external environment without trying to change them. With adolescents it is important to be clear that a nonjudgmental stance does not imply approval. One can mindfully accept a situation that cannot be changed (e.g., parents' divorce, death of a pet) without approving of the situation.

Emotion regulation skills address extreme emotional sensitivity, rapid, intense mood changes, and unmodulated emotional states characterized by depression, anxiety, or problems with either overcontrolled or under-controlled anger. Identifying and labeling emotions, learning how to increase positive emotions, and reducing vulnerability to negative emotions are a few of the emotion regulation skills. These skills build on mindfulness skills in that they teach nonjudgmental observation and description of one's current emotion.

The interpersonal effectiveness skills address patients' difficulties in maintaining consistent and rewarding relationships while maintaining their own self-respect. Skills of "walking the middle path" address nonbalanced thinking and behaviors among family members (Miller *et al.*, in press). These skills involve learning about principles of behavior change, validation, and finding the middle path between common dialectical dilemmas in these families (e.g., authoritarian control vs. excessive leniency.). Both inter-personal effectiveness and walking the middle path require mindfulness skills, specifically the ability to nonjudgmentally observe and describe one's own thoughts and emotions and the thoughts and emotions of the person with whom one is interacting.

CASE STUDY

The following case illustration presents one client's acquisition and use of mindfulness skills in DBT for adolescents. Details of adolescent DBT beyond the use or application of mindfulness are included only when needed to explain the acquisition of mindfulness or to contextualize the use of mindfulness in the overall treatment frame.

PSYCHIATRIC HISTORY

Our client Cassie is a 16-year-old Hispanic female referred to our adolescent outpatient DBT program by her high school guidance counselor after she disclosed having chronic suicidal ideation. Cassie is an eleventh grader who lives with her mother and 14-year-old brother. Upon evaluation at our clinic, Cassie received Axis I diagnoses of major depressive disorder (recurrent, moderate), dysthymic disorder, and generalized anxiety disorder.

Although Cassie did not meet full criteria, she endorsed symptoms of panic disorder and social phobia. Cassie also met criteria for BPD, endorsing affective instability, a pattern of unstable relationships, chronic feelings of emptiness, severe dissociative symptoms, suicidal ideation, and parasuicidal behavior.

Cassie's psychiatric history included significant worry about real-life events for as long as she could remember and feeling depressed since junior high school. Cassie reported that she had been experiencing chronic suicidal ideation for the past year, with a plan (hanging herself with a bed sheet), but with no intent to act on it. Cassie reported that her self-injurious behavior began at age 13 and included superficial cuts with razors and art tools on her arms and legs. Over the past year, self-injury had increased in severity. On several occasions, Cassie had inflicted 10–20 superficial cuts on her forearm during a single episode. Cassie described how the self-injury functioned to re-regulate her emotions in the short term and help her let go of suicidal thoughts. "I tried it the first time when I was really depressed, it helped. ... I felt less sad and I could let go of worry thoughts more easily. Over the past year, I've been doing it more, maybe a few times a week. When I get too sad, I start thinking about killing myself. ... I think I hurt myself sometimes to distract myself from thinking about suicide." Cassie also described a history of relationship patterns characteristic of borderline personality disorder, including frequent conflict with her mother escalating into verbal abuse and then the "silent treatment" for days, and intense friendships with peers formed quickly and then ended precipitously following a perceived infraction or rejection. Family psychiatric history included major depression and social phobia in her father, and social phobia in her brother.

PHASE 1

The individual therapist oriented Cassie to DBT over the initial individual sessions. Cassie agreed to participate in the program, which included 16 weekly sessions of individual therapy (60 minutes) and MFSG (2 hours), along with family sessions and phone coaching, as needed. Cassie also agreed to work on decreasing her self-injurious behavior and building a life worth living. The skills-group leader oriented Cassie and her mother to DBT in their initial group meeting, providing an overview of the structure and philosophy of the DBT treatment program and working to strengthen their motivation for treatment.

Cassie and her therapist agreed on the treatment goals by session 2. These included reducing chronic suicidal ideation and self-injurious behaviors; reducing treatment-interfering behaviors such as not completing diary card and therapy homework assignments; reducing behaviors interfering with quality of life, including depression, anxiety, arguments with mother, and physical altercations with peers; and increasing behavioral skills of core mindfulness, distress tolerance, emotion regulation, interpersonal effectiveness, and walking the middle path.

Individual Therapy

In individual therapy, adolescents learn to apply skills taught in the MFSG to their own lives. Cassie completed a diary card weekly to monitor target behaviors and DBT skill use (including mindfulness). Her therapist reviewed the diary card at the start of each individual therapy session and set the session agenda according to the hierarchically ordered targets. For example, if Cassie had engaged in parasuicidal acts or had experienced suicidal ideation since her last session, the first task in session was to conduct a behavioral and solution analysis of that target behavior.

Over the course of several behavioral analyses that Cassie and her therapist completed collaboratively, it became clear that Cassie often thought about, rather than engaged in, mindfulness and then concluded it did not work. Although Cassie had received formal instruction in mindfulness skills in MFSG, her individual therapist helped her develop these skills through ongoing discussion and in-session practice. This *in vivo* practice enabled Cassie to share her individual observations of her mindfulness practice and to receive immediate feedback and coaching from her therapist on any difficulty in utilizing the skill. Initially, Cassie stated, "I can't do it. My mind wanders too much."

The following paragraphs highlight Cassie's and her therapist's work in individual sessions, first on clarifying and practicing mindfulness, and then on using mindfulness skills in the context of a behavioral analysis and the emotion regulation skill called the "wave." Over time, Cassie was able to generalize her skill use beyond in-session work to more of her daily life.

Story and Metaphor

DBT encourages the use of story and metaphor in general as a way to encourage the patient to consider alternate views of reality and make learning more interesting, humorous, or less threatening. Stories and metaphors are used often in teaching and encouraging the use of mindfulness and are especially useful with adolescents who may be used to shutting down or tuning out standard didactic presentations. For example, Cassie's therapist talked to her about developing her "mindfulness muscle," explaining, "Every time you notice your attention has wandered, and you bring it back to your target, you strengthen your mindfulness muscle." She also addressed Cassie's impatience and self-judgment with the process of learning mindfulness with the metaphor of training for a marathon. A beginning runner does not expect to complete a marathon after a week of training, but trains regularly over a long period, whether he or she feels like it or not, and sees effects gradually over time. Harsh judgments of each training session are likely to lead to frustration and giving up, whereas nonjudgmental participation in each session is more likely to lead to goal attainment.

Practicing Mindfulness

Cassie's therapist led her through the following mindful breathing exercise, providing her with specific instructions on what to do with her attention and wandering mind: "Please get into the mindfulness position— sit comfortably in your chair, in a posture that is comfortable yet dignified. Place your full attention on your breath and let go of any intervening thoughts. If your mind wanders or if judgments intrude, don't try to push them away, but simply label the intervening thought as a thought, or the judgment as a judgment, and let it go, by gently redirecting your attention back to your breath. This wandering mind is not good or bad, but it is a mind doing what minds do. Treat all mental activity, insignificant or highly charged, identically. Instead of turning to and engaging with the thought (and thereby giving it more attention), simply let it go."

Initially, Cassie felt discouraged, stating, "It's too hard, my mind wanders, and there's no way I can treat all thoughts, thoughts about lunch and thoughts about the fight that I had with my boyfriend, the same!" Cassie's therapist asked Cassie if she thought she could be aware, just for a moment, of where she placed her attention, and if she could attend to one thing at a time, just for a moment. Cassie felt this was easy, "if it's just for a few seconds." Cassie's therapist responded, "You're already able to be mindful, perhaps just for a moment, but it's a beginning." Cassie and her therapist then practiced mindfulness of breath for 3 minutes, as described previously. After the practice, they discussed Cassie's observations of the practice, and the therapist reinforced Cassie's collaboration and willingness to participate. Cassie's therapist did not label the mindfulness practices as "good" or "bad" according to Cassie's reported ease or difficulty of being mindful, but simply praised Cassie for her willing participation.

Behavioral Analysis

The behavioral analysis (BA) is a step-by-step examination of a problem behavior, including an exhaustive description of the moment-to-moment chain of environmental and behavioral events, as well as the antecedents and consequences of the target behavior. Conducting the BA draws heavily on the ability to be mindful. Clients are asked to be nonjudgmental observers of the thoughts, emotions, actions, and environmental events that precede and follow their problem behaviors. During the behavioral analysis, thoughts and sensations that arise are observed and described in a detached fashion. In DBT, repeated practice of the BA leads to insight about the functional relationships among thoughts, emotions, and actions. Over repeated behavioral analyses, Cassie practiced the nonjudgmental observation of the cognitive, emotional, and behavioral patterns that informed her understanding of herself, her relationships, and her environment. Cassie observed how her thoughts contributed to her feelings; she observed how the consequences of her behaviors and how her responses to the behaviors of others either maintained or suppressed those behaviors; she observed how she avoided her own emotional experiencing; and she observed her contribution to the relationship chaos she often experienced. Cassie learned to observe these patterns nonjudgmentally and both to validate her valid thoughts, emotions, and behaviors and to replace unskillful behaviors with more skillful ones. Cassie was surprised to learn how her cognitive distortions, misattributions, and unrealistic expectations created a story about herself and her life ("I shouldn't make any mistakes. I'm a bad person. No one likes me. I should always be happy and something bad will happen if I feel sad") and led her to function in the world as if that story were true. For example, Cassie tried to suppress any sad feelings and be happy all the time, was a perfectionist in her school work (often staying up half the night completing academic assignments), and was often socially isolated.

Through this ongoing process of nonjudgmentally observing and describing, Cassie learned how her thoughts and feelings were "just thoughts" and "just feelings" and not necessarily reflections of reality. In this way, the BA and the mindfulness skills that support it helped Cassie begin to break out of cognitive and behavioral habits, or more specifically, the grip of operant and associative conditioning. Over time, Cassie realized options not previously recognized ("You mean it's okay to let myself feel sad sometimes?") and, ultimately, a willingness to take more responsibility for her cognitive and behavioral choices ("I will not hurt myself to distract from the sadness").

The "Wave" Skill

Another DBT skill that relies heavily on mindfulness is the emotion regulation skill known as the wave. This skill is essentially a process of exposure and desensitization to one's own emotional experiences. Mindfulness skills support the patient in sustained experiencing of his or her emotions. During this process, emotions are not disowned, pushed away, or made bigger. Instead, they are observed and experienced. For Cassie, this experiencing with detached observation supported the notion that she was not an emotional state but rather a person who experiences emotional states. Cassie learned to observe her emotions as they increased and then decreased in intensity, and to observe the waxing and waning of action urges associated with the emotions (e.g., self-cutting). Through this process of experiencing and observing, she learned that she had choices about whether or not to act on the urges. Cassie found repeated contact with her previously avoided emotions therapeutic. She had learned through repeated BAs that her self-injury was often an attempt to avoid experiencing her own intense negative emotions or was the result of the dysregulation that resulted from experiencing them. This perceived danger of the negative emotions dissipated as Cassie used the wave skill, essentially putting herself through repeated emotion exposure sessions.

Multifamily Skills Training Group

Cassie and her mother attended the weekly MFSG along with five other adolescents and their parents. Here they received formal instruction and practice in core mindfulness skills. The group format offers several advantages for learning mindfulness. After Cassie overcame her initial fear of participating in the group, she developed camaraderie with the group members that appeared to strengthen her commitment to mindfulness and to treatment in general. Cassie and her mother received formal instruction in mindfulness, practiced mindfulness, and received feedback, coaching, support, and validation in their use of mindfulness from co-leaders and peers in group, as well as from each other outside of group.

The 16-week group is open to new members, and new families start every 4 weeks. This creates a seniority system and a culture within the group in which senior members help orient more junior members to DBT. When Cassie and her mother started group, two other families had been in the group for 8 weeks. These more senior members described and modeled skillful use of mindfulness. This was particularly important as Cassie initially felt extremely skeptical and discouraged about the utility of mindfulness for her difficulties. For example, when Cassie first learned mindfulness in MFSG, she said, "I have real problems, and I get really upset. Watching my breath won't do anything!" The more senior group members validated her doubts, noting, "I felt the same way when I started," and then encouraged her to reserve judgment and keep trying. "You have to just keep doing it. It gets easier, and you'll see it starts to help." The MFSG format allows for this peer support and a culture that fosters the use of mindfulness.

Family Therapy

Cassie and her mother participated in four family therapy sessions. Both were struggling with their own emotional vulnerability and with their own invalidating responses to each other's emotional vulnerability. Interactions between them often led to unskillful, escalating exchanges. During family therapy sessions, Cassie's therapist continually highlighted the importance of using mindfulness skills. She explicitly described the importance of observing one's own reactions to feedback, not judging, doing what works during the interactions, not letting negative emotions make things worse, and staying focused on the topic under current discussion. The therapist explicitly highlighted and reinforced their use of these mindfulness skills during family therapy sessions (e.g., "Cassie, that was a great nonjudgmental description of your mother's reaction when you came home late Friday night") and sometimes called a time-out for a moment of family mindfulness to interrupt escalating exchanges.

Telephone Coaching

Initially, Cassie did not use the telephone coaching modality, as she feared she would bother her therapist. However, over time and with encouragement, she came to make good use of phone coaching. On one occasion, Cassie called in emotion mind, upset and emotionally dysregulated after arguing with her mother. Cassie's therapist realized that Cassie was too dysregulated to participate effectively in any problem-solving discussion, and so she started the coaching call by asking Cassie to breathe mindfully with her for 2 minutes while on the phone. This brief, *in vivo* mindfulness practice helped Cassie re-regulate adequately to participate in a problem-solving discussion. Cassie and her therapist then spent 5 minutes planning what Cassie could do to get through the remainder of the evening. The therapist reviewed with Cassie the importance of doing the selected distress tolerance skills mindfully: placing her full attention on the skill (e.g., listening to music), redirecting her attention back to it as needed, and letting thoughts about the fight with her mother float by "like clouds in the sky."

Therapists' Consultation Meeting

The adolescent DBT therapist consultation team meets weekly for 90 minutes. At these meetings, therapists discuss cases and support each other in conducting DBT. Each meeting begins with a brief mindfulness exercise, which serves several purposes. First, it marks the transition from role of therapist provider to that of DBT therapist colleague. Second, it supports the therapist in bringing his or her attention into the present moment. Third, because therapists rotate leading the mindfulness exercises, it provides an ongoing opportunity for therapists both to enhance these skills and to learn new mindfulness exercises aimed at adolescents. Fourth, after each mindfulness exercise, participants share their individual observations of their practice, as well as provide feedback about the mindfulness exercise itself. This weekly team mindfulness practice fosters the creation of community among the consultation team members. Didactics, including DBT skills, are covered during the last half hour of the meeting. During this time, core mindfulness skills may be reviewed formally or new mindfulness exercises may be taught and practiced.

PHASE 2: GRADUATE GROUP

Cassie graduated from Phase 1 of DBT and entered the optional graduate group, which is led by two therapists and composed of adolescents who have completed the 16-week therapy program (see Miller *et al.,* in press). Here clients often work at deepening their mindfulness practice. The 2-hour format of the group includes several elements. First is a mindfulness exercise, led each week by one of the adolescents or therapists. This provided Cassie with the opportunity to practice taking on the role of mindfulness leader and to increase generalization of mindfulness skills in her daily life. Next, adolescents take turns teaching their peers a DBT skill. The specific skill taught is based on group consensus. Cassie taught core mindfulness skills to her peers and responded to peers' questions about using the skill. After a snack break, sessions continue with consultation and problem-solving in which patients provide peer consultation regarding management of current life problems. Group members must be inter-personally skillful during discussions of often sensitive topics (e.g., avoiding self-injury, managing suicidal ideation, conflict with peers or parents). Cassie practiced skillful use of validation, reinforcement, and other important interpersonal skills (e.g., listening and not interrupting, using a respectful tone of voice, good eye contact) when giving feedback to peers. This portion of the group has a continual and explicit theme of using mindfulness skills to observe and describe one's own reactions to the discussion, stay focused, and refrain from judging one's own and others' behaviors while evaluating the consequences of the behavior. The session ends with each group member sharing one nonjudgmental observation about the day's group. The function of the closing observation is to help the patients practice mindfulness skills, return to wise mind (given frequent discussion of sensitive topics during group, some participants may have entered emotion mind), and practice self- and other-validation skills, as well as reinforcement skills. The observations range from, "Cassie accepted the feedback she received today without judgment" to "I am feeling sad."

CONCLUSION

Cassie and her mother both completed the 16-week treatment. Cassie had learned many of the skills in the five skill modules and had begun incorporating them in her daily repertoire. The graduate group helped Cassie more fully integrate these skills in her daily life. Although initially Cassie was skeptical about the potential utility of mindfulness skills, she ultimately found them extremely helpful. During the second 8 weeks of treatment, Cassie reported that she practiced mindfulness more regularly. At the end of the 16 weeks, Cassie and her mother were regularly incorporating the core mindfulness skills into their daily repertoire, and both described mindfulness as the most helpful of all the skills. Cassie reported that she was experiencing significant benefits from the practice: "I'm able to let go of suicidal thoughts now. I know they're just thoughts, and I don't have to act on them. I'm also more able to 'ride the wave' when I'm feeling sad or feeling an urge to self-injure. I know that I don't have to act on the urge, and that if I continue to observe it, it will eventually go away."

Upon discharge, Cassie no longer met DSM criteria for major depression, and her anxiety symptoms had diminished greatly. Her borderline personality symptoms diminished also (i.e., better affect regulation, improved interpersonal relationships, less impulsivity). Further, Cassie reported she felt more comfortable exploring her feelings and values. Although she continued to experience some fluctuations in her mood, she reported that she was better able to regulate her emotions and to refrain from acting impulsively when emotionally dysregulated. Cassie engaged in one self-injurious behavior during her tenure in the graduate group but did not allow herself another "slip" and maintained her other previous treatment gains.

EMPIRICAL SUPPORT FOR DBT

DBT WITH ADULTS

DBT is the first empirically supported psychosocial treatment for chronically parasuicidal adult women diagnosed with borderline personality disorder. In a randomized controlled one-year treatment trial, DBT participants showed significant reductions in anger, suicide attempts and other parasuicidal acts (in both frequency and medical risk), and number of inpatient psychiatric days, as well as improvement in social adjustment and treatment compliance (Linehan, Armstrong, Suarez, Allmon, & Heard, 1991). Results were generally maintained at one-year follow-up (Linehan, Heard, & Armstrong, 1993; Linehan, Tutek, Heard, & Armstrong, 1994). Promising results have been obtained in the application of DBT to women diagnosed with both a substance use disorder and BPD (Linehan et al., 1999; Linehan et al., 2002). Partial replications by other investigators, at other sites and in other countries, have lent further support to DBT as an effective treatment for this population (Bohus et al., 2000; Koons et al., 2001; McCann & Ball, 2000; Stanley, Ivanoff, Brodsky, Oppenheim, & Mann, 1998; Verheul et al., 2003).

DBT WITH ADOLESCENTS

Based on initial outcome data, DBT also appears to be a promising treatment for suicidal and depressed adolescents with borderline personality features. Pilot data indicate that the short-term treatment program retains multiproblem teens in outpatient care and decreases inpatient hospitalizations (Rathus & Miller, 2002). In this quasi-experimental pilot investigation of suicidal adolescent outpatients diagnosed with borderline personality traits, we compared DBT ($n = 29$) with treatment as usual (TAU) ($n = 82$). At posttreatment, compared with TAU, the DBT group had significantly fewer psychiatric hospitalizations during treatment and a significantly higher rate of treatment completion. Pre–post data within the DBT group showed significant reductions in suicidal ideation, general psychiatric symptoms, and symptoms of BPD.

Employing our adaptation of DBT for adolescents, H. Fellows (personal communication, April 1999) obtained impressive results with her adolescent population in New Hampshire. She and her colleagues evaluated 23 patients who completed their 16-week program. They examined three outcome measures: inpatient psychiatric days, emergency service contacts, and days of respite bed usage during three time periods—6 months prior to treatment, during treatment, and 6 months posttreatment. DBT patients showed significant reductions in all three costly services. For example, prior to treatment, the group had 539 inpatient psychiatric days, compared with 40 days during DBT treatment and 11 days during the 6 months posttreatment. Other researchers (Katz, Gunasekara, Cox, & Miller, 2004) have obtained results that support the feasibility of DBT applied to suicidal adolescent inpatients.

One might wonder whether mindfulness in particular plays a role in treatment improvement from the perspective of adolescents. Interestingly, one study (Miller, Wyman, Huppert, Glassman, & Rathus, 2000) examined adolescent self-reports of helpfulness and overall effectiveness of each DBT skill using pretreatment and posttreatment evaluations. This study found that there were significant reductions in BPD symptoms in all problem areas and that three of the four skills considered most helpful were mindfulness skills.

PRACTICAL ISSUES AND CHALLENGES

Legal and practical considerations influence the application of any intervention with minors. In adolescent DBT, the following issues pertain specifically to working with adolescents and their families during suicidal crises: handling confidentiality, handling family contact, and getting family members involved in a crisis plan. In working with an adolescent patient, one faces the dilemma of working with a minor on the one hand, but risking the loss of the adolescent's trust by breaking confidentiality on the other. Thus, we orient the parents from the outset that we will need to keep the adolescent's confidentiality to maintain his or her trust; otherwise, therapy will not be useful. On the other hand, we also orient the adolescent and the parents as to when we are legally obligated to break confidentiality; then, at least, the parents do not have to worry about whether their child is in imminent danger. For issues of concern that do not *require* breaking confidentiality, we encourage patients to communicate with their parents/ caregivers directly, often following some coaching from the primary therapist to do this skillfully.

When it becomes necessary to engage family members in a crisis plan, it is important to attend to the parents' needs and reactions, as the parents will be a significant part of the adolescent's environment, and their reactions can ameliorate or exacerbate the crisis. Engaging family members in a crisis plan generally involves a combination of soothing, validating, educating, and cheerleading.

We have observed a range of responses from private insurance companies regarding coverage for adolescent DBT. In general, we have found that the individual therapy and group skills components are often covered if the provider is "in-network" or if there is "out-of-network" coverage. In some cases, when there is only in-network coverage and a DBT therapist cannot be identified on the insurance panel, we have been able to secure insurance coverage by providing a letter outlining the patient's clinical needs and the empirical support for adolescent DBT.

In teaching mindfulness skills, it is useful to have parental support regarding the utility of the skill. Parents can provide important reinforcement and modeling of mindfulness, or they can be directly or inadvertently punishing. Although we have observed a range of initial parental reactions to mindfulness skills, from immediate acceptance to skepticism to suspiciousness, we find that parents' concerns are ameliorated through their participation in the MFSG mindfulness practice, as well as through discussion with therapists.

We have found that specific types of mindfulness exercises instruct and engage adolescents especially well, including exercises that are brief (1–5 minutes), that engage multiple sensory systems (e.g., listening, tasting, smelling), or that involve movement. These types of exercises appear to work well with teens who may be impatient or impulsive, and who are often self-conscious about engaging in mindfulness exercises in the presence of adult authority figures and peers. In general, we instruct participants to focus on one thing in the moment (e.g., breathing, eating, a picture, a song) and to continually redirect their attention to that one thing, letting intervening thoughts or feelings go "like clouds in the sky," neither holding on to them, pushing them away, nor judging them. We instruct participants that if they have self-judgments ("I'm not doing this right," I'm making a fool of myself," or "I'm doing better than everyone else at this"), they should "just notice them" and "let them go" by bringing their attention back to the target of the mindfulness exercise. Examples of exercises that appear to engage teens particularly well include observing bubbles, observing the urge to move while sitting in a chair (and not acting on that urge), listening to music without judging it as good or bad (play two very different types of music consecutively), and walking mindfulness (first give instruction to walk very slowly, then to walk quickly, then again very slowly).

A range of options are available for training and professional development in adolescent DBT and in mindfulness skills. Currently, there is no formal certification process for becoming a DBT therapist. However, there is an intensive 10-day training program available that is conducted over 2 weeks with an intervening 6 months for DBT skills practice and program development. While DBT encourages but does not require that therapists have a formal mindfulness practice, all DBT therapists are expected to have learned and practiced all DBT skills, including mindfulness skills. Further, participation in the DBT consultation team (a mandatory modality in the treatment) includes a weekly mindfulness practice that begins each team meeting. Therefore, the structure of the treatment ensures some regular practice with support and discussion of that practice among colleagues.

Finally, we encourage anyone delivering adolescent DBT to develop his or her own mindfulness practice. First, a personal mindfulness practice supports the practitioner's ability to effectively teach mindfulness. Second, although working with suicidal adolescents with borderline features can be enormously gratifying, it can also be enormously challenging, as these patients are often difficult to engage, difficult to retain, intensely emotional, impulsive, demanding, and frequently engaging in suicidal behaviors. A mindfulness practice can support the practitioner's ability to remain effective in the face of this ongoing challenge.

REFERENCES

Adcock, A., Nagy, S., & Simpson, J. A. (1991). Selected risk factors in adolescent suicide attempts. *Adolescents, 26*, 817–828.

Anderson, R. N. (2002). Deaths: Leading causes for 2000. *National Vital Statistics Reports, 50*, 9.

Andrews, J. A., & Lewinsohn, P. M. (1992). Suicidal attempts among older adolescents: Prevalence and co-occurrence with psychiatric disorders. *Journal of the American Academy of Child and Adolescent Psychiatry, 31*, 655–662.

Bohus, M., Haaf, B., Stiglmayer, C., Pohl, U., Bohme, R., Linehan, M. M. (2000). Evaluation of inpatient dialectical behavior therapy for borderline personality disorder: A prospective study. *Behavior Research and Therapy, 38*, 875–887.

Brent, D. A., Johnson, B. A., Perper, J. A., Connolly, J., Bridge, J., Bartle, S., *et al.* (1994). Personality disorder, personality traits, impulsive violence, and completed suicide in adolescents. *Journal of the American Academy of Child and Adolescent Psychiatry, 33*, 1080–1086.

Brent, D. A., Perper, J. A., Moritz, G., Allman, C., Friend, A., Roth, C., *et al.* (1993). Psychiatric risk factors for adolescent suicide: A case-control study. *Journal of the American Academy of Child and Adolescent Psychiatry, 35*, 521–529.

Clarke, G. N., Hawkins, W., Murphy, M., Scheeber, L. B., Lewinsohn, P. M., & Seeley, J. R. (1995). Targeted prevention of unipolar depressive disorder in an at-risk sample of high school adolescents: A randomized trial of a group cognitive intervention. *Journal of the American Academy of Child and Adolescent Psychiatry, 34*, 312–321.

Clarkin, J. F., Friedman, R. C., Hurt, S. W., Corn, R., & Aronoff, M. (1984). Affective and character pathology of suicidal adolescent and young adult inpatients. *Journal of Clinical Psychiatry, 45*, 19–22.

Crumley, F. E. (1979). Adolescent suicide attempts. *Journal of the American Medical Association, 241*, 2404–2407.

Erikson, E. H. (1968). *Identity: Youth and crisis.* New York: Norton.

Fergusson, D. M., & Lynskey, M. T. (1995). Suicide attempts and suicidal ideation in a birth cohort of 16-year-old New Zealanders. *Journal of the American Academy of Child and Adolescent Psychiatry, 34*, 1308–1317.

Huey, S. J., Henggeler, S. W., Rowland, M. D., Halliday-Boykins, C. A., Cunningham, P. B., Peckrel, S. G., et al. (2004). Multisystemic therapy effects on attempted suicide by youths presenting psychiatric emergencies. *Journal of the American Academy of Child and Adolescent Psychiatry, 43*, 183–190.

Katz, L. Y., Gunasekara, S., Cox, B. J., & Miller, A. L. (2004). Feasibility of applying dialectical behavior therapy to suicidal adolescent inpatients. *Journal of the American Academy of Child and Adolescent Psychiatry, 43*, 276–282.

Kienhorst, C., De Wilde, E., Van den Bout, J., Diekstra, R., & Wolters, W. (1990). Characteristics of suicide attempters in a population-based sample of Dutch adolescents. *British Journal of Psychiatry, 156*, 243–248.

Koons, C. R., Robins, C. J., Tweed, J. L., Lynch, T. R., Gonzalez, A. M., Morse, J. Q., et al. (2001). Efficacy of dialectical behavior therapy in woman veterans with borderline personality disorder. *Behavior Therapy, 33*, 371–390.

Lewinsohn, P. M., Rohde, P., & Seeley, J. R. (1996). Adolescent suicidal ideation and attempts: Prevalence, risk factors, and clinical implications. *Clinical Psychology Science and Practice, 3*, 25–46.

Linehan, M. M. (1993). *Cognitive behavioral therapy of borderline personality disorder.* New York: Guilford Press.

Linehan, M. M., Armstrong, H. E., Suarez, A., Allmon, D., Heard, H. L. (1991). Cognitive behavioral treatment of chronically parasuicidal borderline patients. *Archives of General Psychiatry, 48*, 1060–1064.

Linehan, M. M., Dimeff, L. A., Reynolds, S. K., Comtois, K. A., Welch, S., Heagerty, P., et al. (2002). Dialectical behavior therapy versus comprehensive validation plus 12-step for the treatment of opioid dependent women meeting criteria for borderline personality disorder. *Drug and Alcohol Dependence, 67*, 13–26.

Linehan, M. M., Heard, H. L., & Armstrong, H. E. (1993). Naturalistic follow-up of a behavioral treatment for chronically parasuicidal borderline patients. *Archives of General Psychiatry, 50*, 971–974.

Linehan, M. M., Schmidt, H., Dimeff, L. A., Craft, J. C., Kanter, J., Comtois, K. A. (1999). Dialectical behavior therapy for patients with borderline personality disorder and drug-dependence. *American Journal of Addiction, 8*, 279–292.

Linehan, M. M., Tutek, D. A., Heard, H. L., & Armstrong, H. E. (1994). Interpersonal outcome of cognitive behavioral treatment for chronically suicidal borderline patients. *American Journal of Psychiatry, 151*, 1771–1776.

Marttunen, M. J., Aro, H. M., Henriksson, M. M., & Lonnqvist, J. K. (1991). Antisocial behavior in adolescent suicide. *Acta Psychiatrica Scandinavica, 89*, 167–173.

Marttunen, M. J., Henriksson, M. M., Aro, H. M., Heikkinen, M. E., Isometsa, E. T., & Lonnqvist, J. K. (1995). Suicide among female adolescents: Characteristics and comparison with males in the age group 13 to 22 years. *Journal of the American Academy of Child and Adolescent Psychiatry, 34,* 1297–1307.

McCann, R. A., & Ball, E. M. (2000). DBT with an inpatient forensic population: The CMHIP model. *Cognitive and Behavioral Practice, 7,* 447–456.

Miller, A. L., Rathus, J. H., & Linehan, M. M. (in press). *DBT for suicidal multi-problem adolescents.* New York: Guilford Press.

Miller, A. L., Rathus, J. H., Linehan, M. M., Wetzler, S., & Leigh, E. (1997). Dialectic behavior therapy for suicidal adolescents. *Journal of Practical Psychiatry and Behavioral Health, 3,* 78–86.

Miller, A. L., Wyman, S. E., Huppert, J. D., Glassman, S. L., & Rathus, J. H. (2000). Analysis of behavioral skills utilized by suicidal adolescents receiving dialectical behavior therapy. *Cognitive and Behavioral Practice, 7,* 183–187.

Peters, K. D., Kochanek, K. D., & Murphy, S. L. (1998). Deaths: Final data for 1996. *National Vital Statistics Reports, 47,* 1–100.

Rathus, J. H., & Miller, A. M. (2002). Dialectical behavior therapy adapted for suicidal adolescents. *Suicidal and Life-Threatening Behavior, 32,* 146–157.

Shaffer, D., Gould, M., Fisher, P., Trautman, M. P., Moreau, D., Kleinman, M., *et al.* (1996). Psychiatric diagnosis in child and adolescent suicide. *Archives of General Psychiatry, 53,* 339–348.

Shaffer, D., & Piacentini, J. (1994). Suicide and attempted suicide. In M. Rutter & E. Taylor (Eds.), *Child psychiatry: Modern approaches* (pp. 407–424). Oxford: Blackwell Scientific.

Stanley, B., Ivanoff, A., Brodsky, B., Oppenheim, S., & Mann, J. (1998, November). *Comparison of DBT and "treatment as usual" in suicidal and self-mutilating behavior.* Presented at the annual meeting of the Association for the Advancement of Behavior Therapy, Washington, DC.

Verheul, R., van den Bosch, L. M., Koeter, M. W. J., de Ridder, M. A. J., Steijnen, T., & van den Brink, W. A. (2003). A 12-month randomized clinical trial of dialectical behavior therapy for women with borderline personality disorder in the Netherlands. *The British Journal of Psychiatry, 182,* 135–140.

Wood, A., Trainor, G., Rothwell, J., Moore, A., & Harrington, R. (2001). Randomized trial of group therapy for repeated deliberate self-harm in adolescents. *Journal of the American Academy of Child and Adolescent Psychiatry, 40,* 1246–1253.

9

"LIKE WAKING UP FROM A DREAM": MINDFULNESS TRAINING FOR OLDER PEOPLE WITH ANXIETY AND DEPRESSION

ALISTAIR SMITH

Psychology Service, Lancashire Care NHS Trust, Chorley, Lancashire, UK

INTRODUCTION

"Bob" provided this chapter's title 2 weeks after finishing a mindfulness-based cognitive therapy (MBCT) course. A year later he elaborated, "It's shown me what life is all about and given me back my life, which I'd lost." My patients repeatedly demonstrate that given the chance, "old dogs do learn new tricks," and with gusto. A clinical psychologist for older people, I was shocked by the ageism in my initial (mistaken) expectation that few would accept mindfulness training. Since then, participants in courses I have taught in mindfulness-based stress reduction (MBSR) (Kabat-Zinn, 1990) or MBCT (Segal, Williams, & Teasdale, 2002) have expressed their enthusiasm for new learning and experience with the phrase "We'll try anything." My hope is to convey some of the enthusiasm with which they have infected me, and the optimism created by the positive results many have experienced.

191

This chapter will describe the experience of providing six MBSR courses for older people in routine clinical practice, and three MBCT courses as qualitative research. Work with individual clients using these approaches will also be considered. MBSR and MBCT are described in more detail elsewhere in this volume. (See Chapters 1 and 2 for descriptions of mindfulness practices and the sequence of sessions.) In this chapter they are jointly referred to as *mindfulness training* (MT). This chapter does not cover work that construes the term *mindfulness* rather differently, such as that of Langer (e.g., Langer, 1991; 2002) and her associates. *Older people* here means those aged over 65 years, the official beginning of old age in the United Kingdom, with statutory entitlement to retirement and state pension.

WHY OFFER MINDFULNESS TRAINING TO OLDER PEOPLE?

There is no reason *not* to provide MT to older people, if they have needs of the kinds that MBSR and MBCT are designed to address, unless they are deemed incapable of understanding, practicing, or benefiting. As will be seen when reviewing empirical support later, there is little evidence to date to support such provision, but none against it. In other words, this untilled field needs plowing. We will also see that older people with whom I have used MT find it acceptable and useful.

DEPRESSION AND OLDER PEOPLE

Depression is an increasingly common health problem. The World Health Organization projects that by the year 2020, depression will rank second among causes of ill health for all ages. Rates of recurrence are very high (Judd, 1997). Depression (major and minor) has been described as the commonest mental health problem for elders in the United States (Murrell, Himmelfarb, & Wright, 1983) and is as problematic in the UK (Rothera, Jones, & Gordon, 2002). Community studies across Europe report disparate prevalence rates, with a weighted average of 1.8% for major depression in studies reviewed by Beekman, Copeland, and Prince (1999). Osborn *et al.* (2002) found that 3.1% of older people in their large UK study were severely depressed. Older people usually experience similar depressive symptoms as do younger people, yet there are some differences. Lasser, Siegel, Dukoff, and Sunderland (1998) note that depressed older adults often present with more somatic or anxious features and less subjective sadness than is observed in younger groups. Depression may deepen with increasing age: A longitudinal study in a rural sample of people older than age 65 found significant increases in depressive symptoms over time, especially for those aged 85 and over (Wallace & O'Hara, 1992). Each new episode of major depression increases the likelihood of further episodes, and around three-quarters of those who have had two episodes can expect recurrence (Judd, 1997).

Minor depression (depressive symptoms not meeting diagnostic criteria for major depression) is common among older people, with high rates in most cultures and countries studied. Many factors may underlie this high prevalence, including loneliness, poverty, awareness of cognitive impairment, and loss of social status and role (e.g., Blazer, 2002). The phrase "minor depression" adumbrates much human distress, which in addition to affecting quality of life, brings increased utilization of health services (Allen, Agha, Duthie, & Layde, 2004) and risk of developing major depression (Cuijpers, de Graaf, and van Dorsselaer, 2004). As minor depression is characterized by mood symptoms and cognitive symptoms rather than by neurovegetative symptoms (Rapaport *et al.*, 2002), MBCT has potential for helping people with minor depression to come to terms with circumstances while also enhancing their ability to take skillful action to influence those circumstances. Research has focused on major depression, but here perhaps is a way to help many older people before their depression reaches that intensity, plus others whose depression might not deepen but impair their lives long-term in ways that are subjectively far from minor. Since most will be functioning better than many sufferers of major depression, potential exists for offering a cost-effective intervention to large groups, perhaps in primary care or community education settings. Research has yet to examine the efficacy of MT in this context. MBCT, though devised to combat the tendency for depression to recur and delivered between depressive episodes, may also prove effective for some acutely depressed people: We do not yet know how severely depressed or in what ways a person can be before the commitment and intensive practice required by MBCT will prove too demanding, or contemplating their gloomy thoughts too aversive. For example, psychomotor retardation may prevent some from benefiting even if their depression is not very severe, whereas heightened self-criticism may be addressed during an MBCT course.

ANXIETY AND OLDER PEOPLE

Clinically significant anxiety is common, and the old are not immune. Indeed, for reasons including declining health, multiple losses, and the impact of ageism, they are particularly vulnerable. Studies reviewed by Bourland *et al.* (2000) identified 6-month prevalence as high as 6.8%, and their own study of generalized anxiety disorder (GAD) in older people showed that severity of anxiety predicted poorer quality of life. Anxiety may even be as common in older people as is depression (Blazer, 1997).

PHYSICAL HEALTH

Physical health problems, commoner as age increases, are often accompanied by chronic physical pain. This can interact with anxiety and with depression, both experienced by many older people (Flint, 1999; Katona, Manela, & Livingston, 1997; Kipling & Charlesworth, 1997). This adds to the attraction of MT, designed to target just such difficulties, for those working with older people. Recent evidence from outside the MT community (McCracken & Eccleston, 2003) confirms the contribution of acceptance to successful coping with chronic pain.

OTHER CLINICAL PROBLEMS

How far the utility of MT can extend remains to be determined. Work by clinicians such as McBee (2003) and Ross (2004), as well as my MBCT study (described in a later section), suggests that with careful adaptation, MT may benefit people with a wide range of problems prevalent with increasing age, including chronic physical pain, anxiety, agitation associated with progressive cognitive impairment, loneliness, and restriction of activity, and may have other as yet untested applications.

INTERVENTION MATCHED TO CLINICAL NEED
AND AVAILABLE RESOURCES

MBCT, devised to combat the tendency for major depression to recur, provided reduction in relapse rates approaching 50% in clinical trials (Ma & Teasdale, 2004; Teasdale *et al.*, 2000). MBSR, on which MBCT is based, was devised to help people cope with the impact of intractable chronic pain and physical illness, and also has been found effective with anxiety (Miller, Fletcher, & Kabat-Zinn, 1995). Much depression and anxiety in older people is undetected (Bagley *et al.*, 2000; Garrard *et al.*, 1998). It would be easy to blame clinicians for this, yet only effective interventions provide incentive to identify the need for them. MT offers effective treatments, sufficiently cost-effective to offset limited resourcing of older people's mental health care, and may thus ameliorate therapeutic pessimism. Taught to large groups, MT can reach more people than can individual therapy. This matters in the UK, where older people's share of health care resources is less than proportionate to need (Ham & Robert, 2003), and in many other countries for similar reasons. MT, an educational and experiential intervention, more than most therapies, works with people's abilities rather than focusing on "problems." This empowers participants by combating the double stigmatization that many experience as both mental health patients and as old people.

MATURITY AND MEANING IN LIFE

There may be developmental reasons to consider MT suitable for older people. I have provided MT courses to younger and older adults and found that for many younger people, making time to practice mindfulness is at first just another stressor. This is true of some older people, but many find it easy, having more time available than purposeful activity to fill it. There is more to this than the pragmatic issue of finding time for mindfulness practice: Time is passed in subjectively more or less meaningful ways; and passing time has particular significance as the future appears shorter. Writers from many times and cultures have suggested that the appropriate stage in life for attending to spiritual matters is once worldly responsibilities such as child-rearing are completed (Cole & Winkler, 1994). The *Oxford Book of Aging* states:

> [L]ater life in the West today is a season in search of its purposes. ... Between the sixteenth century and the third quarter of the twentieth century ... old age was removed from its place as a way station along life's spiritual journey and redefined as a problem to be solved by science and medicine. ... Older people were removed to society's margins. (Cole & Winkler, 1994, p. 3)

Cole and Winkler note that the tide turned late in the twentieth century, reflecting "growing cultural impulses to explore the experiences of aging, to move towards something as one grows older—a unity of understanding; loving relation with others; the return of wonder; acceptance of mortality; God" (p. 4). This suggests that MT may be an intervention whose time has come, so far as the developed world is concerned—as is reflected in the relationship between psychological well-being and religious involvement (Fry, 2000; Jewell, 2002). Traditionally, religions offered succor to those in mental distress—they still do for many. For others, many psychotherapies fail to address issues of meaning, or meaninglessness, which may be associated with depression (though the importance of these is explicitly addressed by existential therapists and some others). These are highlighted in Erikson's account of developmental stages, with the task in old age of reaching resolution in the face of death. MT is profoundly relevant here. It is an investigation by participants into what it is to each be themselves, conducted in a spirit of sincere and focused inquiry that promotes a degree of detachment from what is observed. Compare this with:

> *Wisdom, then, is detached concern with life itself, in the face of death* itself. ... Only such integrity can balance the despair of the knowledge that a limited life is coming to a conscious conclusion. (Erikson, 1964. Quoted in Cole & Winkler, 1994, p. 44. Italics in original)

MT offers a secular clinical intervention, yet embraces the reality that many people feel that spiritual life matters. Derived from yogic and Buddhist traditions (as well as cognitive therapy in MBCT), MT is nevertheless free of sectarian content or implications. For example, in one of my MBCT courses a Roman Catholic nun, a Methodist lay preacher, a Jehovah's Witness, other religious people, and atheists learned harmoniously together.

TREATMENTS DELIVERED

MINDFULNESS-BASED STRESS REDUCTION

I provide eight-session MBSR courses, usually including the "all day" session in week 6, as part of routine clinical practice, not (to date) formal research. Sessions are 2 hours long, rather than the conventional $2\frac{1}{2}$ hours, to accommodate some frailer people. (Participants often expect that they will struggle to cope with 2 hours, but in the event find that the time passes quickly.) All participants meet me for an hour of precourse assessment. Participants have the option of attending a quarterly 2-hour "reunion." Participants from all courses (including my MBCT research) meet at these reunions, which combine mindfulness practice and discussion, much as do MT course sessions.

My courses adhere closely to Kabat-Zinn's (1990) model of MBSR. Participant numbers have averaged 11 per group, with dropout rates around 25%. I have offered MBSR in two psychiatric day hospitals to day patients and inpatients, but most participants have been outpatients attending only for MBSR. Participants are referred for psychological intervention by general medical practitioners, as well as by psychiatrists, community psychiatric nurses, and other clinical psychologists. Participants are accepted for MBSR if they suffer from any anxiety disorder(s) and have no significant cognitive impairment or psychosis. Many do have other problems, most commonly chronic intractable physical pain or depression. Those whose depression is severe at assessment are excluded and treated individually. In some cases individual therapy, usually cognitive or cognitive behavioral, has preceded or overlapped with participation in an MBSR course.

Although these MBSR courses do not include formal research, participants complete measures of depression and anxiety before and after the courses. Results show wide variation in response following MBSR, confirming my impression (based on participants' comments, actions, amount of mindfulness practice undertaken, and other health care workers' comments) that the course is very beneficial for some and of little use to others. This becomes interesting when we look at who does and does not benefit (though as the courses were not conducted as research, the evidence is anecdotal, not quantitative). Severity of anxiety does not relate in any obvious way to ability to benefit from MT. Even people so agitated that they at first could hardly remain in the room benefited. Participants with comorbid generalized anxiety and obsessive-compulsive disorder (OCD) have found MT more beneficial for their GAD than for OCD symptoms, but numbers are small and no attempt has been made to sample representatively. People with primary chronic physical pain, with secondary anxiety and/or depression, have found MBSR particularly helpful. This may be because their mental health problems are relatively recent and reactive to pain. People whose referrers identified somatization as a major issue have tended not to benefit much, often commenting that MT helped them with stress but not with their main difficulties. It will be worth investigating whether prior socialization into a psychological model may improve outcomes for this group, as in other cognitive-behavioral therapy (e.g., Barsky and Ahern, 2004).

PILOT RESEARCH FOR MINDFULNESS-BASED COGNITIVE THERAPY

This extended pilot study is based on a prepublication version of the curriculum outlined by Segal *et al.* (2002). Three courses were run consecutively so that adaptations indicated to suit older people could be incorporated into succeeding courses. Some alteration of mindful stretching (from yoga sequences used in Kabat-Zinn's MBSR courses) was made before the first course. Cognitive therapy elements of MBCT were not altered. All participants had experienced at least three episodes of unipolar major depression. As MBCT was designed for people who are not currently depressed, a score below 20 on the Beck Depression Inventory II (BDI) (Beck, Steer, & Brown, 1996) was an admission criterion. Significant cognitive impairment was an exclusion criterion.

This pilot study was intended to determine acceptability of MBCT to older people, how it may need adapting, and whether results would support the need for more extensive quantitative research. This was a qualitative study, although BDI scores, recorded before and after the course and at follow-up, provided a minimum indication that MBCT was not making people more depressed. Participants were interviewed at precourse assessment, 2 weeks postcourse, and 12–13 months follow-up. Postcourse interviews included questions about symptom levels, use of mindfulness practices, ease or difficulty of continuing to practice, benefits of the course and of continued use of mindfulness practices, and related topics. Interviews were recorded, and responses transcribed for content analysis to identify the main themes.

Between 11 and 14 people began each course ($n = 38$). Eight people dropped out: four for physical health reasons, four for miscellaneous other reasons. No one dropped out later than session 3. The mean age of completers, of whom 19 (63%) were female, was 70.5 years (range 65–88). Research funds for taxis meant that we could include people who were poor or had some physical disability. No claim is made that participants were a representative sample of older people with recurring depression, nor is there any reason to think that they were unrepresentative.

Responses to the postcourse interviews were classified into one of four categories, labeled (1) *extremely useful, major benefit to life,* (2) *definitely useful, I'm significantly better,* (3) *only slightly useful,* and (4) *no help at all.* Participants included in the *extremely useful* category were those whose comments made it clear that MBCT had been associated not only with absence of symptoms of depression, or even a perception that a person had "more balance in my life," but also with changes that pervaded their lives. Thus Melissa, as detailed in the Case Study to follow, qualified for inclusion because her comments indicated that benefits were global as well as specific. She stated that she felt "more of a whole person" and described positive changes in sociability, calmness, and ability to relax and greatly improved coping with emotional distress. Another participant in this category gave me a letter stating, "How does one find the words to express the gratitude [for] . . . changing my life from desperation to incredible hope?" A year later, he described being "90% better than I was before, accepting things as they are—my wife says I'm a nicer person." He noted that throughout the year he had ceased long-term abuse of analgesics, had stopped antidepressants with no recurrence, was coping well with severe and worsening physical pain, and had resumed long-abandoned leisure activity, and that mind-fulness practice "has just become part of my life." This was confirmed by his letter 21 months postcourse, which stated, "I practice every day and it has been superb for me. . . . The pain is slowly getting worse, but I cope so much better than before. I meditate." Similarly, another participant in this category noted wide-ranging and profound changes. These included, "It's made me more alert, more outgoing. I never seem to put off till tomorrow what I can do today. It used to be the other way round." He also stated, "It gives you energy, a clearer mind—settles you down—a lot of things rolled into one," and "I feel bloody great, at the moment I have a bad chest: at one time I'd have been down, but I'm up here [pointing to the ceiling]. . . . Going back before we ever took this, if not for a religious feeling I think I would have committed suicide. It's really changed me, it's brought me to life. They used to say about sex if he'd made anything better he'd kept it to himself, did God. I can say that about [MT]—if he made anything better, he kept it to himself." These very individual expressions clearly refer to global benefits. Inclusion in the *definitely useful* category required participants' description of important MBCT-related changes, though not such as to reflect transformed lives. In many cases these referred to calmness and relaxation; in others to coping much better at times when depression would formerly have gained the upper hand. Those in the *slightly useful* and *no help* categories reported only small changes or no change at all and that they were unlikely to continue to practice.

At 2 weeks postcourse, 48% of participants fell in the *extremely useful* category. One year later, that proportion had increased to 62%. This increase was surprising, although many participants attending quarterly reunion meetings reported continuing, and in some cases growing, benefits. Only 10–15% of participants found the course to be only slightly useful or of no help. Most participants reported continuing to practice mindfulness regularly, both at 2-weeks postcourse and at 1-year follow-up. The mean daily time spent practicing decreased very little, from 48 minutes 2 weeks postcourse to 43 minutes a year later (though the range was wide). This confirms that many participants valued MT enough to find a significant place for mindfulness practice in their daily routines.

There were many differences in the time course of participants' responses to MBCT. A few found their lives transformed within a few weeks, whereas others struggled to grasp the principles of MT for some time, and were still developing their understanding and use of MT a year postcourse. A range of responses is likely when people learn new ways of relating to thoughts, feelings, and events, leading to change in their perceptions of themselves and their worlds. It is not peculiar to this study, as Ma (2002) illustrates regarding MBCT with younger adults:

> The apparently opposite directions of change in some subjects (e.g., some learned to think more and some to think less before acting) also reflected that they were using the skills of mindfulness . . . to correct their own particular maladaptive patterns. . . . Change in their ways of dealing with stress and depression revealed an intricate interaction amongst the different skills and approaches they learned in the program. There did not seem to be one single path to change. In addition, the benefits of the program were not confined to coping with depression, but were found in life in general. (Ma, 2002, p. 246)

BDI scores averaged 10.37 at precourse and 9.14 at postcourse and fell slightly to 7.84 at 13-month follow-up. As participants were selected to be in remission, a postcourse decline in scores was not predicted. Indeed, we might expect that if MBCT brought no benefit to the group overall, mean scores would increase as some people relapsed. If MBCT offered nonspecific benefits only (for example, due to education about depression and group support), we might expect a decrease postcourse, which might not be maintained at follow-up. If there were specific benefits of MBCT (and if people kept practicing), we might expect a decrease, if benefits of MBCT overcame the tendency for depression to recur, and this was seen, though it was not large. No attempt was made to test the statistical significance of this change, given the small sample size and absence of a control group.

These findings suggest several implications for future research. First, confirmation of the benefits of MBCT for older people will require controlled trials with quantitative outcome measurement. However, the global shifts seen here in emotion, functioning, and subjective perceptions of life certainly constitute sufficient evidence of benefit to justify the cost and labor that controlled trials will entail. Second, long-term follow-up will stand the best chance of detecting the full extent of benefits of MT. Most participants in this research found MBCT so beneficial that they maintained frequent, though not necessarily daily, formal mindfulness practice for at least a year and in many cases much longer. This compares with the finding that up to 90% of MBSR course participants maintained some practice 4 years later (Kabat-Zinn, Lipworth, Burney, & Sellers, 1987). Although many meditative traditions regard daily practice as important for those pursuing spiritual paths, people using mindfulness practice simply to help themselves maintain a sense of perspective and balance in their lives may still benefit from less rigorous regimes. Similarly, Carrington (1987) suggests that even infrequent practice can be useful. Third, the MBCT package has a coherence without which cognitive therapy and MT might conflict. Identifying the contribution to mental health of each component, though desirable, may be impossible, as individuals find varying benefit in different aspects of the course. Most participants (at a reunion) agreed that it was important to retain all the different practices "so we can choose for ourselves."

CASE STUDY: MELISSA—"I FEEL A DIFFERENT PERSON"

Melissa, a widow aged 76 when she joined a course in the MBCT pilot study, had lived alone for 20 years. Medical records confirmed her account of being treated for "nerves" since she was 15 years old, attending hospital then. She had seen an analytical therapist 40 years before, a clinical psychologist 20 years before, had undergone electroconvulsive therapy, and had been treated by psychiatrists for depression and anxiety as an outpatient. Her community psychiatric nurse thought none of this had helped much. She had been offered, but refused, inpatient treatment. At the precourse interview, Melissa hoped for "confidence and an aim in life." She felt "all right at the moment" (her BDI score was 17) and was "willing to try anything to not get depression."

Melissa attended all sessions of her course, participating with a will. She spoke little at first, more at later sessions, yet barely above a whisper. She told me at session 5 that she was becoming more assertive, for example, with tardy taxi drivers. She was clear in stating that attending classes, meeting others "in the same boat," and practicing mindfulness all helped her greatly.

Teaching in the MBCT course emphasizes combining a gentle, self-accepting attitude with sincere effort while learning to practice mindfulness. This worked for Melissa: At the postcourse interview, she said, "I have done everything and been very gentle with everything. I keep doing the things and they are becoming easier." She enjoyed practicing: "I love the exercises [mindful yoga]. I feel completely lost in those and don't think of anything else." She also found the body scan helpful. Informal mindfulness practice was important. She described how moment-to-moment living helped her: For example, "I was peeling carrots one day and I thought, 'I feel sick' [with anxiety], and I thought, 'Oh, automatic pilot. Don't look forward, just think "now" from moment to moment.' And I did feel better." Learning in a group helped: "Being a very nervous person all my life, always keeping in the background, this is the very first time I have really enjoyed meeting the people." Melissa practiced a great deal, with no sense of pressure, maintaining the gentle attitude noted previously. She was assiduous in completing and reviewing practice recording forms. Again, like most others, she liked the audiotapes provided to guide practice. She soon could relax better, and connected this with worrying less: "I've always been a big worrier. I'm now relaxing more and taking things as they come." She found very useful the 3-minute breathing space (which provides a way to "step back" quickly in situations when difficult thoughts and feelings threaten to become overwhelming): "Well, the day when I felt very depressed, and sort of that sick feeling before you feel the depression. When I breathe I feel all right, don't think of past or forward, it's the moment." She used mindfulness very practically: For Melissa the difference between "being" and "doing" modes was about presence and ease in activity, not withdrawing into physical stillness.

Melissa became more aware of precursors to depressive episodes, which enabled her to "nip them in the bud" by focusing on present-moment experiences. Activity scheduling, an explicit cognitive therapy component of MBCT, led her to incorporate more pleasant activities into her daily life: "And this one [points to activity schedule] is what I am doing in my life that nourishes me. So I'm painting, gardening, walking to the shops, talking to my neighbors." Melissa felt confident of maintaining mindfulness practice: "I'll never forget it. I just know I'm going to do it because it has been so helpful," though she wished reunions were more frequent. As well as being enjoyable, mindfulness practice (especially yoga) helped her feel less physical pain. Her close friend had told her, "Oh, you do look better, you have a different look in your eyes." Two weeks after the course, she was spending 2½ to 3 hours daily in formal mindfulness practice. At a reunion 3 months postcourse, she said, "I feel more of a whole person." Others remarked on her stronger voice. Melissa said she now found mindful sitting and yoga very relaxing. At the follow-up interview 13 months postcourse, when asked how she was now in relation to depressive experiences, Melissa said, "I feel I can cope with it. I feel more aware of things and when I feel sort of depressed, it just comes over me to get on with things and it wears off. Now I just do one thing at a time. I'm more sort of orderly, more in control of myself."

Melissa was now enjoying meeting people, saying, "It has opened me up a bit late in life." She said this was the most important benefit (though later she said that being at ease with herself was most important).

Melissa had also followed guidance given in the MBCT course about relapse prevention. She was asked if she had experienced any episodes of depression in the last year:

> Melissa: Yes, when I lost my sister, she died . . . we were very close. I woke up once or twice and I thought, "I can't go through with this—no, get out of bed, as there is plenty to do."

> Interviewer: It sounds more like depressive feelings rather than a full-blown episode?

> M: Well it wasn't a full-blown one. When I woke up, I felt depressed because she wasn't there. One day it was a very dull dark day and I [went shopping, taking a taxi]. A thing I have never done before—I went into a cafe and had a cup of hot chocolate.

She has since begun to do this regularly and meets people in the cafe.

By now others had noticed changes: "Lots of people, to be truthful: 'My word, you look better; you look really well.'" Maintaining practice was easy, with an hour of formal practice most days, plus informal practice and the 3-minute breathing space. This significant commitment of time and energy confirms what Melissa said about the importance of her mindfulness practice. She told the interviewer, "I used to think, 'I'm old now, there is nothing now, I have lost my husband, 21 years I have been alone.' Well, other people are worse off, I'm not ill, I am feeling better in myself even. My whole outlook is different." She still found course material useful, recalling how a story from a course booklet made her realize, "Learn to love a thing. You have bad depression and you have to learn to deal with it."

Like many participants, Melissa did not find it easy to put her experiences during and related to the course into words. "My mind's stronger, sort of clearer . . . it's a difficult thing to explain." At the 21-month reunion, Melissa recalled how she had felt better each session during the course: "I felt ten times higher [by the end]," she said, with eyes sparkling. During the course, "I still felt depressed in the morning, a terrible feeling. But I don't get that any more now. It's marvelous."

Melissa developed more awareness of and better control over her cognitions. "When I start to worry, I think, 'No!' I change my mind and I can do that now. I don't get all nervy. I think, 'Just relax and get on with what you're doing,' and then I go out to the shop and I smile at everybody."

At reunion 31 months postcourse, Melissa was vocal in a group of 25. She reiterated how much formal practices benefited her and that she still used audiotapes to guide practice. She did not think that her depression, lack of confidence, and anxiety (of 60 years standing prior to the MBCT course) would recur: "I think I've risen above it." Melissa has attended nine class reunions up to the time of this writing. She missed the tenth due to injuries sustained in a fall, as she wrote to me, and mentioned that she had experienced other recent illness, was awaiting surgery, and was feeling very well and in good spirits!

In many ways this case study speaks for itself, yet a few points bear elucidation, especially regarding how typical or otherwise Melissa's experiences are. Clearly Melissa found the course beneficial while she was taking it. However, her comments, my observations, and observations by other participants and her family and friends all confirm that the benefits increased over time following the course. This was also true of other participants, unsurprisingly. In many meditation traditions, an 8-week course would seem a scanty introduction to a profound approach to life.

Some other benefits are peripheral yet worthwhile. For example, $2\frac{1}{2}$ years postcourse, Melissa laughed about a recent physical therapy assessment. Asked to bend, she easily touched her toes, to the therapist's astonishment. She could not do this before, but regular yoga had brought suppleness and strength. This common side effect of MT may be at least as valuable for older as for younger bodies.

In summary, Melissa found both MT-specific and nonspecific factors in the MBCT course helpful. She found meeting others who suffered similarly destigmatizing. This might be achieved in other ways, but an educational course in which participants and teacher practiced together, and did not focus on problems, maximized this benefit. Melissa became more comfortable in social situations as her social insecurity, general lack of confidence, and self-esteem improved. Practicing mindfulness, she became more aware of the present, which helped by increasing pleasure and denying processing resources to ruminative tendencies (Teasdale, 1999). She benefited specifically from cognitive therapy aspects of MBCT. She used the 3-minute breathing space to distance herself from escalating distress; made use of activity scheduling; and used relapse prevention strategies successfully in situations when on past evidence, relapse was a real possibility. Melissa's experiences emphasize the relevance of the many ways MBCT supports learning and practice: She made good use of course materials (including teaching stories, audiotapes, practice record forms) and reunions.

OTHER SUPPORT FOR EFFICACY OF MINDFULNESS TRAINING FOR OLDER PEOPLE

There is as yet little material to review regarding the efficacy of MT for older people. Although MBSR courses have included older people (Kabat-Zinn, 1990), their data are not separable from overall results in published reports (e.g., Kabat-Zinn et al., 1987; Kabat-Zinn et al., 1992). The absence of publications in this area specific to older people might be positive if it meant that older people were simply included with other adults, rather than discriminated against, but we cannot trust that this is so. Evidence for ageism in society and in health care is compelling (e.g., Gilchrist, 1999; Roberts, Robinson, & Seymour, 2002), and in my experience in the UK, where focused effort is not made to provide psychological treatment for them, older people tend not to be referred at all. While no age discrimination was intended in trials of MBCT (Ma & Teasdale 2004; Teasdale *et al.*, 2000), the fact that participants were all under age 65 leaves a gap in the evidence base. As a result, older people may be at risk of exclusion from treatment on the grounds that MT is untested with this population.

Several clinicians recently have begun to provide MT courses for older people. However, no research data on outcomes are yet available. McBee (2003) describes several innovative and promising MT-based interventions with older people and with caregivers. She has worked successfully in a nursing home, using a course based on MBSR but modified to accommodate residents' need, with shorter sessions and less emphasis on between-session practice. Given the numbers of older people living in such settings and the paucity of therapeutic provision for them, this highlights an area crying out for study. McBee notes that meditation practice often reminds nursing home residents of their spiritual roots and connection to others, and can provide solace, support, pain reduction, and reduced agitation for those on dementia units. McBee also describes a telephone-based distance learning MBSR course for frail elderly people living at home. Among the results were increasing interaction from participants as sessions proceeded, as well as self-reports that they continued to practice mindfulness following the course. At first glance surprising, the success of this course echoes that of a distance learning MBSR course offered by the North Wales Centre for Mindfulness (see www.bangor.ac.uk/mindfulness) and suggests that older people in a wide range of situations may benefit from this approach, despite illness and frailty. McBee has also provided MT courses for older caregivers (aged 60–85 years) and reports "decrease in stress and somatic complaints as well as an increased satisfaction in the caring role" (2003, p. 262). Since caregivers often experience high levels of stress (e.g., Knight, Lutzky, & Macofsky-Urban, 1993), this is another important pointer for further research.

Ross (2004) described mindfulness training for older mental health inpatients, using extensively adapted MBCT. Sessions last one hour, participants attending for as long and for as many sessions as they wish. Like McBee, Ross places little emphasis on between-session practice, in contrast to standard MT courses. Despite this, results (for 45 participants) were clearly positive: 90% enjoyed attending, 90% found mindfulness practices easy, 70% said MT helped with their difficulties (though only 10% said it "helped a lot"), and 20% went on to meditate regularly, though it is unclear for how long this was maintained. These encouraging results, in a setting that could certainly benefit from effective group-based therapeutic activity, require replication.

DIFFERENT ETIOLOGIES OF EMOTIONAL DISORDERS IN OLDER PEOPLE

We must exercise care about who—with what kinds of difficulties—is offered MT. It may prove vital to distinguish outcomes for older (and younger) people with different anxiety disorders; and with older people, for those with depressive episodes of particular etiology. Evidence suggests that some older people's depression differs from depressive experiences of younger people in etiology as well as presentation, in ways that may affect the potential helpfulness of MT. Kivela, Viramo, and Pahkala (2000) found that high rates of recurrence in depressed old people were related independently to occurrence of major depression and to psychomotor retardation. They suggest that this indicates biochemical etiology, since life stressors and physical illnesses were not relapse predictors. However, others (e.g., Ma and Teasdale, 2004) have pointed out that sensitivity to daily hassles and minor stressors may increase with successive depressive episodes. Heun, Kockler, and Papassotiropoulos (2000) cite studies suggesting that "[t]he higher familial load for affective disorders in early-onset compared to late-onset depressives might indicate a higher importance of genetic factors in early-onset depression" (p. 1138). They also state that increase in cognitive impairment in late-onset depressives supports the idea of a more organic origin. However, it is quite conceivable that the impact of cognitive impairment on quality of life and morale may be depressing for psychosocial reasons. Heun *et al.* (2000) found that old people with younger onset of depressive experience reported low mood and feeling worthless, guilty, and sinful "significantly more often ... than the late-onset depressives" (p. 1140) and cite other findings of differences between early-onset and late-life-onset depression.

Roose and Sackeim (2004, p. xxi) summarize the evidence to date in their recent book on old-age depression by saying that the evidence requires "distinction between the older patient with recurrent depressive illness who had his or her first episode early in life and the older patient with onset of depressive illness during late life.... Late-onset depression has been linked to a lower rate of family history of mood disorder, greater frequency of magnetic resonance imaging abnormalities compatible with ischemic cerebrovascular disease, and possibly the development of dementia.... [P]oststroke depression may present with a different phenomenology and response to antidepressant medication compared to late-life depressive syndromes unrelated to brain injury.... Heterogeneity in the manifestations and course of late-life depression can interfere with accurate diagnosis and treatment selection."

This is an important issue, not yet studied in relation to MT. It emphasizes the need for separate and careful research into the efficacy of MT with older people. This author's current MBCT research included older people on the basis of having had three or more episodes of depression, but the possible need to examine people with first onset in old age separately did not form part of the protocol. Segal, Williams, and Teasdale (2002) suggest that the evidence they reviewed points to depression related to long-standing habits of prolonged rumination being more amenable to MBCT than depression triggered by recent major life events. Future MBCT research with older people should investigate whether it is also the case that people with organically based depression with first onset late in life may be less likely to benefit from MBCT.

Published research has not clearly separated benefits of MT for generalized anxiety from those it may bring for various specific anxiety disorders, for adults of any age, though it is likely that this will be remedied in the next few years. As with depression, so too with anxiety there is some evidence that presentation may differ in late life. Meeks, Woodruff-Borden, and Depp (2003) cite research support for tripartite models of anxiety and depression, with a common factor of negative affect and the unique factors of positive affect and arousal. However, they note, these models are generally based on samples that do not include older adults. Their results, based on large samples, suggest that in older adults, commonly used measures of depression and anxiety are of a unitary distress construct "under which anxiety, depression and related experiences can be subsumed" (Meeks et al., 2003, p. 641).

Comorbidity of anxiety and depression in older adults (e.g., Flint, 1999) and increase in emotional complexity (Knight, 2004) add weight to the importance of ensuring that measures used, as well as interventions, are appropriate for older people. Perhaps future MT research with older people should focus on reduction in both severity and frequency of specific symptoms, as suggested by Chodosh, Buckwalter, Blazer, and Seeman (2004).

PRACTICAL ISSUES

WHO IS QUALIFIED TO OFFER MINDFULNESS TRAINING TO OLDER PEOPLE?

The qualifications required for MT teachers of older people differ little from those required for providing MT to younger adults. Some experience and skill in teaching is desirable, since MT is educative. Ability to manage group dynamics is required: This will form part of the armory of most potential MT facilitators, since they also require clinical qualification and experience. To be qualified as a mindfulness teacher is, of course, also necessary. Routes to such qualification may include training courses for MBSR teachers provided by current and former trainers from the Center for Mindfulness at the University of Massachusetts Medical School, as well as training for MBCT teachers. It is less clear how qualified one should be to teach the form of mindful movement practice used in one's MT courses (e.g., yoga, chi gung, tai chi). A high level of expertise will provide more skill and flexibility in meeting classes' needs but is in my opinion not essential, if caution is exercised. Thus, for example, the sequences of yoga postures used in my courses are based on those described for MBSR by Kabat-Zinn (1990) and are modified in line with the advice of a physical therapist specializing in work with older people. Participants are asked to undertake only what is right for their bodies, but not everyone does this wisely and well, so facilitators retain responsibility for keeping participants safe. Course facilitators should be familiar with relevant clinical issues: When teaching MT to older people, these include awareness of older people's mental health issues, physical aspects of aging, the position of older people in society, and the manifestation of common forms of cognitive impairment. To carry out effective MT with older adults, experience and, ideally, specialist training in working with older people are desirable.

IMPACT OF DISABILITY AND COGNITIVE IMPAIRMENT

Although disability may affect both access to courses and participants' ability to engage in some mindfulness practices, this is not peculiar to older people. Indeed, since MBSR was designed for chronic pain patients in a general hospital, this issue is probably not much different for older participants. Many older people, but not all, have some disability. So do some younger people.

Cognitive impairments must be considered when screening older people. There is potential for adapting mindfulness training to therapeutic work with people with dementia, who may find an approach based on present-moment experience very helpful (McBee, 2003). However, a standard-format MBSR or MBCT course might leave them floundering, as such courses assume ability to retain information from session to session. Two people with early (undiagnosed) dementia were not excluded from my MBSR courses by screening with the 6CIT (Six-Item Cognitive Impairment Test) (Katzman et al., 1983; Brooke, 2000). Their cognitive deficits became apparent during MT, and though they felt that MBSR was beneficial, they required individual support to manage the impact of memory deficits on their learning.

ADJUSTMENTS TO MINDFUL WALKING

Slow mindful walking as conventionally taught suited few participants, and it alarmed me when several people in an early course ignored advice to do this only if their balance was good. This put them at clear risk of falling and prompted immediate revision of this practice. Nonetheless, many MBCT research participants said at follow-up that mindful walking was a favorite part of their informal mindfulness practice—the important differences being that they did not walk very slowly and that they focused on *being present* while walking, rather than on the process of walking itself. In a typical case, one MBCT participant said at interview postcourse, "I am noticing things more, and especially if I go out for a walk I notice things more, if you do things mindfully, even walking mindfully. We practiced that, and you get a different slant on things." Yet, when asked which of the formal practices in the course was least useful to her, this same participant replied, "I think that was probably the slow walking one. I didn't seem to be able to grasp that somehow. I mean, I liked the exercises, but that was a bit like you lost your balance and it was hard to walk slow." This reflects on a related, issue regarding walking, worth reporting here and requiring further study in its own right: Recent research into falls and deliberate attention to posture suggests that people with poor balance, if attending closely to balance-related sensory cues, may overrespond to these and lose balance, as noted by Swan, Otani, Loubert, Sheffert, and Dunbar (2004). In that study, performing a secondary cognitive task at the same time as balancing led to more successful balancing. This supports the work of Gage, Sleik, Polych, McKenzie, and Brown (2003), which suggests that older people who are anxious about falling focus too much attention on walking and disrupt this normally automatic process. Probably MBSR and MBCT teachers should avoid teaching slow walking with focus on the mechanics to anyone with uncertain balance (especially if he or she also suffers from anxiety), in favor of *broader awareness of the current context* while walking.

OTHER EXCLUSION AND INCLUSION CRITERIA

These criteria are not different for older than for younger people. Thus, while I have successfully used MT with two individuals with psychosis (to help them cope with the stress of their situation, not to address delusions directly), it may be risky to include people with active psychotic symptoms in a group. It is important with older as with younger people to assess for sequelae of trauma or abuse. These need not prevent participation, though they may require adaptations, such as prearranged nonparticipation at certain times. One participant dealt with flashbacks by taking cigarette breaks: This did not prevent her from benefiting from the course.

OPTIMAL LENGTH AND NUMBER OF SESSIONS IN MINDFULNESS TRAINING COURSES

Sessions in my MT courses are 2 hours long, compared with the 2½ hours conventional for MBSR, as less robust participants have indicated they felt that this was long enough. Like some other MT teachers, I have found it difficult to deliver MBCT in eight 2-hour sessions without feeling that the cognitive therapy elements were "shoehorned in." By agreement with the MBCT developers, I have redesigned the course to provide the same content in 10 sessions but have not yet run a group using this extended format. There are advantages and disadvantages here. More sessions reduce cost-effectiveness but may enable some participants to grasp the approach more fully, while missing one or two sessions due to illness or vacation will matter less. It is reasonable that older people may take longer to learn MT, since they tend to process information more slowly than younger people (Salthouse, 1996), or possibly learn more slowly due to decreased cognitive inhibition (Chow & Nesselroade, 2004), so may require more time and practice than younger people to develop the full benefits of MT in their lives. Older adults may also learn mindfulness more slowly for other reasons, including cohort differences, as described by Knight (2004). Shorter sessions are less fatiguing but make it hard to deliver the material mindfully at a rate that takes account of the foregoing factors, within eight sessions.

INDIVIDUAL MINDFULNESS TRAINING

Like others, I use mindfulness exercises adjunctively to other therapies. For example, commencing cognitive therapy for posttraumatic stress disorder, sensory focusing often helps with intense posttraumatic recall in-session. However, the varied uses of mindfulness in other therapies, as opposed to focused mindfulness training, cannot be examined within this short chapter.

I have provided approximately a dozen patients with individual MT along the lines of MBSR or MBCT courses. In some cases this was for a patient unwilling to join a group; in others, because no group was available within a reasonable time. Overall, results have been mixed and I now offer one-to-one MT only when it is strongly indicated and there is no way to get the patient to join a group. A few people have benefited greatly from individual MT. For one person it has been life-changing and more effective than previous cognitive therapy. This patient had previous meditation experience and made considerable commitment to practice, as well as reading around the topic. For a larger number, though, individual MT has been of limited benefit for the following practical reasons.

Working in the UK National Health Service (NHS), it is difficult to offer as many hours of therapist contact to an individual as a group MT course provides. Participants in MT groups often comment on the importance of sharing experiences with others "in the same boat," in terms of mental health issues and stigma, and sometimes find fellow participants' comments more helpful than similar remarks by the facilitator. The meaning of lying down on exercise mats is very different in a large group than in a clinic room alone with a therapist—the latter is simply not feasible, with resulting loss of one aspect of the course. Following a period of practice—for example, mindful walking or sitting meditation—mindfulness trainers customarily inquire into participants' experiences. This is important in informing the facilitator, but mainly in helping participants focus more closely on their own experiences. In a group, no one is put "on the spot" by this: It is acceptable to say nothing. Unfortunately, with only one participant there is more potential to feel under pressure. In summary, delivering MT along the lines of the standard course to individuals loses not only the cost-efficiency advantages of a group but also some of the psychoeducational flavor of MT courses, which do not translate well into individual therapy sessions. This also applies to younger people but may be particularly problematic for some older people, for cohort-related (rather than age-related) reasons of politeness and etiquette.

CONCLUSIONS AND FUTURE DIRECTIONS: MINDFULNESS TRAINING IS IDEAL FOR OLDER PEOPLE

It is important to acknowledge that MT is no panacea, yet it may have wide application if used flexibly and in a way that is sensitive to the particular clinical issues being targeted (Teasdale, Segal, & Williams, 2003). This wide-ranging potential reflects the origins of MT in approaches aimed at providing people with more healthy ways of life, not just techniques for managing symptoms.

We need to report research clearly, specifying the salient parameters of disorders and which specific features of our interventions target them and providing evidence of outcomes, all within a scientific paradigm—yet this may influence researchers to focus on the narrower, more easily measured effects of interventions. We must discriminate specific and nonspecific benefits of MT from mere anecdote, yet our accounts must capture participants' experiences fully. This includes reflecting experiences of their lives being changed in significant ways, even when such changes are hard to quantify. Thus, when Melissa (in the Case Study) says she has "risen above" her lifelong difficulties, attributing feelings of being "more of a whole person" to MBCT, this should be considered as the essential context of the fact that she has not suffered recurrence of depression, not just as a welcome epiphenomenon. This is the more important since so many participants express similar views.

It also may be important for researchers studying mindfulness to be practitioners of meditation themselves. As West (1987) notes, "Change resulting from meditation ... is likely to be subtle, demanding sensitivity of measures beyond personality tests and electrodes.... The challenge lies in incorporating and combining meditation with existing methodologies" (p. 209). Thus, researchers who are also meditators may be better able to interpret participants' accounts of their experiences. These accounts are vital to understanding the effects of MT and how they come about. Of course, not all participants can articulate their experiences clearly, and standardized measures will play their part, but to discover the essence of MT we must above all attend to what participants tell us.

MT has been criticized for encouraging increased self-focusing. West (1987) suggests that increased self-awareness in meditation may lead to increased self-evaluation and negative discrepancies between behaviors and standards, creating negative affect. This concern was echoed by Wells (2000), who thought mindfulness training detrimental to people with emotional disorders, as they already self-focus too much. In my view, this long-lived caveat reflects a misunderstanding of how self-focusing is addressed within MT. Participants learn not just to self-focus more, but to self-focus with detachment, without being overwhelmed by streams of ruminative thinking or negative self-evaluation, and with an attitude of compassion for themselves. The difference this makes is the essence of MT. In fact, course participants often tell me that the benefits of passing the light of self-focused attention through a compassionate filter, instead of the harshness of negative self-evaluation, are great. Early in MT, participants often experience negative feelings along the lines of "I can't do this" or "I should be able to empty my mind/feel calmer"—but while they are being gently shown how these are misconceptions of mindfulness, the emphasis on acceptance and witnessing built into MT helps them detach from such ideas. Some kinds of self-focusing may amount to depressive or anxious rumination, but self-focusing of another kind may be essential for aging individuals to establish psychological integrity rather than despair. The literature on reminiscence therapy and life review affirms the value to older people's psychological well-being of particular forms of self-focus (Garland & Garland, 2001; Haight & Webster, 1995) in those cases of facing one's past, rather than current reflection or rumination. Teaching detachment and acceptance as participants learn to attend to the whole of their consciousness in the present, including aspects perhaps long neglected or avoided, MT seems tailor-made to promote enhanced psychological integration and morale in older people.

In conclusion, this chapter has shown that older people are particularly vulnerable to just those mental health difficulties with which MT is effective.

The MBCT pilot research and clinical experience with MBSR described here suggest that older people can benefit at least as much as younger people. Further research to elucidate the significance of differing etiologies and presentations of anxiety and depression between older and younger adults is required to provide appropriate, non-ageist assessment for and provision of MT. MT has potential to make a great contribution to meeting significant underresourced and undertreated mental health needs for older people internationally.

ACKNOWLEDGMENTS

The author acknowledges the financial and other support of his employer. He is particularly grateful for support and guidance from Dr. John Teasdale of the Medical Research Council's Cognition and Brain Sciences Unit in Cambridge, United Kingdom, in respect of the mindfulness-based cognitive therapy research described here.

REFERENCES

Allen, B. P., Agha, Z., Duthie, E. H. Jr., & Layde, P. M. (2004). Minor depression and rehabilitation outcome for older adults in subacute care. *Journal of Behavioral Health Services and Research, 31*, 189–198.

Bagley, H., Cordingley, L., Burns, A., Mozley, C. G., Sutcliffe, C., Challis, D., *et al.* (2000). Recognition of depression by staff in nursing and residential homes. *Journal of Clinical Nursing, 9*, 445–450.

Barsky, A. J., & Ahern, D. K. (2004). Cognitive behavior therapy for hypochondriasis: A randomized controlled trial. *Journal of the American Medical Association, 291*, 1464–1470.

Beck, A. T., Steer, R. A., & Brown, G. K. (1996). *BDI II: Beck Depression Inventory Manual for the 2nd Edition.* New York: The Psychological Corporation/Harcourt Brace.

Beekman, A. T. F., Copeland, J. R. M., & Prince, M. J. (1999). Review of community prevalence of depression in later life. *British Journal of Psychiatry, 174*, 307–311.

Blazer, D. (1997). Generalized anxiety disorder and panic disorder in the elderly: A review. *Harvard Review of Psychiatry, 5*, 18–27.

——— (2002). The prevalence of depressive symptoms. *Journals of Gerontology: Series A: Biological Sciences and Medical Sciences, 57*, M150–M151.

Bourland, S. L., Stanley, M. A., Snyder, A. G., Novy, D. M., Beck, J. G., Averill, P. M., *et al.* (2000). Quality of life in older adults with generalised anxiety disorder. *Ageing and Mental Health, 4*, 315–323.

Brooke, P. (2000). Screening for dementia in the elderly population. *Progress in Neurology and Psychiatry, 4*, 17–19.

Carrington, P. (1987). Managing meditation in clinical practice. In M. A. West (Ed.), *The psychology of meditation* (pp. 150–172). Oxford: Clarendon Press.

Chodosh, J., Buckwalter, J. G., Blazer, D. G., & Seeman, T. E. (2004). How the question is asked makes a difference in the assessment of depressive symptoms in older persons. *American Journal of Geriatric Psychiatry, 12*, 75–84.

Chow, S. M., & Nesselroade, J. R. (2004). General slowing or decreased inhibition? Mathematical models of age differences in cognitive functioning. *Journal of Gerontology, 59B*, 101–109.

Cole, T. R., & Winkler, M. G. (Eds.) (1994). *The Oxford book of ageing: Reflections on the journey of life*. Oxford: Oxford University Press.

Cuijpers, P., de Graaf, R., & van Dorsselaer, S. (2004). Minor depression: Risk profiles, functional disability, health care use and risk of developing major depression. *Journal of Affective Disorders, 79*, 71–79.

Erikson, E. H. (1964). *Insight and responsibility: Lectures on the ethical implications of psychoanalytical insight*. New York: W. W. Norton.

Flint, A. J. (1999). Anxiety disorders in late life. *Canadian Family Physician, 11*, 2672–2679.

Fry, P. S. (2000). Religious involvement, spirituality and personal meaning for life: Existential predictors of psychological well-being in community-residing and institutional care elders. *Ageing and Mental Health, 4*, 375–387.

Gage, W. H., Sleik, R. J., Polych, M. A., McKenzie, N. C., & Brown, L. A. (2003). The allocation of attention during locomotion is altered by anxiety. *Experimental Brain Research, 150*, 385–394.

Garland, G., & Garland, C. (2001). *Life review in health and social care: A practitioner's guide*. London: Brunner-Routledge.

Garrard, J., Rolnick, S. J., Nitz, N. M., Leupke, L., Jackson, J., Fischer, L. R., et al. (1998). Clinical detection of depression among community-based elderly people with self-reported symptoms of depression. *Journals of Gerontology Series A: Biological Sciences and Medical Sciences, 53*, m92–m101.

Gilchrist, C. (1999). *Turning your back on us: Older people and the NHS*. London: Age Concern.

Haight, B. K., & Webster, J. D. (Eds.) (1995). *The art and science of reminiscing: Theory, research, methods and applications*. Washington, DC: Taylor and Francis.

Ham, C., & Robert, G. (Eds.) (2003). *Reasonable rationing: International experience of priority setting in health care*. Maidenhead, UK: McGraw-Hill Education.

Heun, R., Kockler, M., & Papassotiropoulos, A. (2000). Distinction of early- and late-onset depression in the elderly by their life-time symptomatology. *International Journal of Geriatric Psychiatry, 15*, 1138–1142.

Jewell, A. (2002). *Ageing, spirituality and well-being*. London: Jessica Kingsley.

Judd, L. J. (1997). The clinical course of unipolar major depressive disorders. *Archives of General Psychiatry, 54*, 989–991.

Kabat-Zinn, J. (1990). *Full catastrophe living: How to cope with stress, pain and illness using mindfulness meditation*. London: Piatkus.

Kabat-Zinn, J., Lipworth, R. B., Burney, R., & Sellers, W. (1987). Four-year follow-up of a meditation-based program for the self-regulation of chronic pain: Treatment outcomes and compliance. *Clinical Journal of Pain, 2*, 159–173.

Kabat-Zinn, J., Massion, A. O., Kristeller, J., Peterson, L. G., Fletcher, K. E., Pbert, L., et al. (1992). Effectiveness of a meditation-based stress reduction program in the treatment of anxiety disorders. *American Journal of Psychiatry, 149*, 936–943.

Katona, C., Manela, M. V., & Livingston, G. (1997). Comorbidity with depression in older people: The Islington study. *Ageing and Mental Health, 1*, 57–61.

Katzman, R., Brown, T., Fuld, P., Peck, A., Schechter, R., & Schimmel, H. (1983). Validation of a short orientation-memory-concentration test of cognitive impairment. *American Journal of Psychiatry, 140*, 734–739.

Kipling, T., & Charlesworth, G. (1997). Chronic pain in older adults with mental health problems: A survey. *PSIGE Newsletter* 62 (October), 27–32. (Psychologists' Special Interest Group/Elderly). Leicester: British Psychological Society.

Kivela, S. L., Viramo, P., & Pahkala, K. (2000). Factors predicting the relapse of depression in old age. *International Journal of Geriatric Psychiatry, 15*, 112–119.

Knight, B. G. (2004). *Psychotherapy with older adults* (3rd. ed.). London: Sage.

Knight, B. G., Lutzky, S. M., & Macofsky-Urban, F. (1993). A meta-analytic review of interventions for caregiver distress: Recommendations for future research. *The Gerontologist, 33*, 240–248.

Langer, E. J. (1991). *Mindfulness: Choice and control in everyday life.* London. Harvill.

——— (2002). Well-being: Mindfulness versus positive evaluation. In C. R. Snyder & S. J. Lopez (Eds.), Handbook of positive psychology (pp. 214–230). Oxford: Oxford University Press.

Lasser, R., Siegel, E., Dukoff, R., & Sunderland, T. (1998). Diagnosis and treatment of geriatric depression. *CNS Drugs, 9*, 17–30.

Ma, S. H. (2002). *Prevention of relapse/recurrence in recurrent major depression by mindfulness-based cognitive therapy.* Unpublished Ph.D thesis, University of Cambridge, UK.

Ma, S. H., & Teasdale, J. D. (2004). Mindfulness-based cognitive therapy for depression: Replication and exploration of differential relapse prevention effects. *Journal of Consulting and Clinical Psychology, 72*, 31–40.

McBee, L. (2003). Mindfulness practice with the frail elderly and their caregivers: Changing the practitioner-patient relationship. *Topics in Geriatric Rehabilitation, 19*, 257–64.

McCracken, L., & Eccleston, C. (2003). Coping or acceptance: What to do about chronic pain? *Pain, 105*, 197–204.

Meeks, S., Woodruff-Borden, J., & Depp, C. A. (2003). Structural differentiation of self-reported depression and anxiety in late life. *Journal of Anxiety Disorders, 17*, 627–646.

Miller, J., Fletcher, K., & Kabat-Zinn, J. (1995). Three year follow-up and clinical implications of a mindfulness-based stress reduction intervention in the treatment of anxiety disorders. *General Hospital Psychiatry, 17*, 192–200.

Murrell, S. A., Himmelfarb, S., & Wright, K. (1983). Prevalence of depression and its correlates in older adults. *American Journal of Epidemiology, 117*, 173–185.

Osborn, D. P. J., Fletcher, A. E., Smeeth, L., Stirling, S., Nunes, M., Breeze, E., et al. (2002). Geriatric Depression Scale scores in a representative sample of 14,545 people aged 75 and over in the United Kingdom. *International Journal of Geriatric Psychiatry, 17*, 375–382.

Rapaport, M. H., Judd, L., Schettler, P. J., Yonkers, K. A., Thase, M. E., Kupfer, D. J., et al. (2002). A descriptive analysis of minor depression. *American Journal of Psychiatry, 159*, 637–643.

Roberts, E., Robinson, J., & Seymour, L. (2002). *Old habits die hard: Tackling age discrimination in health and social care.* London: Kings Fund.

Roose, S. P., & Sackeim, H. A. (Eds.) (2004). *Late-life depression.* Oxford: Oxford University Press.

Ross, K. (2004, July). *Mindfulness.* Paper presented at Positive Perspectives on Aging conference, University of Durham, United Kingdom.

Rothera, I., Jones, R., & Gordon, C. (2002). An examination of the attitudes and practice of general practitioners in the diagnosis and treatment of depression in older people. *International Journal of Geriatric Psychiatry, 17*, 354–358.

Salthouse, T. A. (1996). The processing speed theory of adult age differences in cognition. *Psychological Review, 103*, 403–428.

Segal, Z., Williams, J. M. G., & Teasdale, J. (2002). *Mindfulness-based cognitive therapy for depression: A new approach to preventing relapse.* New York: Guilford Press.

Swan, L., Otani, H., Loubert, P. V., Sheffert, S. M., & Dunbar, G. L. (2004). Improving balance by performing a secondary memory task. *British Journal of Psychology, 95*, 31–40.

Teasdale, J. D. (1999). Emotional processing, three modes of mind and the prevention of relapse in depression. *Behavior Research and Therapy, 37*(suppl 1), S53–S77.

Teasdale, J. D., Segal, Z. V., & Williams, J. M. G. (2003). Mindfulness training and problem formulation. *Clinical Psychology: Science and Practice, 10*, 157–160.

Teasdale, J. D., Segal, Z. V., Williams, J. M. G., Ridgeway, V. A., Soulsby, J. M., & Lau, M. A. (2000). Prevention of relapse/recurrence in major depression by mindfulness-based cognitive therapy. *Journal of Consulting & Clinical Psychology, 68*, 615–623.

Wallace, J., & O'Hara, M. W. (1992). Increases in depressive symptomatology in the rural elderly: Results from a cross-sectional and longitudinal study. *Journal of Abnormal Psychology, 101*, 398–404.

Wells, A. (2000). *Emotional disorders and metacognition: Innovative cognitive therapy*. Susses, UK: Wiley.

West, M. A. (Ed.) (1987). *The psychology of meditation*. Oxford: Clarendon Press.

10

MINDFULNESS AND DIALECTICAL BEHAVIOR THERAPY (DBT): APPLICATION WITH DEPRESSED OLDER ADULTS WITH PERSONALITY DISORDERS

THOMAS R. LYNCH

Department of Psychology and Psychiatry, Duke University,
Duke University Medical Center, Durham, North Carolina

LESLIE L. BRONNER

Department of Psychiatry, Duke University Medical Center,
Durham, North Carolina

INTRODUCTION

Dialectical behavior therapy (DBT) is a comprehensive intervention originally developed for the treatment of suicidal behavior and borderline personality disorder (BPD). As a treatment, DBT includes the integration or synthesis of behavior therapy strategies aimed at change, and validation strategies aimed at acceptance. These strategies are utilized in weekly outpatient group skills training and individual psychotherapy sessions. There are four behavioral skills modules taught in the group classes and reinforced during individual psychotherapy sessions: mindfulness, emotion regulation, interpersonal effectiveness, and distress tolerance. Mindfulness, the focus of the current chapter, can be considered *the core skill* in DBT because it is integrated throughout other skills modules and is considered an essential component of treatment success. The primary purpose of this chapter is to outline factors associated with the use of mindfulness from a DBT perspective, including a theoretical and conceptual rationale, hypothesized mechanisms of change, and practical issues associated with implementing mindfulness in DBT. We also describe the application of DBT mindfulness skills in a depressed older adult with comorbid personality disorders.

THE TOPOGRAPHY OF MINDFULNESS IN DBT

Mindfulness in DBT was derived from Christian contemplative practices and Zen practice and can be thought of as a state or quality of awareness that involves keeping one's consciousness alive to the present reality (Hanh, 1976). This quality of awareness entails paying attention in a particular way: on purpose, in the present moment, and nonjudgmentally (Kabat-Zinn, 1990). This kind of attention is hypothesized to cultivate patience and gentleness toward oneself. Mindfulness practice in DBT incorporates these principles by teaching specific skills aimed at learning to let go of ineffective attachments and to reduce judgmental thinking, with the ultimate goal of becoming "one" with current experience. While mindfulness practice has been incorporated into a variety of other treatment approaches (Hayes, Strosahl, & Wilson, 1999; Kabat-Zinn, 1990; Marlatt & Gordon, 1985; Segal, Williams, & Teasdale, 2002), the manner in which mindfulness is conceptualized and implemented in DBT is unique and distinguished from other approaches in four ways. *First*, DBT conceptualizes mindfulness as behavior (behavior from a DBT perspective includes thoughts, emotions, and overt action) that is subject to the same reinforcement principles as any other behavior. To our knowledge, with the exception of Hayes and colleagues (1999) and Baer (2003), mindfulness is rarely analyzed from a behavioral perspective. *Second*, DBT distills the broad concept of mindfulness into specific and discrete behavioral skills that can be practiced independently. Although the goal of mindful practice in DBT is full participation in the present moment, particular skills that are relevant to mindfulness can be practiced in isolation, and DBT teaches each of these skills in a step-by-step method. *Third*, although mindfulness practice in DBT includes attentional control and cognitive distancing exercises, the ultimate goal of mindfulness in DBT is to enter into, participate, and become "one" with present experience, not to obtain an

TABLE 10.1   Mindfulness "What Skills" and "How Skills" (Linehan, 1993b)

What Skills	
Observe	Noticing experience without getting caught in the experience or becoming attached to the experience, allowing thoughts or other internal experiences to flow freely with full awareness
Describe	Labeling and putting words on the experience; calling a thought a thought, a feeling a feeling, acknowledging a feeling or thought without necessarily believing it to be literally true
Participate	Participating fully in experience, becoming one with experience, acting without self-consciousness (e.g., an athlete at peak performance)
How Skills	
Nonjudgmentally	Being aware of judgments, taking a nonjudgmental stance, focusing on "just the facts," accepting each moment, acknowledging the helpful or harmful without judgment, not judging yourself when you are judgmental
One-mindfully	Doing only one thing or activity at a time; staying in the present moment and letting go of distractions by concentrating your mind on your chosen focus
Effectively	Behaving in a way that is consistent with one's values and long-term goals, focusing on what works, doing what is needed in any particular situation, letting go of useless anger or ideas that life must always be "fair"

objective "distance" from one's experience (Lynch, Chapman, Rosenthal, Kuo, & Linehan, in press; Chapman & Linehan, in press). *Fourth,* DBT does not require therapists or patients to have a personal formal meditation practice. Although formal practice is valued, patients and therapists are instructed to use mindfulness informally during everyday activities (Linehan, 1993a).

The two basic categories of mindfulness skills are "what skills" and "how skills" (Linehan, 1993b). The "what skills" specifically include the ability to observe, describe, and participate fully in one's actions and experiences. The "how skills" include *nonjudgmentally, one-mindfully,* and *effectively* (see Table 10.1). Mindful practice also involves *radically accepting* a current situation, thought, emotion, or experience while maintaining a stance of *willingness* to enter into life with awakeness and effectiveness. From a DBT perspective, these skills compose mindful *practice,* yet mindfulness itself is a state of awareness and awakeness brought to each moment.

DBT AND WISE MIND: LINKS TO EMPIRICAL DATA

In DBT, the therapist teaches the patient that one goal of mindfulness skills is to achieve a wise state of mind (i.e., "wise mind"), involving a synthesis of reason or logic ("reasonable mind") and emotions and intuition ("emotion mind") (Linehan, 1993a). Wise mind has qualities of direct experience, immediate cognition, and the grasping of the meaning, significance, or truth of an event without relying solely on intellectual analysis (Linehan, 1993a). To access wise knowing, it is necessary to let go of excessively volitional (reasonable mind) or habitualized (emotion mind) modes of knowing. The idea is that all humans have a wise part or center of calmness. Indeed, in DBT the therapist might actively use dialectical strategies to push the patient toward wise mind. For example, a therapist might point out to a patient that he or she is *not* "interested in what you feel" *nor* "interested in what you think," but instead "interested in what you *know to be true*" (Linehan, 1993a).

In a broader sense, wise mind can be related to notions of intuitive knowing or wisdom. Wisdom signifies "the use of the best means for attaining the best ends" (*Webster's Revised Unabridged Dictionary,* 1998). However, despite the importance of this concept in both religious and philosophical thought, it has rarely been the subject of psychological study. One recent approach using more qualitative measures has emphasized the role of *balance*, including one's own interest and the interests of others (Sternberg, 1998). Other research has focused to a greater extent on the cognitive and behavioral aspects of wisdom. For example, Kunzmann and Baltes (2003) have examined evidence for links between wisdom-related knowledge and psychological functioning in three realms: affect, motivation, and social relationships. In general, they found that people with higher wisdom-related knowledge had higher affective involvement (e.g., interest, attentiveness) but lower affective arousal. They concluded that this was related to greater skills at affect modulation. They also observed a value orientation among those high in wisdom-related knowledge that focused both on enhancing others and on personal growth, with a preference for the use of cooperative skills during conflict. A related construct that might also be associated with wise mind is emotional intelligence (EI). Although there has been no research to date examining relationships between wisdom-related knowledge and EI, high levels of EI have been shown to be positively associated with successful social relationships (Lopes *et al.,* 2004). Thus, wisdom-related constructs have been shown to be associated with positive outcomes. Wise mind from a DBT perspective can be conceptualized to include features of both wisdom and emotional intelligence. In addition, as discussed later in the chapter, mindfulness in DBT is not predicted to reduce reactivity (i.e., interest, attentiveness) to emotional stimuli. However, mindfulness practice may result in relatively short-lived emotional experience, similar to the correlation of wisdom-related knowledge and improved affect modulation observed by Kunzmann and Baltes (2003).

HYPOTHESIZED MECHANISMS OF CHANGE
FOR MINDFULNESS IN DBT

Before proceeding with this section, we consider it important to note that it may seem paradoxical to discuss how an acceptance strategy such as mindfulness might function as a mechanism of change. On the other hand, we consider it unlikely that mindfulness as a behavior would have survived throughout centuries of use unless something beneficial occurred for the practitioner (i.e., helpful changes reinforce practice). In addition, certainly when used as a treatment strategy mindfulness implies that something changes. The problem for those teaching mindfulness is that as soon as change is emphasized, then acceptance disappears. Thus, in the following sections we discuss how it may be possible for change to occur within the context of acceptance, and we caution readers to not lose the experiential essence of mindfulness in the details of analysis.

BEHAVIORAL EXPOSURE

Much of the utility of mindfulness in DBT is hypothesized to occur through nonreinforced exposure to previously avoided emotions, thoughts, and sensations (Lynch *et al.*, in press). Indeed, with regard to psychopathology, many disorders can be hypothesized to result from or be exacerbated by classically conditioned experiences (e.g., anxiety, phobia, substance abuse, trauma-related disorders). Although exposure has traditionally been discussed with respect to observable stimuli, the present conceptualization of mindfulness is consistent with the notion of interoceptive exposure (Craske, Barlow, & Meadows, 2000). Nonjudgmental awareness of distressing thoughts, emotions, or sensations in the absence of any dire consequences and without escape or avoidance essentially constitutes nonreinforced exposure to these internal stimuli. In addition, recent research has indicated that the extinction of classically conditioned responses may be considerably influenced by context (Bouton & Brooks, 1993; Bouton, 1993; 2002). For instance, Bouton (1993) has demonstrated that previously extinguished internal responses reemerge following a change in context, and has hypothesized that this is due to a failure to retrieve a memory of extinction in the new context. Interestingly, context can be both external (e.g., room) or internal (e.g., current emotional state, medication) (Otto, Smits, & Reese, 2004). We consider it likely that mindfulness creates an *internal context* that functions as an extinction reminder.

From this perspective, an *extinction reminder* develops as new associations become increasingly dominant through the repeated practice of mindfulness. By allowing emotions, thoughts, and sensations to be experienced without judgment, new associations to a particular stimulus are acquired (the emotion "just is," the thought "just is," the memory "just is"). For example, if a person had been assaulted in an elevator, the thought of being in an elevator may invoke significant anxiety. However, if the person changes his or her response to the thought or experience (e.g., observes rather than avoids the thought), the function or meaning of the thought or experience changes from something to be feared to something to be observed. Thus, elevators "just are," and with repeated mindful practice the new acquired response becomes increasingly dominant and is more likely to be activated than the prior fear-conditioned response. What is particularly exciting about this construct is that because the *context of mindfulness is internal,* these associations are always available.

EMOTION REGULATION

Assuming that mindfulness functions as an extinction reminder suggests that mindfulness may also influence the experience of emotions (Lynch *et al.,* in press). A number of theoretical accounts of emotion have described emotions as *response tendencies* (e.g., Gross, 1998) that have evolved over millennia to serve humans in their quest for survival (LeDoux, 2002). Lang and colleagues have organized these "tendencies" into two motivational response systems:

1. a defensive system, activated by threat, with a basic behavioral repertoire of withdrawal, escape, and attack and
2. an appetitive system, activated by contexts related to sustenance, procreation, and nurturance, with behaviors such as approach, ingestion, and caregiving (Lang, Bradley, & Cuthbert, 1998).

In addition, research has long demonstrated that different appraisal strategies can consistently affect the physiological, experiential, and expressive aspects of emotional responding (e.g., aversive arousal being appraised as "bad," or pleasant arousal being appraised as "good") (Lazarus, 1991; Lazarus, Speisman, Mordkoff, & Davidson, 1962).

Some theorists have emphasized the importance of meanings or appraisals of emotions as mediators of emotional response tendencies. In other words, if an aversive emotion is appraised as "bad," this may lead to avoidance of the emotion and associated aversive stimuli. However, the reverse may also be true; changing the emotion-linked response tendency may change the appraisal. For example, research examining reciprocal inhibition and behavioral exposure has long demonstrated that changing the behavioral response also alters the meaning of the cues eliciting the emotion (Wolpe, 1954).

Reciprocal inhibition is based on the hypothesis that it is impossible to feel two incompatible emotional responses concurrently. Thus, a person's maladaptive emotion can be weakened by repeated exposure to the stimulus that elicits it, while he or she concurrently engages in a response that is incompatible with the maladaptive emotion (e.g., observing the cues that elicit unjustified fear rather than automatically avoiding them). Indeed, Barlow (1988) has suggested that the crucial function of exposure therapy for anxiety disorders is the *prevention of natural action tendencies* associated with anxiety and *promotion of actions incompatible with anxiety*. We believe it likely that mindfulness functions much like reciprocal inhibition/behavioral exposure. Thus, with repeated practice, mindfulness promotes a response of observation (without judgment) with regard to emotion. As with reciprocal inhibition, changing the response tendency (e.g., from avoidance to *observing*) automatically changes the appraisal from "bad" to "just is" without having to directly modify, restructure, or reappraise the associated thought. Thus, a consequence of mindful observation is emotional experience that is less likely to be refired by associated appraisals.

Based on this analysis we would predict mindfulness to not necessarily reduce the overall intensity of the primary emotional response to any particular stimuli, but instead to reduce or eliminate secondary emotional responses that would lead to additional suffering. It may metaphorically be like the principle in physics that states: Any observation of an atomic particle simultaneously changes the momentum of the atomic particle (Gariorowicz, 1995). Thus, mindful *observation* may change what is observed (e.g., the emotional experience) merely through the process of observation itself.

REDUCING RULE-GOVERNED BEHAVIOR

In addition to changes in emotion-linked response tendencies and cognitive appraisals, mindfulness may be associated with reducing the predominance of rule-governed behavior with respect to private experience through nonjudgmental exposure (Lynch *et al.,* in press). Rule-governed behavior occurs in response to a verbal rule that specifies a relationship between a behavior (e.g., saying no to a friend) and a consequence (*that friend will not like me*). Some researchers have suggested that rule-governed behavior reduces the individual's sensitivity to actual contingencies operating in the environment (Hayes, Kohlenberg, & Melancon, 1989). For example, people who always say yes to friends' requests in response to the verbal rule that "If I say no, that person will no longer like me" will never learn that they can maintain a relationship even if they have to say no. Mindfulness teaches individuals to observe these rules as only thoughts that are not necessarily literally true. This is hypothesized to increase sensitivity to the current contingencies in the environment, allowing the opportunity for new learning. Indeed, some have suggested that the development of metacognitive awareness (i.e., seeing thoughts as thoughts, not as literally true) is the salient mechanism of change in cognitive therapy, rather than reappraisal of beliefs in schema (Teasdale, Segal, & Williams, 1995). In this context, mindfulness in DBT would *not* be predicted to reduce the frequency of distressing thoughts but instead decrease the power these thoughts have over subsequent behavior and emotions.

CONTROLLING FOCUS OF ATTENTION

As an acceptance-based strategy, mindfulness involves learning to control the focus of attention, not the object being attended to (e.g., observing a thought as a thought or an emotion as an emotion, without an attempt to change the thought or emotion). In contrast to behavioral change strategies, mindfulness entails acceptance of experience without attempts to alter, suppress, or avoid the experience. Indeed, there is growing empirical support linking psychopathology and chronic attempts to control private experience through inhibition, suppression, or avoidance (e.g., Cheavens et al., 2005; Bijttebier & Vertommen, 1999; Kruedelbach, McCormick, Schulz, & Grueneich, 1993; Lynch, Robins, Morse, & Krause, 2001; Rosenthal, Cheavens, Lejuez, & Lynch, in press), suggesting that acceptance may be an effective alternative approach.

The development of skills that enhance the ability to control attention has been postulated to lead to a "flexibility of attention" (Jersild, 1927; Posner, 1980). This increase in flexibility should promote the ability to shift focus among different aspects of one's experience (emotions, thoughts, sensations, sounds, textures, tastes, etc.) and lead to a more comprehensive awareness of present-moment experience. Attentional control has also been thought to foster nonelaborative awareness of thoughts, feelings, and sensations (Bishop et al., 2004), thereby inhibiting secondary elaborative processing. Teasdale and colleagues (1995) postulated that this ability to redeploy attention should be particularly effective at interrupting streams of thought unrelated to the current moment, thus freeing up the mental resources necessary to support further processing of present-moment experience. Attentional control also may be particularly useful for extreme emotional dysregulation. For example, research has shown that being able to disengage from emotional stimuli may reduce the tendency to experience negative affect (Ellenbogen, Schwartzman, Stewart, & Walker, 2002). Thus, DBT's mindfulness skills may prove useful for patients with extremely intense or reactive emotional experience by enhancing their ability to turn their attention from that which is not useful and attend to what is (Lynch et al., in press).

APPLICATION OF DBT WITH DEPRESSED OLDER ADULTS WITH COMORBID PERSONALITY DISORDERS

There is growing empirical evidence to suggest that elderly depressed individuals with comorbid personality disorders tend to have chronic depression and fail to respond to depression-specific interventions, including pharmacotherapy alone, depression-specific psychotherapy, and combined treatment (Rush, Hollon, Beck, & Kovacs, 1978; Rush & Thase, 1997; Thase & Howland, 1994). In a recent study, older depressed adults diagnosed with a personality disorder were almost four times more likely to experience maintenance or reemergence of depressive symptoms than those without personality-disorder diagnoses (Thase, 1996). Therefore, a novel approach toward treating this population is needed.

DBT was adapted for depressed older adults with personality disorders following the philosophy and protocol of standard DBT. The primary difference between standard DBT and DBT adapted for older adults with depression and personality disorders relates to the theoretical framework and the treatment targets. The theoretical framework was derived from clinical and empirical data from a recent study (Lynch et al., in preparation). This treatment-development study identified a unifying theoretical framework that conceptualized rigidity and low openness to experience as primary barriers to recovery. Essentially, our clinical experience suggested that successful treatment of older adults with personality disorders required a reduction in closed-minded behavior and an increase in flexible situational responding. We believe that being close-minded may reduce compliance with treatments, lower positive treatment expectancies, and reduce the effectiveness of other interventions (i.e., medications and other coping skills) by mitigating the possibility that reinforcers associated with the new experience are attended to. Thus, new learning is less likely to occur.

In terms of the treatment targets, both treatments prioritize life-threatening and therapy-interfering behaviors. However, DBT adapted for depression and personality disorders more specifically targets behaviors functionally related to depression and rigid maladaptive coping styles hypothesized to maintain existing depressive episodes and increase the probability of depressive relapse following remittance. For example, mindfulness specifically focuses on reducing emotional avoidance, thought suppression, and perfectionism/judgmental thinking, which have been shown in prior studies with older adults to be associated with negative mental health outcomes (Lynch et al., in preparation; Chang, 2000). As described earlier in this chapter, mindfulness skills are hypothesized to reduce literal beliefs in maladaptive thinking and encourage the development of metacognitive awareness (i.e., seeing thoughts as thoughts, not as literally true). The following is a case study that describes how mindfulness was utilized in the treatment of a patient who participated in the study of older adults with depression and comorbid personality disorders.

CASE STUDY

This case study is derived from an ongoing research project funded by the National Institute of Mental Health (PI: Lynch) examining the use of DBT to treat comorbid depression and personality disorders in older adults. The structure of this treatment is similar to standard DBT in that patients attend weekly individual and group therapy sessions and therapists attend weekly consultation team meetings.

Mrs. G was a 68-year-old retired female with a history of chronic depression. Her depression and feelings of anger toward others had increased ever since her husband left her 20 years ago. She had never remarried and thought that "it would not be worth it, because men can't be trusted." She met criteria for major depressive disorder, paranoid personality disorder, and obsessive-compulsive personality disorder. Results from diagnostic interviews indicated that she was suspicious and distrustful of others, held persistent grudges (e.g., she remains angry at a dentist who she believed did poor work on her teeth 10 years ago), read demeaning meanings into benign remarks by others or events, felt she was right despite what others said, reported that others had told her she was stubborn, and had a hard time throwing things away.

When Mrs. G presented at her first appointment she was very well dressed and appeared her stated age. Her affect was somewhat flat, and several times throughout the interview she questioned the credentials of the therapist or utility of the therapy. While she endorsed feeling sad, she did not spend a lot of time talking about herself. She talked more about her family and her ex-husband. She stated that she has three daughters and two grandchildren. She indicated that she had poor relations with all of her daughters and that they were all "users." She dismissed any strong desire to reconnect with them, although she admitted feeling lonely at times and that it would be nice to have her grandchildren around. She went on to say that her ex-husband had left her 20 years ago for a younger woman. She had been caught completely off guard and was furious with him for this. She reported feeling fairly bitter about the experience and was unsure whether she would ever recover from it. She had not dated or been interested in dating since the divorce. Finally, she talked about a stroke she had had 2 years ago that left her right side somewhat weak. She also talked about significant pain that she experienced from worsening arthritis. She said that between the stroke and the arthritis it had been very difficult to function. Her eldest daughter had asked her on several occasions to get help but she had refused, saying that "doctors are out to get your money." While she did not know if this therapy would be helpful, she was willing to give it a try.

Over the next few sessions, she described her life. She spent a lot of time talking about her marriage and how horrible she thought it was. The most devastating part, in her mind, was that she had been "fooled by him" because she had not known that he was cheating. When asked about her feelings surrounding this event, she could only say, "I don't know ... I'm just numb." However, she did believe that somehow she should be over this by now. It was clear that this was a devastating event and that she was having severe difficulty in accessing her feelings or thoughts surrounding it.

At around the fourth session, Mrs. G started attending the DBT skills training group, where she was first introduced to concepts related to mindfulness. Mindfulness practice typically occurred for 10 minutes prior to the beginning of each skills training group. Practices included nonjudgmental focus on breath, eating a raisin or pretzel mindfully, walking mindfully, counting breath, etc. Also included was participation in "sound ball," which is an exercise designed to practice participation without judgment: The idea is to "throw" a sound from one group member to another, to "catch" the sound, and then to throw a new sound to another member, etc., like a round-and-round game of catch. The goal during sound ball is to observe any self- or other-judgmental thoughts and to practice turning one's mind back to full participation. Another practice involves the skill of learning that it is not always necessary to respond to every sensation, urge, or emotion. For example, patients are instructed to sit and observe their breath, noticing when urges to scratch an itch occur and to "open and soften" to the irritating sensation, rather than "tensing or resisting." The idea is to breathe into the sensation and turn one's mind to one's breath, over and over again as needed. This practice is similar to what is called "urge surfing," as originally developed by Marlatt and Gordon (1985).

Each practice during skills group was directly linked to individual problems and/or a discussion of how a patient could use the skill to deal with depression or other emotional distress. For example, Mrs. G was asked whether there were activities she would like to be doing but was unable to do because of excessive worry or rumination. She pointed out that she used to like to read. The group skills trainer then discussed how the skill of attentional control in mindfulness could allow her to practice turning her mind back to her reading instead of giving up when distracted. That is, she was taught to first notice that she was no longer really reading, but instead ruminating, and then to turn her mind back to her chosen focus (i.e., the book) without giving herself a hard time.

At the end of each mindfulness practice, patients shared the observations they had experienced during it (e.g., "I noticed the urge to scratch getting more intense and then noticed that when I turned my mind back to my breathing the urge seemed to go away"). In addition, homework was assigned depending on what the practice was that day. For example, after teaching urge surfing, the therapist asked patients to pick three things that they found to be minor annoyances (e.g., going to the airport, making their lunch). Patients were then asked to look for activities during the week and practice noticing the urge to want to avoid the situation, to "breathe" into the sensation, and to nonjudgmentally turn their minds back to being fully present with their current "annoying" activity (e.g., being trapped in an airport due to inclement weather). The goal in this homework exercise was not to make the annoyance go away but to give up on trying to change or avoid a situation that at the moment was unchangeable (i.e., they are trapped in the airport whether they like it or not); in other words, to radically accept that they were in an annoying situation, to not give themselves a hard time about being there, to notice judgmental thoughts or thoughts that "this is unfair," and to turn their minds back to their chosen focus (their breath, their lunch, their book, etc.).

While training in mindfulness skills occurred in the group format, Mrs. G's individual therapist worked with her DBT consultation team in order to functionally examine Mrs. G's problem behaviors and develop treatment targets. For example, it was hypothesized that her suspiciousness functioned to reduce the likelihood of being hurt by others, that holding grudges functioned to validate the belief that she had been wronged, and that not confiding in others validated her beliefs that the world was an unsafe place (because she was never confronted with any contradictory evidence).

The individual therapist then used these treatment targets to guide instruction and practice of mindfulness skills. Mrs. G was encouraged to use the "what skills" and "how skills" of mindfulness in order to practice nonjudgmental participation in relationships with others. She was given behavioral assignments that focused on individual treatment targets such as mindfully observing judgmental thinking but not judging her judgment (in order to increase empathy and reduce grudges) and mindfully practicing prosocial behaviors (e.g., engaging in three practices of "chit-chat" per week while turning her mind from judgmental thoughts). In addition, metaphor was used to enhance learning. For example, it was pointed out to Mrs. G that her approach to relationships for the past 20 years had been like a person who desires to go swimming but instead walks endlessly around the swimming pool, never jumping in because she cannot be certain how deep the water is (i.e., she is afraid to participate because she is afraid of being hurt again).

The group skills training in mindfulness, in-session practice, and homework assignments continued throughout the remainder of the treatment, during which the therapist also focused on behavioral change strategies for other problems (e.g., improving interpersonal skills, use of self-soothing skills, cognitive restructuring). Mrs. G was encouraged to incorporate mindfulness into all aspects of her life, including times that she might be practicing other skills. Often mini-practices were done in session, or she was instructed to practice mindfulness in the waiting room prior to session in order to get accustomed to using this skill outside of session.

During session 12, she reported that she had used mindfulness skills to participate without judgment in singing hymns with other church members. Normally she would never have done this, as she felt it was "stupid." She used her mindfulness skills to notice thoughts that arose during the singing (e.g., "This is dumb," "Everyone is watching me") and to notice those thoughts as "just thoughts" while turning her mind back to participating in the singing. She noted that she had to "turn her mind" many times, and her therapist explained that this was part of practicing mindfulness in that context. During this session, the patient was encouraged to use the same technique when interacting with a potential date the following week. Here too, the goal was to notice her judgmental thoughts regarding her date but without trying to fix the thoughts, get rid of the thoughts, or dwell on the thoughts. Instead, as with the singing, she was encouraged to note the thoughts and then nonjudgmentally turn her mind back to her chosen focus; in this case, her date. Over time, the patient reported greater success with this. She indicated that she was able to note harsh judgments about others and say to herself, "Well, look at that," and then turn back to attending to the relationship instead of dwelling on the negative thought as she had in the past. Thus, she became more proficient at participating in relationships without judgment, maintaining attentional control, and reducing literal beliefs in rules governing her behavior (e.g., *if people are nice to you they want something*). She was also encouraged to practice mindfulness during moments of pleasure or times that positive emotions might be experienced (e.g., while playing with her new puppy, eating a delicious meal, taking a walk). Thus, although formal meditation practice was never prescribed, she was asked to develop a habit of looking for times in her life when she could practice being "in the moment."

Mrs. G continued to improve over the next several weeks. She had started incorporating mindfulness into her daily routine, which included a 15-minute mindful breathing practice every morning. Her relationships with her daughters started to improve as she became more proficient at noticing judgmental thinking. She began to date successfully and saw more of her grandchildren. By the end of treatment, she reported less critical thinking regarding others, improved social relations, improved social support from her family, less bitterness and hostility, and significantly less depression.

EMPIRICAL SUPPORT

According to guidelines established by Chambless and Hollon (1998), DBT is the only well-established treatment for BPD, having been evaluated in seven well-controlled randomized clinical trials (RCTs) conducted across four independent research teams (Koons *et al.*, 2001; Linehan, Armstrong, Suarez, Allmon, & Heard, 1991; Linehan *et al.*, 1999; Linehan *et al.*, 2002; Turner, 2000; Verheul *et al.*, 2003). It has also demonstrated efficacy in RCTs for eating-disordered individuals (Telch, Agras, & Linehan, 2001) and for chronically depressed older adults (Lynch, Morse, Mendelson, & Robins, 2003).

Lynch *et al.* (2003) investigated DBT as an augmentation of antidepressant medication for treatment of chronic depression in the elderly. Thirty-four (largely chronically) depressed individuals aged 60 and older were randomly assigned to receive 28 weeks of antidepressant medication (MED) or medication plus DBT skills training and scheduled telephone coaching sessions (MED + DBT). Results showed that 71% of MED + DBT patients were in remission (≤ 7 on the Hamilton Rating Scale for Depression) at posttreatment, in contrast to 47% of MED patients. At 6-month follow-up, 75% of MED + DBT patients were in remission compared with only 31% of MED patients, a statistically significant difference. Secondary analyses of the Lynch *et al.* (2003) study were conducted by Rosenthal, Cheavens, Compton, Thorp, and Lynch (2005). Interestingly, regression analyses indicated that *higher levels of thought suppression* were associated with higher depressive symptoms at follow-up after controlling for pretreatment severity and chronicity of depression. These findings, although preliminary, may prove particularly relevant for the utility of mindfulness training in DBT, which is designed to specifically target experiential avoidance.

PRACTICAL ISSUES

MYTHS

Mindfulness in the Buddhist traditions has been around for about 2500 years, but only in the past 20–25 years has there been an effort to incorporate aspects of this tradition into clinical practice. Therefore, more people than ever have been exposed to the concept of mindfulness, and they have undoubtedly formed impressions about what it is. As stated by Kabat-Zinn (1990), for those who come in with the attitude that "this won't work" or that "this is the right path for me/meditation is the answer," chances are that treatment will not be very helpful. Thus, it is imperative to work with patients early on to debunk any myths that they may have

TABLE 10.2 Myths about Mindfulness

Mindfulness: What It Is Not	Mindfulness: What It Is
A mystical or mysterious state of mind	Awareness; attention; choosing to focus on something without judgment
Blocking or pushing away a thought or feeling	Noticing a thought or feeling (then maybe choosing to focus on something else)
A quick fix; a cure-all	A part of living an effective life; often a first step in using other skills
A skill you learn all at once, in an "aha!" moment	A skill that requires much practice
Something that only Zen Buddhists do or can do	A capacity everyone has (whether you know it yet or not)
Having perfect focus; never getting distracted	Choosing to try to keep your focus even though distractions will probably arise again and again. Mindfulness involves noticing the wandering, and gently guiding your attention back to your chosen focus
A relaxation exercise	An exercise that involves full participation and acceptance of "what is," which at any given time could be a state of tension
An attempt to change yourself or the world	A nonjudgmental acceptance of reality (even though it may lead you to make changes)

about mindfulness that could hinder progress toward their goals. We have listed several myths about mindfulness from a DBT perspective in order to facilitate these discussions (see Table 10.2).

FORMAL SITTING PRACTICE

Sitting practice was originally proposed by Kabat-Zinn (1990) when he introduced mindfulness as a part of his mindfulness-based stress reduction (MBSR) program, which was later incorporated by Segal and colleagues (2002) into mindfulness-based cognitive therapy (MBCT). As described in Chapter 1 of this book, the formal sitting practice consists of daily sessions that last about 45 minutes and directs clients to focus their attention in various ways (on breathing, on bodily sensations, etc.). Formal practice by the therapist is emphasized so that he or she may teach mindfulness from direct experience and knowledge that will enhance interactions with the client. Mindfulness as a part of DBT does not emphasize formal practice for the therapist or the client. However, DBT often includes mindfulness practice at the beginning of each outpatient DBT skills training group. Typically this practice is tied to whatever skill is being taught that day in the group. For example, if interpersonal effectiveness is a focus for that particular group, then the practice that day might include pairing up group members and having each partner observe the shoes of the other. The goal of the practice is to observe and describe the other's shoes and to notice any judgmental thoughts that arise. Practices usually last 5 minutes, with 5 minutes of discussion and observation afterward. This brief duration allows practice of mindfulness skills while decreasing the likelihood of causing undue distress for severely disturbed clients. However, it is also important to note that a number of patients may choose to develop a formal mindfulness meditation practice during the course of DBT and this is not discouraged.

CHOSEN FOCUS VERSUS CHOICELESS AWARENESS

Since DBT mindfulness skills are taught during times when a patient might be depressed or emotionally dysregulated, the majority of mindfulness practices emphasize full attention on a chosen focus rather than choiceless awareness. *Choiceless awareness* is a type of meditative practice in which the participant is open and receptive to anything that crosses the field of awareness. For depressed or emotionally dysregulated patients, often what crosses the field of awareness are distressing or hopeless thoughts or emotions. Thus, DBT mindfulness practices, particularly during the early stages of therapy, involve choosing a focus and practicing directing the attention back to that focus. This improves a patient's ability to not be attached to distressing thoughts or emotions.

SUMMARY AND CONCLUSIONS

DBT is a comprehensive treatment intervention that integrates behavior therapy and validation strategies. In DBT there are four modules for teaching behavioral skills (mindfulness, emotion regulation, interpersonal effectiveness, and distress tolerance). Mindfulness is considered the core skill that is integrated throughout the other modules. Mindfulness is a state or quality of awareness that has been conceptualized in DBT as a type of behavior and distilled into specific and discrete skills. The idea is to identify treatment targets that guide specific mindfulness practices. These skills are taught and practiced in session and as homework assignments. The ultimate goal is for the patient to participate fully in life experience without judgment in order to facilitate the expression of effective and skillful behavior.

The ultimate goals of DBT mindfulness skills are to allow individuals to

- achieve a "wise" integration of emotional and rational thinking,
- increase conscious control over attentional processes, and
- experience a sense of unity or oneness with themselves, others, and the universe.

Interestingly, mindfulness may function to create a new sense of self (i.e., a *benign sense of self*) by deliteralizing harsh judgmental observations and imperatives.

We reviewed four overlapping principles or mechanisms that may be associated with mindfulness practice in DBT. First, based on recent animal research regarding classical conditioning (e.g., Bouton, 1993), we consider mindfulness to function as an *internal context* and *extinction reminder*. Second, we consider it likely that *changing the automatic response tendency* of an emotion influences the appraisal associated with the emotion automatically, without having to consciously restructure, reframe, or modify the appraisal. Third, we hypothesize that mindfulness enhances *attentional control,* which improves the ability to disengage from emotional stimuli. Fourth, we consider it likely that being an impartial witness to present-moment experience leads to the formation of new associations to thoughts, emotions, and sensations and *reduces literal belief in self-governing rules.* We hope that this excavation of the clinical and basic science literature provides a platform for continued exploration into this important topic. The identification of specific mechanisms of action for this important therapeutic tool may lead to more effective implementation of mindfulness and better treatment outcomes.

DBT is unique from other mindfulness approaches in that it is designed to be used with emotionally dysregulated patients. Thus, including the work done with BPD, we also presented recent work with older adults with chronic depression and comorbid personality disorder in this chapter. Future research needs to continue to examine the mechanisms associated with DBT mindfulness skills in patients with severe psychopathology.

ACKNOWLEDGMENTS

Manuscript preparation was supported by NIMH MH01614 to the first author (PI: Lynch) and by NIDA R01 DA017372-02S1 (PI: Lynch) to the second author.

REFERENCES

Baer, R. A. (2003). Mindfulness and behavior analysis. In K. S. Budd & T. F. Stokes (Eds.), *A small matter of proof: The legacy of Donald M. Baer.* Reno, NV: Context Press.
Barlow, D. (1988). *Anxiety and its disorders: The nature and treatment of anxiety and panic.* New York: Guilford.
Bijttebier, P., & Vertommen, H. (1999). Coping strategies in relation to personality disorders. *Personality and Individual Differences, 26,* 847–856.
Bishop, S. R., Lau, M., Shapiro, S., Carlson, L., Anderson, N. D., Carmody, J., et al. (2004). Mindfulness: A proposed operational definition. *Clinical Psychological Science Practice, 11,* 230–241.

Bouton, M. (1993). Context, time and memory retrieval in the interference paradigms of Pavlovian learning. *Psychological Bulletin, 114*, 80–99.

—— (2002). Context, ambiguity, and unlearning: Sources of relapse after behavioral extinction. *Biological Psychiatry, 52*, 976–986.

Bouton, M., & Brooks, D. (1993). Time and context effects on performance in a Pavlovian discrimination. *Journal of Experimental Psychology: Animal Behavior Process, 19*, 165–179.

Chang, E. C. (2000). Perfectionism as a predictor of positive and negative psychological outcomes: Examining a mediation model in younger and older adults. *Journal of Counseling Psychology, 47*, 18–26.

Chambless, D. L., & Hollon, S. D. (1998). Defining empirically supported therapies. *Journal of Consulting and Clinical Psychology, 66*, 7–18.

Chapman, A. L., & Linehan, M. M. (in press). Dialectical behavior therapy for borderline personality disorder. In M. Zanarini (Ed.), *Borderline personality disorder*. New York: Marcel Dekker.

Cheavens, J. S., Rosenthal, M. Z., Daughters, S. D., Novak, J., Kossen, D., Lynch, T. R., et al. (2005). An analogue investigation of the relationships among perceived parental criticism, negative affect, and borderline personality disorder features: The role of thought suppression. *Behaviour Research and Therapy, 43*, 257–268.

Craske, M. G., Barlow, D. H., & Meadows, E. (2000). *Mastery of your anxiety and panic (MAP-3): Therapist guide for anxiety, panic, and agoraphobia* (3rd ed.) San Antonio, TX: The Psychological Corporation.

Ellenbogen, M. A., Schwartzman, A. E., Stewart, J., & Walker, C. (2002). Stress and selective attention: The interplay of mood, cortisol levels, and emotional information processing. *Psychophysiology, 39*, 723–732.

Gariorowicz, S. (1995). *Quantum physics* (2nd ed.). New York: Wiley.

Gross, J. J. (1998). The emerging field of emotion regulation: An integrative review. *Review of General Psychology, 2*, 271–299.

Hanh, T. N. (1976). *Miracle of mindfulness*. Boston: Beacon.

Hayes, S., Kohlenberg, B., & Melancon, S. (1989). Avoiding and altering rule-control as a strategy of clinical intervention. In Hayes, S. (Ed.), *Rule-governed behavior: Cognition, contingencies and instructional control* (pp. 359–385). New York: Plenum.

Hayes, S., Strosahl, K. D., & Wilson, K. G. (1999). *Acceptance and commitment therapy: An experiential approach to behavior change*. New York: Guilford Press.

Jersild, A. T. (1927). Mental set and shift. *Archives of Psychology, 14*, 81.

Kabat-Zinn, J. (1990). *Full catastrophe living: Using the wisdom of your body and mind to face stress, pain and illness*. New York: Delacorte.

Koons, C., Robins, C. J., Tweed, J. L., Lynch, T. R., Gonzalez, A. M., Morse, J. Q., et al. (2001). Efficacy of dialectical behavior therapy in women veterans with borderline personality disorder. *Behavior Therapy, 32*, 371–390.

Kruedelbach, N., McCormick, R. A., Schulz, S. C., & Grueneich, R. (1993). Impulsivity, coping styles, and triggers for craving in substance abusers with borderline personality disorders. *Journal of Personality Disorders, 7*, 214–222.

Kunzmann, U., & Baltes, P. B. (2003). Wisdom-related knowledge: Affective, motivational, and interpersonal correlates. *Personality and Social Psychology Bulletin, 29*, 1104–1119.

Lang, P. J., Bradley, M. M., & Cuthbert, B. N. (1998). Emotion, motivation and anxiety: Brain mechanisms and psychophysiology. *Biological Psychiatry, 44*, 1248–1263.

Lazarus, R. S. (1991). *Emotion and adaptation*. New York: Oxford University Press.

Lazarus, R. S., Speisman, J. S., Mordkoff, A. M., & Davidson, L. A. (1962). A laboratory study of psychological stress produced by a motion picture film. *Psychological Monographs: General and Applied, 76*, 1–34.

LeDoux, J. (2002). *Synaptic self.* New York: Viking.

Linehan, M. M. (1993a). *Cognitive-behavioral treatment of borderline personality disorder.* New York: Guilford Press.

—— (1993b). *Skills training manual for treating borderline personality disorder.* New York: Guilford Press.

Linehan, M. M., Armstrong, H., Suarez, A., Allmon, D., & Heard, H. (1991). Cognitive-behavioral treatment of chronically parasuicidal borderline patients. *Archives of General Psychiatry, 48*, 1060–1064.

Linehan, M. M., Dimeff, L., Reynolds, S., Comtois, K., Welch, S., Heagerty, P., et al. (2002). Dialectical behavior therapy versus comprehensive validation plus 12 step for the treatment of opioid dependent women meeting criteria for borderline personality disorder. *Drug and Alcohol Dependence, 67*, 13–26.

Linehan, M. M., Schmidt, H., Dimeff, L., Craft, C., Kanter, J., & Comtois, K. (1999). Dialectical behavior therapy for patients with borderline personality disorder and drug dependence. *American Journal of Addictions, 8*, 279–292.

Lopes, P. N., Brackett, M. A., Nezlek, J. B., Schutz, A., Sellin, I., & Salovey, P. (2004). Emotional intelligence and social interaction. *Personality and Social Psychology Bulletin, 30*, 1018–1034.

Lynch, T. R., Chapman, A. L., Rosenthal, M. Z., Kuo, J. R., & Linehan, M. M. (in press). Mechanisms of change in dialectical behavior therapy: Theoretical and empirical observations. *Journal of Clinical Psychology.*

Lynch, T. R., Cheavens, J. S., Bronner, L. L., Beyer, J. L., Thorp, S. R., Rosenthal, M. Z., et al. (in preparation). *Treatment of depression in older adults with personality disorders: A pilot study of medication and dialectical behavior therapy.*

Lynch, T. R., Morse, J., Mendelson, T., & Robins, C. (2003). Dialectical behavior therapy for depressed older adults: A randomized pilot study. *American Journal of Geriatric Psychiatry, 11*, 33–45.

Lynch, T. R., Robins, C. J., Morse, J. Q., & Krause, E. D. (2001). A mediation model relating affect intensity, emotion inhibition, and psychological distress. *Behavior Therapy, 32*, 519–536.

Marlatt, G., & Gordon, J. (Eds.). (1985). *Relapse prevention: Maintenance strategies in the treatment of addictive behaviors.* New York: Guilford Press.

Otto, M. W., Smits, J. A. J., & Reese, H. E. (2004). Cognitive-behavioral treatment for anxiety disorders. *Journal of Clinical Psychiatry, 65*, 34–41.

Posner, M. I. (1980). Orienting of attention. *Quarterly Journal of Experimental Psychology, 32*, 3–25.

Rosenthal, M. Z., Cheavens, J. S., Compton, J. S., Thorp, S. R., & Lynch T. R. (2005). Emotion inhibition and treatment outcomes in late-life depression. *Aging and Mental Health, 9*, 35–39.

Rosenthal, M. Z., Cheavens, J. S., Lejuez, C. W., & Lynch, T. R. (2005). Thought suppression mediates the relationship between negative affect and borderline personality disorder symptoms. *Behaviour Research and Therapy, 43*, 1173–1185.

Rush, A. J., Hollon, S., Beck, A. T., & Kovacs, M. (1978). Depression: Must pharmacotherapy fail for cognitive therapy to succeed? *Cognitive Therapy and Research, 2*, 199–206.

Rush, A. J., & Thase, M. E. (1997). Strategies and tactics in the treatment of chronic depression. *Journal of Clinical Psychiatry, 58*(suppl 13), 14–22.

Segal, Z., Williams, G., & Teasdale, J. (2002). *Mindfulness-based cognitive therapy.* New York: Guilford Press.

Sternberg, R. J. (1998). A balance theory of wisdom. *Review of General Psychology, 2*, 347–365.

Teasdale, J. D., Segal, Z., & Williams, M. G. (1995). How does cognitive therapy prevent depressive relapse and why should attentional control (mindfulness) training help? *Behavior Research and Therapy, 33*, 25–39.

Telch, C. F., Agras, W. S., & Linehan, M. M. (2001). Dialectical behavior therapy for binge-eating disorder. *Journal of Consulting and Clinical Psychology, 69*, 1061–1065.

Thase, M. E. (1996). The role of axis II co-morbidity in the management of patients with treatment resistant depression. *Psychiatric Clinics of North America, 19*, 287–309.

Thase, M. E., & Howland, R. H. (1994). Refractory depression: Relevance of psychosocial factors and therapies. *Psychiatry Annals, 24*, 232–240.

Turner, R. (2000). Naturalistic evaluation of dialectical behavior therapy–oriented treatment for borderline personality disorder. *Cognitive and Behavioral Practice, 7*, 413–419.

Verheul, R., van den Bosch, L. M., Koeter, M. W., de Ridder, M.A., Stijnen, T., & van den Brink, W. (2003). Dialectical behavior therapy for women with borderline personality disorder. *British Journal of Psychiatry, 182*, 135–140.

Webster's Revised Unabridged Dictionary (1996, 1998). Plainfield, NJ: MICRA, Inc.

Wolpe, J. (1954). Reciprocal inhibition as the main basis of psychotherapeutic effects. *Archives of Neurology & Psychiatry, 72*, 205–226.

PART IV

APPLICATIONS
WITH MEDICAL
POPULATIONS

11

MINDFULNESS-BASED STRESS REDUCTION (MBSR) AS AN INTERVENTION FOR CANCER PATIENTS

MICHAEL SPECA AND LINDA E. CARLSON

*Department of Oncology, University of Calgary,
Department of Psychosocial Resources, Tom Baker Cancer Centre,
Alberta Cancer Board, Calgary, Alberta, Canada*

MICHAEL J. MACKENZIE AND MAUREEN ANGEN

*Department of Psychosocial Resources, Tom Baker Cancer Centre,
Alberta Cancer Board, Calgary, Alberta, Canada*

THEORETICAL AND CONCEPTUAL RATIONALE

CHALLENGES OF CANCER DIAGNOSIS AND TREATMENT

Cancer is a term denoting a spectrum of diseases characterized by uncontrolled and abnormal proliferation of cells in the body. It is the second leading cause of death in developed countries and accounts for 12.6% of deaths worldwide (World Health Organization, 2003). In the United States the lifetime risk of being diagnosed with cancer is 46% for men and 38% for women, and the overall 5-year relative survival rate is 64% (Ries *et al.*, 2004). Surgery, radiation therapy, and chemotherapy, used alone or in combination, remain the predominant forms of cancer treatment. Recently, specifically targeted therapies and biologic treatments offering the possibility of effective treatment with fewer side effects have been introduced (Baselga & Hammond, 2002; van der Poel, 2004). However, both cancer and its treatment often cause significant physical and psychological morbidity.

Symptoms of cancer and side effects of treatment are variable in range, severity, and duration and correspond to numerous factors such as the type, site, and extent of disease, as well as the specific course of treatment undertaken and the patient's preexisting health status and life adjustment. Upon diagnosis, many patients face daunting choices concerning treatment options, the prospect of debilitating and protracted treatment protocols, and an uncertain future. Cancer taxes the coping resources of patients and their families to the extreme, as burdens multiply, life routines are disrupted, and mortality is often unavoidably confronted. Understandably, emotional distress following receipt of a cancer diagnosis is common (Strain, 1998). Fears about the future, social role changes, and physical symptoms or functional losses resulting from the disease or its treatment contribute to an experience that is aptly described as an emotional roller coaster.

Among one large sample of cancer patients, researchers found a prevalence rate for psychological distress of 35% (Zabora, BrintzenhofeSzoc, Curbow, Hooker, & Piantadosi, 2001). The rate varied from 43.4% for lung cancer to 29.6% for gynecological cancers. Another study examined 215 randomly accessed new patients at three collaborating cancer centers for the presence of formal psychiatric disorder (Derogatis, Morrow, & Fetting, 1983). All were assessed by psychiatric interview and standardized psychological tests and classified according to the criteria of the *Diagnostic and Statistical Manual of Mental Disorders*, 3rd ed. (DSM-III) (American Psychiatric Association, 1980). Forty-seven percent of the patients received a DSM-III diagnosis. Approximately 68% of the psychiatric diagnoses were adjustment disorders and 13% were major affective disorders. Approximately 85% of those patients with a psychiatric condition were experiencing a disorder with depression or anxiety as the central symptom.

Although cancer-related posttraumatic stress disorder appears to be uncommon, a substantial minority of cancer patients do respond with intense fear, feelings of helplessness, or horror (Palmer, Kagee, Coyne, & DeMichele, 2004). Long after treatment is over, difficulties involving body image, fear of recurrence, and sexual problems are reported by a large proportion of survivors (Kornblith & Ligibel, 2003). Cancer often exacerbates stresses in key relationships, and there can be profound effects on spouses and other relatives and caregivers as normal life trajectories and day-to-day routines are disrupted (Pitceathly & Maguire, 2003). In addition to psychological distress or physical disability ensuing from cancer diagnosis, submitting to arduous treatment—though hoped-for outcomes cannot be guaranteed—often awakens the realization that control over one's own destiny is severely limited. Life priorities, purpose, and meaning are among the existential concerns that must be visited as cancer patients' sense of identity is renegotiated in the face of ongoing and sometimes dramatically life-altering circumstances.

APPLICABILITY OF MBSR TO THE CHALLENGES OF CANCER

Training in mindfulness meditation develops an individual's capacity for the intentional self-regulation of attention and harnesses this capacity toward the cultivation of insight regarding the basic processes whereby each of us construe identity and meaning from experience. The skills and understandings thus developed have broad applicability for the cancer patient, which includes but is not limited to the ostensible goal of stress reduction.

A fundamental aspect of mindfulness meditation that has particular salience for cancer patients is its here-and-now orientation, that is, the radical insistence on paying attention to present-moment reality. Some sources of stress for cancer patients relate to concerns about the past. These might include attributions about cancer causation or regrets about past decisions or life priorities. Other worries relate to future expectancies such as enduring pain or suffering or the loss of life itself. The practice of mindfulness provides a powerful antidote to these sources of stress, which lie in memory and imagination, by anchoring awareness in present experience and providing a relatively conflict-free sphere from within which the nature of disturbing thoughts and emotions can be examined, understood, and integrated. The aphorism "one day at a time" is commonly embraced by cancer patients as a keystone of their coping efforts, and by extension, the notion of applying mindfulness to moment-by-moment experience is sensible and often has initial intuitive appeal. However, a range of delightful insights, foreshadowed by germinal instances of calmness and clarity, await patients who develop the intention, commitment, and skill to put this principle into meaningful practice. During meditation, for example, the sense of time itself becomes plastic and each moment may serve as a timeless refuge from the inexorable demands of life as a cancer patient.

Many cancer patients' initial interest in mindfulness-based stress reduction (MBSR) derives from their belief that their cancer may have been caused by stress, emotions, or other psychological factors, though causal relationships between these factors and cancer initiation or progression have not been convincingly demonstrated (Fox, 1995; Tomatis, 2001). This is a notoriously difficult area of study, and in the absence of definitive science many patients are determined to explore these connections as they may relate to their own life situation. MBSR, with its holistic orientation to healing, provides a suitable framework for these patients' explorations as they experience and directly observe the relationships among their behavior, thoughts, and feelings and bodily responses. Didactically presented information also supports patient learning relating to physiologic functioning and the stress response cycle. Though MBSR promotes an orientation of nondoing, highlighting awareness of *being* rather than goal-oriented behavior, patients do often learn experientially how to moderate their level of arousal. This knowledge can assist them in managing symptoms of cancer and side effects of treatment such as pain and nausea that are exacerbated by anxiety (Mundy, DuHamel, & Montgomery, 2003) and allows them to assume an active and effective role in the healing process.

The frank uncertainty ushered into the lives of those affected by cancer and submission to the routines and rigors of cancer treatment pose an immense challenge to preexisting perceptions of personal control over one's future and one's own body. Perceived loss of control and reductions in one's sense of self-efficacy are strongly associated with psychological distress and diminished psychosocial adjustment to cancer (Lev, Paul, & Owen, 1999; Lowery, Jacobsen, & DuCette, 1994). MBSR addresses these factors in several ways. Adopting the attitude and practice of acceptance, that is, holding experience in awareness while relinquishing identification with the felt imperative to react or respond, frees patients from frantic and futile efforts to control the uncontrollable. Attachment to threatened aspects of the conditioned temporal sense of self, one's social identity, becomes leavened by a growing awareness that we embody deeper currents of being, whose sources we share with the larger universe. Facing and accepting the totality of one's experience as it is, including losses and limitations, provides an authentic grounding for expressions of personal choice and control that can serve to enhance self-efficacy in meaningful domains of experience such as self-care and relating to others.

A heightened awareness of mortality and death is typically evoked in persons diagnosed with cancer. But rather than being a wholly traumatic experience, cancer may be seen to precipitate a life transition offering the possibility of both positive and negative psychosocial outcomes. Many people diagnosed with cancer describe personal growth consequent to their illness experience (Cordova & Andrykowski, 2003). Those impacted by challenging life events like cancer often perceive associated benefits such as improved relationships, greater appreciation of life, and increased resilience. Such benefit finding has piqued much recent research interest (Katz, Flasher, Cacciapaglia, & Nelson, 2001; Lechner et al., 2003; Schulz & Mohamed, 2004; Sears, Stanton, & Danoff-Burg, 2003). Studies of a cognitive-behavioral stress management intervention, for example, have demonstrated increases in benefit finding over the course of treatment that were associated with other beneficial outcomes in cancer patients (Antoni et al., 2001; Cruess et al., 2000; McGregor et al., 2004). Because the practice of mindfulness involves acceptance and honest acknowledgment of things as they are, yet encourages us to experience them with a beginner's mind, that is, devoid of preconceptions and expectations, the immanence of infinite possibilities inherent in each moment of life becomes more apparent. A range of options for perceiving, understanding, and responding to one's life situation can be apprehended that heighten one's sense of both freedom and responsibility for choices made. The following poem, written by one of our MBSR program participants, provides an illustration of how exquisite awareness may combine with the freshness of perspective characterized by the beginner's mind to transmute seemingly mundane experience into something more sublime.

Tea Ceremony

Shaun Hunter

> *They serve tea at the cancer centre*
> *in fine china cups*
> *with scalloped edges*
> *and delicate pink flowers*
> *like the cups your grandmother used*
> *long ago*
> *when you were just*
> *starting out*
> *on your life*

> *This long dark hallway of cancer*
> *feels like the end*
> *of everything*
> *you wait*
> *keep your eyes down*
> *tuck into the ache of your self*
> *wrap your body*
> *in the cold comfort*
> *of fear*

> *You will hear the tea trolley before*
> *you see it*
> *the fine gentle music*
> *of tea cups and silver spoons*
> *rattling on saucers*

> *Take the offered cup*
> *taste the tea as if*
> *for the first time*

> *This is your new life*

> *Drink it in*

Several other features of mindfulness practice are pertinent to those facing life-altering circumstances associated with cancer. Though for many patients life will never return to what had been considered normal, sustained practice of mindfulness leads to an appreciation that change and impermanence are ubiquitous in consciousness and in our lives generally. Practitioners develop the capacity to accept even unwelcome change with greater equanimity and thus reduce the dimension of suffering associated with pain and illness. They also learn to question the nature of the self and the degree to which it can be solely identified with the process and content of shifting thoughts and feelings. For some, burgeoning curiosity about the nature of the self leads to greater awareness of the interconnectedness of all beings and the development of insights regarding purpose and meaning in life that relate to an appreciation of the self as part of a larger whole.

Though MBSR does not explicitly emphasize the strengthening of cancer patients' social support networks, as do some models of psychotherapeutic intervention, mutual understanding and meaningful bonds do develop between group members out of their shared experience. The practice of loving-kindness meditation fosters the strengthening of social bonds both within the group and in the patient's preexisting social context. If opportunities for continued mindfulness practice extending beyond the initial program involvement are afforded to participants, such as through an ongoing drop-in group, mutual support among participants is further facilitated.

COMPARISON WITH OTHER TREATMENT APPROACHES

Several psychosocial interventions that effectively ameliorate the distress or improve the quality of life of cancer patients have been developed. These interventions have been thoroughly reviewed several times over the past decade (Andersen, 1992; Blake-Mortimer, Gore-Felton, Kimerling, Turner-Cobb, & Spiegel, 1999; Bottomley, 1996; 1997; Cunningham, 1995; 2000; Fawzy, 1999; Fawzy, Fawzy, Arndt, & Pasnau, 1995; Fawzy, Fawzy, & Canada, 1998; Fobair, 1997; Greer, 1995; Iacovino & Reesor, 1997; Meyer & Mark, 1995; Newell, Sanson-Fisher, & Savolainen, 2002; Schneiderman, Antoni, Saab, & Ironson, 2001; Trijsburg, van Knippenberg, & Rijpma, 1992). Though the methodology of many trials has been less than optimal, most reviewers have concluded that psychosocial interventions can effectively decrease distress and improve the quality of life of cancer patients.

Cunningham (1999) has identified a hierarchy of different types of therapy, based on increasingly active participation by the recipient.

These five types are:

1. information providing (psychoeducation),
2. emotional support,
3. behavioral training in coping skills (cognitive-behavioral therapy),
4. psychotherapy, and
5. spiritual/existential therapy.

Most of these modalities have been provided in both individual and group formats. Interventions are usually targeted to one of three periods across the illness trajectory: at diagnosis or pretreatment; immediately post-treatment or during extended treatment (such as radiotherapy or chemo-therapy) and follow-up; and during latter phases of illness (Schneiderman et al., 2001). Certain modes of treatment have been shown to be more efficacious during one or more of these time periods. For example, psycho-education may be most effective early on, when patient information needs are high. However, for later-stage adjustment with more advanced disease, group support may be more effective, while cognitive-behavioral techniques such as relaxation, stress management, and cognitive coping may be most useful during extended treatments (Bottomley, 1997; Fawzy, 1995). All of these modes of intervention are supported by research demonstrating their efficacy, although the bulk of the research is in the area of supportive and cognitive-behavioral interventions.

MBSR may be considered to fit into this scheme both at the level of group training in a specific set of coping skills and also as a spiritual/existential therapy in that it attunes participants to the quality of moment-by-moment lived experience and the interdependence of all worldly manifestations. Trials directly comparing MBSR with other treatment modalities for cancer patients have not been reported; thus, an evidence base for drawing distinctions concerning the differential effectiveness of MBSR is not available. Comparing MBSR with other validated psychosocial treatments for cancer patients would be a useful avenue for future research.

SPECIAL CONSIDERATIONS IN TEACHING MBSR TO CANCER PATIENTS

The timing of a cancer patient's enrollment in an MBSR program is an important parameter to consider in both research and clinical contexts. Whether patients are referred by health care providers or are self-referred, it is advisable to review with the patient how participation in the program might be affected by current or anticipated health states especially in relation to the treatment plan. This would typically take place during a pre-intervention interview at which prospective participants are introduced to the program format, evaluated for motivation and suitability, and assessed psychometrically. If patients are to be included as subjects in a research protocol, informed consent may be obtained at this time.

Undertaking MBSR during the course of a demanding chemotherapy regime may be overly taxing for some patients, and treatment schedules that interfere with MBSR program attendance may be difficult or impossible to alter. Notwithstanding inclusion and exclusion criteria relating to a specific research protocol, it may be preferable to defer program initiation to the postchemotherapy time frame, when patient vitality typically rebounds. Each patient may be considered on a case-by-case basis. For those patients whose motivation is high and whose life circumstances permit it, cancer treatment and MBSR training may proceed concurrently. Indeed, many cancer patients take an extended sick leave from work during treatment, and this time away from work may represent their best opportunity to immerse themselves in learning new skills. With appropriate tailoring of expectations and concern for safety, even vulnerable or debilitated patients are able to meaningfully engage in MBSR training. Similar considerations apply specifically to the yoga component of MBSR practice. Moving with awareness, acknowledging current limitations, and accepting responsibility to ensure one's own safety are fundamental expectations that are clearly communicated to all participants. MBSR instructors typically assist patients to modify standard yoga *asanas* (i.e., postures) as necessary in ways that are tailored to individual circumstances and abilities. Patients are encouraged to discuss any doubts they may have regarding their suitability for MBSR training with their treating physician. For some, MBSR may be most helpful in the posttreatment phase, when patients are reconstituting their lives and may wish to alter aspects of their lifestyle to promote health (Kabat-Zinn, Massion, Hebert, & Rosenbaum, 1998).

Cancer often significantly and adversely affects members of cancer patients' families. So, at patient request and when adequate resources are available, we at our center sometimes allow family members or other close confidants to enroll in our MBSR groups along with the patient. This is considered only if they demonstrate sufficient motivation and are willing to commit to full and equal participation. In the first class, the participants, including those without cancer, are each invited to identify the unique aims and hopes that brought them to enroll in the program.

Given that many patients' initial interest in MBSR derives from their belief that their cancer may have been caused by stress, emotions, or other psychological factors, it is frequently useful and necessary to respond to this issue forthrightly during the initial interview. Gaps in understanding and limitations in the state of knowledge concerning links between psychosocial factors and cancer incidence or progression can be readily acknowledged, and patients who are interested in learning more can be directed to reliable sources of relevant and valid information.

There are questions concerning which cancer patients are likely to benefit from an MBSR program. Preexisting personality traits may influence recruitment, compliance, and the ability to use meditation to ease stress and mood symptoms (Bishop, 2002). The effectiveness of the MBSR program is likely to depend, at least in part, on how useful patients find the particular techniques within the program structure. In all likelihood, the most useful aspects will vary from person to person depending on individual needs, background, and personality. Kabat-Zinn, Chapman, and Salmon (1997) found that patients with anxiety disorders displayed either a cognitive or a somatic orientation that corresponded to preferences for particular meditation techniques. This observation points to the likelihood that some program components may be more useful for a given patient or subgroup of patients than others. Teaching experience and knowledge of these factors may assist instructors to optimize MBSR program fit and adherence for each participant.

CASE STUDY

INTRODUCTION

Although MBSR has been shown to benefit cancer patients as assessed with validated psychometric instruments, the range of subjective benefits experienced by program participants has not been well documented. The following Case Study was developed as part of a larger qualitative research investigation conducted at the Tom Baker Cancer Centre in Calgary, Alberta. Interviews were held with a number of cancer patients who had completed an 8-week MBSR program offered through the Centre's Department of Psychosocial Resources. The case of Sharon was selected for presentation because it illustrates a number of pertinent issues common to the application of MBSR in the context of cancer treatment. It is formatted as a qualitative research report in which thematically categorized research findings are integrated with the subjectively reported experience of the patient in her own words. (See Chapter 1 in this volume for a more detailed discussion of the MBSR protocol.)

PERSONAL BACKGROUND AND DISEASE CONTEXT

Sharon is a 43-year-old married woman with two children, ages 12 and 14. She works as both an editor and a writer. Sharon was diagnosed with a stage IIA, Clark level IV, 1.73-mm thick malignant melanoma in October 2000. Melanoma, which means "black tumor," is a malignant mole, or skin cancer. It is among the most malignant of all cancers and can spread to nearly every organ and tissue of the body. The incidence rates of malignant melanoma have increased dramatically in recent decades. More than half of all malignant melanomas are diagnosed in women, and the risk of being diagnosed increases with age.

Sharon underwent surgical excision of her melanoma. It is possible that this treatment was curative; however, given the depth and thickness of her tumor, her prognosis can be considered guarded. Once the melanoma has recurred or reaches the lymphatic and blood vessels in the dermis, cure is unlikely, but a long period of quiescence may be achieved by surgery, immunoaugmentive therapy, or other experimental approaches. It is therefore difficult to determine any individual melanoma patient's prognosis with certainty. Living under this threat and uncertainty is a central challenge for melanoma patients. Sharon began the 8-week MBSR program approximately 10 months after her diagnosis and surgical treatment. Part of her motivation for enrolling in the program was that she did not feel her cancer experience was completely over, even though she viewed her prognosis as hopeful and her surgery had been completed. She believed that her initial cancer experience marked a turning point in her life that required her to change aspects of how she had been living. She was also interested in exploring what she could do to prepare in the event she had to deal with another crisis, such as a recurrence of her cancer. After completing the 8-week program, Sharon began attending weekly drop-in sessions open to cancer patients who wish to continue their practice in a group context. She had been practicing meditation for almost 3 years by the time of her interview for this Case Study. She had not engaged in previous meditation prior to enrolling in the 8-week MBSR program, with the exception of a yoga class she had taken in the early 1980s. At the time of the interview for this Case Study, Sharon had not participated in any other support program in relation to her cancer diagnosis, treatment, or recovery.

METHODOLOGY

This qualitative research followed an approach based upon a grounded theory model. A semistructured interview was administered on site at the Tom Baker Cancer Centre. The interview was tape-recorded with permission of the participant. The data were analyzed using QSR N6 software (QSR International, 2002) to identify themes the patient brought forward concerning the effects of meditation in her life.

FINDINGS

Three major themes capturing meaningful aspects of Sharon's MBSR experience emerged through analysis of her interview data. These were themes of: group dynamics, self-regulation, and personal change.

Group Dynamics

Group dynamics refers to the interaction between the group members during the meditation class and any interactions they have outside of class. These social relationships buffer individual perceptions of stressors, provide resources to modify the environmental demand, and help manage individual affective responses (Roberts, Cox, Shannon, & Wells, 1994). Cancer diagnosis may challenge the integrity of one's ideas about oneself and long-held concepts about one's life trajectory and relationships. Patients often confront existential issues, such as trying to make sense of the illness in their lives and confronting issues around death and dying (Spiegel, 1999). In this context, Sharon describes her initial experience of cancer as quite isolating: "When you're in your circle of friends, most people don't want to talk about it. Even in the eye of the storm, people don't want to talk about it. It scares people. So you don't talk about it. When you do want to talk about it, nobody is there to talk. There aren't a lot of outlets."

Regarding group participation, Sharon related that it was extremely important to be in a room full of others who, like herself, were coming to terms with living and surviving with cancer. Being together with others sharing a similar diagnosis in a supportive context creates a sense of community that alleviates the deep sense of isolation commonly experienced by patients with cancer (Spiegel, Bloom, & Yalom, 1981). These group settings empower patients by providing a sense of connection and shared meaning (Fobair, 1997): "It's a very powerful experience sitting in a circle of people who have been affected by cancer. I find in it a very profound understanding because we all share a similar experience. We all know what it means to have cancer and live with it. You've had this deep experience and there are others who have had a similar experience. You're constantly reminded of your own humanity and the humanity of others."

Participants share not only in their cancer diagnoses but also in the practice of meditation. By listening to and observing one another, patients share in the discovery of solutions to common dilemmas and thus increase their repertoire of effective coping skills (Spiegel *et al.*, 1981). In Sharon's words: "That's what is really special about the group, hearing about what people are coping with. You can listen to someone talk about their suffering and you can accommodate that. I'm really happy I have an opportunity to know about those things."

The most effective group strategies involve accepting cancer as a diagnosis and facing the problems related to cancer directly (Nezu *et al.*, 1999) Patients establish meaningful social support, confront fears, express their emotions, seek control over what can be improved, and let go of what cannot be controlled (Spira, 1998). Handled well, such confrontation enhances patients' abilities to cope, manage symptoms, and reorder priorities in life (Spiegel, 2001). Upon completing the 8-week program Sharon immediately joined an ongoing weekly MBSR drop-in class intended to facilitate continued practice by program graduates. Because of their continuity over time, such groups provide an opportunity to build greater intimacy and cohesion.

Sharon felt that the drop-in group was extremely welcoming toward her, at a time when she was feeling isolated: "Within a couple of weeks of my first time in the group, Ed [fellow participant, now deceased] presented me with a pin. It was a really overwhelming experience. It was very moving. I had been afraid of coming up to this building for a long time. All of a sudden, I was being welcomed to this building. That was quite beautiful. The next week, Dawn [fellow participant] passed out invitations to her party. I couldn't believe it! You didn't have to do anything for this group to accept you. You just had to show up, which was quite exceptional and very different from any other group experience I'd been involved in."

Self-Regulation

Self-regulation refers to patients' regulation of their own behaviors to maximize well-being. It requires patients to pay attention to the consequences of their behavior and make corrective adjustments as needed. When self-regulation breaks down, patients' habitual behaviors, which produce poor results, are chronically repeated. A case can be made that self-regulation is a crucial mechanism through which the changes in psychological and physical health produced by MBSR interventions are effected (Shapiro & Schwartz, 2000).

Sharon describes the process of self-regulation in terms of creating space in her life and responding mindfully to events rather than reacting habitually or with volatility. The most important step in breaking free from stress reactivity is to be mindful of what is happening in each moment. This allows us to see our life situation more clearly and to influence the level of stress associated with our habitual reactions in difficult situations (Kabat-Zinn, 1990). As Sharon says: "You can sit in silence and get some space from your own life. It's not about this whole act/react thing we talk about in class. Kabat-Zinn shares [that] you can actually breathe and get space from what's going on. I'm not sure I know how to use that tool very effectively yet. I've only experienced that in a few moments. I'm not at the stage where I can sit down and just invoke space for 20 or 30 minutes. I can get a sense of it enough that I'm committed to go the next day and sit back down. For a few moments, I can sit and not be overwhelmed. That's a valuable tool."

Sharon stated that she does not believe her meditation practice is a cure for her cancer. She is cognizant of the limited scientific evidence supporting the ability of complementary therapies to cure cancer and is realistic in her use of the MBSR program as an adjunctive, rather than as a replacement to conventional care (Balneaves, Kristjanson, & Tataryn, 1999). In her own words: "You can make your life better, but I've never been under the illusion I'm cured of cancer. Do I think my chances are better because I'm eating differently, meditating and doing yoga? Yes, I think my chances are good. Am I going to cure it? I don't think so. You just have to live with that."

Sharon conveyed that she thinks of her time spent meditating, in some ways, as an investment in her life. Meditation in this framework is practiced as a *way of being* rather than as a technique. It emphasizes bringing mindfulness to all aspects of life experience, including physical illness, emotional turbulence, and the activities of everyday living (Kabat-Zinn et al., 1998): "I think of this as an investment. I want to be able to draw on it when I need it. It could be in an hour or it could be in 10 years. I don't want to lose the tools. The more it becomes part of what I do, the better I get at using these tools. I'll know what to do and I'll draw on the reserve I've been investing."

A key to Sharon's ability to self-regulate is her capacity to integrate the practice into daily life. In this respect she has taken a flexible approach toward maintaining her practice in her home environment: "I live in a house with three other people. There's not always silence. There's not always space. When there is, I take advantage of it. If there isn't, I don't fight it. I accept that it will change over the years. That's where I'm at right now."

Patients with chronic medical conditions who participate in MBSR are able to effect positive changes in their physical and mental health status as a result of an increased ability to cope with stress, pain, and illness (Reibel, Greeson, Brainard, & Rosenzweig, 2001). This capacity to respond mindfully to stress develops during meditation practice (Kabat-Zinn, 1990). Through the repeated experience of recognizing the patterns of one's mental processes, patients' realize their role as writer-director of inner dramas and discover an element of choice in the perception of reality. Subsequently, patients are less at the mercy of mental responses and are therefore less stereotyped in reactions and behavior (Kutz, Borysenko, & Benson, 1985).

Personal Change

Cancer patients may enroll in an MBSR program seeking an experience of transformative change. Meaningful changes in patients' perceptions and behavior may begin before, during, or after MBSR program participation. Changes specifically associated with enhanced health and well-being are facilitated by meditation (Bonadonna, 2003). Sharon had made a conscious choice to change certain aspects of her life prior to her enrollment in the MBSR program: "I'd come through the immediate crisis of my diagnosis. I was looking at what I could be doing in the event I had to deal with another crisis. I didn't feel it was completely over, although my prognosis was good and the surgery was finished. It was such a huge life change. I decided I wasn't going to walk back into my old life."

Meditation provides a powerful psychological framework and accessible methods for coming to terms with one's personal situation in ways that provide comfort, meaning, and direction in times of high stress and uncertainty (Kabat-Zinn et al., 1998). In the MBSR program, Sharon found new ways of perceiving her life situation: "In reading Kabat-Zinn's book Full Catastrophe Living, there were ideas he was putting forth that certainly echoed with my own experience of cancer diagnosis. The whole concept of the mind and body and trying to get a handle on what causes stress and how you can deal with it made a lot of sense. This whole notion of embracing change as the constant, I'd never really thought of it that way before."

The practice of mindfulness encourages a willingness to look deeply into all emotional states and life circumstances as they arise. This emphasis on self-observation can help people to perceive conditioned patterns of behavior more clearly (Kabat-Zinn, Lipworth, & Burney, 1985). In this context MBSR can assume an especially meaningful role for cancer patients. Through the developing capacity for self-observation, Sharon began to make distinctions between her more scholastically based knowledge and her more experiential or intuitive knowledge: "I'm a thinking person and spent a lot of my life in school. I don't know that it ever really turned the lens on my own life. In the book and in this program were tools I knew when I was diagnosed with cancer that I didn't have. I didn't know what to do. These are tools I now have and there are more I haven't even discovered."

Paying attention to the breath and bodily sensations develops a sense of coherence between mental and physical modes of experiencing. Mindfulness is a practice that dissolves the discontinuity we may perceive between mind and body, awareness and its objects, and allows us to yield to an experience of wholeness (Bonadonna, 2003). Sharon appreciates this crossover between the psychological component of the program and its physical embodiment: "The ideas actually have a physical embodiment. That's what is so powerful about this—you don't just read it. It's about how you take those ideas and actually do what you have to do. It's very simple what you have to do. You have to sit, you have to be quiet and you have to listen to your breathing. That is really beautifully simple."

Awareness is the critical element in learning how to free ourselves from stress reactions (Kabat-Zinn, 1990). Sharon has a means of meta-awareness, or reflecting upon herself, that she felt she did not have previously: "I'm much more aware of how I'm moving through this life. Organizing things is a form of control. I was under the impression I could control most things. That was completely blown out of the water with a cancer diagnosis, which left me paralyzed. I didn't know what else I could rely on. Incorporating this program in my life has given me opportunity and time to reflect on what I'm doing."

Sharon relates that her first thought of coming to the Cancer Centre was one of fear. This fear has been transformed, in part due to the program, which suggests that responding mindfully to change and loss will make a difference in the perception of stressful events, and that having cancer can become an event rather than the defining characteristic of the patient (Coker, 1999). In the process, MBSR programs can evoke a greater sense of partnership in patients undergoing medical treatments (Kabat-Zinn *et al.*, 1998). Sharon now finds being a part of the Centre an important thing: "I was afraid to come into this building. This was like a leper colony. I've lived in the city a long time and you just do not want to come into the Cancer Centre. When I had to come up here on a weekly basis for this group, I didn't think I could do it. I've found since that, in fact, it's a very positive experience. It's a constant reminder of the fragility of things."

Sharon's perspective has even changed in regard to her treatment: "Now I just come up here for my follow-ups and I don't really care. I just walk in looking forward to a cup of tea and a cookie. I realized not everyone up here was the bearer of bad news."

From the perspective of mindfulness, any situation, even illness, provides an opportunity to learn and grow. Examining one's lived experience with awareness and acceptance can lead to insights that significantly transform its meaning. Sharon has made this transformation in viewing her cancer as a motivating force: "The way I look at cancer is that once you get through the awfulness, it's a very powerful motivator to live your life. I'm grateful I can come up here and be reminded of that."

Trevino (1996) suggests that worldviews are the essential framework in which our experiences are rooted and through which we develop our basic perceptions and understandings of the world. The individual is exposed to a variety of different experiences, both generally, through one's culture, and specifically, via unique experiences. Through the practice of mindfulness, each individual begins to hold his or her unique constellation of thoughts and experiences in new ways, at both general and specific levels. This initiates practitioners into a process of self-examination that stems from their own expertise and self-witnessing, without having to appeal to an ideological or cultural shift in perspective (Kabat-Zinn & Santorelli, 1999).

For example, as Sharon continues to practice, her orientation remains largely secular. It should be noted that although mindfulness is a practice derived from a philosophical-religious tradition, specifically Buddhist meditation, its practice requires no particular religious orientation or belief system (Roth & Creaser, 1997): "The word 'spirituality' is a loaded one. It's one of those words people are tossing about daily. I have trouble talking about myself in terms of that. Definitely there is a lot in the material that's been presented that addresses those kinds of concerns and interests."

From the outset of developing this model, Kabat-Zinn endeavored to take the heart of mindfulness practice into the world in a way that was not locked into a culturally bound framework that made it impenetrable to the vast majority of people, who were nevertheless suffering (Kabat-Zinn *et al.*, 1998). Sharon relates to the program because of its nondoctrinal stance: "It appeals to me because it's not doctrinal. I have a real resistance to that. To someone telling me I have to believe this or that. This seems much more open-ended. It's wise, there's this universality about it. You don't have to come from a certain faith tradition to take some of these things away."

Within the MBSR program, patients work with the body, breath, and mind and their accompanying physiological, psychological, affective, and spiritual states (Moore, 1998). This leads to a participatory learning environment in which the fundamental constituents of what it is to be human are cultivated directly by the client according to her or his own innate capacities. Within the context of the practice, clients access their own inner resources for learning, growing, and healing (Kabat-Zinn, 1996). As Sharon continues to practice, now 3 years after her initial experience, she feels she continues to grow.

REVIEW OF EMPIRICAL SUPPORT

The literature investigating the effects of MBSR on cancer patients is in an incipient stage. Although some of the patients with mixed medical diagnoses treated at the University of Massachusetts Medical Center had cancer diagnoses, the first study to appear specifically with cancer patients was published by our group in 2000 (Speca, Carlson, Goodey, & Angen, 2000) and remains the only randomized controlled trial (RCT) reported in the literature. Patients in this study had a wide range of cancer diagnoses of all stages and were not restricted in terms of treatment-related variables. Compared with control subjects, participants in the intervention group had significantly less overall mood disturbance, tension, depression, anger, or concentration problems and more vigor following the intervention. They also reported fewer symptoms of stress, including peripheral manifestations of stress, cardiopulmonary symptoms of arousal, central neurological symptoms, gastrointestinal symptoms, habitual stress behavioral patterns, anxiety/fear, and emotional instability compared with those still waiting for the program. Results of a 6-month follow-up, including both experimental and wait-list participants who had by then completed the program, indicated a maintenance of these gains over the follow-up period (Carlson, Ursuliak, Goodey, Angen, & Speca, 2001).

The next study conducted by our group was a pre-post MBSR intervention study with early-stage breast and prostate cancer patients who were all at least 3 months posttreatment. Outcomes included biological measures of immune, endocrine, and autonomic function, in addition to similar psychological variables as previously (Carlson, Speca, Patel, & Goodey, 2003; 2004). Briefly, 59 and 42 patients were assessed preintervention and postintervention, respectively. The 59 patients attended a median of eight of a possible nine sessions over the 8 weeks (range 1–9). They also practiced at home as instructed, reporting an average of 24 minutes/day of meditation and 13 minutes/day of yoga over the course of the 8 weeks. Significant improvements were seen in overall quality of life, symptoms of stress, and sleep quality. Although there were no significant changes in the overall number of lymphocytes or cell subsets, T cell production of interleukin (IL)-4 increased and interferon gamma decreased, whereas natural killer cell production of IL-10 decreased. These results are consistent with a shift in immune profile from one associated with depressive symptoms to a more normal profile. Significantly, IL-4 has been identified as potentially having antitumor activity against breast cancer, and these levels increased more than threefold postintervention (Carlson et al., 2003). Hormone profiles also shifted preintervention to postintervention, with fewer evening cortisol elevations found post-MBSR and some normalization of abnormal diurnal salivary cortisol profiles occurring (Carlson et al., 2004). This is very significant given that abnormal profiles have been associated with shorter survival time in breast cancer patients (Sephton, Sapolsky, Kraemer, & Spiegel, 2000).

In other work with biological outcomes, an innovative study by Kabat-Zinn's group looked at the effects of combining a dietary intervention with MBSR on levels of prostate specific antigen (PSA), an indicator of the level of oncological activity, in men with prostate cancer (Saxe et al., 2001). They found that the combined program resulted in a slowing of the rate of PSA increase in a pilot sample of 10 men, and are currently conducting a larger RCT to verify this significant impact on such an important marker of biochemical recurrence in prostate cancer.

Our recent work has focused on sleep problems in cancer patients and how MBSR may be beneficial in treating this common problem in them. Similar to what others have reported, we found a very high proportion of our cancer patients with disordered sleep (~85%) in a general sample attending the MBSR program. In these patients, sleep disturbance was closely associated with levels of self-reported stress and mood disturbance, and when stress symptoms declined over the course of the MBSR program, sleep also improved (Carlson, Speca, Goodey, & Garland, 2004). Improvements were seen on the Pittsburgh Sleep Quality Index subscales of subjective sleep quality, sleep efficiency, and hours of sleep. On average, sleep hours increased by $\frac{1}{2}$ to 1 hour per night.

A study by Shapiro, Bootzin, Figueredo, Lopez, and Schwartz (2003) also examined the relationship between participation in an MBSR program and sleep quality and efficiency, but it did not find statistically significant relationships between participation in an MBSR group and sleep quality. They did, however, find that those who practiced more informal mindfulness reported feeling more rested.

Other groups are also applying modifications of the MBSR program to cancer patients, and beginning to present results at scientific meetings. For example, Bauer-Wu and Rosenbaum (2004) have adapted MBSR for individual use in isolated hospitalized bone-marrow transplant patients, finding immediate effects on levels of pain and anxiety. Another group is investigating a shortened four-session MBSR program for cancer patients in Florida (Moscoso, Reheiser, & Hann, 2004). Clinical work is ongoing in other regions as well, including through the Wellness Community (e.g., Baum & Gessert, 2004), but no publications have yet resulted from these programs.

Overall, the body of empirical research supporting the use of MBSR with cancer patients is compelling, but very preliminary. According to Bishop (2002), "Although the efficacy of MBSR to self-manage stress and mood symptoms associated with cancer seems particularly promising, it would be difficult based on a single randomized controlled trial (the Tom Baker study) to strongly recommend it at this time. This study is significant however as it represents the first rigorous test of the efficacy of this approach to foster adaptation to a medical illness. Replication is clearly needed to firmly establish its efficacy in this population" (76). In addition to replication efficacy studies, studies comparing MBSR with other psychosocial interventions, and research designed to explicate the relative contributions of various components of this multifaceted intervention, are now needed.

PRACTICAL ISSUES

Clinical practice in all health-related disciplines is increasingly being shaped by the ethical imperative that evidence of the efficacy of interventions offered to patients will be developed (Grol & Grimshaw, 2003). Therefore, in the oncology setting, early consideration should be given to integrating a well-conceived program of research and evaluation with the clinical MBSR program.

The context in which MBSR is to be offered to cancer patients must be carefully considered in order to maximize patient access and ensure the receptivity of those who may be in a position to refer patients or provide other forms of program support. Opportunities to inform health care providers and administrators about the nature of the intervention, its adjunctive or complementary role in relation to cancer treatment, and the potential benefits to patients should not be neglected. In institutional settings, such as hospitals or clinics providing cancer treatment, this may be done both through informal networking and by taking advantage of opportunities to participate in more formal contexts such as hospital rounds and scientific or professional conferences and seminars. Health professionals or administrators who have personal meditation or yoga experience may be natural allies whose support can be elicited for efforts to establish or maintain an MBSR program.

The ideal qualifications for an MBSR facilitator in an oncology setting would include an appropriate combination of MBSR training and relevant supervised experience in facilitating similar groups, as well as some working familiarity with the unique challenges faced by cancer patients. Facilitators must make an ongoing commitment to maintain a personal mindfulness practice in order to ensure a credible experientially grounded basis for responding to participants' questions and needs. In our locale, MBSR groups are led by pairs of co-facilitators with shared responsibilities for conducting the group. This minimizes any difficulties attendant to facilitator illness and allows for the sharing of support, feedback, and new learning between facilitators.

Health professionals established in traditional disciplines such as psychology, medicine, and nursing who are already working with cancer patients and have obtained requisite additional training in MBSR may be ideally situated to introduce mindfulness practices into the oncology setting. Currently, our services are provided through a universal, publicly funded health care system as a component of an integrated multidisciplinary approach to cancer treatment that adheres to a biopsychosocial model of care.

REFERENCES

American Psychiatric Association. (1980). *Diagnostic and statistical manual of mental disorders* (3rd ed.). Washington, DC: Author.

Andersen, B. (1992). Psychological interventions for cancer patients to enhance the quality of life. *Journal of Consulting and Clinical Psychology, 60*, 552–568.

Antoni, M. H., Lehman, J. M., Kilbourn, K. M., Boyers, A. E., Culver, J. L., Alferi, S. M., *et al.* (2001). Cognitive-behavioral stress management intervention decreases the prevalence of depression and enhances benefit finding among women under treatment for early-stage breast cancer. *Health Psychology, 20*, 20–32.

Balneaves, L. G., Kristjanson, L. J., & Tataryn, D. (1999). Beyond convention: Describing complementary therapy use by women living with breast cancer. *Patient Education and Counseling, 38*, 143–153.

Baselga, J., & Hammond, L. A. (2002). HER-targeted tyrosine-kinase inhibitors. *Oncology, 63*, 6–16.

Bauer-Wu, S. M., & Rosenbaum, E. (2004). Facing the challenges of stem cell/bone marrow transplantation with mindfulness meditation: A pilot study. *Psycho-Oncology, 13*, S10–S11.

Baum, C., & Gessert, A. (2004). Mindfulness-based stress reduction (MBSR) classes as a tool to decrease the anxiety of cancer patients. *Psycho-Oncology, 13*, S13.

Bishop, S. R. (2002). What do we really know about mindfulness-based stress reduction? *Psychosomatic Medicine, 64*, 71–83.

Blake-Mortimer, J., Gore-Felton, C., Kimerling, R., Turner-Cobb, J. M., & Spiegel, D. (1999). Improving the quality and quantity of life among patients with cancer: A review of the effectiveness of group psychotherapy. *European Journal of Cancer, 35*, 1581–1586.

Bonadonna, R. (2003). Meditation's impact on chronic illness. *Holistic Nurse Practitioner, 17*, 309–319.

Bottomley, A. (1996). Group cognitive behavioural therapy interventions with cancer patients: A review of the literature. *European Journal of Cancer Care, 5*, 143–146.

———— (1997). Where are we now? Evaluating two decades of group interventions with adult cancer patients. *Journal of Psychiatric and Mental Health Nursing, 4*, 251–265.

Carlson, L. E., Speca, M., Goodey, E., & Garland, S. (2004). Improvements in sleep quality in cancer outpatients participating in mindfulness-based stress reduction. *Psychosomatic Medicine, 66*, A-80.

Carlson, L. E., Speca, M., Patel, K. D., & Goodey, E. (2003). Mindfulness-based stress reduction in relation to quality of life, mood, symptoms of stress, and immune parameters in breast and prostate cancer outpatients. *Psychosomatic Medicine, 65*, 571–581.

———— (2004). Mindfulness-based stress reduction in relation to quality of life, mood, symptoms of stress and levels of cortisol, dehydroepiandrostrone-sulfate (DHEAS) and melatonin in breast and prostate cancer outpatients. *Psychoneuroendocrinology, 29*, 448–474.

Carlson, L. E., Ursuliak, Z., Goodey, E., Angen, M., & Speca, M. (2001). The effects of a mindfulness meditation based stress reduction program on mood and symptoms of stress in cancer outpatients: Six month follow-up. *Supportive Care in Cancer, 9*, 112–123.

Coker, K. H. (1999). Meditation and prostate cancer: Integrating a mind/body intervention with traditional therapies. *Seminars in Urological Oncology, 17*, 111–118.

Cordova, M. J., & Andrykowski, M. A. (2003). Responses to cancer diagnosis and treatment: Posttraumatic stress and posttraumatic growth. *Seminars in Clinical Neuropsychiatry, 8*, 286–296.

Cruess, D. G., Antoni, M. H., McGregor, B. A., Kilbourn, K. M., Boyers, A. E., Alferi, S. M., et al. (2000). Cognitive-behavioral stress management reduces serum cortisol by enhancing benefit finding among women being treated for early stage breast cancer. *Psychosomatic Medicine, 62*, 304–308.

Cunningham, A. J. (1995). Group psychological therapy for cancer patients: A brief discussion of indications for its use, and the range of interventions available. *Supportive Care in Cancer, 3*, 244–247.

———— (1999). Mind–body research in psychooncology: What directions will be most useful? *Advances in Mind Body Medicine, 15*, 252–255.

———— (2000). Adjuvant psychological therapy for cancer patients: Putting it on the same footing as adjunctive medical therapies. *Psychooncology, 9*, 367–371.

Derogatis, L. R., Morrow, G. R., & Fetting, J. (1983). The prevalence of psychiatric disorders among cancer patients. *Journal of the American Medical Association, 249*, 751–757.

Fawzy, F. I. (1995). A short-term psychoeducational intervention for patients newly diagnosed with cancer. *Supportive Care in Cancer, 3*, 235–238.

———— (1999). Psychosocial interventions for patients with cancer: What works and what doesn't. *European Journal of Cancer, 35*, 1559–1564.

Fawzy, F. I., Fawzy, N. W., Arndt, L. A., & Pasnau, R. O. (1995). Critical review of psychosocial interventions in cancer care. *Archives of General Psychiatry, 52*, 100–113.

Fawzy, F. I., Fawzy, N. W., & Canada, A. L. (1998). Psychosocial treatment of cancer: An update. *Current Opinion in Psychiatry, 11*, 601–605.

Fobair, P. (1997). Cancer support groups and group therapies: Part I. Historical and theoretical background and research on effectiveness. *Journal of Psychosocial Oncology, 15*, 63–81.

Fox, B. H. (1995). The role of psychological factors in cancer incidence and prognosis. *Oncology, 9*, 245–253.

Greer, S. (1995). Improving quality of life: Adjuvant psychological therapy for patients with cancer. *Supportive Care in Cancer, 3*, 248–251.

Grol, R., & Grimshaw, J. (2003). From best evidence to best practice: Effective implementation of change in patients' care. *Lancet, 362*, 1225–1230.

Iacovino, V., & Reesor, K. (1997). Literature on interventions to address cancer patients' psychosocial needs: What does it tell us? *Journal of Psychosocial Oncology, 15*, 47–71.

Kabat-Zinn, J. (1990). *Full catastrophe living: Using the wisdom of your body and mind to face stress, pain and illness*. New York: Delacorte.

——— (1996). Mindfulness meditation. What it is, what it isn't and its role in health care and medicine. In Y. Haruki & M. Suzuki (Eds.), *Comparative and Psychological Study on Meditation* (pp. 161–170). Delft, Netherlands: Erubon.

Kabat-Zinn, J., Chapman, A., & Salmon, P. (1997). Relationship of cognitive and somatic components of anxiety to patient preference for different relaxation techniques. *Mind-Body Medicine, 2*, 101–109.

Kabat-Zinn, J., Lipworth, L., & Burney, R. (1985). The clinical use of mindfulness meditation for the self-regulation of chronic pain. *Journal of Behavioral Medicine, 8*, 163–190.

Kabat-Zinn, J., Massion, A. O., Hebert, J. R., & Rosenbaum, E. (1998). Meditation. In J. F. Holland (Ed.), *Psycho-Oncology* (pp. 767–779). New York: Oxford University Press.

Kabat-Zinn, J., & Santorelli, S. (1999). *Mindfulness-based stress reduction professional training resource manual*. Worchester, MA: Center for Mindfulness in Medicine, Health Care, and Society.

Katz, R. C., Flasher, L., Cacciapaglia, H., & Nelson, S. (2001). The psychosocial impact of cancer and lupus: A cross validation study that extends the generality of "benefit-finding" in patients with chronic disease. *Journal of Behavioral Medicine, 24*, 561–571.

Kornblith, A. B., & Ligibel, J. (2003). Psychosocial and sexual functioning of survivors of breast cancer. *Seminars in Oncology, 30*, 799–813.

Kutz, I., Borysenko, J. Z., & Benson, H. (1985). Meditation and psychotherapy: A rationale for the integration of dynamic psychotherapy, the relaxation response, and mindfulness meditation. *American Journal of Psychiatry, 142*, 1–8.

Lechner, S. C., Zakowski, S. G., Antoni, M. H., Greenhawt, M., Block, K., & Block, P. (2003). Do sociodemographic and disease-related variables influence benefit-finding in cancer patients? *Psycho-oncology, 12*, 491–499.

Lev, E. L., Paul, D., & Owen, S. V. (1999). Age, self-efficacy, and change in patients' adjustment to cancer. *Cancer Practice, 7*, 170–176.

Lowery, B. J., Jacobsen, B. S., & DuCette, J. (1994). Causal attribution, control, and adjustment to breast cancer. *Journal of Psychosocial Oncology, 10*, 37–53.

McGregor, B. A., Antoni, M. H., Boyers, A., Alferi, S. M., Blomberg, B. B., & Carver, C. S. (2004). Cognitive-behavioral stress management increases benefit finding and immune function among women with early-stage breast cancer. *Journal of Psychosomatic Research, 56*, 1–8.

Meyer, T. J., & Mark, M. M. (1995). Effects of psychosocial interventions with adult cancer patients: A meta-analysis of randomized experiments. *Health Psychology, 14*, 101–108.

Moore, N. G. (1998). The Center for Mindfulness in Medicine: Meditation training for the body's innate wisdom. *Alternative Therapies in Health and Medicine, 4*, 32–33.

Moscoso, M., Reheiser, E. C., & Hann, D. (2004). Effects of a brief mindfulness-based stress reduction intervention on cancer patients. *Psycho-Oncology, 13*, S12.

Mundy, E. A., DuHamel, K. N., & Montgomery, G. H. (2003). The efficacy of behavioral interventions for cancer treatment–related side effects. *Seminars in Clinical Neuropsychiatry, 8,* 253–275.

Newell, S. A., Sanson-Fisher, R. W., & Savolainen, N. J. (2002). Systematic review of psychological therapies for cancer patients: Overview and recommendations for future research. *Journal of the National Cancer Institute, 94,* 558–584.

Nezu, C. M., Nezu, A. M., Friedman, S. H., Houts, P. S., DelliCarpini, L. A., Bildner, C., *et al.* (1999). Cancer and psychological distress: Two investigations regarding the role of social problem-solving. *Journal of Psychosocial Oncology, 16,* 27–40.

Palmer, S. C., Kagee, A., Coyne, J. C., & DeMichele, A. (2004). Experience of trauma, distress, and posttraumatic stress disorder among breast cancer patients. *Psychosomatic Medicine, 66,* 258–264.

Pitceathly, C., & Maguire, P. (2003). The psychological impact of cancer on patients' partners and other key relatives: A review. *European Journal of Cancer, 39,* 1517–1524.

QSR International (2002). QSR N6 [Computer software]. Melbourne, Australia: QSR International Pty Ltd.

Reibel, D. K., Greeson, J. M., Brainard, G. C., & Rosenzweig, S. (2001). Mindfulness-based stress reduction and health-related quality of life in a heterogeneous patient population. *General Hospital Psychiatry, 23,* 183–192.

Ries, L. A. G., Eiser, M. P., Kosary, C. L., Hankey, B. F., Miller, B. A., & Clegg, L. (2004). *SEER cancer statistics review, 1975–2001.* Bethesda, MD: National Cancer Institute.

Roberts, C. S., Cox, C. E., Shannon, V. J., & Wells, N. L. (1994). A closer look at social support as a moderator of stress in breast cancer. *Health and Social Work, 19,* 157–164.

Roth, B., & Creaser, T. (1997). Mindfulness meditation–based stress reduction: Experience with a bilingual inner-city program. *Nurse Practitioner, 22,* 150–152, 154, 157.

Saxe, G. A., Hebert, J. R., Carmody, J. F., Kabat-Zinn, J., Rosenzweig, P. H., Jarzobski, D., *et al.* (2001). Can diet in conjunction with stress reduction affect the rate of increase in prostate specific antigen after biochemical recurrence of prostate cancer? *Journal of Urology, 166,* 2202–2207.

Schneiderman, N., Antoni, M. H., Saab, P. G., & Ironson, G. (2001). Health psychology: Psychosocial and biobehavioral aspects of chronic disease management. *Annual Review of Psychology, 52,* 555–580.

Schulz, U., & Mohamed, N. E. (2004). Turning the tide: Benefit finding after cancer surgery. *Social Science and Medicine, 59,* 653–662.

Sears, S. R., Stanton, A. L., & Danoff-Burg, S. (2003). The yellow brick road and the emerald city: Benefit finding, positive reappraisal coping and posttraumatic growth in women with early-stage breast cancer. *Health Psychology, 22,* 487–497.

Sephton, S. E., Sapolsky, R. M., Kraemer, H. C., & Spiegel, D. (2000). Diurnal cortisol rhythm as a predictor of breast cancer survival. *Journal of the National Cancer Institute, 92,* 944–1000.

Shapiro, S. L., Bootzin, R. R., Figueredo, A. J., Lopez, A. M., & Schwartz, G. E. (2003). The efficacy of mindfulness-based stress reduction in the treatment of sleep disturbance in women with breast cancer: An exploratory study. *Journal of Psychosomatic Research, 54,* 85–91.

Shapiro, S. L., & Schwartz, G. E. (2000). Intentional systemic mindfulness: An integrative model for self-regulation and health. *Advances in Mind-Body Medicine, 16,* 128–134.

Speca, M., Carlson, L. E., Goodey, E., & Angen, M. (2000). A randomized, wait-list controlled clinical trial: The effect of a mindfulness meditation–based stress reduction program on mood and symptoms of stress in cancer outpatients. *Psychosomatic Medicine, 62,* 613–622.

Spiegel, D. (1999). Embodying the mind in psychooncology research. *Advances in Mind–Body Medicine, 15,* 267–273.

——— (2001). Mind matters: Group therapy and survival in breast cancer. *New England Journal of Medicine, 345,* 1767–1768.

Spiegel, D., Bloom, J. R., & Yalom, I. (1981). Group support for patients with metastatic cancer: A randomized prospective outcome study. *Archives of General Psychiatry, 38,* 527–533.

Spira, J. L. (1998). Group therapies. In J. Holland (Ed.), *Textbook of Psych-oncology* (pp. 701–716). Oxford: Oxford University Press.

Strain, J. J. (1998). Adjustment disorders. In J. F. Holland (Ed.), *Psycho-oncology* (pp. 509–517). New York: Oxford University Press.

Tomatis, L. (2001). Between the body and the mind: The involvement of psychological factors in the development of multifactorial diseases. *European Journal of Cancer, 37*(suppl 8), S148–S152.

Trevino, J. G. (1996). Worldview and change in cross-cultural counselling. *The Counselling Psychologist, 24,* 198–215.

Trijsburg, R. W., van Knippenberg, F. C., & Rijpma, S. E. (1992). Effects of psychological treatment on cancer patients: A critical review. *Psychosomatic Medicine, 54,* 489–517.

van der Poel, H. G. (2004). Smart drugs in prostate cancer. *European Urology, 45,* 1–17.

World Health Organization (2003). *Global action against cancer.* Geneva: Author.

Zabora, J., BrintzenhofeSzoc, K., Curbow, B., Hooker, C., & Piantadosi, S. (2001). The prevalence of psychological distress by cancer site. *Psychooncology, 10,* 19–28.

12

MINDFULNESS-BASED STRESS REDUCTION (MBSR) WITH SPANISH- AND ENGLISH-SPEAKING INNER-CITY MEDICAL PATIENTS

BETH ROTH

Mindfulness Meditation Consulting, New Haven, Connecticut

LIA CALLE-MESA

Independent Consultant, Hamden, Connecticut

INTRODUCTION

Effective and culturally appropriate health care options for low-income minority groups in the United States are urgently needed. Mindfulness-based stress reduction (MBSR) is an educational intervention in behavioral medicine that is growing in popularity. This chapter is based on our work teaching MBSR to Spanish- and English-speaking inner-city medical patients at the Community Health Center in Meriden, Connecticut (CHC-Meriden). The history, philosophy, and curriculum of this program have been previously described (Roth, 1994; 1997), and research findings have been published elsewhere (Roth & Creaser, 1997; Roth & Stanley, 2002; Roth & Robbins, 2004). This chapter includes four sections: a case study, theoretical framework, literature review, and practical issues for teaching MBSR in an inner-city health care setting. More detailed information about the MBSR protocol is provided in Chapter 1 of this volume.

CASE STUDY

PRESENTATION

Miguel is a Spanish-speaking Puerto Rican man who was 48 years old when he participated in the Spanish-language MBSR program at CHC-Meriden. He had been diagnosed 5 years before with rheumatoid arthritis, and the disease had steadily progressed. At the time that he presented for the MBSR intake interview, he had chronic pain and dysfunction in his legs. He walked with the assistance of a cane and wore a metal brace on his left leg. The illness had affected all aspects of his life. He experienced a great deal of anxiety and depression related to the physical pain and to the uncertain prognosis of his disease. As a result of the physical pain, anxiety, and depression, he suffered from insomnia and anorexia, which further exacerbated his fatigue and weight loss. He was in treatment with a family physician and a rheumatoid arthritis specialist, and was taking seven different medications daily and one injection weekly to manage his symptoms. Despite this treatment regimen, Miguel described a very poor quality of life, including low self-esteem, marital discord, difficulty socializing, and a sense of "having lost his identity" due to his illness.

In the first class session Miguel heard an in-depth presentation of the philosophy of the MBSR program, the curriculum, and the commitment to home meditation practice that was expected of patients. He participated in a brief eating meditation and a body scan meditation and discussed his initial experiences and impressions with the group. He left with the Spanish-language audiocassette and instructions to do the 30-minute guided body scan daily. In the second class, we discussed patients' experiences with attempting to incorporate meditation practice into daily life, and the value of self-awareness and self-care. We did another body scan and introduced a short awareness-of-breathing meditation. The home practice assignment was to continue the body scan and add 10 minutes of breathing practice daily.

Miguel was adherent to home meditation practice. He said that since he had tried everything else that was available without much improvement, he owed it to himself to make a sincere effort with the MBSR program. By the third week, Miguel reported a significant reduction in physical pain. He described how he was often awakened before dawn by pain in his legs. His custom was to take a variety of medications in a usually unsuccessful attempt to get back to sleep. Now, although he continued to be awakened by physical pain, he got out of bed and did 10–15 minutes of breathing meditation. He could then fall back to sleep without any medication. He was also sleeping better at night. He had decreased his pain medication and eliminated the medication for insomnia. As the course progressed, Miguel's face, countenance, body language, and posture gradually took on a more peaceful and relaxed appearance. Although still recognizable as the same man who had entered the program a few weeks before, class members and personal friends commented about his changed physical appearance.

Miguel attended six of the eight MBSR classes, as well as the pre-intervention and postintervention meetings. He continued to practice the body scan and the breathing meditation in class and at home, and added to this repertoire walking meditation and gentle yoga. He participated in class discussions about the relevance of meditation practice and mindfulness to stress, physical pain, illness, and difficult mind states. He discovered that mindfulness could also help him more fully experience the pleasant moments of his life. The far-reaching effects of meditation practice surprised him. The changes he experienced served to heighten his curiosity about himself and about mindfulness and strengthened his commitment to home meditation practice.

During the course of the MBSR program Miguel became increasingly vocal in sharing his experiences in class discussions. In subsequent months, he volunteered to participate in videotaped panel presentations where he described his experiences, through an interpreter, to audiences of medical and mental health professionals, and to graduate students at Yale University. Miguel was articulate about how meditation practice helped him to change his life. It was his desperation about his health and his life that finally caused him to overcome his hesitation to contact us and attend the orientation session. He explained that men in general, and Hispanic men in particular, are taught to think that they do not have any problems, and to attribute to their wives and girlfriends whatever problems they are unable to deny. This belief system made it difficult for him to consider participating in the intervention. However, since the program was offered in Spanish, he decided to inquire about it. He said that it was the immediate rapport he felt with the program instructor at the orientation meeting that caused him to enroll. The instructor was a white female nurse practitioner fluent in both English and Spanish, who is the first author listed of the current chapter.

Miguel's description of his first impressions of the program reflects how formally cultivating mindfulness through meditation practice can be immediately relevant to daily life:

> The first couple of classes felt strange. I was doing things I'd never done before and talking about things I'd never before discussed. The meditation practices were initially a little boring and monotonous, doing the same thing for so many minutes at a time. But I could see the value right away. I had a chance to think about myself in

new ways. I learned to really pay attention to my mind and my body. I learned to
breathe more consciously, and to calm down with the awareness of my breath.
I realized I could experience immediate benefit from even one long conscious breath
at any time during the day.

The types of changes that Miguel experienced as a result of his participation in the MBSR program are illustrative of how mindfulness practice
affects both physical and mental health. His physical pain diminished in
frequency and severity. He decreased his daily use of medication from seven
medications to one and decreased his weekly injections to one per month.
Because these significant physical changes occurred in a short period, he
developed a new understanding of the pivotal role of the mind in the mind–
body relationship:

> More important than the decrease in physical pain is what happened to me mentally.
> I've learned how to live with the pain. The mind is the main thing. I now have
> a different relationship with my own mind.

As his physical condition improved, his anxiety also diminished. In
addition to feeling less anxious about everyday things, he was able to travel
for the first time in a long time, flying without anxiety to Puerto Rico to visit
friends and family. As Miguel developed new strengths and capabilities, he
became aware of inner resources that he never knew he had. This realization
further boosted his growing self-confidence:

> Before the meditation program, I occasionally prayed, but I never meditated. I asked
> God for help. I didn't know how to help myself. Now I still pray to God, but I also
> know how to help myself.

Prior to entering the MBSR program, Miguel assumed that his happiness
was dependent upon eliminating the sources of his stress. What he discovered was quite different. Miguel spoke eloquently about how meditation
did not take away his suffering but did change his perspective and his
relationship to it:

> My problems haven't disappeared, and I'm not trying to hide from them either. I've
> learned to bring myself closer to my problems than I did before, but with a very
> different result. Daily life is easier. I have the same problems I always had, but now
> I can see them coming. Because I see my problems coming, I am able to soften them
> as they approach.

Miguel said that his health improvement was more than he had hoped for
or could have imagined, yet it was just a small part of more global personal
change. Although not cured of his illness, he described himself as "being
well again." He explained how his perception of himself had dramatically
shifted from feeling helpless and worthless to regaining a more positive
identity:

> What I gained from this course is self-esteem, to feel good about myself. I am almost
> 50 years old and I feel young again. I've wanted to grow a beard for a long time, but I

always felt embarrassed about it. Now I've grown a beard. And because I don't speak English, I never felt confident socializing with English-speaking people. Now I go places where there are English-speaking people. I talk about myself with others. I discuss my meditation experiences with professionals and students. I'm more comfortable with my family and friends too. Because of meditation practice, I know myself and understand myself better. I am more open within myself, so I can be more open with others. I'm not as rigid or dogmatic as I used to be. I can consider another person's point of view and other people's needs. I'm more communicative with my wife and my children. My marriage has improved. I had completely lost my identity because of my illness, and now I've got it back again. I am well again. I've even got my sense of humor back!

As with any effective group intervention, social support is inherent to the success of MBSR. Yet the specific ingredients of this support, and their mechanisms of action, are not entirely understood. Miguel's experience of the group changed during the course of the program. Initially he was self-conscious about being in it, since his presence there indicated that he had problems and needed help. He explained that this was a difficult position to be in as a Hispanic male, accustomed to denying his problems even as they threatened to overwhelm him completely. His self-consciousness was further heightened by the fact that there were so few men in the group. He reported that it took a little while to feel comfortable in a room of mostly women. It was the trust he felt in the instructor that helped him to move beyond these initial obstacles and that the instructor's kindness and sincerity and her confidence in his ability to benefit from the MBSR program had made a significant impression on him. The skill of the instructor, the opportunity to speak openly and listen sincerely to others, and practicing meditation in a group setting enabled him to become an integral member of the class. His personal suffering also took on a different meaning in the context of the group. He was able to see the universal nature of human suffering. He reflected on this aspect of his experience:

The group is very positive. We don't just complain or talk about our problems. We are actually confronting our problems and solving them. We are learning things together and supporting one another. I used to think that my problems were very different from other people's problems, and that Puerto Ricans or Latinos had different problems than Americans. Now I know that all people are the same. We're all in the same boat. Of course there are some differences, but we're all basically the same. We all have problems and we are all looking for solutions.

Miguel's experience with the MBSR program also challenged his former passivity as a medical patient and health care consumer. When he spoke with medical professionals about MBSR, he noticed a variety of responses:

My rheumatoid arthritis doctor noticed such a change in me that she wanted to know more about the MBSR program. But most doctors aren't so interested. I've mentioned it to other doctors, and their responses indicate that they really can't be bothered. They don't want to hear about it. Doctors really should be more open-minded.

Miguel talked with many people in his community about MBSR. Believing it could help others as it had helped him, he was distressed that this intervention was considered "alternative" and was not more readily available, especially to the Latino population. His experience with the MBSR program caused him to confront shortcomings of the health care system:

> Wealthy people have so many health care options available to them, so many treatments and services, and a variety of "alternative" programs to help them with lifestyle changes. The people who will suffer the most if MBSR programs are not made more available are working-class and poor people, and the Latino communities. I think it's time that the government, health care providers, administrators, and policymakers recognize the value of programs like MBSR. We need to convince the government to fund more programs like this, and to make them available in Spanish to Latinos.

Some months after completing the MBSR program, Miguel was asked if he was still practicing meditation. He responded that he gained so much during the 8 weeks of the program that he rarely misses a day of practice. The techniques he does the most are the body scan and awareness-of-breathing meditation, often with the assistance of audiotapes. But as important as these practices are to him, even more important is the skill these practices taught him—the skill of mindfulness. He has learned how to pause in his life, to take 1, 2, or 3 minutes a few times each day to simply feel his own breath. In this way he can immediately calm himself amidst the changing circumstances of daily life. He said it was easier to maintain a daily meditation practice after the course ended, because by then he had learned how to meditate, and he was fully aware of the benefits of meditation practice. Miguel also mentioned that since his family had seen how much meditation helped him, they were very supportive of his practice and encouraged him to dedicate himself to it.

Many months after the MBSR program ended, Miguel spoke privately with us. He said the time had come to share something he had hesitated to say. He reminded us of the total desperation that had almost completely overwhelmed him prior to enrolling in MBSR:

> I never told you just how desperate I was. I had decided there was no point in continuing to live. My physical health was poor and continuing to deteriorate, the physical pain was constant, and my depression and anxiety prevented me from eating or sleeping normally. I felt worthless, and my social life had disintegrated because of all this. I had no hope. I had made the decision to take my own life. I had purchased a thick rope with which to hang myself from a large pipe in the basement of my apartment building. I had chosen a date the following week to execute this plan. Because of the continued insistence of my wife's friend, I finally called you and went to the orientation session. I decided this would be my final attempt to improve things before committing suicide. I remember that during that initial interview, you asked me lots of questions about my health and my life. You asked me if I had any recent thoughts of suicide. I lied. I thought that if I told you the truth, you would exclude

me from the meditation program. So I lied. At that first meeting I trusted you immediately. I felt a glimmer of hope that this program might help me, even a little. And now I can say that the meditation program literally saved my life.

DISCUSSION

Although the experience of Miguel is quite dramatic, it is by no means unique. The majority of inner-city MBSR patients enter the program feeling desperate, having tried years of medications, treatments, and therapies to improve their health. While some of these treatments may have helped stabilize medical or psychological symptoms, patients are experiencing a poor quality of life.

It is common for patients to find the MBSR program initially strange, unlike anything they have ever done before. The majority of patients who drop out of the program do so in the first 2 weeks. Among those who continue, health improvements occur quite quickly. By the second or third week, patients often experience a decrease in physical pain and improved quality of sleep. These initial improvements create a positive feedback loop that increases patients' motivation to attend class sessions and practice meditation at home. These early changes also challenge patients' assumptions about their physical condition, limitations, and prognosis.

As the program continues, patients generally experience improvement in mental and emotional states, such as a decrease in anxiety, a more positive mood, and enhanced appreciation for life. Patients realize that although they joined the program for stress reduction, they are actually involved in a profound process of self-discovery and personal transformation. Mindfulness meditation teaches patients to perceive physical pain and discomfort as pure sensation, separate from mental and emotional reactions to the sensation. When patients can uncouple mental reactions from physical sensation, their physical pain often diminishes. The realization that thinking itself can be observed as a process distinct from the content of thoughts is another pivotal insight. Patients realize that their identity need not be defined by their thoughts. A significant shift in identify occurs when patients learn to experience body sensations and thoughts as the ever-changing, impermanent processes they actually are.

During the latter half of the program, patients begin to comprehend how their own habits of perception and reaction contribute to their stress. Patients learn to replace habitual reactions with consciously chosen responses. They discover that more choice means more freedom, and that this freedom can be exercised only through a willingness to assume greater responsibility for their own health and happiness.

These changes in self-perception and personal identity correspond to changes in how patients perceive their place in the world. Mindfulness creates greater self-awareness and understanding, which in turn facilitates a greater understanding of others. Interpersonal communication and relationships often improve. Patients feel less separate and isolated from others. Greater intimacy with oneself enables greater intimacy with others and with life itself. The patients' problems and suffering become less acutely personal. Both suffering and the desire for happiness are revealed to be universal attributes of all human beings. The growing sense of connection with a larger community of humanity contributes to the personal healing. Thus, it may be that the reduction in stress reported by many MBSR participants is a side effect of more profound intrapersonal and interpersonal change. For patients who continue to practice meditation when the MBSR program ends, the skill of mindfulness continues to grow. Mindfulness is increasingly woven into the tapestry of daily life and integrated into the ongoing process of human development.

CONCEPTUAL FRAMEWORK

OVERVIEW OF THE FOUR NOBLE TRUTHS

Numerous sound theoretical frameworks inform MBSR work in general, and with inner-city patient populations in particular. These frameworks come from a variety of disciplines, including philosophy, psychology (especially the study of stress), nursing, medicine, and education. It is a philosophical or contemplative framework that has most authentically served as the foundation for our MBSR work at CHC-Meriden. This framework is a fundamental Buddhist teaching called the Four Noble Truths. Although the Four Noble Truths are not explicitly discussed with patients, the instructor's understanding of this teaching is a guide and companion as the MBSR program unfolds with each group of patients.

The First Noble Truth acknowledges that there is suffering in life. The Second Noble Truth says that there are causes for our suffering. The Third Noble Truth asserts that freedom from suffering, also known as liberation, happiness, or well-being, is possible. The Fourth Noble truth describes the path from suffering to greater health and happiness.

Jon Kabat-Zinn, founder of the original MBSR program at the University of Massachusetts Medical Center in Worcester, Massachusetts, skillfully created a curriculum that presented Eastern meditation practices in a way that was immediately accessible and useful to Western medical patients (Kabat-Zinn, 1990). While he made no attempt to hide its roots in the Buddhist tradition, he promoted MBSR without direct reference to Buddha or Buddhism, and without the "trappings" of Buddhism as a religion (Gates & Nisker, 1993). As MBSR programs proliferated and grew in popularity, most instructors followed Kabat-Zinn's lead in acknowledging that mindfulness meditation comes from the Buddhist tradition, while at the same time keeping Buddhism per se out of the classroom.

In the 25 years since the founding of the first MBSR program, discussion of mindfulness meditation's roots in the Buddhist tradition has become more commonplace among researchers and scientists exploring the psychological and physiologic mechanisms by which this practice exerts its healing effects. Buddhist philosophy, psychology, and meditation techniques have also become more familiar to Westerners in North America and Europe. Research documenting the health benefits of mindfulness meditation is reported in the media and lay press (Goleman, 2003; Hall, 2003; Stein, 2003), as are results of meetings between Western scientists and the Dalai Lama that explore the interface of science, psychology, and Buddhism (Goleman, 2003).

It is worth noting that MBSR teachers, much like their students, come from a variety of religious and secular backgrounds. While they all have extensive personal experience with mindfulness meditation, their familiarity and identification with Buddhism varies greatly. Professionals and laypeople alike now recognize that it is possible to extract teachings and practices from the Buddhist tradition without adopting Buddhism as a religion and that doing so may be beneficial to one's health. Thus, the current climate is more conducive to a sincere exploration of the Four Noble Truths as a conceptual framework for MBSR.

An explanation of the Four Noble Truths was the Buddha's first public teaching, given to a small group of disciples after his enlightenment. In the subsequent 45 years until his death, he delivered a vast number of teachings on many topics, yet continued to emphasize the vital importance of the Four Noble Truths. Although the Four Noble Truths is a Buddhist teaching, it has profound and universal application to human existence. It is variously considered a cosmology, a philosophy, a psychology, or a means for directly investigating and understanding the nature of human consciousness. As psychiatrist Mark Epstein (1995) commented, "The teachings of the Four Noble Truths are less about religion (in the Western sense) than they are a vision of reality containing a practical blueprint for psychological relief" (p. 45).

THE TEACHING OF THE FOUR NOBLE TRUTHS

The First Noble Truth names birth, illness, aging, and death as the four types of suffering inherent to every human life. Suffering also refers to physical pain and discomfort, and to emotions and mind states that preclude the possibility of coexistent happiness or well-being. Common examples are sorrow, fear, anger, hatred, greed, jealousy, aversion, confusion, anxiety, disappointment, shame, and guilt. The Pali word *dukkha* is most often translated into English as "suffering." Other common translations point to the comprehensive meaning of *dukkha:* illness, unhappiness, discomfort, pervasive unsatisfactoriness, or simply stress (Kabat-Zinn, 1990; Harrison, 1994; Epstein, 1995; Olendzki, 2000).

The Second Noble Truth says that there are reasons for our suffering. There are causes and conditions that give rise to unhappiness. The primary cause is ignorance, which refers not to a lack of intelligence but to a misperception of reality. For example, due to ignorance of the law of cause and effect, people tend to seek happiness through actions that could not possibly lead to happiness but instead lead to suffering. Ignorance about impermanence and the nature of change causes people to suffer by assigning permanence to what is by nature impermanent, such as the human body, material possessions, and transient emotions and mental states. Ignorance about the nature of the self causes suffering because people mistake their perceptions, opinions, and experiences for a solid entity of personality. According to Buddhist teaching, we fail to perceive that the self is more a changing process than a static entity. It is constructed anew in each moment through the individual's interaction with the constant flow of sensory perceptions. This false sense of a solid self also creates suffering because it gives rise to painful feelings of separation from other beings and from the natural world.

The Third Noble Truth proclaims that freedom from suffering is possible, that happiness can be found in this lifetime. The happiness that is referred to is often called "genuine happiness," which means well-being, inner peace, or peace of mind. This is contrasted with the more "ordinary happiness" that can be gained from sensory pleasure, acquisition of material possessions, money, fame, good fortune, or good luck. This is not to say that sensory pleasures, material possessions, etc., are not legitimate types of enjoyment. Rather, distinguishing genuine happiness from ordinary happiness simply points to the truth that seeking inner peace through ordinary happiness will inevitably lead to disappointment and suffering. While transient enjoyment dependent on material objects and external circumstances is certainly pleasurable, it is entirely different from abiding inner peace, cultivated through intention, discipline, and practice.

The Fourth Noble Truth offers a path toward the end of suffering. Understanding this path, and choosing to journey along it, is the first step toward genuine happiness, precisely because it sets one's intention to live with greater awareness. The Fourth Noble Truth is also known as the Noble Eightfold Path, because it is made up of eight interrelated aspects. These eight components are: skillful thought, skillful view, skillful speech, skillful action, skillful livelihood, skillful effort, skillful concentration, and skillful mindfulness. *Skillful,* in this context, simply means "leading to happiness and well-being." These eight components can be divided into three groupings: the behavioral, or ethical, group, which includes speech, action, and livelihood; the meditative group, which contains effort, concentration, and mindfulness; and the wisdom group, which is made up of thought and view.

The teaching of the Four Noble Truths posits health to be a far larger concept than we ordinarily take it to be, and proposes that we can consciously influence both the physical and mental aspects of health. By proclaiming that optimum health depends more on genuine inner peace than any other factor, the definition of health is extended far beyond the absence of pain, symptoms, or disease. "Physical health is indeed a blessing, but if it is no longer an option, freedom can still be claimed by the 'coming to terms with things as they are' that constitutes mental health" (Olendzki, 2000).

The Buddha's teaching of the Four Noble Truths rests on the assumption that the attainment of happiness is available to all, and that every human being has an equal right to achieve this happiness. Furthermore, despite the differences among people due to age, gender, nationality, ethnicity, religion, language, educational background, and socioeconomic status, it is the experience of suffering and the innate drive for happiness that unite all human beings. The Four Noble Truths assert that every human being belongs to one family of humanity.

Although the MBSR curriculum does not include explicit discussion of the Four Noble Truths, patients generally discover for themselves the immediate relevance of this teaching. In the inner-city medical setting, examples of personal and community *dukkha* fill the MBSR classroom: a vast array of medical and psychological diagnoses among patients; the illness, death or incarceration of family members; and a constellation of stressors related to poverty, low academic achievement, unemployment, community violence, and marginalization from mainstream culture and society. When patients enter the MBSR program, they are manifesting the First Noble Truth: There is suffering in life.

Over the course of the program, patients experience many and varied benefits. These changes come about through the patient's own efforts, accomplished by engaging in a variety of mindfulness meditation practices and exploring the direct application of mindfulness to all aspects of one's life. Many patients experience a noticeable improvement in symptoms during the first weeks of the program. Initial changes such as decreased physical pain and improved quality of sleep enable patients to gain glimpses of the Third Noble Truth, that relief from suffering is possible. This taste of the Third Noble Truth generally occurs with little understanding of the Second Noble Truth, which explains the causes of suffering.

Toward the middle of the 8-week program, when patients experience a significant decrease in stress, they suddenly realize how their own habits of reactivity exacerbate their stress. This realization marks their awakening to the Second Noble Truth: There are reasons for our suffering. As the course unfolds, patients become more skillful in replacing habitual reactions with more conscious responses to stress. The Third Noble Truth is further confirmed, and the Fourth Noble Truth becomes evident. There is a path that leads to decreased suffering; happiness is possible. In the last weeks of the program, patients learn more about the Noble Eightfold Path that is the Forth Noble Truth. The meditation techniques taught throughout the MBSR program belong to the meditative group of the Noble Eightfold Path. As effort, concentration, and mindfulness of the meditative group improve with meditation practice, patients gain greater insight into how the components of the wisdom group affect their health. Patients learn to influence their thoughts and beliefs in the service of their healing. As patients are increasingly able to choose conscious responses to stress, they gain an experiential understanding of the role of speech, action, and livelihood, the behavioral group of the Noble Eightfold Path, in achieving greater happiness and well-being.

Patients who participate fully in the MBSR program discover precisely what the Four Noble Truths proclaim: Health improvement comes about more by changing our relationship to our experience of suffering than by changing the nature of the suffering itself. In the MBSR program, inner-city medical patients come to know through their own experience that *dukkha,* whether defined as suffering or as stress, is essentially "a remediable attitude that affects all aspects of human existence" (Olendzki, 2000).

LITERATURE REVIEW

SOCIOECONOMIC STATUS, STRESS, AND HEALTH

Low socioeconomic status (SES) is associated with poorer health outcomes, and the largest groups of minority citizens in the United States are found in lower SES brackets (Baum, Garofalo, & Yali, 1999). Approximately 22% of African Americans live in poverty, compared with 13% for the United States as a whole and 8% of whites (U.S. Department of Health and Human Services [DHHS], 2002a). The poverty rates for Hispanics are 14% for Cuban Americans, 31% for Puerto Ricans, and 27% for Mexican Americans (DHHS, 2002b). Members of minority groups have higher rates of morbidity and mortality than do whites (DHHS, 2002a; 2002b). Depression, mental health problems, and other indices of personal and social distress are also more prevalent in minority groups (Baum *et al.,* 1999).

Two interrelated factors are believed to contribute to the poorer health outcomes of low-SES, minority-group populations: chronic stress and racism (Baum *et al.,* 1999; Williams, 1999). Chronic stress is defined as stress that "lasts for a long time, either because it occurs repeatedly, episodically, or continuously, or because it poses severe threats that are not easily adapted or overcome" (Baum *et al.,* 1999). Stress exerts its deleterious effects on health and well-being through a variety of neural, neuroendocrine, and immune-system pathways (Baum *et al.*, 1999). It is important to note that stress is not simply the result of a difficult external event. The ways in which a person perceives and handles a difficult experience will determine the degree to which the experience is stressful (Kabat-Zinn, 1990).

Racism is an ideology of inferiority that is used to justify unequal treatment of members of minority groups. Racism gives rise to prejudice (negative attitudes and beliefs) toward racial minorities. It also creates damaging policies of discrimination within the institutional structures of society. The subjective experience of racism is also believed to be an additional important stress that adversely affects physical and mental health (Baum *et al.*, 1999; Williams, 1999).

The stress burden associated with low SES consists of several environmental, institutional, and psychological factors. Residential segregation of minorities is a key mechanism by which racial inequality is reinforced in this country (Massey & Denton, 1993). The resulting concentration of poverty in residential areas creates pathogenic housing and living conditions (Williams, 1999). High population density, poor sanitation, high levels of noise, crime, and violence, and increased rates of incarceration and homicide are endemic to inner-city neighborhoods. Adverse environmental conditions also contribute to insufficient quality and quantity of restorative nightly sleep among low-SES groups (Van Cauter & Spiegel, 1999). Behavioral components of the poorer health status of low-SES groups include constrained diet and inadequate nutrition, increased tobacco, alcohol, and drug use, and a sedentary lifestyle lacking adequate physical exercise (Baum *et al.*, 1999).

Residential segregation has also led to racial differences in the quality of elementary and high school education. Segregation, educational inequality, and patterns of urbanization and industrialization have contributed to decreased employment opportunities, high unemployment, and underemployment in minority communities.

Disparities in medical care also adversely affect the health status of low-SES groups (Baum *et al.*, 1999). Members of low-SES groups are less likely to have adequate health insurance, which leads to decreased access to health care, reliance on emergency room visits over continuity of care, delays in the detection and diagnosis of disease, and the differential management and treatment of illness (Baum *et al.*, 1999; Williams, 1999). Members of low-SES groups are also disproportionately exposed to unrelieved physical pain due to inadequate medical treatment (Edwards, Fillingim, & Keefe, 2001). In addition, a growing body of research suggests that racial discrimination is responsible for differential and inadequate medical treatment after accounting for differences in SES, health insurance, and clinical status (Williams, 1999).

In summary, racial minorities are overrepresented in low-SES groups, and low SES increases stress and adversely affects health. It follows that successful stress reduction strategies for racial and ethnic minorities could improve their health status. The literature is beginning to provide evidence for the utility of MBSR with these populations.

MBSR WITH INNER-CITY MEDICAL PATIENTS

Most of the research to date on the effectiveness of MBSR for patients in health care settings has been conducted with working- and middle-class populations and has focused on subjective reports of symptom reduction following completion of the program. Although variability of rigor of study design and methodology has made definitive conclusions difficult, the results of these studies are promising. The bulk of this research has been summarized in an excellent review article by Baer (2003).

Since Baer's review article, a study examining changes in biological processes that are associated with reported improvements in mental and physical health has added valuable information to the literature. A randomized study comparing subjects in an MBSR program with wait-list controls documented positive changes in brain and immune function (Davidson et al., 2003). Results indicated significant increases in left-sided anterior brain activation in the intervention group and not in the control group, as measured by electroencephalogram. This pattern of electrical activity is associated with positive mood and affect. Members of the intervention group also demonstrated a significantly greater rise in antibody titers to the influenza vaccine, compared with the control group. Furthermore, the magnitude of increase in left-sided brain activation predicted the magnitude of antibody titer rise to the influenza vaccine. These results indicate that an 8-week MBSR program has demonstrable effects on brain and immune function and suggest the need for further research using larger sample sizes and functional magnetic resonance imaging of the brain.

A few research studies have explored the effects of MBSR among inner-city, minority-group patient populations. Two uncontrolled studies, one at the Worcester City Campus Program (Kabat-Zinn, 1994), a satellite of the Stress Reduction Clinic at the University of Massachusetts, and the other at the Community Health Center in Meriden, Connecticut (Roth & Creaser, 1997), documented the positive effects of the MBSR intervention with Spanish- and English-speaking inner-city medical patients. Participants in both studies demonstrated significant reduction in medical and psychological symptoms, and improvement in self-esteem. Both studies reported a 60% completion rate for patients in the MBSR programs.

Another study at the Meriden, Connecticut, site compared the subjective self-report of health-related quality of life (HRQoL) of 68 inner-city medical patients completing an MBSR program in English or Spanish with a comparison group of 18 Spanish-speaking patients who received no intervention (Roth & Robbins, 2004). The demographic profile of patients in this study revealed an inner-city, low-SES, largely Hispanic, primarily female population with significant comorbidity of medical and mental health diagnoses. Patients in this study reported significantly poorer health status and health-related quality of life than the general United States population.

There was a 66% completion rate for the MBSR program among patients in the intervention group. This study was the first to report adherence to home meditation practice among inner-city patients completing an MBSR program. Fifty (94%) of the 53 patients who provided data on their meditation practice reported meditating regularly at home, with 34 (64%) indicating that they practiced meditation 4–7 days per week.

The Short-Form 36 (SF-36) questionnaire was used to assess general health status and HRQoL. This widely used instrument measures eight health concepts: general health, physical functioning, role limitations caused by physical health problems, bodily pain, vitality (energy and fatigue), social functioning, role limitations caused by emotional problems, and general mental health (psychological distress and psychological well-being). Results demonstrated significant improvements among members of the intervention group in five of the eight health concepts, and a trend toward significance in two other areas, with no change in the comparison group.

The only published study to compare the health care utilization patterns of medical patients before and after completion of an MBSR program was also conducted at the Meriden, Connecticut, inner-city site (Roth & Stanley, 2002). A medical chart review of MBSR program completers compared the number and type of health center visits made during the year before entering the MBSR program with those of the year following completion of the program. Patients' health center visits were assigned to one or more categories according to the diagnosis for each visit: well-adult or routine care, chronic illness care, and episodic or acute care. A significant decrease in the number of chronic care visits was found among the 47 patients for whom complete data were available, and the 36 patients who completed the Spanish-language MBSR courses demonstrated a significant decrease in total medical visits and chronic care visits. These findings suggest that MBSR may help contain health care costs by decreasing the number of visits made by inner-city medical patients to their primary care providers.

MBSR research is moving in the direction of more rigorously designed studies that explore the biological and psychological mechanisms of action responsible for health improvements associated with the intervention. It is hoped that as MBSR becomes more available to minorities, low-SES groups, and Spanish-speaking communities, future research will clarify how MBSR might help ameliorate the deleterious effects of stress on these populations.

PRACTICAL ISSUES

PLANNING AND STAFF INVOLVEMENT

A thorough and well-conceived planning phase is vital to the success of an MBSR program in an inner-city setting. It is worth delaying instruction of patients in order to ensure that critical components of success are in place. Adequate staff orientation is of utmost importance. Ideally, the administration would allow the MBSR instructor to offer the full 8-week program during work time for all interested health center staff. Offering the MBSR program to staff allows the administration to demonstrate its interest in helping employees to reduce their stress and improve their health and well-being. Additionally, when health care providers and support staff have firsthand experience of the MBSR program, they may more enthusiastically promote it to patients. Authentic support and "ownership" of the MBSR program by medical and mental health providers and other staff will help to ensure the success of the program. With strong staff support, the MBSR program can claim its rightful place as an integral component of the health care services offered to patients. Without this support, the MBSR instructor is likely to be considered an outsider, and the program will become marginalized, excluded from the domain of "real" health care. If this occurs, medical and mental health providers may be unwilling to take an extra minute during a patient visit to discuss the program. Support staff may resent any additional work associated with the MBSR program. If offering the MBSR program during the workday is not possible, staff members might be able to attend a course that is taught in the evening. Alternatively, some staff may be able to attend sessions of patient courses in order to have a "taste" of the MBSR program.

Health center staff can also be included in other aspects of the planning phase, such as choosing a name for the MBSR program, setting up efficient procedures for referring patients to the program, designing posters and patient education materials to promote the program, and mounting a media campaign in the local community. Patient education materials must be written at a grade level appropriate for the educational background of the target patient population.

CHILD CARE AND TRANSPORTATION

At CHC-Meriden, child care and transportation issues were major obstacles to patients' ability to enroll in and complete the MBSR program. Solutions to the child care problem included the use of student volunteers, the reassignment of support staff for the necessary hours, and the funding of a part-time child care position. Medicaid-insured patients were eligible for taxi service for their MBSR sessions, since these health center visits were scheduled and billed as any other medical appointment. Reminder phone calls to all patients the day before each MBSR session also helped to maintain attendance and decrease program attrition.

PUBLICITY AND MEDIA COVERAGE

Local media coverage in English- and Spanish-language newspapers heightened the profile of the CHC-Meriden MBSR program. This included press releases, newspaper articles, letters to the editor, and interviews with MBSR program staff and patient completers of the program. Outreach to local hospitals, mental health centers, and large private medical practices also helped generate interest in the program.

BILLING AND REIMBURSEMENT

Billing and reimbursement issues are of major importance to the successful implementation of an inner-city MBSR program. MBSR is a legitimate health care intervention and a billable service. How it is billed will depend on a variety of factors, including whether the MBSR program instructor is a medical or mental health provider or other health care professional, and whether the majority of the patients are insured by Medicaid, have private insurance, or are uninsured. MBSR instructors who are mental health therapists generally use CPT (Current Procedural Terminology) billing codes for individual and group therapy. Instructors who are primary care providers, such as nurse practitioners, nurse midwives, and physicians, can use Preventive Medicine Group Counseling CPT code 99412 for patients without a medical illness or diagnosis, and 99078 for patients with established symptoms or diagnosis. In 2002 a new category called Health and Behavior Assessment/Intervention was created, with CPT codes 96150 through 96155. These codes are well suited to MBSR work and can be used whether the MBSR instructor is a physician, nurse practitioner, nurse midwife, physician associate, psychologist, licensed clinical social worker, registered nurse, or other health care professional. These Health and Behavior codes are reimbursed by Medicaid in nearly all states and can be used for reimbursement of sessions in 15-minute intervals up to 90 minutes or more. Not all health care facilities are familiar with these CPT codes. Administrators may doubt whether the MBSR services will qualify, or whether the rate of reimbursement will be worth the effort of the billing department to familiarize itself with the use of these codes and add the new codes to their data system. Adequate reimbursement for MBSR will contribute to greater acceptance of the program and ensure its wider implementation. For MBSR programs taught by instructors who are not health care professionals, other avenues such as grant funding will likely need to be utilized. Uninsured patients can pay a sliding-scale fee based on income. Ideally, arrangements can be made so that no patient will be turned away from the MBSR program for financial reasons.

GUIDED MEDITATION AUDIOCASSETTES

Guided meditations in audiocassette and CD format must be given to patients for home practice. The guided meditations should be created in the patients' native language, taking into account the variations of the language depending on patients' countries of origin and educational background. Although the tapes that accompanied the original University of Massachusetts program were 45 minutes long, we decided that adherence to home practice would be improved by the use of shorter recordings. We decreased the body scan and yoga to 30 minutes and offered guided awareness of breathing meditation in both 15- and 30-minute durations. We also provided inexpensive tape recorders to patients who did not own a tape recorder.

THE MBSR INSTRUCTOR

A significant obstacle to enrolling in an inner-city MBSR program is the patient's mistrust or lack of rapport with health care professionals. Many patients are accustomed to an alienating aloofness or professional distance from medical and mental health professionals. The initial rapport that the patient feels with the MBSR instructor may determine whether the patient decides to participate in the program. The continued development of an authentic relationship with the instructor is essential to the patient's compliance with and successful completion of the program. In addition to being an experienced meditation practitioner and a skilled teacher, the instructor must be able to establish a genuine personal connection with patients. The instructor's comfort with a particular patient population and fluency in the patients' native language are important to this relationship. Equally important is the instructor's recognition of a shared humanity that is palpable and perceptible to the instructor and patient alike. The ability of the instructor to establish this type of relationship with patients is an individual matter, determined more by the instructor's personality and life experience than by his or her gender, race, nationality, ethnicity, native language, educational background, or professional training. There is no substitute for this most human attribute, and it is vital to the success of the MBSR program.

EXCLUSIONARY CRITERIA

We initially excluded from the MBSR program patients who were actively suicidal and/or abusing drugs or alcohol. As described previously in the case study, we discovered that a patient could be actively suicidal and have an extraordinarily successful experience with the MBSR program. Over time, our policy regarding exclusionary criteria became one of considering each interested patient on an individual basis, and consulting with the patient's other care providers and mental health therapists as needed. We found that patients who were abusing substances or living in situations of domestic violence were generally unable to exercise enough control over themselves or their environment to participate successfully in the program. In such cases, patients were advised to obtain the services or treatment most immediately needed, and consider the MBSR program as a future option.

ADAPTING THE CURRICULUM

An attitude of flexibility and experimentation with the MBSR curriculum was helpful to the success of the inner-city program. Many patients had traumatic histories, including childhood physical or sexual abuse, or posttraumatic stress disorder due to combat in the armed forces, an experience of community violence, or political persecution in their country of origin. Because of such experiences, patients were often uncomfortable lying on the floor or were unable to sustain their focus on the body for extended periods. Thus, the body scan was sometimes introduced in the second class rather than the first. Many patients chose to sit in a chair rather than lie on the floor for the body scan, especially the first time it was introduced. And we occasionally taught the body scan in short segments rather than scanning the whole body at once. Meditation instruction and home practice were individualized by group or even for particular patients in a group.

At CHC-Meriden the educational level among patients varied, and patients in the English-language MBSR classes generally had more formal schooling than patients in the Spanish-language classes. Due to the educational background of the majority of patients, we avoided class handouts and written homework assignments. Instead, this content was explored during class sessions, or through a home practice assignment to pay close attention to a particular aspect of one's experience that we would discuss in class the following week. The all-day weekend session that is generally part of an MBSR program was never included, due to logistical difficulties of providing child care and opening the health center on a weekend. The theme of the sixth class (interpersonal communication) was changed to an exploration of anger and other strong emotions. Forgiveness or lovingkindness was the theme of the seventh class, which included a discussion of these attributes and their health benefits, and a guided forgiveness or loving-kindness meditation. In the final class session, a certificate of completion was presented to each patient. The distribution of these certificates became an emotional graduation ceremony, as patients accepted this symbol of their sincere effort in the MBSR program. Some patients commented that this certificate was the first diploma of their life.

SPANISH-LANGUAGE COURSES

There are a number of issues specific to teaching MBSR in Spanish. Because of significant variations in the Spanish language spoken by people of Caribbean, Mexican, Central American, and South American origin, it is important to use both spoken language and audio materials that will be understood by the target population. Since any given group of patients may include Spanish speakers of different origins, it may be necessary to offer more than one term to convey the corresponding concept in English. As MBSR is being introduced in Spanish into more settings in the United States and Latin America, key concepts and the names of the meditation practices themselves are being translated in different ways by different instructors. For example, the term *mindfulness* has been translated as *atención intencional, atención enfocada, conciencia del momento, presencia mental, atención vigilante, visión cabal, atención consciente,* and *atención plena.* The recent publication of the first Spanish translation of *Full Catastrophe Living* (Kabat-Zinn, 1990) may lead to greater standardization of terminology. Fernando de Torrijos, former instructor of the Worcester City Campus Program, is currently the international coordinator for MBSR in Spanish. He has chosen "REBAP," or "Reducción del estrés basados en la atención plena," as the translation of MBSR. (For more information, visit www.rebapinternacional.com).

Prior to implementing the CHC-Meriden MBSR program, we had concerns about how the meditation practices would be received by a largely Catholic Spanish-speaking population. We did little to adapt the program to this particular concern other than to substitute the terms *gentle stretching* (*estiramientos suaves*) or *body movements* (*movimientos del cuerpo*) for the word "yoga." Rarely did a patient object to the MBSR program or to the meditation practices due to conflicts with religious beliefs. On the contrary, many patients described how meditation and mindfulness enhanced their religious practices.

As explained by Miguel in the case study, many Spanish-speaking patients found the first MBSR class strange and could not initially see the potential benefit of the program. Knowing this, Miguel and other Spanish-speaking program graduates often arrived unannounced at the first session of a new Spanish-language MBSR course. They offered personal testimony about the benefits of the program. They encouraged patients to stick with the course, to practice meditation at home, and to have confidence in themselves and the instructor. This endorsement was very meaningful to patients new to the program.

SUPPORTING MBSR PROGRAM GRADUATES

At CHC-Meriden we experimented with different ways of offering support to graduates of the MBSR program. We taught 8-week "advanced" courses for graduates, as well as weekly and monthly drop-in group meditations. Graduates of the MBSR program who are continuing to practice meditation can also be trained to facilitate or co-facilitate (with the instructor or another experienced patient) drop-in sessions for graduates. It is important to provide continued support and guidance to patients who complete the MBSR program. Some experimentation may be necessary to discover what format works best in a particular setting.

CONCLUSION

Mindfulness-based stress reduction is a unique and promising health care intervention for low-income, minority, and non–English-speaking populations. Public and private funding for program development and research is urgently required. Teacher training and support is needed for individuals who wish to offer MBSR programs in inner-city settings. An active communication network among MBSR teachers in inner-city settings could help prevent instructor burnout and contribute to program success through the sharing of ideas and experiences. High-quality, positive media coverage of inner-city MBSR programs could increase visibility and funding for existing programs and encourage their replication to more health care settings. A significant expenditure of energy, effort, commitment, and creativity is required to establish and sustain MBSR programs in inner-city settings, but the potential benefit to the health and well-being of their recipients warrants just such an endeavor.

ACKNOWLEDGMENTS

We wish to thank Margaret Flinter, vice president and clinical director of The Community Health Center, for administrative support of the Mindfulness-Based Stress Reduction Program at the Community Health Center of Meriden, Connecticut. We also wish to express our gratitude to the patients who participated in the inner-city MBSR program. We admire their strength, courage, and wisdom and offer them our heartfelt thanks for the richness of all that we learned together.

REFERENCES

Baer, R. (2003). Mindfulness training as a clinical intervention: A conceptual and empirical review. *Clinical Psychology: Science and Practice, 10*, 125–143.

Baum, A., Garofalo, J., & Yali, A. (1999). Socioeconomic status and chronic stress: Does stress account for SES effects on health? *Annals of the New York Academy of Sciences, 896*, 131–144.

Davidson, R., Kabat-Zinn, J., Schumacher, J., Rosenkranz, M., Muller, D., Santorelli, S., et al. (2003). Alterations in brain and immune function produced by mindfulness meditation. *Psychosomatic Medicine, 65*, 564–570.

Edwards, C., Fillingim, R., & Keefe, F. (2001). Race, ethnicity and pain. *Pain, 94*, 133–137.

Epstein, M. (1995). *Thoughts without a thinker: Psychotherapy from a Buddhist perspective.* New York: Basic Books.

Gates, B., & Nisker, W. (1993). Bringing mindfulness into the mainstream of America: An interview with Jon Kabat-Zinn. *Inquiring Mind: A Semi-Annual Journal of the Vipassana Community* (pp. 8–12). Berkeley, CA: n.p.

Goleman, D. (2003, February 4). Finding happiness: Cajole your brain to lean to the left. *New York Times*, p. F5.

Hall, S. (2003, September 14). Is Buddhism good for your health? *New York Times Magazine*, 46–49.

Harrison, G. (1994). *In the lap of the Buddha.* Boston: Shambhala.

Kabat-Zinn, J. (1990). *Full catastrophe living: Using the wisdom of your body and mind to face stress, pain, and illness.* New York: Dell.

———— (1994). *Mindfulness-based inner city community stress reduction clinic: Unpublished final narrative and financial report.* Worcester, MA.

Massey, D., & Denton, N. (1993). *American apartheid: Segregation and the making of the underclass.* Cambridge, MA: Harvard University Press.

Olendzki, A. (2000). Meditation, healing, and stress reduction. In C. Queen (Ed.), *Engaged Buddhism in the West* (p. 544). Boston: Wisdom Publications.

Roth, B. (1994). Anchoring in the present moment: Meditation in the inner city. *Nurse Practitioner News, 2*, 12–14.

———— (1997). Mindfulness-based stress reduction in the inner city. *Advances: The Journal of Mind-Body Health, 13*, 50–58.

Roth, B., & Creaser, T. (1997). Mindfulness meditation-based stress reduction: Experience with a bilingual inner-city program. *The Nurse Practitioner, 22*, 150, 152, 154, 157, 161–162, 164, 170–171, 174, 176.

Roth, B., & Robbins, D. (2004). Mindfulness-based stress reduction and health-related quality of life: Findings from a bilingual inner-city patient population. *Psychosomatic Medicine, 66*, 113–123.

Roth, B. & Stanley, T. (2002). Mindfulness-based stress reduction and health care utilization in the inner city. *Alternative Therapies in Health and Medicine, 8*, 60–66.

Stein, J. (2003, July 27). Just say om. *Time*, 48–55.

U.S. Department of Health and Human Services (2002a). *Fact sheet: African Americans. Culture, race, and ethnicity.* Washington, DC: Author.

———— (2002b). Fact sheet: Latinos/Hispanic Americans. Culture, race, and ethnicity. Washington, DC: Author.

Van Cauter, E., & Spiegel, K. (1999). Sleep as a mediator of the relationship between socioeconomic status and health: A hypothesis. *Annals of the New York Academy of Sciences, 896*, 254–259.

Williams, D. R. (1999). Race, socioeconomic status, and health: The added effects of racism and discrimination. *Annals of the New York Academy of Sciences, 896*, 173–188.

1 3

ACCEPTANCE AND COMMITMENT THERAPY (ACT) IN THE TREATMENT OF CHRONIC PAIN

JoAnne Dahl and Tobias Lundgren

Department of Psychology, University of Uppsala, Uppsala, Sweden

INTRODUCTION: PAIN AND SUFFERING

Human beings, unlike animals, seem capable of suffering in the midst of abundance. If animals are given food, warmth, shelter, and care, they seem perfectly content, while human beings, on the other hand, with far greater luxuries, mostly seem discontent. This paradox of human suffering can be illustrated by Sweden's example. Citizens of Sweden enjoy one of the highest standards of living and best working environments in the world. Everyone is fully covered by free and high-quality health care. Excellent education, including university study, is free and open to everyone. Nowhere else in the world is there more vacation time, a shorter working week, a greater number of holidays, or longer paid maternity leave. At the same time, Sweden has more workers on sick leave and work-related disability due to chronic pain and stress-related disorders than anywhere else in the world. Sweden also has one of the world's highest rates of suicide. This paradox suggests that human suffering is not easily reduced by higher standards of living, free access to high-quality health care and education, and good working environments. In fact, attempting to reduce human suffering in these ways may lead to other problems.

Clients with chronic pain suffer greatly, as do many professionals in their attempts to help them. Most traditional medical treatments for chronic pain aim at reducing or managing the pain sensations. Painkillers, muscle relaxants, and anti-depressant drugs are the most common treatments. In recent years, several meta-analyses evaluating the established pain treatments used today (Bigos *et al.*, 1994; Morley, Eccleston, & Williams, 1999; van Tulder, Goossens, Waddell, & Nachemson, 2000) have shown that these medical treatments, which may be effective in acute pain, are not effective with chronic pain and may, in fact, be causing further problems. A radical and provocative conclusion drawn by the authors of a Swedish government evaluation (van Tulder *et al.*, 2000) of all established medical treatments offered today was that the best treatment a primary care physician could give a patient with chronic pain was nothing. Providing no treatment at all had far better results than any of the medical solutions offered today for chronic pain. Most of the pain treatments are designed for and useful for acute pain but, used in the long run, may create more problems, such as substance abuse and avoidance of important activities. Pain, in itself, is an inevitable part of living. Without it we could not survive. The common element in most of the pain treatments developed in Western cultures over the past 50 years has been an emphasis on avoiding pain or fighting to reduce pain. When pain was unavoidable, we tolerated it. When pain became avoidable, it became intolerable. What we have created, with all of our painkillers and pain management strategies, is an intolerance and increased sensitivity to pain.

OVERVIEW OF ACT FOR CHRONIC PAIN

Acceptance and commitment therapy (ACT) (Hayes, Strosahl, & Wilson, 1999) is an acceptance- and mindfulness-based approach that can be applied to many problems and disorders, including chronic pain. It appears to be a powerful therapeutic tool that can reduce suffering both for the client and for the treating professional. ACT emphasizes observing thoughts and feelings as they are, without trying to change them, and behaving in ways consistent with valued goals and life directions. ACT has shown promising results in several recent studies (Bach & Hayes, 2002; Bond & Bunce, 2000; Dahl, Wilson, & Nilsson, 2004; McCracken, Vowles, & Eccleston, 2004; Zettle, 2003).

The basic premise of ACT as applied to chronic pain is that while pain hurts, it is the struggle with pain that causes suffering. The pain sensation itself is an unconditioned reflex serving the function of alerting us to danger or tissue damage. The noxious sensation of pain is critical for our survival.

The same applies to emotional pain, such as the "broken heart" we feel from the death of a loved one or loss of a relationship. We know that it is natural and necessary to feel such pain in the mourning process in order to heal and go on with our lives. In the case of chronic pain, causal and maintaining factors may be unclear, and efforts to reduce or eliminate the pain may be unsuccessful. In these cases, continuing attempts to control pain may be maladaptive, especially if they cause unwanted side effects or prevent participation in valued activities, such as work, family, or community involvement (McCracken et al., 2004).

McCracken et al. (2004), in their development of the Chronic Pain Acceptance Questionnaire (CPAQ), have shown that two primary aspects of pain acceptance are important: (1) willingness to experience pain and (2) engaging in valued life activities even in the face of pain. Acceptance of pain was correlated with lower self-rated pain intensity, less self-rated depression and pain-related anxiety, greater physical and social ability, less pain avoidance, and better work status. This study also showed that acceptance of pain was not correlated with pain intensity. In other words, it was not those persons with less pain who were more willing to accept pain. In addition, laboratory studies with clinical and nonclinical populations (e.g., Gutierrez, Luciano, Rodriguez, & Fink, 2004; Hayes et al., 1999; Levitt, Brown, Orsillo, & Barlow, 2004) have shown that acceptance techniques used in ACT (such as observing and accepting thoughts and feelings as they are) produce greater tolerance of acute pain and discomfort than do more traditional techniques of pain control, such as distraction and cognitive restructuring. In these studies, pain tolerance was measured as the duration of tolerance and time to recuperation from different forms of discomfort such as holding a hand in ice water or inhaling carbon dioxide–enriched air, which causes panic-like physiological sensations.

In ACT and other mindfulness-based approaches, pain is seen as an inevitable part of living that can be accepted, whereas struggling to avoid inescapable pain causes more suffering. The struggle with pain is seen as a form of nonacceptance or resistance to "what is." The intensity of the suffering depends on the extent of the client's fusion with thoughts and feelings associated with the pain. Fusion is the extent to which the client believes the pain-related thoughts (e.g., "I can't do anything useful or enjoyable because of my pain" and "I have to get rid of my pain before I can do anything I value in life") and acts in accordance with these thoughts and related emotions. In this way, most of the suffering in chronic pain is self-created and unnecessary. The more the client struggles to escape the pain, the more he or she suffers. The aim of ACT in the treatment of chronic pain is to help the client to develop greater psychological flexibility in the presence of thoughts, feelings, and behaviors associated with pain.

MINDFULNESS IN ACT

Mindfulness is a key element used in ACT to establish a sense of self that is greater than one's thoughts, feelings, and other private events. By practicing mindfulness exercises, clients learn to develop an "observer-self" perspective, in which they can examine previously avoided thoughts and feelings in a nonreactive and nonjudgmental way. Adopting this observer perspective facilitates cognitive defusion, in which the client learns to notice thoughts without necessarily acting on them, being controlled by them, or believing them. Thus, pain-related thoughts that tell the client to avoid particular situations or activities can be seen for what they are (thoughts), rather than what they say they are (truth or reality). The observer-self perspective also allows exposure to previously avoided emotions and sensations to take place. Exposure generally reduces fear of these phenomena and leads to greater behavioral flexibility in their presence. Finally, mindfulness helps the client maintain awareness of the present moment and develop persistence in taking steps in valued directions.

The use of mindfulness is critical in helping clients to identify valued life directions that are intensely personal and deeply important to them and that will provide natural positive reinforcement. Clients who are "stuck" in chronic pain are mostly active in the nonvital struggle of reducing pain rather than living the vital lives of their choice. Most clients with chronic pain will come to the pain clinic saying that all they want is to become pain free. Much of their focus in life is on pain management. There is not much vitality in nursing pain symptoms. On the other hand, valued directions, which have probably been put on hold in the service of reducing pain, contain the positive reinforcement or vitality needed to motivate the behavior change to resume living a valued life. From an individual point of view, valuing is something intensely personal, and in a deep sense of the term, freely chosen. Valuing is a term used in ACT that means acting in your valued directions, in spite of having thoughts and feelings that may be unpleasant or painful.

OTHER ELEMENTS OF ACT IN THE TREATMENT OF CHRONIC PAIN

The traditional cognitive-behavioral therapy (CBT) approach to treatment of chronic pain attempts to reduce pain behaviors and increase healthy behaviors. ACT takes a different approach to the phenomena of chronic pain, characterized by building psychological flexibility in the context of the client's values. Several concepts are important in understanding the ACT approach to chronic pain.

Experiential Avoidance of Pain

Experiential avoidance is the negative evaluation of and unwillingness to maintain contact with internal experiences, such as bodily sensations, emotions, cognitions, and urges, and efforts to avoid, escape, change, or terminate these experiences, even when doing so is harmful (Hayes, Wilson, Gifford, Follette, & Strosahl, 1996). Typically, when we feel pain sensations, the sympathetic nervous system is alerted and we avoid or escape pain before having time to think. This reflex is essential for survival. In addition, however, human beings can imagine pain and react to it as if it were truly present. For example, we cringe at the thought of having our teeth drilled, although no drill is present. We may get frightened when we feel our own heart palpitations, or tense and apprehensive if we expect pain. If we react to these thoughts, sensations, and expectations about pain with avoidance, escape, or resistance, we may create more problems. For example, we may avoid situations or activities that are necessary for our well-being, such as going to the dentist or engaging in aerobic exercise.

The more we attempt to avoid pain and the associated situations, thoughts, and activities, the more restricted our lives become. One of the aims of ACT in the treatment of chronic pain is for the client to accept that pain is a normal and inevitable sensation that will come to all of us who live. Anxiety and fear are natural reactions to pain and are normal and inevitable as well. Using mindfulness exercises, the client can learn to see pain sensations as normal physical warning signals alerting attention, or as part of their ongoing chronic pain condition. The client learns to observe the natural tendency to escape or avoid pain. Being present to this process improves ability to make active choices about whether avoidance or exposure to the pain experience is more functional.

Pain Mindscripts

In the ACT model, the human mind is sometimes called the "don't-get-eaten machine." Its job is to compare, evaluate, make judgments, remember past dangers and failures, and warn about potential future catastrophes. As soon as pain sensations have been perceived by the brain, the mind starts producing cognitions, or "scripts," about the pain. These *mindscripts* include thoughts regarding the causes of pain and rules aimed at protection from further pain. Common rules include the following: "A person with your pain cannot work," "Take care of your pain first before you do anything else," "Any physical exertion might cause more pain," and "Avoid any stress or demands until you have gotten rid of your pain." Rules like these contribute to a life characterized by pain avoidance and inability to move in valued directions. If the client is fused with these beliefs, his or her behavior is unlikely to change, regardless of the treatment. One of the aims of ACT is to defuse the client from these mindscripts. The client learns through the practice of mindfulness exercises to adopt the observer-self perspective. From this perspective, the client learns to observe and detach from the scripts that the mind produces. That is, the client learns, "I have thoughts, but I am not my thoughts. I have feelings, but I am not my feelings. I am much greater than all of these components, and I do not have to be controlled by my thoughts and feelings."

Values Illness

In the ACT model, *values illness* is a condition that develops when a person puts valued activities on hold in the service of reducing symptoms—in this case, pain. As pain management occupies more and more of the person's time, other valued activities are neglected. For most people, valued activities such as social contact, exercise, intimate relationships, parenting, professional work, or community involvement give meaning to life. By neglecting these naturally reinforcing activities, we risk losing that which is meaningful and becoming depressed. When pain management becomes our main occupation, we are likely to suffer from values illness.

Several exercises can be used to help the client identify long-standing consistent values. One method frequently used in ACT is establishing the client's life compass. This method will be illustrated in the Case Study later in the chapter. The purpose of making the compass is to help the client to express consistently valued directions for his or her life *and* to look at how he or she is actually living today. The life compass also clarifies the verbal barriers or reasons why the client believes he or she cannot move in those valued directions.

Another exercise that we have developed for identifying valued directions is the funeral exercise. The client is asked to imagine being present at his or her own funeral. The client is asked to invite the five or six persons he or she would most want to be present. The exercise has three parts. In the first part, the client expresses what he or she fears the loved ones present will be thinking about the client as they say farewell. In the second part, the client listens to the loved ones as they express the fears of the client. In the final part, the client gets a second chance and is instructed to speak directly to each of the loved ones. The client is asked to express what type of relationship he or she wants to have with each of the loved ones and also make a commitment with regard to what he or she is now willing to do to create that relationship. Committed action or "valuing" refers to making public statements about doing whatever needs to be done to start moving in that valued direction, and then taking these steps.

For the client who has been occupied by pain management, this exercise brings to light the discrepancy between deeply important values and the activities of pain management. The fears are commonly described around the following themes: "I'm afraid my children are thinking that I only thought about my pain during the past year and wasn't there for them," "I'm afraid my friends will think that I didn't care about them because I didn't take the time for them," "I'm afraid my husband (partner) would think that I let my marriage go down the drain and didn't take the time to develop it," and so on. The client clearly sees the discrepancy between his or her vital valued directions (being there for children, working to maintain a marriage, keeping the vitality in friendships) and the nonvital dominating activities done in the service of pain management.

For most clients, seeing the huge discrepancy between what we value and how we act can be enough to motivate significant behavior change in the valued directions. The client's valued directions are the natural positive reinforcers that motivate the hard work of exposure in therapy. Pain management cannot be a valued direction in itself because it contains no natural positive reinforcers. The client who has been occupied by pain reduction thoughts and behaviors probably needs to reconnect to deeply important life directions. In sum, all three of these components— experiential avoidance, pain mindscripts, and values illness—should be addressed with the aim of creating psychological flexibility.

Clean Pain and Dirty Pain

Clean pain (unconditioned pain) is the hurting sensation itself alerting us that something is wrong. It is natural to avoid and escape clean pain. *Dirty pain* (conditioned pain), on the other hand, is created as a result of our resistance to thoughts, expectations, and emotions associated with pain. When we lower our tolerance to thoughts and feelings associated with pain and get involved in activities focused on avoiding future pain, we develop dirty pain. ACT distinguishes between avoiding dangerous events or injury (which is usually adaptive) and avoiding feelings and thoughts about dangerous events (which is often maladaptive). The ACT therapist may say, "Pain flourishes in your absence." The client who is "absent" from the present because of living in the pain mindscripts of the past or future has little control over his or her life. Becoming present to the actual pain sensations and discriminating clean from dirty pain is an essential part of the treatment, because it facilitates active choices about how to move in valued directions.

HOW THE ACT APPROACH DIFFERS FROM TRADITIONAL COGNITIVE-BEHAVIORAL THERAPY

In general the difference between the traditional CBT treatment model and the ACT model of chronic pain lies in the contextualistic philosophy underlying ACT. The underpinnings of functional contextualism, with its unique theory of language and cognition (relational frame theory) (Hayes, Barnes-Holmes, & Roche, 2001), leads to a treatment model of chronic pain that, like traditional CBT, is exposure-based but looks quite different. The traditional CBT approach to chronic pain emphasizes reducing pain behaviors and increasing healthy behaviors. Traditional behavioral techniques such as shaping, graduated physical training, pain education, social skills training, cognitive restructuring, and contingency management are used to reduce pain behaviors, increase muscle relaxation, and encourage normal movements and ergonomic working techniques. Common rehabilitation goals in CBT include improving physical fitness, improving social skills such as assertiveness, increasing pain coping skills, and improving ergonomic skills. This multidimensional approach to rehabilitation has been acknowledged as a generally effective treatment for chronic pain (Turk, Rudy, & Sorkin, 1992).

The ACT approach differs primarily in the use of mindfulness skills and the contextual framework that emphasizes close examination of the client's values. Clients in ACT reconnect to their own values context, which then serves as the motivation for behavior change in valued directions. In the ACT approach, positive reinforcement (or what we call vitality) is identified through the use of the values context and mindfulness exercises. In this way, the values context provides the meaning and motivation for the client to develop willingness to make the changes that are needed to get back on life's track. The ACT approach focuses on empowerment of the individual's own resources for rehabilitation. The therapeutic relationship differs from the traditional CBT model in that the client is regarded as competent and able to take charge of his or her own rehabilitation. In sum, the ACT model differs from traditional CBT in its focus on moving toward a vital life rather than on pain management. This creates differences in the purposes for which treatment strategies are implemented. For example, traditional CBT strategies generally are implemented with the explicit goal of pain reduction or improved pain management. Conversely, in ACT, treatment strategies are never linked to pain management, reduction, or coping per se. Instead, they are methods of enhancing a vital life.

CASE STUDY

The following is a case of a 46-year-old woman, Susan, who has been diagnosed with fibromyalgia. When Susan came to the clinic, she had been on disability for the past year and had little hope of ever returning to work. In the first part of this section Susan tells her story. The second part is a transcript of much of Susan's first ACT session, which illustrates fundamental therapeutic components. The third part illustrates how specific mindfulness exercises are used within the ACT context.

Susan's Story

I can begin by saying that I feel disappointed and deserted by medical professionals. I have been let down by everyone in the health care services who have promised to help me. I have done everything I was told to do by every sort of health care professional and I am today far worse off than I was at the start. I hurt all over my body and I am depressed. I feel like I have lost almost everything that meant anything to me, all because of my pain. If I could just find a cure I could start living again. I have tried everything in order to get rid of it. I went on sick leave and avoided the lifting and the stress that was causing my pain. I reduced all demands so that I could give myself a break. I even stopped seeing my friends so that I could completely focus on getting better. Essentially, I put my life on hold in the service of getting rid of my pain, but strangely enough, the opposite happened. The more I gave up and the more I tried to manage my pain, the worse it got and the more depressed I became. Taking care of my pain became a full-time occupation. I tried painkillers, antidepressants, muscle relaxers, sleeping pills. I tried physical therapy, massage therapy, acupuncture, and acupressure. I went to a counselor and talked about my pain. I tried to change my way of thinking and be more positive. I went to the fibromyalgia self-help group and learned more about my illness. I tried health foods and even went to a healer. And despite having spent the past two years doing nothing but trying to get rid of my pain, I have never felt worse. I have more pain now than before I went for help *and* I have lost virtually everything in my life. I have lost my job and my self-confidence and have little chance of getting back to work. I have gained 40 pounds and feel bad about myself. I have lost my friends and my social life. I have lost my sexual interest and my husband is not interested in any intimate relationship with me. I have stopped going to my kids' activities and my relationship with them is worse. I don't have the energy to invite anyone home or even go out if I get invited, so I feel isolated. Right now I have no hope of ever getting better. So the best thing you can do to help me is to write an evaluation saying that I am unable to work so that I can get permanent disability.

SESSION 1

Following is a transcript of the first session with Susan. The aim of the session is to identify and reconnect to her valued life directions, to examine the verbal barriers stopping her from moving in these directions, and to examine the workability of the strategies she is using to solve her problems.

Therapist: From your description, Susan, it sounds like your pain is squeezing the life out of you.

Susan: Yes, I am desperate. I don't know what else to do. That is why I came to you. I was hoping maybe this clinic had something I haven't tried.

T: I get the sense of your suffering and your losses. It sounds like you have given up almost everything that meant anything to you in the service of quieting that pain down.

S: That's the strange thing. The more I tried and the more I sacrificed, the worse the pain got. It just makes no sense.

T: Let me tell you a metaphor that is related to what you are talking about. Imagine when you go home tonight that you find a baby tiger in your kitchen. Can you see him there sleeping by the stove? When you come in, he wakes up and snarls at you. You know that tigers are meat eaters and you instinctively know that he is hungry. You go to the fridge and find some meat to give him. He is satisfied for a little while and you relax and get ready to go on with your activities when he snarls again. Again, you know what to do and this time you give him a bigger portion of meat and hope that he stays quiet a longer time. But what happens is that the more you give him, the hungrier he gets. And soon you are doing nothing else but feeding that tiger. Finally, you have given the tiger everything you have in your fridge and there is nothing else to give. You turn around to tell the tiger that there is no more meat to give him. To your horror, you see that the little baby tiger has become a huge hungry tiger and YOU are his next meal. What have you created?

S: A monster!

T: Think of that baby tiger snarling at you as your pain when it started. In the service of quieting down your pain, you started sacrificing activities that are important to you. You might have sacrificed meeting your friends or exercising, or your job, all in the service of getting control over your pain.

S: Yes, I did that, but that's what I was told to do. My doctor told me to go on sick leave and rest up and get better before I went back to work. My physical therapist told me to not do anything that hurt.

T: I know that the health care system gives these instructions and you did your best. Let's just look at what happened. From what you have said, you put one valuable activity after another on hold in the service of getting control over your pain. But instead of getting rid of your pain, it looks like you got a big and hungry pain and lost much of your quality of life.

S: Yes, that is exactly what happened. I thought by focusing on my pain and getting rid of it, I could get back to my life. That's what I was told by everyone I went to. Everyone told me, prioritize getting well. They told me to cut down on my activities and think about myself for a change. That's what I did and look what happened! I lost everything! I thought the health care system knew what they were doing!

T: In order for me to help you, I need to know more about the life that you want and that you have lost. I want to know about what you have put on hold while you have been feeding the tiger.

S: [pause] That hurts to think about. I've tried not thinking about my losses. I've tried to adapt to the way things are now.

T: And where has that thinking led you?

S: I've just tried to be realistic and accept the fact that pain rules my life and do the best I can within those limits.

T: And where has that thought gotten you?

S: That's not a thought, it is reality.

T: And thinking that thought, where has that led to?

S: Why do you keep talking about thoughts? I am talking facts! I have lived with this pain for years now and I have accepted that my life as I knew it before I got this illness is over.

T: I can feel that you are suffering, Susan, and it seems to me from what you have conveyed that your pain is suffocating your life.

S: [tears in her eyes] That's the right word!

T: If it is okay with you, I would like to put aside pain for a moment and hear more about the life you want to live. Let's say I have a magic wand and your pain is now gone. What would your life look like? What would you want your life to stand for?

S: I don't really see the sense in thinking about a fantasy that could never happen, but okay. If I could, I would get back important parts of my life, like activities with my children, my close relationship with my husband, meeting my friends again, and developing my own interests. I would also go back to work and maybe get more education and a more advanced job within special education. But I know that none of that is possible, so I don't know why you want to talk about dreams that never can come true. I have really tried to *not* think about those dreams.

T: I understand that it hurts to care about directions you would like to go in your life, especially if you feel the door to them is shut for you. Would you be willing, here and now, to feel that hurt by looking more carefully at those dreams that you care about? Doing that might give you the possibility of getting closer to what you want. Would you be willing to bring those hurt feelings into this room here and now?

S: I guess so, if that helps you help me.

T: You have mentioned that, if it weren't for your pain, you would like to get closer to your children, your husband, your friends, your own interests, and possibly more education that might lead to a more advanced job. I am going to write these directions down in what I will call your "life compass." On this compass, there are four more areas as well: community involvement, spirituality, your own parents and siblings, and your health. Let's do an exercise in which you think about each of these life dimensions and what is important about them. Think about the very essence of how you want to be in that dimension. Think about what are the most important components that you want in each dimension. Write down your "intentions" for each one. When you are done with that, I want you to think about what stands between you, today, and following those intentions you have described. You can write these as barriers.

S: Okay. [Susan writes on the white board. Her responses are reproduced in Table 13.1]

T: As you look at what you have written here on your life compass, I want you to allow yourself to really look at the difference between your intentions or how you

TABLE 13.1   Susan's Intentions and Barriers in Life Dimensions

Life Dimension	Intentions	Barriers
Parenting	Be present and mindful with my children	Tired
Health	Exercise regularly, eat healthy foods, sleep 8 hours per night	Pain
Social relations	Give and receive support, sense of belonging	No time
Intimate relations	Give and receive physical and emotional closeness	Too fat, afraid
Family	Give and receive support, sense of belonging	No energy
Community	Contribute to the well-being of children	No time
Work	Contribute to the well-being of children with developmental disabilities	Pain
Spiritual life	Reflect on my place in life, give myself time, show myself compassion	No time
Education/development	Develop my knowledge/skills in special education	Too old
Leisure	Develop my creative interests	No time

deeply want your life to be *and* how you are, in fact, living today. It might be easier for you to think of your intentions as the directions you want your life to go and how you are acting today as your feet. Now look at your life dimensions and see in how many of them your feet are consistently in the direction you want to go. Or you could think of it this way: If your feet were your intentions, which way would they be walking?

S: My God, that is depressing! My feet are going frantically in the opposite direction of where I want them to go. What happened? I guess I had a picture of the way I was supposed to be, supposed to live, that influenced my feet more than my own dreams. I did what I thought was expected of me rather than what I really felt was important. I ended up doing what others wanted of me and I let my own dreams down.

T: And how does that feel?

S: Empty and meaningless. I feel like my feet have just been running around in circles trying to please everyone else but losing my own direction.

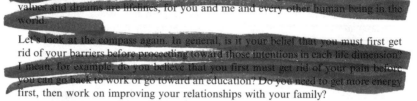

T: Your dreams, values, and visions are what make living worthwhile, Susan. Those values and dreams are lifelines, for you and me and every other human being in the world.

Let's look at the compass again. In general, is it your belief that you must first get rid of your barriers before proceeding toward those intentions in each life dimension? I mean, for example, do you believe that you first must get rid of your pain before you can go back to work or go toward an education? Do you need to get more energy first, then work on improving your relationships with your family?

S: Yes, that is what I believe. If I just could get rid of my pain, get more energy, lose weight, and get more time, I might be able to regain some of that life back. That is what I have been trying to do! Solve those problems.

T: Let's write down all of the strategies that you have worked with over the years to do just that, getting rid of your pain. I can set up a table and you can fill in everything that you have worked with. [Susan's responses are shown in Table 13.2.]

Table 13.2   Susan's Pain Control Strategies and Their Outcomes

Strategy	Short-Term Results	Long-Term Results Relative to Intentions
Sick leave	Fewer demands	Further from work intentions
Avoid physical activity	Less strain/stress	Further from health intentions
Avoid places where one must sit	Fewer demands, less stress	Further from social, leisure, education, spiritual intentions
Avoid intimacy	Fewer demands	Further from intimacy intentions
Rest	Less stress	Further from all intentions
Massage	Relief	Further from all intentions
Physical therapy	Relief	Further from activity intentions
Alternative therapy	Relief	Further from all intentions
Painkillers	Relief	Further from health and social intentions
Stop activity	Relief	Further from all intentions

T: Now we have listed all the ways in which you have tried to manage your pain. You have worked very hard for a very long time in trying to prevent or directly control your pain. What does your experience say about all of these strategies as far as getting rid of your pain? And secondly, what does your experience say about how these pain management strategies influence your quality of life? I mean, the life you have described in your life compass. Has your focus on pain management got you any closer to that life you want to live?

S: I know the answer to that. I don't want to say it because it makes me feel that I have wasted countless time and money and energy and lost most everything in my life besides all that. I have been disappointed so many times; I don't even want to think about it.

T: I am asking you now if you would be willing to examine your experiences and let yourself feel the hopelessness of this struggle.

S: I don't understand, I came here to feel better not worse.

T: I understand that your margins are worn thin and the last thing you want right now is more pain and suffering. But it may be so that in order to get better, you may need to feel worse for a while. Would it be worth it to you to feel more pain and confusion a while with me in order to find a new path that might lead you closer in those directions that you want to go?

S: But what if there are new and better ways to get rid of my pain? Who knows what new research might bring? Maybe they will find a cure for pain. Then all my struggling might be worthwhile.

T: Maybe they will, Susan, who knows? The question remains, what does your experience tell you about your pain and suffering and the strategies you have tried in the service of getting rid of your pain? When is enough? At what point have you suffered enough?

S: Yes, I definitely have. I want to get out of this struggle and be left alone.

T: Be left alone with your pain, letting pain run your life, is that what you want?

S: What choice do I have? My pain has occupied my life. If I just cut down on all other demands and stress, I could probably get by and be okay.

T: Is that what you want for yourself in life? To count your losses and just get by?

S: I have no choice. There is no solution to getting rid of my pain. I can see that today when we have listed all the things I have done to try to manage my pain. There is no solution.

T: Susan, I think you are right. I don't think there is a solution either.

S: You mean I am a hopeless case? Now I really feel lousy.

T: Not you, Susan. You are not hopeless, but the strategies of getting rid of your pain so that you can get back to your life are probably as hopeless as you have experienced.

S: What can I do?

T: Imagine that I have two packages in my hands. In the one package, you have complete freedom from pain. And that you know from your own experience is perfectly possible. You can keep yourself drugged all the time. You can drink yourself numb. There are all kinds of ways to numb yourself and be pain free 24 hours a day. But in that package you do not have the life that you want. In the other package, you get the chance to come closer to that life that you want back. You have the chance to get closer to your old or new friends, get closer to your kids again, and get started toward those dreams you had with your husband, get closer to that community work that you have visions about and so on. *And* you have your pain, more or less as you have it today. Which of these packages would you choose?

S: That's not much of a choice. Of course I would choose the chance to get my life back. I don't want to be drugged all the time.

T: What I hear you saying, Susan, is that you are choosing your valued life and you are willing to make a space for your pain and take it along on your journey?

S: Yes, I am willing to do that.

SUMMARY OF SUSAN'S FIRST SESSION

In the ACT approach to chronic pain, a context of values is identified and used as the motivation for the hard work of rehabilitation. As can be seen in the example of Susan, there is an initial and consistent focus in the treatment sessions on finding the ultimate values in each life dimension. Examining these values is a step toward empowering Susan to take responsibility for her own life direction. Once these values are identified, often described in terms of feelings of vitality, they are used as reference points for behavior change. The second therapeutic component is examining the verbal barriers that Susan's mind has produced as reasons why she cannot take steps in her valued directions. With the help of the therapist, Susan learns to analyze the function of her verbal reasons rather than dispute their content. The focus is on what these thoughts lead to rather than whether they are true or probable. By viewing her verbal barriers functionally, rather than by content, she can see that these rules lead her in directions that she does not want to go. Mindfulness will be used in the next session as a tool for helping Susan to see those verbal barriers as products of her mind attempting to make sense of her pain. A third component in this session is creative hopelessness, which aims at undermining reason-giving and exposes the unworkability of Susan's strategies for solving her problem. Susan is asked to examine the strategies she has used to solve her pain problem. The therapist validates Susan for the hard work of pain management she has done and that has cost her economically and personally. Once again, Susan performs functional analyses on these pain management strategies, which shows clearly that they have led her further away from her vital life. She can see from her experience that the strategies of trying to prevent, reduce, or control her pain have actually backfired and she has lost out on all counts. This is usually a difficult insight. Susan is asked to face the possibility that the solutions she has invested so much in actually may be part of the problem. Clients in ACT are often taken aback by the insight that doing what seemed logical, rational, and normal is clearly unworkable or even pathological. The paradox brought to light here is that Susan is experiencing more suffering, because trying to get rid of pain is painful in itself. Seeing and experiencing the hopelessness of these strategies from her own experience helped Susan to let go of ineffective strategies and opened up space for new ways of approaching rehabilitation.

At the end of the session, an alternative focus of therapy was presented in the form of willingness and acceptance of the pain experience *and* taking steps toward her valued life. Susan is asked if she is willing to make a commitment to be willing. Commitment to stepping up to what needs to be done is a key component in ACT. Therapy is now focused on moving toward a vital life, rather than on fighting against pain. Before this journey begins, Susan will need a safe place where she can expose herself to previously avoided private events. The next session uses mindfulness exercises to help Susan to develop a new perspective on her thoughts and feelings.

MINDFULNESS AND DEFUSION IN SUSAN'S CASE

Mindfulness exercises are a key element used in ACT to establish a sense of self that exists in the present and to provide a context for the work of cognitive defusion. In the second session, the observer exercise (Hayes *et al.,* 1999) is used to help Susan create a space of flexibility where she can observe her pain-related thoughts and feelings and see how they lead her away from her valued directions and reduce her quality of life. The aim of this exercise is also to empower Susan to see that she has full control over her behavior regardless of what her thoughts and feelings are telling her.

> Therapist: Susan, if I have your permission, I would like to do an exercise with you in which we bring those difficult thoughts and feelings into this room.
>
> Susan: I don't know how that would be possible, but we can try.
>
> T: I would like to do what is called a mindfulness exercise. Start by closing your eyes and just listen to my voice.
>
> S: Okay.
>
> T: I want you to take a deep breath and slowly breathe out. Notice your breathing. Imagine that you are being breathed by the air. Just be passive and let yourself be breathed by the air. Notice that you do not have to be involved in your breathing; your body takes care of itself without any effort on your part. Now, I want you to observe yourself sitting in the chair in this office. I want you to feel whatever you feel in your body. Notice any sensations in any parts of your body. You might notice your heart beating or some tension in a muscle. Just sense whatever you sense. I want you also to observe the thoughts that come into your head as you are sitting now. If you can, try just to observe your thoughts, the way a cat watches a mouse hole. Just watch each new thought and let it go. If you can, try not to argue with or resist your thoughts that come, just acknowledge each of your thoughts and let it go and watch for the next one that comes [silence for one minute]. Now, I want you to observe your

feelings. Notice how your feelings might have changed during the time you have been here today. Just notice your feelings as they come and go. If you can, try not to pass judgments on your feelings, just allow them to come forward, acknowledge them and let them go and watch for new feelings [silence one minute]. I want you now to notice who it is that is doing this noticing. Notice that it is you in a special state that is here right now noticing your thoughts and feelings and bodily sensations. I want you to be aware of that person behind your eyes who has the ability to observe thoughts, feelings, and sensations. We can call this person, who is you, the "observer-self."

I want you now to remember something that happened to you last summer. Something that was significant for you. When you have that picture, I want you to look around you in that situation. If there were people there, I want you to look into their faces, into their eyes. I want you to feel what you were feeling at that moment. I want you to think the thoughts you had just then. I want you to feel what bodily sensations you had at that moment. See if you can capture the smells that were present and the sounds [silence for one minute]. Now see if you can notice that it was YOU, the observer-self, noticing all these experiences. It is you, the observer-self, who has the ability to re-create a picture from the past like you just did. You were there then and you are here now. The person who we can call the observer-self was aware of your thoughts and feelings then and is the same person who is here today, aware and noticing your thoughts and feelings and bodily sensations.

We can take a situation even farther back in time. I want you to go back as far as possible to the first memory that you remember very clearly. Go back to the first memory that is very clear to you. Something that was very significant to you [silence for one minute]. Take your time and look around. See what you see, hear what you hear, and feel what you feel. What are the thoughts of that little girl? Try to feel what she was feeling. Look at her hand and see that it is your hand, although it is the hand of a child. See that her body is the body of a child, but it is the same body as is here today. Notice that it was the same observer-self that was there then that is here today. You have been YOU your whole life. Notice that even though your body has changed and your thoughts and feelings have changed, the observer-self is the same. Everywhere you have been, everything you have felt, every thought you have had, YOU have been there noticing.

From your observer-self perspective we are going to examine some important areas of your life. We can start with your body. Your body was once a little baby and it has grown as big as it is today. Sometimes your body is sick and sometimes it is healthy. Sometimes your body is tired and sometimes it is rested. Your body can be in pain or it can feel fine. You have experienced that bodily sensations come and go, yet YOU remain constant. You may have already lost parts of your body, through operations, but YOU remain the same. You have experienced that your body is in constant change and will continue to change. Yet, from your observer perspective YOU remain constant. Your body is very important to you and you are responsible for taking care of your body, but YOU are NOT your body. You are much more than your body. Sometimes you may forget this and think that you are your body. You might even think that you are your pain. When this happens, you make yourself vulnerable and can feel hopelessly stuck inside your painful body. You have the ability to observe all your bodily sensations from the observer perspective, and pain is no exception. You can observe your pain without becoming your pain. Pain might get very loud and demand your attention the way a screaming child throws a temper tantrum in order to get you to buy candy. You know that candy is not healthy for the child and you do not want to give in, but because you can't stand his screaming you give in and buy this child the candy. When you do this, you teach him that screaming and temper tantrums are effective for getting candy. In the same way, if you yield to your screaming pain by doing what it tells you rather than what you know is healthy and good for you, you create a body that is going to act up everywhere you go. Give yourself a minute to notice the sensations in your body come and go. And as your body changes, notice that your observer-self remains the same. This means that while you have a body and you can observe pain in your body, you are more than your painful body. Notice that YOU are the one noticing.

Let's take a look at your feelings. You have experienced that your feelings are in constant change. You may have had strong feelings about someone or some issue a while back that you hardly feel anything about today. Today you may observe strong feelings about some things that may be gone tomorrow. One thing is certain. Your feelings, regardless of how strong they are, will change. Feelings are in constant movement. Your feelings are important to you. With your feelings you are able to feel closeness, love, joy, sadness, and other vital dimensions in life. Notice who is noticing those feelings. The you who is noticing is much greater than your feelings. Despite the dramatic changes in your feelings from one second to the next, you remain constant. Your observer-self can monitor feelings without being automatically controlled by them. Your observer-self can feel your feelings and decide from a larger perspective whether to go with a feeling or not. Sometimes you forget this and believe that you ARE your feelings. You can tell when this happens. It happens when you feel that you cannot resist an impulse. You can feel like a victim or slave to a feeling and that you have no choice but to follow what a feeling tells you. When you yield like this to a feeling, you blow life into that feeling and give it power over you. Always remember that it is YOU who gives feelings power. It is only through you that feelings can gain or lose strength. NO feeling can bully you off your set course. Only you are in charge of where your feet go. You are not a victim to your feelings. You are much greater than your feelings.

Let us look at the last and most difficult area, your mind and your thoughts. Your mind has a great analytic ability to solve problems, create structure, organize into categories, evaluate, and make logical judgments. You have experienced how well your mind works in helping you to control or influence external events in your life, such as painting a room, or sewing clothes, or fixing the car. Your mind is very important to you and does an excellent job at what it does. But you also have experience that your mind does not do so well in trying to control internal areas within you. Internal things, such as thoughts and feelings, just don't seem to be controllable. Your thoughts are in constant change. At some time in your life you may have had definite thoughts about something and then you got an education or more experience and your thoughts changed. Even as we have been sitting here today, your thoughts may have changed. Even though you have observed your thoughts in constant change, YOU have remained the same. Sometimes you forget this and believe you are your thoughts. When you identify yourself with your thoughts you may become more vulnerable. You can easily be insulted or threatened when your thoughts are questioned by others. From the observer perspective you can monitor your thoughts and see them as they are; products of your mind, your past learning experience. You have experience that when you come into a new situation or feel a pain sensation, your mind produces thoughts to try and make sense of the situation. Your mind produces reminders of similar past dangers and warns you to beware. From the observer perspective, you can appreciate your mind's efforts in trying to protect you and make the choice of what action you will take. You are much greater than your mind.

Just as a matter of experience, you have noticed that you are not just your body, not just your feelings, not just your pain, and not just your thoughts. All of these things are the content of your life, while you are the arena or the context or the space from which all this content unfolds in your life. As you think about that, notice that the pain, which you have been struggling with, and the treatments and the work issues are not you. No matter what happens with all those battles, you will remain the same, unchanged, just noticing what happens. See if you can use this observer perspective to let go of some of this content and give yourself space. You can feel secure that however things turn out, you will remain you. Maybe you don't need to invest yourself in fighting because you have seen these fights all your life, and whether one side wins or loses doesn't much matter in the long run. You will remain the same.

In this mindfulness exercise, Susan finds a transcendent part of herself where she can be aware of difficult or painful feelings, sensations, or thoughts without being threatened by them. From this observer position, Susan is more ready to expose herself to pain and associated emotions and thoughts.

Other mindfulness exercises may be used to discriminate vital from nonvital life directions. Exercising mindfulness helps the client to be present in all activities and make active choices about whether these activities are consistent with valued directions or not. For example, by exercising mindfulness in her daily life, Susan discovered that many of her activities were in nonvital directions. Susan did an exercise program daily because the physical therapist required her to do so; she was following a diet because her doctor told her she must lose weight; and she was going to pain management lectures because her insurance company demanded it. Such behaviors exemplify an ACT concept called "pliance," a type of rule-governed behavior controlled by the social consequences of rule-following. These behaviors are likely to be nonvital. In ACT, one of the most important aims is to find the vitality of natural positive reinforcers in the activities we choose. The activities of rehabilitation, such as exercising, eating nutritious food, and learning about pain, all may be naturally reinforcing, but Susan was doing them primarily because she had been told to. The use of mindfulness helped Susan to make active choices about which activities coincided with her own values.

HOW MINDFULNESS HELPED SUSAN

Susan started taking steps in her valued directions after the first session. Reconnecting to her deeply held values and seeing the discrepancy between how she wanted to live her life and how she, in fact, was living was enough to get her back on track in a couple of dimensions. Susan called her two best friends and told them how much they meant to her and initiated a meeting. She also visited her former workplace and told her coworkers how much her work meant to her and that she wanted to come back. During the second session of mindfulness, Susan was able to adopt the observer-self perspective and monitor her thoughts and feelings without being fused to them. As soon as she was able to change the context and not identify herself with her pain and associated thoughts and feelings, she created flexibility for herself. This flexibility helped Susan to let go of what she could not influence and see the possibilities in the here and now that she could influence. Susan started taking steps toward finishing her college degree so that she could pursue her professional goals. As she took those steps, she encountered verbal barriers that attempted to stop her. Susan's experience with mindfulness exercises allowed her to recognize those barriers and accept them compassionately without letting herself get pushed off track.

EMPIRICAL SUPPORT FOR ACT WITH CHRONIC PAIN

There is growing evidence for the effectiveness of ACT in the treatment of several problems (Hayes, Masuda, Bissett, Luoma, & Guerrero, 2004). Applications of ACT to the treatment of chronic pain have only recently been empirically evaluated. To date there are two group studies. McCracken, Vowles, and Eccleston (in press) conducted an ACT-based 3- to 4-week residential treatment program with 108 patients with complex, long-standing chronic pain and long histories of unsuccessful treatment. Findings included statistically and clinically significant improvements on a range of outcome measures, including pain; depression; pain-related anxiety; disability; ability to sit, stand, and walk; number of medical visits; time spent resting due to pain; use of pain medication; and acceptance of pain. Most improvements were maintained at 3-month follow-up. Increases in acceptance predicted positive changes in depression, pain-related anxiety, physical and psychosocial disablity, and the ability to move quickly between sitting and standing. Changes in pain were small compared with improvements in functioning, and increased acceptance of pain appeared to be the primary process responsible for improved functioning.

In an randomized controlled study, Dahl *et al.* (2004) investigated the effects of a brief ACT intervention for the treatment of caretakers and practical nurses working in the public health sector who showed chronic stress and/or pain and were at risk for high sick-leave utilization. ACT was compared in an additive treatment design with medical treatment as usual (MTAU). A group of 19 participants were randomly distributed into two groups. Both conditions received MTAU. Additionally, the ACT condition received four one-hour weekly sessions of ACT. At posttreatment and 6-month follow-up, the ACT participants showed fewer sick days and used fewer medical treatment resources than those in the MTAU condition. Quality-of-life measurements showed a nonsignificant trend favoring ACT. These improvements could not be accounted for by remission of stress and pain in the ACT group, since no between-group differences were found for pain or stress symptoms.

Several recent case studies illustrate the use of ACT with individuals with severe chronic pain. Montesinos, Hernández, and Luciano (2001) reported encouraging results for a male cancer patient with severe pain, anxiety, and experiential avoidance. Luciano, Visdómine, Gutiérrez, and Montesinos (2001) noted positive findings for two young women with chronic pain and concurrent behavioral problems. Wicksell, Dahl, Magnusson, and Olsson (in press) investigated the effect of ACT for an adolescent with debilitating pain. In this study, it was hypothesized that avoidance of pain and pain-related stimuli was a central theme in the disability. Treatment emphasized increasing activity in valued directions, rather than symptom reduction. As the client moved in valued directions, exposure to avoided pain stimuli took place naturally. The results of this study showed improvement in valued life activities such as school attendance and individual goal achievement, as well as reduced pain ratings. These results suggest that acceptance-based treatments might be a promising alternative for young clients who do not show improvement in the traditional pain management programs.

IMPLEMENTING MINDFULNESS WITH THE TREATMENT TEAM

Mindfulness can be used in consulting with rehabilitation teams in a numbers of ways. Clinical work in chronic pain is frustrating for rehabilitation professionals, because clients who have gotten stuck in the vicious cycle of pain management rarely get unstuck and move forward. Rehabilitation team members often get stuck themselves over time and lose much of their initial flexibility, empathy, and compassion. The practice of mindfulness can help team members in the same way that it helps clients. It aims at creating psychological flexibility, reconnecting to deeply held values, and defusing from unhelpful cognitions. Here is an excerpt from the exercise we have created for this purpose.

> Now I want you to go back to the time when you first started your job working in rehabilitation. Can you see yourself there full of optimism and energy, full of compassion for helping clients with different disabilities come back to their lives? Notice the thoughts and the feelings you had at that time, the feeling that you wanted to make a difference for these people, a difference in this world. Notice the person behind your eyes who can notice those feelings and see those thoughts. See if you can notice the difference between the optimism you felt then and what you feel today. Perhaps you hadn't worked very long before you started to see that some clients did not get better, despite your best efforts. A feeling of hopelessness emerged around certain clients. In vain, you gave homework assignments, training programs, and evidence-based advice tailored especially for them. Some clients appeared to function better as long as you worked with them but quickly fell back into old destructive

patterns when they were left on their own. Notice these feelings of hopelessness and how they affected your ability to work with these individuals. Is it possible for you to feel those feelings of frustration when you have worked hard to prepare a client for a better life that he or she never gets the chance to experience? Perhaps you also can feel the frustration of seeing clients who seem to have no illness at all but who see themselves as incapable of working or living a vital life. Let us work together today to create a space of flexibility around these "stuck" thoughts and feelings so that we can together reclaim our compassion and vitality as the therapists we want to be.

Much of the work in consulting or supervising rehabilitation teams using ACT is no different than working with clients. The aim of an ACT supervisor could be summarized as follows: Help the team to reconnect to deeply held values, both individually and collectively; identify the verbal barriers standing in the way of moving in valued directions; reduce cognitive fusion through the use of mindfulness and role-playing; undermine experiential avoidance by illustrating its unworkability and how it conflicts with valued directions; teach acceptance and willingness as alternative coping responses; practice defused exposure to difficult, frustrating thoughts and feelings; and take steps in valued directions.

REFERENCES

Bach, P., & Hayes, S. C. (2002). The use of acceptance and commitment therapy to prevent the rehospitalization of psychotic patients: A randomized controlled trial. *Journal of Consulting and Clinical Psychology, 70,* 1129–1139.

Bigos, S., Bowyer, O., Braen, A., Brown, K., Deyo, R., Haldeman, S., *et al.* (1994). Clinical Practice Guideline No. 14. AHCPR Publication No. 95-0642. Rockville, MD: Agency for Health Care Policy and Research, Public Health Service, U.S. Department of Health and Human Services.

Bond, F. W., & Bunce, D. (2000). Mediators of change in emotion-focused and problem-focused worksite stress management interventions. *Journal of Occupational Health Psychology, 5,* 156–163.

Dahl, J., Wilson, K., & Nilsson, A. (2004). Acceptance and commitment therapy and the treatment of persons at risk for long-term disability resulting from stress and pain symptoms: A randomized controlled clinical trial. *Behavior Therapy, 35,* 785–801.

Gutièrrez, O., Luciano, C., Rodrìguez, M., & Fink, B. C. (2004). Comparison between an acceptance-based and a cognitive-control-based protocol for coping with pain. *Behavior Therapy, 35,* 767–784.

Hayes, S. C., Barnes-Holmes, D., & Roche, B. (Eds) (2001). *Relational frame theory: A post-Skinnerian account of human language and cognition.* New York: Kluwer Academic/Plenum.

Hayes, S. C., Masuda, A., Bissett, R., Luoma, J., & Guerrero, L. (2004). DBT, FAP, and ACT: How empirically oriented are the new behavior therapies? *Behavior Therapy, 35,* 35–54.

Hayes, S. C., Strosahl, K. D., & Wilson, K. G. (1999). *Acceptance and commitment therapy: An experiential approach to behavior change.* New York: Guilford.

Hayes. S. C., Wilson, K. G., Gifford, E. V., Follette, V. M., & Strosahl, K. D. (1996). Emotional avoidance and behavioral disorders: A functional dimensional approach to diagnosis and treatment. *Journal of Consulting and Clinical Psychology, 64,* 1152–1168.

Levitt, J. T., Brown, T. A., Orsillo, S. M., & Barlow, D. H. (2004). The effects of acceptance versus suppression of emotion on subjective and psychophysiological response to carbon dioxide challenge in patients with panic disorder. *Behavior Therapy, 35,* 747–766.

Luciano, C., Visdómine, J. C., Gutiérrez, O., & Montesinos, F. (2001). ACT (acceptance and commitment therapy) and chronic pain. *Análisis y Modificación de Conducta, 27,* 473–502.

McCracken, L. M., Carson, J. W., Eccleston, C., & Keefe, F. J. (2004). Acceptance and change in the context of chronic pain. *Pain, 109,* 4–7.

McCracken, L. M., Vowles, K. E., & Eccleston, C. (2004). Acceptance of chronic pain: Component analysis and a revised assessment method. *Pain, 107,* 159–166.

———(in press). Acceptance-based treatment for persons with complex, long-standing chronic pain: A preliminary analysis of treatment outcome in comparison to a waiting phase. *Behaviour Research and Therapy.*

Montesinos, F., Hernández, B., & Luciano, C. (2001). Application of acceptance and commitment therapy in cancer patients. *Análisis y Modificación de Conducta, 27,* 503–523.

Morley, S., Eccleston, C., & Williams, A. (1999). Systematic review and meta-analysis of randomized controlled trials of cognitive behavior therapy for chronic pain in adults excluding headache. *Pain, 80,* 1–13.

Turk, D. C., Rudy, T. E., & Sorkin, B. (1992). Chronic pain: Behavioral conceptualizations and interventions. In S. M. Turner, K. S. Calhoun, & H. E. Adams (Eds.), *Handbook of clinical behavior therapy* (2nd ed.) (pp. 373–396). New York: John Wiley & Sons.

van Tulder, M., Goossens, M., Waddell, G., & Nachemson, A. (2000). Kroniska länd-ryggsbesvär-konservativ behandling. In *Ont I ryggen, ont I nacken* (Vol. II, pp. 17–113), Stockholm: SBU.

Wicksell, R. K., Dahl, J., Magnusson, B., & Olsson, G. L. (in press). Using acceptance and commitment therapy in the rehabilitation of an adolescent female with chronic pain: A case example. *Cognitive and Behavioral Practice.*

Zettle, R. D. (2003). Acceptance and commitment therapy (ACT) vs. systematic desensitization in treatment of mathematics anxiety. *Psychological Record, 53,* 197–215.

PART V

APPLICATIONS FOR INTERPERSONAL RELATIONSHIPS

14

MINDFULNESS-BASED RELATIONSHIP ENHANCEMENT (MBRE) IN COUPLES

JAMES W. CARSON AND KIMBERLY M. CARSON

Department of Psychiatry and Behavioral Sciences, Duke University Medical Center, Durham, North Carolina

KAREN M. GIL AND DONALD H. BAUCOM

Department of Psychology, University of North Carolina, Chapel Hill, North Carolina

INTRODUCTION: STRESS, RELATIONSHIPS, AND MINDFULNESS

Enduring human partnerships inevitably entail adjustment to a course of stressful events and situations, both minor and major. Stress, however, has not been as widely studied as other risk factors for marital dissatisfaction (e.g., poor communication skills, low sexual satisfaction). Nonetheless, numerous cross-sectional, longitudinal, and treatment efficacy studies have confirmed a link between stress and relationship quality (see Carson, 2002). In fact, a recent meta-analytic review of 115 longitudinal studies examining the course of marriages offers compelling evidence that relationship functioning is bolstered in couples with good stress coping abilities (i.e., those who are able to respond well to challenging or difficult situations) (Karney & Bradbury, 1995). However, established approaches to the prevention of marital dissatisfaction, such as the Prevention and

Relationship Enhancement Program (PREP) (Markman, Floyd, Stanley, & Storaasli, 1988) and Relationship Enhancement (Guerney, 1977), have not targeted stress coping abilities. Building on the notion that healthy individual functioning is important to successful marriages, current reviewers of the couples literature (Halford, Sanders, & Behrens, 1994; Sayers, Kohn, & Heavey, 1998) have begun to advocate for the development of programs aimed in part at boosting individual partners' stress coping skills.

Given that mindfulness meditation group interventions have been demonstrated to be efficacious in helping individuals cope more effectively with stress in a variety of nonclinical (e.g., Shapiro, Schwartz, & Bonner, 1998) and clinical populations (depression, Teasdale et al., 2000; cancer, Speca, Carlson, Goodey, & Angen, 2000; psoriasis, Kabat-Zinn et al., 1998), adaptation of mindfulness training into a relationship enhancement format, with a focus on improving dyadic as well as individual stress coping abilities in nondistressed couples, was a logical next step. The theoretical basis for applying mindfulness to boost partners' stress coping skills and enhance their relationships is based on at least four salient processes frequently activated by this type of intervention.

First, the act of being mindful—that is, of incorporating all experiences, whether enjoyable or difficult, into nonjudgmental presence of mind—appears to generate a process of insight that is highly applicable to optimal interpersonal functioning. As practitioners' self-observation skills increase, they typically report gaining insight into the automaticity of many patterns of thought, emotion, and behavior, and also of the consequences of these for both themselves and their partners. In many relationship-related contexts, such insight appears to place meditators in a better position to interrupt overlearned maladaptive responses and to experiment with an increased range of response options. Notably, Halford et al. (1994) and other marital experts (e.g., Sayers et al., 1998) have urged the cultivation of self-monitoring and self-regulation skills in couples programs.

Second, mindfulness training places an emphasis on the acceptance of one's experiences as they are. This acceptance might contribute to increases that practitioners often report in the compassion they feel for themselves and their empathy for others (Shapiro et al., 1998). Notably, theorists in the area of enhancement of healthy relationships endorse the importance of acceptance (Wenzel & Harvey, 2001), as do numerous marital therapy researchers (e.g., Christensen & Jacobson, 2000).

Third, while mindfulness does not aim at inducing relaxation per se, nonetheless it appears that, similar to other meditation techniques (Benson, Beary, & Carol, 1974), mindfulness, in fact, often does promote the relaxation response (Carson, Carson, Gil, & Baucom, 2004; Kabat-Zinn, 1990). Psychophysiologically the relaxation response results in changes that are the mirror opposite of stress-induced hyperarousal, and subjectively is often experienced as feelings of calm, clarity, and well-being. Interpersonally, such changes may translate into a calmer approach to shared difficulties. Several researchers have suggested that psychophysiologically soothing techniques are likely to be helpful to couples (e.g., Gottman, 1993).

Fourth, the practice of mindfulness is often experienced as self-broadening, leading to attitudinal transformations that are expressed in terms of a greater sense of trust, love for others, and connectedness with a greater *whole* (Astin, 1997; Carson *et al.,* 2004; Kabat-Zinn, 1993; Shapiro *et al.,* 1998). Such changes fit well with a prominent perspective on close relationships, Aron and Aron's (1997) self-expansion model. This model proposes that expansion of "self" is a fundamental human motivation and that close relationships are an especially satisfying means to self-expansion. These authors' studies have shown that relationship satisfaction increases through mutual engagement in exciting, self-expanding activities, including those leading to "the discovery of linkages, wisdom, [and] their position in the universe" (p. 252). These are precisely the types of experiences that mindfulness meditators often report.

INTERVENTION DESCRIPTION

Mindfulness-based relationship enhancement (MBRE) is directly modeled on Kabat-Zinn's mindfulness program in terms of format, teaching style (e.g., use of poetry), sequence of techniques, composition of topics, and homework assignments (for a complete description of MBRE, see Carson, 2002). Like mindfulness-based stress reduction (MBSR), programs consist of eight weekly 2½-hour meetings plus a full-day (7-hour) weekend retreat session during the sixth week.

MBRE was developed to strengthen the relationships of couples who are relatively happy and is not intended as a group therapy for distressed couples. A number of leading relationship researchers have reasoned that it is much easier to prevent marital problems and promote optimal partnerships by working with couples when they are relatively happy and emotionally engaged than to modify negative interactional patterns after they have become destructive and entrenched (e.g., Markman *et al.,* 1988; Van Widenfelt, Markman, Guerney, & Behrens, 1997). It cannot be assumed that MBRE would work in a similar way with distressed couples.

COUPLE-FOCUSED ADAPTATIONS

Along with standard MBSR components, MBRE incorporates several modifications to encompass issues specific to working with nondistressed couples to enhance their relationships. These adaptations are first evident in the screening interviews, which are conducted on a couples basis and emphasize potential relationship-related, as well as individual, benefits of the program (e.g., joint mindfulness training highlights important information about partners' mutual interactions and each partners' thoughts, feelings, and behaviors within the context of their relationship, thereby allowing couples to better understand themselves, their relationship, the nature of any problems, and potential solutions). Several of the principal adaptations involve extending already extant elements of MBSR sessions in a specifically dyadic manner. For example, the seventh session of MBSR typically includes a loving-kindness practice known as *metta,* a method for developing compassion involving the use of silent mental phrases to direct feelings of love and kindness toward a loved one, toward oneself, and toward various other targets (Salzberg, 1995). In MBRE, beginning with the first session, greater use is made of loving-kindness practices, with a particular focus on directing compassion toward one's partner (see the Case Study discussed later in this chapter). Also, given that interpersonal communication is a central concern in dyadic functioning, MBRE places greater emphasis than MBSR on applying mindful attention to communications during sessions. As in MBSR courses taught by Kabat-Zinn (1990) and colleagues, the Native American "council" communication model forms the basis of mindful communication in MBRE—i.e., one person speaks at a time while others listen attentively; the person speaks "from the heart" spontaneously without mental rehearsal and expresses himself or herself succinctly so that others may have their turn (see Zimmerman & Coyle, 1996). Interestingly, similar communication guidelines have also been incorporated into empirically supported cognitive-behavioral couple interventions (Baucom, Shoham, Mueser, Daiuto, & Stickle, 1998). Another salient extension of MBSR components involves employing partner versions of yoga exercises, in which this "meditation in movement" is transformed from an individual endeavor into a sort of dyadic dance in which partners physically support and facilitate one another in the performance of therapeutic, often pleasurable postures. In addition, in the latter MBRE sessions—after the fundamentals of mindfulness practice have been established—several new, uniquely dyadic exercises are introduced into the mindfulness training process. These include a mindful touch exercise, with each partner paying close attention to the giving and receiving of a gentle back rub, followed by dyadic discussion of the implications of mindful touch for enhancing their sensual intimacy (i.e., sensate focus; Spence, 1997). Another unique component is a two-part dyadic eye gazing exercise (adapted from Levine & Levine, 1995). During the first part, partners enter into a brief "facing stress" experiment in which they gaze into one another's eyes without diverting their attention. In many partners this sustained gazing soon elicits a vague sense of discomfort and vulnerability. Rather than react based on these feelings, couples are encouraged to simply take notice of whatever feelings and urges come up, while remaining attentive and open to any shifts that occur in their experience. In the second part of the exercise, couples are asked to continue their gaze, while now doing their best to recognize and inwardly welcome a "deep-down goodness" present within their partner and also within themselves. The exercise ends with a group discussion of its implications for learning to remain mindfully nonreactive and receptive to one's partner in the face of stress-inducing circumstances that might otherwise lead to hurtful arguments or withdrawal from one another.

More globally, in MBRE the context for practicing various mindfulness skills, both in-session and at home, is tailored to bring couples' relationships into sharp focus—for instance, partners are encouraged to be more aware during *shared* pleasant activities, unpleasant activities, and stressful interactions and to discuss and keep daily records about new understandings arising from such interactions. Also, group discussion and didactic components of the program provide opportunities to highlight the impact of all the various exercises on relationship functioning.

COMPARISON OF MBRE WITH ESTABLISHED PROGRAMS

The overall structure of MBRE bears some resemblance to standard cognitive-behavioral programs designed to enhance relationships and prevent relationship distress in that sessions include such common elements as skills instruction, didactic presentations, couples exercises, and group discussions and rely strongly on homework assignments for skills development. However, the contents of each of these elements differ in important ways in the mindfulness program. Chief among these differences is in the area of skills. Programs such as Relationship Enhancement (Guerney, 1977) and PREP (Markman *et al.,* 1988) focus on teaching an assorted set of relational skills, with each skill targeted at specific issues (e.g., modification of inappropriate expectations, joint problem solving, how to enhance friendship and sexual functioning). In contrast, MBRE emphasizes continual development of a single generic skill, that of careful, nonjudgmental attention to one's ongoing in-the-moment experiences, whatever their nature. This single skill is practiced in a formal manner across a spectrum of common activities, such as sitting, reclining, and walking, and also is applied in an informal manner in all types of situations. As in other programs, situations considered important to relationship functioning are targeted in MBRE (e.g., both mutual and individual pleasant experiences and stressful communications), but by means of mindfulness, and without pursuing any specific goal. Thus, rather than prescribing diverse behavioral or cognitive strategies targeted at specific changes, it is assumed that as the scope of partners' mindfulness practice continues to expand, this will contribute to a variety of positive changes, such as enhanced insight into the nature of challenges and difficulties (e.g., to what extent they are situationally determined, in what way one's own or a partner's ways of thinking and behaving may have contributed to them); greater acceptance of self, partner, and circumstances; greater calmness of mind and body; and greater feelings of love and interconnectedness. Partners will thereby tend to find themselves in a better position to explore ways of resolving relationship or individual difficulties in their own manner. For this process, a patient, nonstriving attitude is advocated as most effective to overall reduction of tensions and eventual resolution of relational and individual problems.

Along with MBRE's emphasis on distinct skills, the program stands out relative to standard relationship enhancement programs in regard to the exercises couples engage in during classes. Thus, in place of exercises such as brainstorming (PREP), MBRE couples engage in activities such as partner versions of yoga postures and mindful touch exercises. Didactic presentations in MBRE also differ from those in other programs. Nearly all didactic material is based on the stress and coping literature (e.g., fight/flight reactions, role of appraisal in stress reactivity), as contrasted to presentations in cognitive-behavioral programs on such issues as problem-solving skills or sexual functioning (PREP). Also, in teaching MBRE, important didactic points are drawn out from couples' own observations whenever possible, rather than introduced as something new that they need to learn. And as a consequence of all the previous distinctions between MBRE and other cognitive-behavioral programs, group discussions during this intervention typically revolve around somewhat different foci than in other programs, such as insight into appraisal-making processes versus various options for solving a problem. However, the vital functions that such discussions serve, such as clarification and reinforcement of skill learning processes, and mutual sharing and learning from others' experiences, are common to most couples intervention programs.

Finally, MBRE differs from standard interventions in that it includes a rather unique component, a full day of mindfulness practice conducted largely in silence. To those unacquainted with silent meditation retreats, it may appear that such an event would hold little promise of benefiting couples' relationships. However, most couples who have participated in MBRE report quite the opposite. Partners often tell of discovering a previously unsuspected sense of spontaneous closeness and interconnectedness, made possible by the heightened state of awareness and sensitivity generated by the day's silent mindful activities.

Naturally, the differences outlined previously between MBRE and other couples programs contribute to a variety of treatment-related changes that have been commonly reported by mindfulness couples but are not typically observed elsewhere. In the only existing research study of MBRE (see Empirical Support section), along with improvements in standard dyadic outcomes (e.g., relationship satisfaction, autonomy, relatedness), mindfulness couples demonstrated changes in processes more specifically linked to mindfulness work, such as increased acceptance, relaxation, and spirituality. Moreover, apart from statistically analyzed outcomes, qualitative data collected from MBRE couples indicate that they often describe changes that may not be typical of standard couples interventions. For example, as illustrated in the Case Study discussed later, we have found that it is not uncommon for partners in MBRE to report greater awareness of the value of each shared moment, a heightened sensory acuity, stronger feelings of closeness to nature, and more playfulness in lovemaking.

EMPIRICAL SUPPORT

This section will present the empirical data collected from a case couple (described in detail in the following section) and relate the changes they reported to the overall set of outcomes from the only existing randomized controlled trial of MBRE (Carson *et al.*, 2004). The trial included 44 nondistressed, mostly well-educated heterosexual couples. Mean (*M*) age of women was 37; of men, 39. *M* duration of relationships was 11 years. All participants were white except for 1 African American woman. Thirty-seven couples were married, 7 were cohabiting. Twenty-two couples were in the intervention condition (6–8 couples per group), and 22 were in the wait-list condition. Two distinct sets of self-report measures were collected during the study: *questionnaires* were administered before and after the intervention and 3 months later, and *data diaries* were recorded each day for 2 preintervention weeks and the final 3 weeks of the 8-week program. Both sets of measures tapped domains not only of relationship functioning but also of individual well-being. The questionnaires measured relationship satisfaction with the Quality of Marriage Index (Norton, 1983), acceptance of partner with the Acceptance of Partner Index (Carson *et al.*, 2004), relationship distress with the Global Distress Scale from the Marital Satisfaction Inventory–Revised (Snyder, 1997), autonomy and relatedness with the Autonomy and Relatedness Inventory (Schaefer & Burnett, 1987), closeness with the Inclusion of Other in the Self Scale (Aron, Aron, & Smollan, 1992), relaxation with the Individual Relaxation Index (Carson *et al.*, 2004), psychological distress with the Brief Symptom Inventory (Derogatis & Melisaratos, 1983), spirituality with the Index of Core Spiritual Experiences (Kass, Friedman, Leserman, Zuttermeister, & Benson, 1991), and optimism with the Revised Life Orientation Test (Scheier, Carver, & Bridges, 1994). The diaries measured daily relationship stress, relationship happiness, overall stress, and stress coping efficacy.

The case couples' responses to relationship measures showed posttreatment improvements in nearly all domains assessed. Most dramatic were changes in acceptance of partner, average daily relationship stress, and average daily relationship happiness. Also notable were improvements in relationship satisfaction and relationship distress. Positive changes were also recorded in autonomy and relatedness. The one exception to this pattern was in closeness, which showed no change in the female partner and a slight decrease in the male partner. The couple's individual measures likewise indicated posttreatment improvements in nearly all cases. The strongest changes were in relaxation, psychological distress, and average daily stress coping efficacy. Improvements were also observed in spirituality and optimism. On average daily overall stress, the male partner decreased somewhat, whereas the female partner showed an increase. Examination of follow-up scores indicated that 3 months after the intervention, this couple's improvements in relationship, as well as individual measures, continued at approximately the same levels (with some dips and further gains). The only exception was in the male partner's psychological distress score, which at follow-up was somewhat increased relative to pretreatment (but still far from the clinically distressed range).

The changes observed in empirical measures of this case couple's functioning largely mirror the overall pattern of improvements seen in our MBRE trial. Results from this study suggested that the program had a favorable impact on couples' levels of relationship satisfaction, relationship distress, daily relationship happiness, daily relationship stress, autonomy, relatedness, acceptance of partner, and closeness (see Carson et al., 2004, for means, etc.). Because the probability of encountering ceiling effects is high when intervening with relatively happy couples (Christensen & Heavey, 1999), these findings are very encouraging. Individually, partners significantly benefited, as indicated by measures of spirituality, optimism, relaxation, psychological distress, daily stress coping efficacy, and daily overall stress. In addition, diary recordings of daily mindfulness practice showed that couples who practiced mindfulness more had better outcomes, and within-person analyses of diary data showed that greater mindfulness practice on a given day was associated on several consecutive days with improved levels of relationship happiness, relationship stress, stress coping efficacy, and overall stress. Furthermore, our results provided empirical support for the rationale of adopting a mindful approach to enhancing relational functioning in that measures showed improvements in several proposed mindfulness-related processes of change, including acceptance of partner, individual relaxation, and self-broadening (e.g., spirituality). Measures of mindfulness per se were not included, as none were available at the time the study was conducted.

It is important to note several limitations to this empirical work. First, although the 3-month follow-up results offer encouragement, longer-term follow-up would be needed to examine the durability of changes. Limits also come from the fact that like most research with couples, this study's sample was almost entirely white, well educated, middle-class, and heterosexual. Caution is in order, therefore, in generalizing these results to diverse populations. Additional limitations come from lack of control for non-specific factors (e.g., attention from an intervention provider), the utilization of only one team of intervention leaders, and reliance on self-report data. Further investigations are needed to establish more definitively the efficacy of MBRE.

AN ILLUSTRATIVE CASE STUDY

Given that MBRE is a group intervention, in tracing the progress of a sample couple encountering and responding to the challenges and opportunities offered by the program, we will necessarily also describe the unfolding of aspects of an important group process across the intervention. To us, the group context appears crucial for much of the learning and changes that occur in couples. Also, please note that rather than attempt to describe this sample couple's responses to every element of the program, we will highlight especially salient processes. Like other interventions, some elements of MBRE may be especially good in sparking change in one couple but not in another; in virtually no cases are all elements likely to be equally effective.

SCREENING INTERVIEW

As with all couples who have taken MBRE, we first met Kathy and John at their screening interview (real names and other identifying information have been altered throughout this chapter). Kathy, age 26, was a Ph.D. student at a major university, and John, 34, worked as a manager for a rapidly expanding consulting firm. Kathy and John had been married for 4 years, and for both, this was their first marriage. They had no children but expected to one day. Both were white. They said their motivation to take the program came from the fact that although they loved one another very much, they felt they were drifting apart, particularly as a result of work-related stress and demands. As part of the screening process, we asked them to complete self-report measures of relationship distress (Global Distress Scale) and individual distress (Brief Symptom Inventory) to ascertain that they were not clinically distressed in either regard (a procedure in place as part of the outcomes study we were conducting; see Carson *et al.,* 2004). Although both spouses qualified as nondistressed, John was close to the cutoff on the relationship measure, and Kathy was relatively high on the individual measure. As we described to them the substantial commitment to daily mindfulness practice required to gain much of value from the program, Kathy and John expressed hesitation because of their very full schedules. We emphasized that although at first they might experience the program as an added stress, most likely their view of it would be transformed as they learned to encounter stressful events in a new way. We also underscored our assumption that if a couple is not able to commit to the program, probably this is an indication that MBRE is not a good fit at that particular point in their relationship, and we suggested to Kathy and John that they might want to consider putting off participation in MBRE for the time being. They consulted with one another for a few minutes, and then reaffirmed their determination to take the program in order to improve their relationship.

SESSION 1

After introductory remarks, in session 1, couples were guided in an exercise based on loving-kindness, in which partners were asked to recall the days when they first fell in love and decided to be together, and observe whether they could actually *feel* again in the present moment the sense of discovery, closeness, trust, sweetness, or fun that they had at that time. Strong emotional responses to this exercise are not uncommon, and in this case it was especially notable that Kathy had tears in her eyes as the exercise ended. Afterward, partners were invited to introduce themselves, including saying something about what their relationship was like when they were at ease with one another (this differs from MBSR, in which participants are asked to say something positive about themselves). Most couples named commonalities of good times in a good relationship, such as a sense of easy comfort with one another, playfulness and laughter, or greater attentiveness to the preferences and needs of one another. Kathy and John were the last to introduce themselves. Kathy remarked that during the earlier exercise she had suddenly sensed vividly the sweet closeness that she and John had once shared so frequently. But she said this vivid feeling was immediately followed by a wave of sadness as she realized how long it had been since they last felt that way. She said stress was getting in their way, and expressed strong hope that being in this group would help them restore their previous closeness.

Toward the end of the session, couples were guided through a short breath-focused meditation and then a more extended body scan meditation. Afterward, when partners were invited to comment on their experience of these exercises, Kathy was quite pointed in her remarks: She described sitting with eyes closed as "sheer torture," and the body scan as only slightly more tolerable. She said she could hardly bear the idea of doing these exercises every day. We encouraged her and the other couples to be patient with this process ("you don't have to like it, you just have to do it") and reemphasized that although at first mindfulness training could be stressful because of the extra demands on partners' time and attention, most likely they would soon notice valuable changes beginning. The session ended with a description of home practice assignments, principally a daily body scan meditation, done jointly at least once with awareness of points of contact with one's partner's body (lying down facing opposite directions, with right sides lightly touching), and informal mindfulness of a shared activity such as dinner.

SESSION 2

Following a joint body scan, the value of mindful communication was introduced, and partners were invited to apply the "council" method during the group discussion of mindfulness practice experiences (see Couple-Focused Adaptations section). As have most MBRE participants, these couples adopted the council method quite readily, and it appeared to produce the desired effect of heartfelt, pithy, orderly communication. Portions of subsequent discussions throughout the program followed the council method, and even at other times speaking and listening mindfully was emphasized.

During the discussion about the past week's practice, Kathy said that the body scan had usually made her even more anxious and uptight, but she had done it each day anyway. John said he had not been able to do the practice more than once because of being out of town most of the week. He added, "I don't know how this is going to work. It felt like adding mindfulness might be taking away from the little time we had together this week." Fortunately, however, most of the group reported otherwise, saying that although they had often found the body scan challenging—revealing how busy and distracted their minds could be—overall it was a positive experience, which at times was deeply relaxing. One couple reported that doing the body scan together had made them feel more at ease with one another. Those with children appeared to have greater difficulty finding a suitable time to practice, and especially to do the joint practice. One couple found that the solution was to practice it together after the children were asleep. Another couple invited their two small children to participate in the body scan with them. We drew on these other couples' comments in a gentle way to encourage Kathy and John to bring an attitude of open-minded curiosity to the challenges they were encountering in doing the body scan—perhaps there was something to be learned from observing how they felt—and we also emphasized patience once again. Patience, in fact, was a topic on our agenda for the day (along with other principles supporting mindfulness, such as nonjudgment and nonstriving), so we took advantage of the concerns being raised to segue into a discussion of the centrality of patience for the fruitful practice of mindfulness. Utilizing the material arising from the group to illustrate important points was, in fact, pivotal to our intention as program leaders to not simply teach *about* mindfulness, but rather to teach in an especially mindful, in-the-moment manner. The remaining group discussion in this session centered mostly around experiences of engaging in the week's assignment to be become mindful, in an informal way, in the midst of a shared activity such as dinner. While some couples, including Kathy and John, found that bringing this intention to a shared activity had the effect of enhancing their enjoyment of it (e.g., the food, their conversation), others remarked mostly on their discovery of how "out to lunch" they often were—not really mentally present to taste the food, or to hear what their partner was saying—because their minds were elsewhere, caught up in passing worries, or in wondering about some past event or imagined future. We emphasized the fact that becoming aware of the wanderings of our minds, over and over again, is an integral part of the process of waking up to how our lives—including the ways we relate to one another—are often being lived on "automatic pilot." We highlighted the fact that heightened awareness of our absent-minded tendencies opens up many possibilities for learning to live, and love, more fully and spontaneously.

SESSION 3

After starting out with a short sitting meditation, yoga posture exercises—done individually in a gentle, mindful fashion—were introduced in this session. We intentionally instructed couples in working with a selected sequence of postures on an individual basis first, before having them engage in partner versions of the same sequence (in session 6). We did this because it is important that each person gain a measure of flexibility, strength, and familiarity with a set of postures before attempting to do it as a couple. Partner versions of yoga postures offer advantages in terms of extra support for opening up our bodies, and for interpersonal fun and intimacy, but they also in some cases carry greater risk of injuries if not executed properly.

After yoga practice, Kathy opened up the group discussion by telling about her first "breakthrough." She said insomnia had plagued her for years, and more so during the past few months. Using the body scan just before going to bed this week, she said, had allowed her to have several really good nights of sleep. She reported she was feeling much better during the day as well. Kathy appeared notably more at ease and cheerful than in previous sessions, and others in the group remarked on how well she looked. John, on the other hand, said he was still having a hard time fitting mindfulness into his daily schedule. Nonetheless, he had managed to practice 3 days during the week. His comments prompted Kathy to follow up by saying, "John, this is really important for us, but you're not doing it." Looking noticeably uncomfortable, John responded that he was doing his best. After a few moments of awkward silence, we offered comments directed to the full group, gently emphasizing patience once again—patience not only with oneself, but also with others, accepting that each person has to find out for himself or herself.

Much of the discussion again revolved around what couples had learned while doing the week's informal mindfulness assignment, which had been to keep a "Pleasant Events Calender" with a special emphasis on shared enjoyable activities. Kathy and John both spoke of how hearing various couples' comments the previous week about how absent-minded they often were had sparked an interesting conversation between them about focusing on this issue in their own relationship. This intention was then reflected in their Pleasant Events entries, which expressed their amazement about how often they assumed that they were "together" in some activity, but now realized how often that was not really the case. They said it seemed that they had needed to hear this process described by another couple first before they could see it in themselves. Half-jokingly, John also expressed a measure of chagrin at the fact that "the spotlight of mindfulness seemed to be creeping" into more and more of his moments, making it difficult for him to mentally compartmentalize activities or to find any "escape from reality." We followed up on John's comment by asking if others in the group knew firsthand the feeling John was expressing, and there were several nods. We drew on these acknowledgments to highlight that much of what we learn about ourselves through mindfulness is common to us all; we also remarked on the valuable contribution that honest observations such as John's make to the learning process.

SESSION 4

Group discussion following the opening meditation centered on couples' experiences while keeping track of shared *unpleasant* events this week. Kathy relayed a particularly insightful discovery. She began by saying that she seemed to be taking notice of her thoughts and feelings in a new way. On Sunday she and John had been working in the garden, something they both valued. Kathy, however, found herself feeling quite irritated rather than at ease, and she began to wonder why. Suddenly she noticed how frequently her thoughts were about John not doing things "right"— not tilling the soil correctly, not spacing the seedlings right, etc. Noticing this seemed to temporarily suspend these kinds of thoughts. She said tears came to her eyes, followed soon after by a dawning realization: She saw that in so many other situations in her life, activities that could be enjoyable frequently turned into "downers" due to the way she was thinking about them: critically judging what John, or someone else, or often she herself, was doing. "I know I have a long way to go with this, but already I'm finding myself starting to lighten up, and I'm enjoying being with John more."

SESSION 5

The session began with sitting meditation with a focus on recognizing thoughts as "events" in one's consciousness and distinguishing thought events from their particular contents. Home assignments this week had included keeping a stressful communications calendar. Several participants described a pattern of noticing that when arguments happened between themselves and their partner, usually it was well under way before it dawned on them that they had any choice in the matter. Couples also noted how often stressful communications revolved around rather petty disputes, which in retrospect were seen as trivial but nonetheless could lead to disrespecting one another and significantly hurting one another's feelings. In the ensuing discussion, we highlighted our general human tendency, when feeling threatened, to fall back into the rut of our long-standing defensive conditioning, into a mode in which we react to one another in a very driven, almost unconscious way. We also emphasized the role of mindfulness in waking us up, at least in some degree, to a choice we have in our manner of responding to an argument.

Group discussion led directly into a didactic component on communication styles, such as aggressive, passive, passive-aggressive, and assertive (Kabat-Zinn, 1990), followed by a dyadic communication exercise in which partners took turns enacting each communication style, based on aikido strategies (Kabat-Zinn, 1990), and discussed bringing mindfulness to bear on habitual ways of communicating. Most participants recognized a communication style (usually *not* the assertive style) as a common pattern for themselves, and also a pattern they often observed in their partner. As they enacted the various styles, often in a lighthearted way, they exaggerated their tendencies, eliciting laughter around the room. Many were intrigued by the possibility of discovering how to be mindfully assertive in the service of effectively resolving thorny issues.

SESSION 6

The session began with the couples' first experience of partner yoga. As has been our typical experience when conducting MBRE, this was a lot of fun! Playfulness abounded on all sides as the sound of laughter and "oohs" and "ahhs" filled the air. Many of the postures required a good deal of mutual contact and close coordination of movement while standing on one leg, leaning against or away from one another, or in other stretching positions couples had never engaged in together. Partners frequently joked, half-seriously, about issues of supporting or being supported, and couples traded humorous comments across the room. As the yoga sequence ended in a prone relaxation pose, the jovial atmosphere gave way to a sense of almost tangible quiet and stillness. This was followed by a period of sitting meditation.

In the discussion that followed, all couples commented on enjoying the partner yoga. As we moved into the topic of the week's assignment of paying attention to broader areas of life—such as work, family, and diet—that can have a stressful impact on relationships, John told of a crucial interaction with his boss. For months he had wanted to talk to his boss about having more structure in the hours he was available to work. He had been putting this off, feeling torn between his boss's requests that he put more time into new responsibilities, involving frequent travel, and his and Kathy's wish to spend more time together. Inspired by the previous week's focus on communication styles and being mindfully assertive, he asked for a meeting with his boss and successfully negotiated an agreement for additional specific, fixed times off. Clearly elated, John said, "It wasn't just what I learned here last week that helped me get this worked out, I've also been getting more out of the daily practices. Lately I've been doing more of the sitting and also the yoga, and both have helped me feel calmer and clearer and more in control of how I react to things that come up, including things with Kathy. After last week, I realized that I often have avoided dealing with issues that come up, not only at work but also between us. I usually prefer to put off talking about whatever it might be. But I've made a decision to change that now, and it seems to be working. Mindfulness finally seems to be making sense to me."

John's comments provided us with a fitting segue into a presentation on the difference between mindful "stress responses" versus automatic "stress reactions" and the importance of continued daily practice in cultivating this skill. In further discussion, another couple, Bill and Ardith, spoke at length about the challenges they were facing, "the most prolonged stressful period in 40 years of marriage," due to multiple ailing in-laws. They concluded by saying, "The mindfulness work has helped us survive all this in a way not possible without it."

DAY OF MINDFULNESS

For most partners, to spend a full Saturday engaged mostly in silent mindfulness practice is unlike anything they have ever done, either individually or together. Quite commonly participants start the day out with anxious expectations about not being able to handle 7 hours of continual practice, or of not being able to bear being in silence, especially in the company of their partner. The same was true of this group. Yet, as with other MBRE groups we have conducted, once we had introduced the day as a rare opportunity to explore being with one's self and one's partner in an atmosphere of peace and quiet, participants fell fairly easily into the flow of alternating periods of sitting meditations, walking meditations, and yoga practice. During the sixth hour, couples were guided in a series of dyadic exercises, including a mindful touch exercise, with each partner paying close attention to the giving and receiving of a gentle back rub, ending with an embrace. Silence was then broken, first through quiet discussion within dyads, followed by group discussion focused on what the day was like.

Most couples had a favorable reaction to the mindful massage, which appeared to elicit a strong feeling of mutual affection between partners. A few partners said they had never felt comfortable in giving a massage, but this time enjoyed both the giving as well as the receiving. Several couples commented on at first feeling awkward about keeping silence but later sensing a strong connection to one another while enjoying the quiet and feeling no need to speak. Kathy and John remarked that especially while sharing lunch they felt a sweet sense of togetherness, which was quite the opposite of what they had assumed, since mealtime conversations were an important part of their relationship. John added that he had a hard time deciding to come for the day because he was scheduled to do a major presentation to a corporate group on Monday morning, but he was sure now that he had made the right choice in coming.

The location where these MBRE sessions, including the day of mindfulness, were held has well-kept lawns and shrubbery and is surrounded by woods. Many participants commented on experiencing a highlighted sense of closeness to nature during the walking practice. Kathy said, "I really loved the walking meditations; they made me feel very grounded, yet simultaneously free in some inexplicable way." Later, after the program ended and couples were exiting, Kathy approached us and said, "I didn't want to say this in front of everyone, but during the last sitting meditation I had an amazing experience—I felt connected to the universe through all of my pores, I felt in rhythm with all of life. It was so real. I've never felt anything like that before."

SESSION 7

Much of the group discussion in this session focused on aftereffects from the day of mindfulness. Several couples spoke of sharing especially enjoyable dinners that evening, feeling lighthearted and affectionate and noticing that their sense of taste and other senses seemed unusually acute. Kathy and John described being "filled with love," so much so that the next day when they saw some ducklings at a pet shop, they could not resist taking two ducklings home, even though they had never considered having ducks. John also described how well his Monday morning presentation had gone, saying he was calm, focused, energized, and effective despite spending much less time preparing for it than usual.

Following another mindful touch exercise (ending with dyadic discussions on its implications for sensual intimacy) and a loving-kindness meditation (focused especially on directing feelings of love toward one's partner and the relationship as a unit), group discussion centered on the week's topic of attention regarding aids and obstacles to mindfulness. Several couples spoke about realizing that long-established habits of attempting to split their attention across multiple tasks at once—such as jogging while trying to plan the day's job activities—usually prevented a clear sense of present-mindedness, and a growing inclination to devote their attention to the activities at hand whenever multitasking was not necessary. John told about a gradual change in his TV viewing habits, saying that on most workday evenings he used to "turn on the TV and mindlessly watch just whatever" for several hours because it provided him with an escape from his stressed-out mind. Now, however, he said he was drawn to spend more time with Kathy, and reading, and doing mindfulness practices; and when he did watch TV, it was usually because there was something specific he wanted to see.

SESSION 8

Much of the session involved a final council-style group discussion focused on partners' accounts of the relationship-related and personal changes they had experienced over the past 7 weeks. Following are some of the comments that were shared:

Kathy: "It makes such a difference for me to be able to chill and relax now.... I was so stressed out when we started. And I see John much more often now—and he's not only present, he's more considerate, and spontaneously sweet."

John: "Mindfulness is a tool we can use any time something between us gets out of whack. It gives us a way to step back and get centered. And being in this group really has been important, hearing from other couples what they go through and what they're learning. This past weekend, we had a pretty stressful visit from some relatives. Having heard what Bill and Ardith said a couple of sessions ago about mindfulness helping them handle all the stress in their families, I was able to keep focused on what had to be done at each moment and avoided overreacting to the rude things my relatives said and did. I could just see that they aren't very conscious of how they are; they're on auto pilot, and there's no point in my getting upset."

Others in the group: "Doing the mindfulness practice on a regular basis altered the rhythm of our life—we're more serene, less reactive to things. This has given me greater awareness of how valuable each moment we share is, and that it is not worth ruining the present moment by dwelling on the past."

"Partner yoga was surprising because it was very intimate, we didn't know we could have such greater intimacy than we already had, it definitely improved our lovemaking, it put us more in synch and also we're more playful now."

"There's been a big change in my ability to not get pulled off kilter by a disruption that comes up between us. Now I can sense that whatever comes up in the moment doesn't have to have all kinds of implications for future moments and future conflicts, and I have a greater capacity to sense what my partner is going through."

At the end of the session, at the suggestion of one of the couples, the participants decided to form a group and continue to meet on their own once a month. Some in this group continue to meet now, 4 years later, to share mindfulness practice and insights into "the mindful life."

SUMMARY

Apart from idiosyncratic details, the types of processes and improvements seen in Kathy and John as they moved through the MBRE course are rather typical of what we have observed in other couples. As suggested in our Introduction, growth in at least four areas—capacities for insight, acceptance, relaxation, and self-broadening—were evident in this couple. In Kathy's case the first changes corresponded with an increased ability to relax (including sleeping better), followed by a growing capacity for insight into her thinking and behavior patterns (particularly when being judgmental). This was accompanied by a shift toward greater feelings of acceptance and love toward John, herself, and others; and eventually Kathy began to sometimes experience a deeply meaningful sense of expansive interconnectedness ("in rhythm with all of life"). In John, the process was initially slower. The first important changes involved insight ("the spotlight of mindfulness," awareness of avoiding interpersonal issues). With time, his capacity for love also grew ("filled with love"), as did abilities to remain calm and relaxed (successful job presentation) and to accept people and circumstances as they are (visit from relatives).

As a closing note to this Case Study, we want to make clear that mindfulness is not a panacea that will produce ideal relationships in all couples, even those who are apparently nondistressed. We know of at least one couple who decided to break up about 6 months after completing MBRE. This couple had previously gone through a course of marital therapy. At the time they entered MBRE, unknown to us they had agreed that this would constitute their last effort to stay together. According to their feedback, the mindfulness training *did* help them communicate better about the decision to break up, but it did not prevent it.

PRACTICAL ISSUES IN OFFERING MINDFULNESS TO COUPLES

In this section we will address several challenges and important practical concerns related to establishing an MBRE program and leading groups.

RECRUITMENT AND FEASIBILITY

Although recruitment for our research study was relatively easy, this was likely related to the fact that we offered MBRE for free, and within a community composed largely of staff, faculty, and students of large research-oriented universities. Despite the apparent appeal of this program to the couples in our study, recruitment under different circumstances could be difficult. At present much of the public has yet to have any exposure to what mindfulness is and how it could be helpful. Even if an effort were to be made to familiarize the public with the benefits of couples-based mindfulness, it is not obvious that its appeal would necessarily be broad. And MBRE has yet to be offered for payment in the way that MBSR usually is, so we do not know that an MBRE program can be offered on a sustained basis. Perhaps the most promising possibility would be to begin offering MBRE through established MBSR clinics, of which there are now quite a number in the United States. A final challenge to recruitment comes from the requirement that not just one individual be interested and committed, but so must their partner, which is surely less common.

MOTIVATING PRACTICE

Impatience for desired results and initial failure to realize the value of mindfulness practice are the chief obstacles to progress in mindfulness training, couples-based or otherwise. In this we echo many others (e.g., Kabat-Zinn & Santorelli, 1999) in highlighting that if teachers are able to motivate participants to engage in regular mindfulness practice for at least several weeks running, then an appreciable degree of valuable change is possible for most people. Thereafter the gains, both personal and inter-personal, that flow from daily practice become largely self-reinforcing.

At least two factors seem crucial to successfully motivating couples to practice: First and foremost, the teachers themselves must have sufficiently experienced the value of their own persistent mindfulness practice, including going through periods in which they lost their footing and regained it. In the absence of this sort of steady groundedness in mindfulness practice, teachers will not be able to embody the sort of insightful clarity required to inspire others. And we want to emphasize that in couples-based mindfulness training, it is critical that *both* teachers be steeped in living mindfully. Otherwise, as they interact dyadically while leading the group, they will not provide an appropriate model of mindful relatedness. In the various MBRE groups conducted thus far, couples frequently have commented on what they have learned from watching the two teachers interact and complement one another's teaching style through mindful attention to their joint teaching role. The second crucial factor in motivating mindfulness practice comes from the synergistic momentum that gradually emerges within the group of couples. As illustrated in the previous account, as one couple describes the changes and insights they are encountering, this often generates the impetus for others to experience similar openings. The succession of related changes continues to build throughout the program.

In our work with couples, at times a partner has expressed frustration regarding their counterpart's failure to engage in mindfulness practice, as did Kathy in the previous case. We have successfully defused these situations by reemphasizing the importance of patience and nonjudgment and the need for each individual to take personal responsibility for his or her own process. We have not encountered a couple expressing open conflict in the group about this or other issues and consider this unlikely.

ATTENDANCE AND COMPLETION ISSUES

Differential attendance by partners can quite frequently become a problem. Assuming that the partner who is missing sessions is engaged regularly in daily mindfulness practice, and does not miss more than half of the meetings, then in most cases the couple's mutual learning process can remain sufficiently robust and worthwhile. There will of course be some loss of exposure to opportunities to broaden and deepen their practice. Nonetheless, a solitary partner can still gain a good deal from participating in sessions with the other couples, and from observing other couples when a session includes dyadic exercises. If, however, one or both partners miss at least half of the sessions, we recommend that they discontinue MBRE until they can commit to regular attendance. In our research study, the average attendance rate was 80% (range, 61–100%).

Couples' completion rate in the MBRE study, 76%, was quite good. Historically, however, completion rates for group-based relationship programs have been low in the United States. For example, the average rate for the widely used PREP program was reported as 39% (Van Widenfelt et al., 1997). Clearly, sustained efforts to boost couples' commitment to completing the program are crucial. At least three factors appear to be important. First, like MBSR, in screening couples for MBRE there appears to be a motivation-boosting advantage to providing a description of the program as a challenging opportunity to develop inner resources for growth and change, and in emphasizing commitment to attend sessions and complete daily home practice assignments. Second, incorporation of strategies to accommodate children's needs, including child care services, could make the program more accessible to many couples. In our research study, attrition was related to number of children, with those who dropped out likely to have more children. Third, several authors (e.g., Sayers et al., 1998; Van Widenfelt et al., 1997) have suggested that it is probably advantageous to recruit and offer programs in settings such as universities, hospitals, and employee wellness programs as opposed to religious settings, which has been routine in most distress prevention programs. In our study, most couples were recruited from a hospital employees' wellness program, and the program was conducted in campus meeting rooms. Perhaps, as these authors hypothesized should happen, recruitment from this venue resulted in couples who were less influenced by attitudes that have interfered with other programs, such as taboos on sharing information about intimate relationships and the feeling that a successful marriage should come naturally to partners, without help from others (Bradbury & Fincham, 1990; Van Widenfelt *et al.*, 1997).

INTERVENTION LEADERS' QUALIFICATIONS

In our study, all intervention sessions were jointly led by a married couple composed of a clinical psychology doctoral student (J.W.C.) and a health educator (K.M.C.) who is a certified yoga instructor. Both intervention leaders had extensive experience practicing and teaching mindfulness and met the recommended minimum standards for provision of MBSR (see the introductory chapter of this book). We endorse the importance of the MBSR teaching standards, especially the requirements for a well-established daily mindfulness practice, and completion of a residential professional training program in MBSR. It is preferable that MBRE be offered by a single couple, but potentially two qualified teachers who are in separate long-term relationships could also be very effective, assuming that these two share good rapport. As the availability of well-qualified MBSR and MBCT teachers continues to increase, pairing of teachers to offer MBRE should become uncomplicated.

REFERENCES

Aron, A., & Aron, E. N. (1997). Self-expansion motivation and including other in the self. In S. Duck (Ed.), *Handbook of personal relationships: Theory, research and interventions* (pp. 251–270). Chichester, UK: Wiley.

Aron, A., Aron, E. N., & Smollan, D. (1992). Inclusion of Other in the Self Scale and the structure of interpersonal closeness. *Journal of Personality and Social Psychology, 63*, 596–612.

Astin, J. A. (1997). Stress reduction through mindfulness meditation. Effects on psychological symptomotology, sense of control, and spiritual experiences. *Psychotherapy and Psychosomatics, 66*, 97–106.

Baucom, D. H., Shoham, V., Mueser, K. T., Daiuto, A. D., & Stickle, T. R. (1998). Empirically supported couples and family therapies for adult problems. *Journal of Consulting and Clinical Psychology, 66*, 53–88.

Benson, H., Beary, J. F., & Carol, M. P. (1974). The relaxation response. *Psychiatry, 37*, 37–46.

Bradbury, T. N., & Fincham, F. D. (1990). Preventing marital dysfunction: Review and analysis. In F. D. Fincham & T. N. Bradbury (Eds.), *The psychology of marriage: Basic issues and applications* (pp. 375–401). New York: Guilford Press.

Carson, J. W. (2002). *Mindfulness-based stress reduction for relationship enhancement.* Unpublished dissertation, University of North Carolina.

Carson, J. W., Carson, K. M., Gil, K. M., & Baucom, D. H. (2004). Mindfulness-based relationship enhancement. *Behavior Therapy, 35,* 471–494.

Christensen, A., & Heavey, C. L. (1999). Interventions for couples. *Annual Review of Psychology, 50,* 165–190.

Christensen, A., & Jacobson, N. S. (2000). *Reconcilable differences.* New York: Guilford Press.

Derogatis, L. R., & Melisaratos, N. (1983). The Brief Symptom Inventory: An introductory report. *Psychological Medicine, 13,* 595–605.

Gottman, J. M. (1993). A theory of marital dissolution and stability. *Journal of Family Psychology, 7,* 57–75.

Guerney, B. (1977). *Relationship enhancement.* San Francisco: Jossey-Bass.

Halford, W. K., Sanders, M. R., & Behrens, B. C. (1994). Self-regulation in behavioral couples therapy. *Behavior Therapy, 25,* 431–452.

Kabat-Zinn, J. (1990). *Full catastrophe living: Using the wisdom of your body and mind in everyday life.* New York: Delacorte.

——— (1993). Mindfulness meditation: Health benefits of an ancient Buddhist practice. In D. Goleman & G. Gurin (Eds.), *Mind/Body Medicine* (pp. 259–275). New York: Consumer Reports Books.

Kabat-Zinn, J., & Santorelli, S. F. (1999). *Mindfulness-based stress reduction professional training resource manual.* Worcester, MA: Center for Mindfulness in Medicine, Health Care, and Society.

Kabat-Zinn, J., Wheeler, E., Light, T., Skillings, A., Scharf, M. J., Cropley, T. G., et al. (1998). Influence of a mindfulness meditation-based stress reduction intervention on rates of skin clearing in patients with moderate to severe psoriasis undergoing phototherapy (UVB) and photochemotherapy (PUVA). *Psychosomatic Medicine, 60,* 625–632.

Karney, B. R., & Bradbury, T. N. (1995). The longitudinal course of marital quality and stability: A review of theory, methods, and research. *Psychological Bulletin, 118,* 3–34.

Kass, J. D., Friedman, R., Leserman, J., Zuttermeister, P. C., & Benson, H. (1991). Health outcomes and a new index of spiritual experience. *Journal for the Scientific Study of Religion, 30,* 203–211.

Levine, S., & Levine, O. (1995). *Embracing the beloved: Relationship as a path of awakening.* New York: Doubleday.

Markman, H. J., Floyd, F. J., Stanley, S. M., & Storaasli, R. D. (1988). Prevention of marital distress: A longitudinal investigation. *Journal of Consulting and Clinical Psychology, 56,* 210–217.

Norton, R. (1983). Measuring marital quality: A critical look at the dependent variable. *Journal of Marriage and the Family, 45,* 141–151.

Salzberg, S. (1995). *Lovingkindness.* Boston: Shambhala.

Sayers, S. L., Kohn, C. S., & Heavey, C. (1998). Prevention of marital dysfunction: Behavioral approaches and beyond. *Clinical Psychology Review, 18,* 713–744.

Schaefer, E. S., & Burnett, C. K. (1987). Stability and predictability of quality of women's marital relationships and demoralization. *Journal of Personality and Social Psychology, 53,* 1129–1136.

Scheier, M. F., Carver, C. S., & Bridges, M. W. (1994). Distinguishing optimism from neuroticism (and trait anxiety, self-mastery, and self-esteem): A reevaluation of the Life Orientation Test. *Journal of Personality and Social Psychology, 67,* 1036–1078.

Shapiro, S. L., Schwartz, G. E., & Bonner, G. (1998). Effects of mindfulness-based stress reduction on medical and premedical students. *Journal of Behavioral Medicine, 21,* 581–599.

Snyder, D. K. (1997). *Manual for the Marital Satisfaction Inventory–Revised.* Los Angeles: Western Psychological Services.

Speca, M., Carlson, L. E., Goodey, E., & Angen, M. (2000). A randomized, wait-list controlled clinical trial: The effect of a mindfulness meditation-based stress reduction program on mood and symptoms of stress in cancer outpatients. *Psychosomatic Medicine, 62*, 613–622.

Spence, S. H. (1997). Sex and relationships. In W. K. Halford & H. J. Markman (Eds.), *Clinical handbook of marriage and couples intervention* (pp. 73–105). Chichester, UK: Wiley.

Teasdale, J. D., Segal, Z. V., Williams, J. M., Ridgeway, V. A., Soulsby, J. M., & Lau, M. A. (2000). Prevention of relapse/recurrence in major depression by mindfulness-based cognitive therapy. *Journal of Consulting and Clinical Psychology, 68*, 615–623.

Van Widenfelt, B., Markman, H., J., Guerney, B., & Behrens, B. C. (1997). Prevention of relationship problems. In H. Markman & W. K. Halford (Eds.), *Clinical handbook of marriage and couples interventions* (pp. 651–675). New York: John Wiley & Sons.

Wenzel, A., & Harvey, J. (2001). Introduction: The movement toward studying the maintenance and enhancement of close romantic relationships. In J. Harvey & A. Wenzel (Eds.), *Close romantic relationships: Maintenance and enhancement* (pp. 1–10). Mahwah, NJ: Lawrence Erlbaum Associates.

Zimmerman, J. M., & Coyle, V. (1996). *The way of council*. Las Vegas: Bramble.

15

Dialectical Behavior Therapy (DBT): A Mindfulness-Based Treatment for Intimate Partner Violence

Jill H. Rathus

*Department of Psychology, Long Island University/C.W. Post Campus,
Brookville, New York*

Nicholas Cavuoto

Long Beach Reach, Inc., Long Beach, New York

Vincent Passarelli

*Department of Psychiatry, Mood and Personality Disorders Research Program,
Mount Sinai School of Medicine, New York, New York*

INTRODUCTION

Mindfulness is "paying attention on purpose, in the present moment, and nonjudgmentally to the unfolding of experience moment by moment" (Kabat-Zinn, 2003, p. 145); it originates from meditation practices developed in Buddhist spiritual traditions. In the last decade, mindfulness and acceptance-based approaches have permeated and expanded the cognitive-behavioral therapy tradition to such an extent that they have been referred to as the third generation or third wave of behavior therapy (Hayes, 2004), following traditional behavior therapy and cognitive therapy.

Numerous randomized trials support the effectiveness of a variety of mindfulness-based treatments, such as dialectical behavior therapy (DBT) (Linehan, Armstrong, Suarez, Allmon, & Heard, 1991), mindfulness-based stress reduction (MBSR) (Kabat-Zinn *et al.,* 1992), acceptance and commitment therapy (ACT) (Hayes, Strosahl, & Wilson, 1999), and mindfulness-based cognitive therapy (MBCT) (Teasdale *et al.,* 2000). Versions of these treatments have addressed such clinical conditions as borderline personality disorder (BPD) (Linehan *et al.,* 1991), psychotic thinking (Bach & Hayes, 2002), depressive relapse (Segal, Williams, & Teasdale, 2001), substance abuse (e.g., Linehan *et al.,* 1999; Marlatt *et al.,* 2004), and eating disorders (Wilson, 2004). The present chapter presents the rationale for and application of a mindfulness-based treatment—an adaptation of DBT—for intimate partner violence.

THEORETICAL AND CONCEPTUAL RATIONALE

INTIMATE PARTNER VIOLENCE

Male-to-female domestic violence is a significant social concern in the United States. While specific estimates of its prevalence vary, they all highlight the seriousness of the problem. For example, the National Institute of Justice estimates that domestic violence occurs in 2.5 to 4 million American homes each year. The FBI has reported that husbands and boyfriends were responsible for nearly one-third of the women murdered in 1995, and that battering was the leading cause of injury to women between the ages of 15 and 44, making it responsible for more injuries to women than car accidents, muggings, and stranger rapes combined (Emery & Laumann-Billings, 1998). "Common couple violence" and violence in same-sex couples pose significant concerns as well (e.g., Johnson, 1995; Renzetti, 1997).

Despite the pervasiveness of intimate partner violence, research suggests that the standard treatment approaches show small effect sizes at best (see Babcock, Green, & Robie, 2004). Treatments evaluated in controlled studies have failed to reduce recidivism rates and fare poorly in retaining individuals in treatment. Dropout rates in the first 3 months of treatment have been observed to range between 40% and 60% (Taft, Murphy, Elliott, & Morrel, 2001). Further, generic treatment programs offer a one-size-fits-all approach that does not address the differences among batterer subtypes in terms of clinical characteristics and functions of relationship violence (Holtzworth-Munroe, Meehan, Herron, Rehman, & Stuart, 2000; Babcock, Costa, Green, & Eckhardt, 2004). Investigators have thus called for the development of new treatments that take into account both the difficulty of treating relationship aggression and the diversity of perpetrators of relational violence (Babcock *et al.,* 2004). Thus, we propose a new treatment approach, DBT, for intimate partner violence.

OVERVIEW OF DBT

DBT was developed by Linehan (1993a) as a treatment for chronically suicidal individuals with BPD. DBT blends behavioral and crisis intervention strategies with a dialectical philosophy and Zen practice. This blending is represented by DBT's ongoing emphasis on behavior change balanced with acceptance and validation of patients as they are. The treatment is based on Linehan's biosocial theory, which suggests that BPD arises from a transaction between a biologically based difficulty with emotion regulation and a pervasively invalidating environment. DBT is comprehensive and flexible, designed to:

1. improve patients' behavioral capacities,
2. increase patients' motivation to change,
3. help patients generalize new behaviors to all relevant aspects of their lives,
4. support therapists, and
5. structure the environment to promote the success of both patients and therapists.

Each of these functions is addressed through at least one mode of treatment, which typically includes individual therapy, a skills training group, telephone consultation, and a case consultation team for therapists. The behavior therapy aspect of treatment is framed by the hierarchy of treatment targets and the chain analysis procedure. Stage one targets are:

1. decreasing life-threatening behavior;
2. decreasing therapy-interfering behavior;
3. decreasing quality-of-life interfering behavior; and
4. increasing behavioral skills (Linehan, 1993a).

In order to identify problem behaviors, the patient fills out a daily diary card to track the frequency, intensity, and times at which they occur (Linehan, 1993a). Patients bring the diary card with them to therapy and together with the therapist identify the behaviors taking place during the week that are highest on the treatment hierarchy. To examine target behaviors, the DBT therapist then employs a chain analysis, which follows a standard behavior therapy "A-B-C" format (i.e., antecedents-behavior-consequences). Once the target is identified, the therapist and patient exhaustively examine it in terms of precipitating events, that is, the patient's feelings, bodily sensations, thoughts, images, behaviors, and ensuing events, with each representing a link in the chain (Linehan, 1993a). After exploring each precipitant, they fully consider the function of the behavior, examining all consequences. During this stage of the chain analysis, the patient and therapist also engage in problem-solving efforts such as skill strengthening, contingency management, cognitive restructuring, or exposure, as needed.

The skills training group runs concurrently with individual therapy, although it does not need to be run by the individual therapist. The skills group is divided into four didactic modules: mindfulness, distress tolerance, emotion regulation, and interpersonal effectiveness.

HOW MINDFULNESS TRAINING IS LIKELY TO BE HELPFUL

DBT approaches mindfulness as "psychological and behavioral versions of meditation skills usually taught in Eastern spiritual practices" (Linehan, 1993a, p. 114), particularly Buddhist traditions. Why should mindfulness be applied in the treatment of batterers? Many aspects of mindfulness training, and in particular, its utility for enhancing emotion regulation, point to its relevance.

Bishop et al. (2004) recently operationalized the concept of mindfulness as (1) the self-regulation of attention, focused and sustained on immediate experience, while (2) relinquishing the goal of changing the experience and instead accepting each thought, emotion, sensation, and urge as it arises. This process is expected to alter the subjective meaning of these experiences. They state, "mindfulness in contemporary psychology has been adapted as an approach for increasing awareness and responding skillfully to mental processes that contribute to emotional distress and maladaptive behavior" (p. 230). In particular, targets of mindfulness-based treatment share qualities of emotional distress and maladaptive behavior that can be conceptualized as outgrowths of problems of emotion regulation.

One could argue that partner-directed aggression may stem from difficulties with emotional regulation. Linehan (1993a) describes emotion dysregulation as the frequent and intense experience of strong emotions brought on by emotional vulnerability (a tendency to be sensitive to emotional triggers and to experience strong, long-lasting emotional reactions) combined with a deficit in the capacity to modulate emotions. As Linehan (1993a) argues, extreme maladaptive behaviors typically either result directly from dysregulated emotions (which are inevitably accompanied by cognitive and behavioral dysregulation, such as impulsive explosions of anger) or represent attempts to re-regulate intolerably aversive affective states (which could be impulsive or planned; such as by blocking a partner from leaving before an argument is settled).

Problems with emotional dysregulation can result in two main maladaptive coping strategies: emotional (or experiential) avoidance and emotional preoccupation (Hayes & Feldman, 2004). Both represent ends of a continuum of controlling or trying to manage one's emotional experience. Experiential avoidance is an attempt to push away experience whereas emotional preoccupation is an attempt to hold on to it. Hayes (2004; Hayes et al., 1996) and others have identified experiential avoidance as lying at the core of many forms of disordered behavior; that is, symptoms arise and are maintained as a result of avoiding painful emotions through whatever means possible (e.g., binge eating, substance abuse, self-injurious behavior). Similarly, partner-violent individuals might aggress against a partner to relieve an aversive state of internal arousal, such as rage resulting from a partner's verbal aggression (Babcock *et al.,* 2004; Fruzzetti & Levensky, 2000; Tweed & Dutton, 1998). Even instrumental functions of partner-directed violence include escape from negative affect. For example, a partner's compliance with a demand might reduce the mate's frustration.

On the other hand, emotional preoccupation can also occur, wherein individuals get stuck dwelling on emotions by clinging to positive experiences or ruminating about negative ones (Hayes & Feldman, 2004). For example, an individual might demand continued contact with a partner as a love interest becomes an obsession. Or, ruminating about the potential threats to a relationship might lead to excessive dysphoria and jealousy, in turn leading to behaviors such as monitoring, controlling, and stalking. Such emotional preoccupation could potentially develop into experiential avoidance, for example, when isolation and restriction of a partner function to reduce the painful experience of anxiety about threats of loss of the partner. That is, emotions produce associated action urges (e.g., anger typically occurs with the urge to attack). When one becomes preoccupied with one's emotions, action urges grow stronger. Failure to act on these urges tends to increase negative arousal (Bishop *et al.,* 2004; Carver & Scheier, 1990), whereas satisfying the action urge of an emotion tends to decrease it, at least in the short run (e.g., feeling jealous leads to the urge to keep a partner out of situations one finds threatening). Of course, to the extent that satisfaction of the action urge temporarily reduces negative arousal, acting on urges becomes negatively reinforced (Adams, 1988). Bishop *et al.* (2004) make a case for a mindfulness-based batterer treatment when they state, "Mindfulness approaches thus may be particularly effective for clinical syndromes in which intolerance of negative affect and subsequent behavioral avoidance play a central role" (p. 237).

In the practice of mindfulness, one learns to cease controlling one's emotional experience, by neither pushing it away nor clinging to it (Linehan, 1993a). One learns to notice emotions and urges without acting on them. One also learns to observe thoughts, bodily sensations, and surroundings without feeling a mandate to change them. Rather, one simply observes present-moment experience nonjudgmentally, as it enters awareness. Implicit in the notion of observing without altering experience is the notion of accepting this experience.

Linehan (1993a; 1993b) has delineated a set of component skills for practicing mindfulness. The "what" skills indicate *what to do*, and consist of observing, or just noticing experience; describing, or putting experience into words; and participating, or throwing oneself into one's experience without rumination or self-consciousness. The "how" skills indicate *how* to do each "what" skill, and consist of acting one-mindfully (focusing on one thing in the moment), nonjudgmentally, and effectively (focusing on what works, keeping long-term goals in mind). Men who engage in intimate partner violence have been shown to lack these capacities. For example, many are poor at putting experience into words, suffering from what has been termed *normative male alexithymia* (Levant, 2001). Many cannot let go of ruminating (e.g., Sonkin, Martin, & Walker, 1985). They have trouble responding nonjudgmentally, for example, making overly negative attributions for partners' behaviors (Holtzworth-Munroe & Hutchinson, 1993). And they frequently have difficulty responding effectively, drawing on limited social decision-making repertoires and poor communication skills (e.g., Anglin & Holtzworth-Munroe, 1997).

Practicing mindfulness thus has clear relevance for individuals with problems of relationship aggression. In terms of basic processes, mindfulness suggests the ability to separate thought ("She's disrespected me") and emotion (anger) from action (aggression). It also enhances the ability to observe and describe emotions—a key to regulating them (Linehan, 1993a). In terms of higher-level cognitive processes, mindfulness training teaches the ability to pause from automatic responding, to reflect, and, with awareness, to select a response, rather than react impulsively. This switching from reacting to noticing experience allows one to break the cycle of overlearned, habitual responding. Mindfulness also aids in inhibiting secondary elaborative processing of emotions (Bishop *et al.,* 2004). This inhibition is useful, since secondary emotions, rather than primary ones, often lead to maladaptive cognitions and behaviors (Fruzzetti & Iverson, 2004).

WHY DBT FOR INTIMATE PARTNER VIOLENCE?

Several important arguments for adapting DBT for batterers can be made. First, DBT has been effective in treating people with severe problems of behavioral and emotional dysregulation (Fruzzetti & Levensky, 2000), such as BPD and substance abuse. Fruzzetti and Levensky (2000) note that the parasuicidal behaviors of the BPD patient and the violence of the batterer may have similar functions, as both result in instrumental gains and diminished negative emotional arousal. DBT's efficacy in reducing cutting and other parasuicidal acts indicates that it may be similarly efficacious in reducing aggressive behavior. In addition, DBT skills modules specifically target problems in emotion dysregulation, interpersonal dysregulation, behavioral and cognitive dysregulation (i.e., impulsivity), and self-dysregulation (e.g., unstable identity, confusion about self) (Linehan, 1993a; 1993b). Evidence suggests that partner-violent men generally have difficulties in each of these areas. For example, they show much higher levels of emotional distress and reactivity and poorer affect regulation than nonviolent married men (e.g., Babcock, Jacobson, Gottman, & Yerington, 2000; Cohen, Rosenbaum, Kane, Warnken, & Benjamin, 1999; Dutton, 1999; Holtzworth-Munroe & Smutzler, 1996; Scott, 2004). Many have a history of trauma, which may contribute to their problems of emotional dysregulation (Dutton, 1995a; 1995b; Rosenbaum & Leisring, 2003). Additionally, partner-violent men have deficits in interpersonal skills, are significantly poorer at selecting or applying effective solutions during stressful situations, and show evidence of behavioral and cognitive dysregulation and impulsivity (Cohen *et al.,* 2003; Dutton & Browning, 1988; Holtzworth-Munroe, 1992; Holtzworth-Munroe & Anglin, 1991; Tolman & Bennett, 1990). Finally, studies pointing to the dependency, abandonment fears, and loss of self of batterers in intimate relationships (e.g., Babcock *et al.,* 2000; Goldstein & Rosenbaum, 1985) suggest that they also suffer from self-dysregulation/confusion about self. Thus, in addition to mindfulness training, the remaining three skills modules seem highly tailored for addressing batterers' behavioral and emotional dysregulation.

A second reason for applying DBT to a batterer population is to address the problem of treatment dropout, which can be as high as 90% between time of first contact and program completion (Gondolf & Foster, 1991). Since women tend to stay with partners who enter treatment, it is vital to the safety of women that the men stay in treatment until completion (Babcock & Steiner, 1999). In addition, completion has been associated with higher commitment to treatment, which may also result in lower recidivism rates (Babcock *et al.,* 2004; Rondeau, Brodeur, Brochu, & Lemire, 2001). DBT has several methods for increasing the likelihood of treatment completion. For example, the commitment strategies target investment in the treatment process from the outset (Linehan, 1993a). The therapist's use of relationship-enhancing techniques such as radical acceptance, validation, empathy, and a nonjudgmental stance may help clients develop more trust in the therapeutic alliance, thereby allowing a more honest examination of behavior. Additionally, by targeting therapy-interfering behaviors, the therapist and patient have the opportunity to address impediments to treatment completion before they cause premature discontinuation. Finally, the hierarchy of treatment targets provides both patient and therapist with a clearly agreed upon set of treatment goals. Epperson, Bushway, and Warman (1983) have reported that level of perceived agreement on treatment goals is positively correlated with treatment retention.

Third, the batterer treatment field has largely acknowledged that the heterogeneity of the battering population likely relates to the poor success of unitary approaches to treatment (Babcock *et al.,* 2004; Babcock *et al.,* 2004; Holtzworth-Munroe *et al.,* 2000). A comprehensive and flexible multipronged approach such as DBT may be better equipped to address this heterogeneity than other treatment approaches. In individual therapy in DBT, behavioral analyses of targeted behaviors continually

assess and address idiosyncratic contexts and functions of physical aggression and related behaviors, rather than assuming uniform functions of
violence (e.g., to control the partner, as in the Duluth model [Pence
& Paymar, 1993]).

A fourth rationale for conducting DBT with partner-violent men is to
help generalize newly learned capacities to the client's natural environment.
DBT's policy of phone calls to the therapist allows for *in vivo* coaching of
clients in challenging situations. Thus, clients are more likely to apply what
they have learned in therapy to difficult real-life scenarios.

Finally, an important feature of DBT is its provision of support to
therapists, for whom working with this population can be very stressful.
Therapists may be unable, or even unwilling at times, to validate or feel
empathy toward someone whose behavior may shock or outrage. Therefore,
the therapists' consultation team can provide a forum for addressing
these issues in a nonjudgmental manner before they become a problem
in the treatment.

HOW DBT DIFFERS FROM EXISTING MODELS FOR TREATING
INTIMATE PARTNER VIOLENCE

Most batterer treatment conducted today falls into one of two categories: feminist treatment and treatments based on principles of cognitive-
behavioral clinical psychology, with many combining these two to varying
degrees. The feminist approach attempts to teach men to take full
responsibility for the violent acts they commit and to challenge the ways
in which our patriarchal society has contributed to the justification of
violence as a means of maintaining power and control over one's
partner (Mederos, 1999; Pence & Paymar, 1993). This aim is addressed
not only through *education groups* (note that they are not referred to as
"treatment" or "therapy" groups) but also through a systemwide coordinated community response designed "to diminish the power of batterers
over their victims and to explore with each abusive man the intent and
source of his violence" (Pence & Paymar, 1993, p. 1). The template for the
feminist approach is the Duluth Domestic Abuse Intervention Project
(DAIP), more commonly referred to as the "Duluth model." There are two
distinct components to the Duluth model—the education group and the
coordinated community response (CCR). The education group is a 26-week
program based on a curriculum with eight themes: (1) nonviolence, (2) nonthreatening behavior, (3) respect, (4) support and trust, (5) accountability
and honesty, (6) sexual respect, (7) partnership, and (8) negotiation and
fairness (Pence & Paymar, 1993). The CCR consists of community organizations such as family court, probation, clinicians, and victims' advocates
working together to treat and monitor the men and ensure the future
safety of the women. The cognitive-behavioral therapy (CBT) approach

(e.g., Adams, 1988; Dunford, 2000) includes such treatment components as anger management, self-initiated time-outs, arousal reduction strategies, cognitive restructuring, and assertiveness skills (e.g., teaching the difference among passive, aggressive, and passive-aggressive behavior and replacing these with direct and appropriate communication skills). This approach is typically offered in groups but has also been conducted with couples (e.g., O'Leary, 2001b; O'Leary, Heyman, & Neidig, 1999).

DBT differs from these approaches in several ways. First, functions of violence, across and within individuals, are not assumed *a priori,* but rather are assessed on an ongoing basis. Thus, a DBT therapist would not assume the function of a violent act to be a mode of anger expression (implicit in the CBT model) or an attempt to assert power (implicit in the Duluth model) but would conduct a behavioral analysis to investigate its function. This is of critical importance, as research demonstrates that violence serves a range of functions. For example, although functions vary across different acts of aggression, Babcock, Costa, *et al.* (2004) found that antisocial men more often use violence to control, and borderline men more often use violence in response to the experience of jealousy. Second, the therapeutic style blends validation and acceptance with an emphasis on behavioral change. Third, as explicated previously, much improvement would be hypothesized to occur because of an increased ability to observe and accept present-moment experience without the need to *change* this experience. In other such treatments, the therapist attempts to directly change clients' experiences (e.g., confronting patriarchal attitudes, calming arousal, or challenging cognitions). Fourth, additional change would be expected to occur based on the comprehensive set of skills taught, which would enhance clients' capability deficits in these areas. While both of the other major models address skills deficits (e.g., negotiation, communication), DBT does this more broadly, with a greater emphasis on self-regulatory abilities. Fifth, separating treatment into group and individual components allows for peer support and a standardized didactic component while concurrently addressing individual contingencies, motivational issues, and therapeutic relationship issues. Sixth, the DBT team approach builds in an element of therapist support to enhance treatment effectiveness and reduce burnout.

ADAPTATIONS MADE FOR THIS POPULATION

In its standard form, DBT is structured to treat the problems faced by individuals with BPD, most of whom are women. While it has been demonstrated that partner-violent males share many personality and behavioral characteristics with women with BPD, such as poor treatment retention, significant emotional dysregulation, problems with anger, confusion about self, impulsivity, and poor interpersonal skills, a variety of modifications were deemed necessary to adapt DBT to the male partner-violent population.

The first adaptation was to expand the treatment hierarchy to include targets relevant to a partner-violent population. Specifically, the category of "life-threatening behavior" has been expanded to include not only self-injurious behavior but also other-directed violent behavior (particularly toward one's partner and children). In addition, the category "quality-of-life interfering behavior" now includes behaviors that affect the quality of life of others—for instance, psychological abuse, verbal abuse, controlling behaviors, stalking, and violating orders of protection. Authors such as O'Leary (2001a) insist that a focus on forms of partner aggression other than physical aggression is imperative in batterer treatment, as these forms of abuse might actually increase in the absence of physical aggression (Gondolf, Heckert, & Kimmel, 2002).

We also modified the DBT diary card to include conflict tactics (such as physical, psychologically aggressive, and positive or negative verbal tactics; urges to be aggressive; and partner injury) and a greater number of emotions to monitor on a daily basis (anger, fear, jealousy, happiness, misery, sadness, guilt, and shame). The remaining minor alterations were made to the skills themselves and to the skills-related handouts. First, we added a module titled "Domestic Partner Education," which provides psychoeducation regarding definitions of physically, verbally, and psycho-logically abusive behavior; the impact of domestic violence on children; family-of-origin violence; common patriarchal attitudes or myths justifying abusive behavior; and the link between substance use and domestic violence. Other changes include a greater emphasis on a partner's experiences in addition to one's own (e.g., being mindful of others' experiences, or "relational mindfulness" [Fruzzetti & Levensky, 2000]), increased emphasis on empathy and partner respect in the interpersonal effectiveness module, a rewording of some of the decidedly feminine content to be more masculine (such as within the self-soothing and pleasant activities handouts), an expansion of the acceptance skills to include explicit acceptance of the partner, as well as a list of difficult relationship truths that must be accepted (e.g., a partner might choose to end the relationship), and an added focus on the emotion of jealousy, which has been shown to be a significant emotional precursor to male abusive behavior (e.g., Babcock *et al.*, 2004).

CASE STUDY: MR. C

CLIENT BACKGROUND

Mr. C was a 25-year old white male at the time he presented for treatment. He was somewhat below average height and of slender but muscular build. Mr. C resided with his mother and younger sister in a suburb of New York City. He had earned some college credits but had not received a degree. He had been unemployed for the year prior to treatment. He had been dating his girlfriend, Ms. W (age 25), for several years. At intake, Mr. C was well groomed and casually but neatly dressed, wearing a baseball cap. He was polite and friendly and displayed appropriate eye contact. He was well related, verbal, and coherent and expressed interest in starting the DBT program. Mr. C exhibited some insight and the ability to reflect on his behavior, and so appeared to be an appropriate treatment candidate.

Mr. C's parents divorced when he was 7 years old. He described his father as physically and emotionally abusive toward the family and as having been incarcerated as a result. Mr. C's mother remarried after the divorce. He stated that his stepfather was also physically brutal and emotionally abusive toward the family. His stepfather had moved out approximately 6 years prior to Mr. C's intake meeting. Mr. C believed that his own use of physical aggression, which began in high school, was the result of being bullied (physically and emotionally) for most of his childhood and adolescence. In fact, he was able to articulate that as a small-framed young man, physical aggression had paid off for him, as it taught peers to fear and respect him.

Mr. C was self-referred to the men's program. On assessment of physical aggression toward his partner using the Conflict Tactics Scale 2 (CTS2) (Straus, Hamby, Boney-McCoy, & Sugarman, 1996), he reported that in the year preceding the program intake he had grabbed his girlfriend on multiple occasions while also punching walls (sometimes making holes) several times during arguments. In addition, he had been even more violent prior to the past year and recounted times when he had twisted his girlfriend's arm; pushed, grabbed, and slapped her; spit at her; flipped over tables; and slammed her against a wall. He had also once picked up a chair and thrown it across the room; Ms. W had been struck in the eye by the thrown chair and required stitches. She suffered other injuries, such as bruises, as a result of the other behaviors. Ms. W corroborated Mr. C's long history of partner aggression.

In the week prior to the program intake, Ms. W also witnessed a violent physical altercation occurring between Mr. C and his brother that involved punching, choking, threatening, intimidating with a knife, and destruction of property. As a result of this incident, Mr. C was arrested and a "do not harass" order was filed against him by his brother and sister-in-law. On separate and unrelated occasions in the past, Mr. C had been arrested for attempted assault (i.e., street fighting) and had been required to make a court appearance for possession of marijuana. Although he was not mandated to treatment for assaulting his brother, the incident helped Mr. C recognize that he needed help controlling his dangerously escalating aggression, so he contacted our program.

On assessment of psychological aggression using the Psychological Maltreatment of Women Inventory (PMWI) (Tolman, 1999), Mr. C reported that during the year prior to program intake, he had frequently used verbally aggressive behaviors. On the Emotional and Verbal Abuse (EVA) subscale of the PMWI, he endorsed acting insensitively to his girlfriend's feelings, changing his moods radically, yelling and screaming, calling her names, and saying things to spite her. Mr. C also reported using dominating, isolating, and controlling behaviors during the year prior to program intake. On the Dominance and Isolation (DI) subscale of the PMWI, he reported acting jealous of other men, acting jealous or suspicious of his girlfriend's friends, discouraging her from socializing or doing things for her own self-improvement, and asking her to account for her time.

On interview, Mr. C reported symptoms of depression and posttraumatic stress disorder. He also met full criteria for borderline and antisocial personality disorders. Mr. C reported being on no medication and had never been hospitalized for a mental health–related problem. As a teen, he had once been hospitalized for accidental alcohol poisoning. During the intake, Mr. C reported drinking approximately three to four beers 3 days a week when with friends. He occasionally smoked marijuana, and reported last smoking 3 weeks prior to intake. He also reported experimenting with various other drugs (e.g., ecstasy, mushrooms) while in high school.

Mr. C's girlfriend, the 25-year-old Ms. W, was a white female who, like Mr. C, also resided with her parents in a suburb of New York City. She had a bachelor's degree and worked in an administrative position. Mr. C described her as "loving." He also described her as reclusive and very anxious and reported that she had a clinical diagnosis of obsessive-compulsive disorder (OCD), for which she was receiving treatment. She had no history of hospitalizations for mental health–related or substance-related problems.

TREATMENT

Mr. C was a participant in a study of DBT for batterers described in a later section. Along with three other men, he participated in a 20-week protocol that included weekly individual therapy sessions and skills group meetings. He also completed individual assessment sessions at pretreatment and posttreatment and at 9-month follow-up. Ms. W also participated in assessments at these times. The DBT program targeted Mr. C's violent and intimidating behaviors toward his girlfriend and others, his psychological/verbal aggression, and his difficulties managing emotions, tolerating distress, and maintaining interpersonal relationships.

Individual sessions each began with a mindfulness exercise to practice the skill and to cue a different mindset for participation in therapy. These were followed by review of Mr. C's diary card, which he completed in a highly detailed manner each week. Based on the DBT target hierarchy and consultation with Mr. C, the therapist selected a behavior for analysis. Mr. C then provided an exhaustive account of the moment-to-moment antecedents and consequences of the targeted behavior. The therapist and Mr. C began by identifying common vulnerability factors, such as a poor night's sleep or excessive drinking the night before. Next, precipitants to the chain of emotion dysregulation were actively explored, such as an argument with Ms. W over his going out with friends or his feeling controlled by her. Links in the chain leading to the problem behavior were then identified, such as his subjective sense of "heating up" and feeling like he was "about to explode." The problem behavior itself, such as pounding his fists on his dashboard while sitting next to her in the car, was then discussed in light of these precipitating factors. Finally, the reinforcing and punishing consequences were looked at and their role in maintaining the problem behaviors was explained, such as immediate relief from the tension buildup and her temporarily desisting in her demand, as well as pain in his hands, a sense of feeling out of control and ineffective, and a negative impact on Ms. W. Solution analysis then focused on intervening at one or more links in the chain to yield a more desirable outcome, using one or more DBT problem-solving strategies, such as skills enhancement, contingency management, cognitive restructuring, or exposure, as needed. Mindfulness played a particularly critical role in working to change the course of events. For example, Mr. C was taught to observe and describe his thoughts of being controlled, his feelings of rising anger and tension, and his urges to pound his car's dashboard. He was taught to participate fully in this experience without judging it or trying to change it. He was also taught to focus on effectiveness; that is, to identify his goal and think about behaving in a manner that would make him most likely to reach it. For example, one goal in this situation was to communicate to Ms. W his discomfort at feeling controlled, without intimidating or abusing her. Thus, after learning to slow his chain of action through mindful contemplation, he gradually became able to elect to use interpersonal effectiveness skills to express his feelings to his girlfriend. Conducting behavioral analyses repeatedly across sessions helped Mr. C gain insight into his patterns of aggressive and otherwise maladaptive behavior and strengthen alternative responses.

Group skills training sessions each began with a mindfulness exercise as well. The men then discussed their experiences of the exercise and shared their observations. Group leaders then taught additional skills corresponding to the current module. Mr. C learned essential information in these modules. For example, in the domestic partner education module, he learned about the impact of the family-of-origin violence he experienced. In the mindfulness module, he learned of the difference between "emotion mind," when his emotions took over, and "reasonable mind," when he pushed out emotions and responded only with logic. In the distress tolerance module, he learned skills for self-soothing, distracting, improving the moment, and considering the pros and cons of using aggressive behavior; and radical acceptance skills that helped him accept both his painful abuse history and his girlfriend and her OCD symptoms. In the interpersonal effectiveness module, he learned to validate his partner, to better articulate his wants, to say no while avoiding conflict escalation, and to maintain respect for his girlfriend and himself. Finally, in the emotion regulation module, he learned to identify and label his emotional experiences other than anger, to mindfully observe his emotions rising and falling like waves, to reduce his emotional vulnerability through self-care, to reduce his emotional suffering by building positive experiences, and to act opposite to his destructive action-urge emotions, particularly jealousy.

TREATMENT OUTCOME FOR MR. C

Physical Aggression

The average intensity level of Mr. C's urges to be aggressive (as measured by the DBT diary cards) decreased from pretreatment to follow-up by approximately 45%. In addition, he reported no acts of physical aggression, as measured by the diary cards and the CTS2, toward Ms. W over the entire duration of the treatment and follow-up period. Interestingly, although his urges to be aggressive showed a downward trend, Mr. C's weekly anger ratings varied little across treatment, indicating an enhanced capacity to experience anger without acting aggressively in response to it. In addition, Ms. W reported a significant improvement in her sense of personal safety.

Psychological Aggression

Mr. C demonstrated a notable decrease in psychological aggression following treatment. On the emotional and verbal abuse subscale of the PMWI, Mr. C had a pretreatment score of 29 (out of 40) and posttreatment and follow-up scores of 10 (the scale's floor) and 12, respectively. This improvement was corroborated by Ms. W at follow-up. On the dominance and isolation scale of the PMWI, Mr. C showed similar decreases. His scores fell from 29 at pretreatment to 13 at posttreatment and 12 at follow-up. Ms. W again substantiated these decreases. Moreover, at her posttreatment and follow-up interviews, Ms. W identified notable improvements in Mr. C's level of jealousy and isolating behaviors.

Mr. C's use of negative verbal tactics and psychologically aggressive tactics as monitored on the daily diary cards showed a downward trend as treatment progressed. In particular, 82% of his total use of negative verbal tactics occurred during the first 10 weeks of treatment. Similarly, 80% of his total use of psychologically aggressive tactics occurred during the first 7 weeks of treatment. In addition, Mr. C's diary card assessment showed a consistently high level of positive verbal tactics, with a slight increase across treatment.

Confusion about Self, Impulsivity, Emotional Dysregulation and Interpersonal Chaos

The Life Problems Inventory (LPI) assesses four core aspects of BPD: confusion about self, interpersonal chaos, emotional dysregulation, and impulsivity (Rathus & Miller, 2002). It was used to assess the level of skill acquisition in the group participants across the treatment modules. Mr. C reported a significant decrease in each of these targeted areas. His improvement was noticeable shortly after treatment began and may be a reflection of his moderately high baseline scores and steadfast connection to treatment that was apparent throughout his time in the program. Mr. C's gains were maintained at follow-up. In addition, the improvements were substantiated by Ms. W's interview data, which she provided at pretreatment, posttreatment, and follow-up assessments. For example, during the pretreatment interview, Ms. W was asked to describe Mr. C's emotion regulation. She stated: "[He] doesn't know how [to regulate his emotions] or just can't walk away from things. He punches walls or car dashboards, drinks at times, yells and screams with bugged out eyes. If it has something to do with me, I will try to walk away. Sometimes he grabs my arms and won't let me [walk away]."

She also reported that although Mr. C made attempts to communicate with her, he lacked the skills to do so effectively and would usually "end up making false promises." At other times he would have an impulsive "screw you, I'm going to do it anyway" attitude. She reported that the two things that helped Mr. C tolerate painful emotions were drawing and playing video games, although the video games tended to be graphically violent.

A posttreatment interview with Ms. W included the following information about the targeted treatment areas: "Before the program, [he] used to lie or joke to communicate with me. Now he actually voices his feeling instead of sulking, and will tell me if something is bothering him." Ms. W also expressed that on several occasions, Mr. C had appropriately asked her for "alone time and time-outs" so that he could "take the time to think about what he wants to say." She reported that Mr. C was more supportive of her decisions and now validated her with "respect and awareness for her feelings." In addition, he would often ask Ms. W, "What can we do to prevent this [argument/disagreement] from happening again?" Mr. C was also reported to be less impulsive and less angry than he was at pretreatment. Ms. W summarized the improvements by stating: "Overall, [he] is less rigid and seems to be less sensitive to criticism from others. Instead of walking home and leaving, or waiting in his car, punching his dashboard, he will talk about things openly and calmly."

Ms. W reported that the interpersonal and emotion regulation gains that Mr. C made over the course of treatment were maintained and further improved at follow-up. Her follow-up assessment included the following: "The last nine months were a real test for us. It was full of plenty of opportunities for fights and disagreements between [him] and me because my OCD has gotten worse and I have been stressed out. However, [he] has been very flexible and understanding with me and is assertive where he can express his feelings to me without being aggressive or yelling." In addition, she reported that Mr. C continued to be supportive of her decisions "rather than tell her what to do." Meanwhile, Mr. C had found a job, and Ms. W described several scenarios that demonstrated his ability to walk away from others at work who were "pushing his buttons" and how he had learned to use humor (e.g., "laughing at himself or a situation") as a means to cope with stress. Ms. W described an apparent increase in Mr. C's mindfulness skills, stating that he was "more aware of what he is doing and why." She also described him as more secure, confident, and "no longer needing to intimidate others."

Problem Solving

Mr. C demonstrated marked improvement following treatment on a social skills measure designed to test competency of responses to hypothetical provocative couple interaction scenarios (Holtzworth-Munroe & Anglin, 1991). At pretreatment, Mr. C's responses indicated below-average competency, that is, behavior that makes the situation worse, escalates the situation, or may harm the relationship (e.g., negative attributions; passive aggressive behavior; negative speaker and listener skills). At posttreatment and follow-up, Mr. C's responses indicated above-average competency. Some responses were emblematic of positive behaviors that may not necessarily enhance the situation but keep the interaction positive or solve the situation constructively (e.g., expressing feelings; making requests, not demands; talking about what may be going wrong; "stopping the action"). Other responses were indicative of positive behaviors that were likely to enhance the relationship or make problems of the same type less likely in the future (e.g., validating the partner's feelings even if one does not agree with them, empathic statements, avoiding defensiveness) (Holtzworth-Munroe & Anglin, 1991).

SUMMARY

Over the course of treatment, Mr. C reported no acts of physical aggression toward his partner. In addition, his use of psychological aggression improved markedly as treatment progressed. These improvements were largely maintained at follow-up and were corroborated by Ms. W's posttreatment and follow-up reports. Mr. C also demonstrated change on the other areas under investigation, namely the "life problems" common to BPD (e.g., confusion about self, impulsivity, emotion dysregulation, interpersonal chaos), problem-solving skills, and urges to be aggressive.

At posttreatment, Mr. C stressed the importance of having a "powerful" connection to the older male group members. The two older men in his life previously, his father and stepfather, had both been physically and emotionally abusive toward him and his family. Thus, he may never have had the experience of identification with an older male upon whom he could model prosocial relationship behaviors. Since he had described himself as a "loner," the connection he felt to the other members and the value he placed upon this came as a surprise to him. Another surprise was the strong connection he felt to the treatment team, particularly with his male individual therapist. He stated, "A male therapist may have made me more comfortable. Like a male camaraderie." Mr. C added that he was "amazed" at how many skills he learned, but more importantly about the times and places to apply them.

At the follow-up assessment, Mr. C and Ms. W were still in a dating relationship. Both stated that although they had occasional disagreements, they were able to compromise and not argue as they had in the past. Mr. C, who was still working, was preparing to return to trade school to become an electrician. He reported that he felt very much in control of his emotions and had a newfound trust in himself that he could overcome conflicts without being aggressive. When asked his opinion about the DBT skills, Mr. C. stated that he continued to find them helpful and to use them on an ongoing basis, particularly mindfulness, validation, and weighing the pros and cons. He also noted that he misses the men's program because it gave him a sense of belonging.

EMPIRICAL SUPPORT FOR DBT FOR INTIMATE PARTNER VIOLENCE

Two studies utilizing DBT for partner-violent men have been carried out by treatment teams at a university-based counseling center on Long Island. Both studies employed a quasi-experimental repeated single case design (Kazdin, 2003). All therapists except the principle author, who is a clinical psychologist intensively trained in DBT, were doctoral students in clinical psychology.

STUDY 1

Our first study was conducted as a group-only treatment over a 22-week period in 2001. Each weekly group session included both behavioral analyses of target behaviors and instruction in skills. In addition to mindfulness, the three skills modules were distress tolerance, interpersonal effectiveness, and emotion regulation. Participants were 5 men between the ages of 23 and 45 who had been identified as physically and emotionally abusive toward their present or past partners. The only exclusionary criteria were clear neurological impairment, psychotic disorder, and a primary alcohol- or other substance-abuse disorder. The participants were both self-referred and court mandated. None of these latter were specifically mandated to this DBT treatment program, but to partner-violence treatment in general.

It was hypothesized that treatment would result in decreases in urges to be aggressive toward partners, as well as in physically, psychologically, and verbally abusive behaviors. The results indicate that most of the men experienced an increase in either the frequency or the intensity of urges to be aggressive from module 1 to module 2, followed by decreases during module 3. However, while the urge to be aggressive increased for the first two-thirds of treatment, the level of physical aggression did not. Specifically, physical aggression for the group showed substantial improvement from pretreatment to posttreatment, as the men did not report any use of physical aggression toward a partner during the final assessment period. Daily diary card ratings of partner injury and physically aggressive tactics lend strong support to the claim of reduced aggressiveness. First, no partner injury was reported by any of the men throughout the treatment. This fact was corroborated by two of the partners contacted at posttreatment. Next, only four instances of mild physical aggression (such as partner restraint and slamming a fist on a kitchen counter) were reported during the treatment. There was one instance of moderate to severe physical aggression by one participant, but this was not directed toward a partner.

Emotional and verbal abuse also showed substantial improvement, while dominance and isolation behaviors improved moderately. Emotional and verbal abuse behaviors were some of the most improved, as they decreased by at least 40% at posttreatment for 4 of the 5 participants. Daily diary card ratings of psychologically aggressive tactics and negative verbal tactics generally support this claim. The men reported only four instances of psychologically aggressive behavior during module 3, with three of these coming from the same man.

The fact that the various forms of emotional abuse were distinctly lower at posttreatment is important. As noted earlier, emotional and verbal abuse can be as damaging as physical abuse (Gondolf et al., 2002; O'Leary et al., 2001a) and have previously been shown to increase while men are taking part in batterers treatment programs, even while physical abuse decreases (Gondolf et al., 2002). Thus, a treatment that does not take these forms of abuse into account cannot be viewed as complete. These behaviors were directly monitored and targeted in the treatment protocol, which may explain the improvements seen.

Other results included a moderate decrease in confusion about self and substantial decreases in interpersonal difficulties, emotional dysregulation, and impulsivity. Anxious attachment to one's partner showed moderate improvement from pretreatment to posttreatment, although these results were least uniform between men. In addition, by the third module the men were reporting very high levels of positive verbal tactics and effective DBT skill use on their daily diary card ratings. This is an important finding in that men in battering relationships have been shown to lack relevant communication and anger management skills (Anglin & Holtzworth-Munroe, 1997; Holtzworth-Munroe, 1992). Anger management showed moderate improvement for the group as a whole.

STUDY 2

Four men participated in our second study (including Mr. C). Their ages ranged from 25 to 47 years. Two were self-referred and two were court mandated. They participated in a 20-week protocol that included both group and individual sessions. Study 2 also differed from Study 1 in the inclusion of *systematic* partner data, 9-month follow-up data, and a social skills assessment measure.

The results of Study 2 were similarly promising. At posttreatment and follow-up, all four participants reported no use of physical aggression toward their partners. However, as research has suggested that partner-violent men consistently underreport aggressive behaviors (e.g., Heckert & Gondolf, 2000; Dutton, 1986b), partner reports were included to enhance validity. The three female partners who participated in the posttreatment and follow-up assessments confirmed that no physical aggression (pushing, grabbing, slapping, or use of weapons) had occurred. In addition, self-reports regarding verbally aggressive behaviors and use of dominating, isolating, and controlling behaviors (as measured by the PMWI) showed an overall downward trend at posttreatment. The three female partners who participated in posttreatment assessment corroborated this information. Of the three male participants who were available at follow-up, two maintained their gains regarding use of psychological aggression. The maintenance of these gains was once again consistent with partner reports.

Improvements also were noted in emotional dysregulation, impulsivity/poor distress tolerance, interpersonal chaos, and confusion about self at posttreatment, as measured by the LPI. Finally, all four participants showed notable improvements in ability to generate competent solutions for hypothetical, provocative partner interactions, and gains were maintained by each of the three men participating in follow-up assessment.

CONCLUSIONS REGARDING EMPIRICAL SUPPORT

A recent meta-analysis of batterer treatments as commonly practiced (Babcock *et al.,* 2004) suggests that no standard treatment can claim superiority over any other and that the effects are small at best—often no more than 5% greater than no treatment at all. Although a 5% decrease would result in 42,000 fewer battered women per year in the United States, the enormity of the problem suggests that more effective treatments are badly needed. Our two studies of DBT adapted for intimate partner violence, though preliminary, offer support for the feasibility and accept-ability of this intervention. The maintenance of improvements at follow-up and the high retention rates are especially promising when compared with the existing literature. Similar findings were reported in an uncontrolled study by Fruzzetti (2002), whose participants showed high rates of treat-ment retention and were all found to be nonviolent at follow-up assessment. Additional controlled studies of DBT for intimate partner violence are clearly warranted.

PRACTICAL IMPLEMENTATION OF DBT
FOR INTIMATE PARTNER VIOLENCE

Practical issues in applying DBT to batterers include the cost-effectiveness of the treatment, the dissemination of the treatment and training practitioners, the difficulty in teaching mindfulness to batterers, the challenge of selling the notion of acceptance and validation to practitioners working with a violent population, and the difficulty of introducing novel treatments that might not adhere to state guidelines.

DBT is more time intensive than standard treatments for batterers, which typically are offered in weekly groups running approximately 90 minutes over 3–6 months. DBT is conducted for a minimum of 5–6 months across multiple modalities, including individual sessions, 2-hour group skills training, phone coaching as needed, and therapist consultation team meetings. Controlled studies are needed that include a comparison condition matched for attention and contact or that show substantial improvement over standard treatment, indicating that costs are saved in the long run (in reductions in emergency-room visits, legal involvement, workdays missed, etc.). Similar evidence has been presented demonstrating the cost-effective-ness of DBT for BPD clients despite its time-intensive format (see Jones, 2000; Linehan, Kanter, & Comtois, 1999).

Another point concerns the dissemination of treatment and training of practitioners. Implementation of DBT requires a high level of training, and few practitioners working with intimate partner violence have had exposure to the approach. Yet, if additional research supports the efficacy of

DBT for this form of physical violence, practitioners in growing numbers will likely seek out the widely available training in DBT. This phenomenon has occurred with the treatment of BPD. Begun in a university research setting, DBT for BPD has proliferated in community mental health centers and other treatment settings across the country.

Regarding difficulty teaching mindfulness to partner-violent men, we have observed that the "packaging" of mindfulness to a partner-violent population is important in its perceived credibility as a core treatment strategy. As the concepts being discussed may be quite novel to a Western, male audience, the therapist teaching mindfulness to batterers may want to keep the following points in mind:

- Begin with easier, concrete exercises, e.g., observation of breath, mindfulness of the position of the body, noticing thoughts without trying to change them.
- Build to more complex exercises, but use materials that will make them more concrete and evocative, e.g., food, lighting, music, scents, magazines/books.
- In keeping with the DBT stylistic strategies, use a lot of validation when eliciting experiences of doing mindfulness exercises. Batterers may have difficulty discussing "intimate" experiences, such as bodily sensations, as this may lead to increased feelings of vulnerability. Reinforce openness in the group by being highly validating and especially nonjudgmental.
- Gradually alter the approach by adding a focus on being mindful of other people's experiences, particularly one's partner. This emphasis on paying attention to the experience of one's partner, which Fruzzetti and Levensky (2000) refer to as relational mindfulness, can be carried on throughout the modules. The aim is to increase the emphasis on empathy and perspective taking, which is imperative for a batterer treatment program.

Regarding the difficulty in selling validation and acceptance to those working with a violent population, practitioners must remember to validate only the valid; for instance, emotions, urges, and experiences may be valid, but violent behavior is never a valid response to these emotions. Practitioners must keep in mind that DBT always balances acceptance with change strategies. There is growing evidence that approaches emphasizing the therapeutic relationship improve retention and outcome. As Taft *et al.* (2001) and Brown and O'Leary (2000) have found, motivational techniques that are designed to enhance treatment retention and improve therapeutic alliance are associated with less violence recidivism.

The final issue concerns the difficulty of introducing novel treatments that might not adhere to state guidelines. After reviewing the treatment literature, one comes away with the feeling that stagnation has set into the batterer treatment field—that treatment innovation is a rare thing. This state of affairs may have to do with the fact that batterer treatment has become a highly political issue. Victims' advocates have had a substantial impact in influencing what types of treatment are considered acceptable. As a result, state legislatures have written restrictive standards about these, making it difficult for clinical researchers to implement new treatment methods that are not expressly permitted by their state (Holtzworth-Munroe, 2001). For example, Massachusetts prohibits both couples group therapy and psychodynamic therapy for batterers, even though there is no evidence to suggest that these treatments are less effective than the standard feminist/CBT ones (Hamberger, 2001).

In noting the presence of rigid standards for implementing new batterer treatments, it is important to point out that these standards exist to protect the victims from "questionable practices" (Hamberger, 2001, p. 271). As Babcock and Steiner (1999) caution, inadequate batterer treatment may actually increase the risk of partner violence. Treatment has been shown to provide the female partner with a false sense of security. That is, the male partner entering treatment is the single biggest predictor of a couple reconciling, even after the woman has been in a shelter. Therefore, experimental treatment evaluations, utilizing comparison groups and participant randomization, of which there have been few, are of the utmost importance for both batterer and victim (Babcock & Steiner, 1999; Dunford, 2000). Unfortunately, many authors have noted that the batterer treatment literature is so marred by inconsistency—in its methods, measurement, dropout rates, and, most importantly, its results—that batterer treatment *standards* are impossible to set with any degree of certainty (e.g., Dunford, 2000; Gondolf, 1999; Hamberger, 2001; Rosenfeld, 1992). Thus, the promising preliminary data on DBT for intimate partner violence suggest the value in evaluating the treatment through controlled empirical approaches, to work toward enhancing the effectiveness of programs aimed toward eliminating intimate partner violence.

ACKNOWLEDGMENTS

The authors wish to thank the following individuals for their input in this work: Eva Feindler, David Pelcovitz, and Dan Wagner. This work was supported by a grant awarded to the first author from the Long Island University/CW Post Research Committee.

REFERENCES

Adams, D. (1988). Treatment models of men who batter: A profeminist analysis. In K. Yllo & M. Bograd (Eds.), *Feminist perspectives on wife abuse* (pp. 176–199). Newbury Park, CA: Sage.

Anglin, K., & Holtzworth-Munroe, A. (1997). Comparing the responses of maritally violent and nonviolent spouses to problematic marital and nonmarital situations: Are the skill deficits of physically aggressive husbands and wives global? *Journal of Family Psychology, 11*, 301–313.

Babcock, J. C., Costa, D. M., Green, C. E., & Eckhardt, C. I. (2004). What situations induce intimate partner violence? A reliability and validity study of the Proximal Antecedents to Violent Episodes (PAVE) Scale. *Journal of Family Psychology, 18*, 322–442.

Babcock, J. C., Green, C. E., & Robie, C. (2004). Does batterers' treatment work? A meta-analytic review of domestic violence treatment. *Clinical Psychology Review, 23*, 1023–1053.

Babcock, J., Jacobson, N., Gottman, J. M., & Yerington, T. (2000). Attachment, emotional regulation, and the function of marital violence: Differences between secure, preoccupied, and dismissing violent and nonviolent husbands. *Journal of Family Violence, 15*, 391–409.

Babcock, J. C., & Steiner, R. (1999). The relationship between treatment, incarceration, and recidivism in battering: A program evaluation of Seattle's coordinated community response to domestic violence. *Journal of Family Psychology, 13*, 46–59.

Bach, P., & Hayes, S. C. (2002). The use of acceptance and commitment therapy to prevent the rehospitalization of psychotic patients: A randomized controlled trial. *Journal of Consulting and Clinical Psychology, 70*, 1129–1139.

Bishop, S. R., Lau, M., Shapiro, S., Carlson, L., Anderson, N. D., Carmody, J., et al. (2004). Mindfulness: A proposed operational definition. *Clinical Psychology, Science and Practice, 11*, 230–241.

Brown, P. D., & O'Leary, K. D. (2000). Therapeutic alliance: Predicting continuance and success in group treatment for spouse abuse. *Journal of Consulting and Clinical Psychology, 68*, 340–345.

Carver, C. S., & Scheier, M. F. (1990). Principles of self-regulation: Action and emotion. In E. T. Higgins & R. M. Sorrentino (Eds.), *Handbook of motivation and cognition: Foundations of social behavior* (Vol. 2, pp. 3–52). New York: Guilford.

Cohen, R., Brumm, V., Zawacki, T., Paul, R., Sweet, L., & Rosenbaum, A. (2003). Impulsivity and verbal deficits associated with domestic violence. *Journal of International Neuropsychological Society, 9*, 760–770.

Cohen, R. A., Rosenbaum, A., Kane, R. L., Warnken, W. J., & Benjamin, S. (1999). Neuropsychological correlates of domestic violence. *Violence and Victims, 14*, 397–411.

Dunford, F. W. (2000). The San Diego Navy experiment: An assessment of interventions for men who assault their wives. *Journal of Consulting and Clinical Psychology, 68*, 468–476.

Dutton, D. G. (1999). Traumatic origins of intimate rage. *Aggression and Violent Behavior, 4*, 431–447.

——— (1995a). Intimate abusiveness. *Clinical Psychology: Science and Practice, 2*, 207–224.

——— (1995b). Male abusiveness in intimate relationships. *Clinical Psychology Review, 15*, 567–581.

——— (1986b). Wife assaulter's explanations for assault: The neutralization of self-punishment. *Canadian Journal of Behavioral Science, 18*, 381–390.

Dutton, D. G., & Browning, J. J. (1988). Concern for power, fear of intimacy, and aversive stimuli for wife assault. In G. Hotaling, D. Finkelhor, J. T. Kirkpatrick, & M. A. Straus (Eds.), *Family abuse and its consequences: New directions in research*. Newbury Park, CA: Sage.

Emery, R. E., & Laumann-Billings, L. (1998). An overview of the nature, causes, and consequences of abusive family relationships: Toward differentiating maltreatment and violence. *American Psychologist, 53*, 121–135.

Epperson, D. L., Bushway, D. J., & Warman, R. E. (1983). Client self-termination after one counseling session: Effects of problem recognition, counselor gender, and counselor experience. *Journal of Counseling Psychology, 30*, 307–315.

Fruzzetti, A. (2002, November). *DBT adapted for partner violent men.* Paper presented at the roundtable discussion "Application of DBT for intimate partner violence" (J. H. Rathus, chair), at the annual meeting of the Association for the Advancement of Behavior Therapy, Philadelphia.

Fruzzetti, A., & Iverson, K. M. (2004). Mindfulness, acceptance, validation, and "individual" psychopathology in couples. In S. C. Hayes, V. M. Follette, & M. M. Linehan (Eds.), *Mindfulness and acceptance: Expanding the cognitive-behavioral tradition.* New York: Guilford Press.

Fruzzetti, A. E., & Levensky, E. R. (2000). Dialectical behavior therapy for domestic violence: Rationale and procedures. *Cognitive and Behavioral Practice, 7,* 435–447.

Goldstein, D., & Rosenbaum, A. (1985). An evaluation of the self-esteem of martially violent men. *Family Relations, 34,* 425–428.

Gondolf, E. W. (1999). A comparison of four batterer intervention systems. *Journal of Interpersonal Violence, 14,* 41–61.

Gondolf, E. W., & Foster, R. (1991). Wife assault among V.A. alcohol rehabilitation patients. *Hospital and Community Psychiatry, 42,* 74–79.

Gondolf, E. W., Heckert, D. A., & Kimmel, C. M. (2002). Nonphysical abuse among batterer program participants. *Journal of Family Violence, 17,* 293–314.

Hamberger, L. K. (2001). Musings of a state standards committee chair. In R. Geffner & A. Rosenbaum (Eds.), *Domestic violence offenders: Current interventions, research, and implications for policies and standards* (pp. 265–283). New York: The Haworth Maltreatment and Trauma Press.

Hayes, S. C. (2004). Acceptance and commitment therapy and the new behavior therapies: Mindfulness, acceptance, and relationship. In S. C. Hayes, V. M. Follette, & M. M. Linehan (Eds.), *Mindfulness and acceptance: Expanding the cognitive-behavioral tradition.* New York: Guilford Press.

Hayes, A. M., & Feldman, G. (2004). Clarifying the construct of mindfulness in the context of emotion regulation and the process of change in therapy. *Clinical Psychology, Science and Practice, 11,* 255–262.

Hayes, S. C., Strosahl, K. D., & Wilson, K. G. (1999). *Acceptance and commitment therapy: An experiential approach to behavior change.* New York: Guilford Press.

Hayes, S. C., Wilson, K. G., Gifford, E. V., Follette, V. M., & Strosahl, K. (1996). Experiential avoidance and behavioral disorders: A functional dimensional approach to diagnosis and treatment. *Journal of Consulting and Clinical Psychology, 64,* 1152–1168.

Heckert, D. A., & Gondolf, E. W. (2000). Assessing assault self-reports by batterer program participants and their partners. *Journal of Family Violence, 15,* 181–197.

Holtzworth-Munroe, A. (2001). Standards for batterer treatment programs: How can research inform our decisions? In R. Geffner & A. Rosenbaum (Eds.), *Domestic violence offenders: Current interventions, research, and implications for policies and standards* (pp. 165–180). New York: Haworth Maltreatment and Trauma Press.

———— (1992). Social skill deficits in maritally violent men: Interpreting the data using a social information processing model. *Clinical Psychology Review, 12,* 605–617.

Holtzworth-Munroe, A., & Anglin, K. (1991). The competency of responses given by maritally violent versus nonviolent men to problematic marital situations. *Violence and Victims, 6,* 257–269.

Holtzworth-Munroe, A., & Hutchinson, G. (1993). Attributing negative intent to wife behavior: The attributions of maritally violent versus nonviolent men. *Journal of Abnormal Psychology, 102,* 206–211.

Holtzworth-Munroe, A., Meehan, J. C., Herron, K., Rehman, U., & Stuart, G. L. (2000). Testing the Holtzworth-Munroe and Stuart (1994) batterer typology. *Journal of Consulting and Clinical Psychology, 68,* 1000–1019.

Holtzworth-Munroe, A., & Smutzler, N. (1996). Comparing the emotional reactions and behavioral intentions of violent and nonviolent husbands to aggressive, distressed, and other wife behaviors. *Violence and Victims, 11,* 319–339.

Johnson, M. P. (1995). Patriarchal terrorism and common couple violence: Two forms of violence against women. *Journal of Marriage and the Family, 57,* 283–294.

Jones, A. S. (2000). The cost of batterer programs: How much and who pays? *Journal of Interpersonal Violence, 15,* 566–586.

Kabat-Zinn, J. (2003). Mindfulness-based interventions in context: Past, present, and future. *Clinical Psychology: Science and practice, 10,* 144–156.

Kabat-Zinn, J., Massion, A. O., Kristeller, J., Peterson, L. G., Fletcher, K. E., & Pbert, L. (1992). Effectiveness of a meditation-based stress reduction program in the treatment of anxiety disorders. *American Journal of Psychiatry, 149,* 936–943.

Kazdin, A. E. (Ed.) (2003). *Methodological issues and strategies in clinical research* (3rd ed.). Washington, DC: American Psychological Association.

Levant, R. (2001). Desperately seeking language: Understanding, assessing, and treating normative male alexithymia. In G. R. Brooks & G. E. Good (Eds.), *The new handbook of psychotherapy and counseling with men: A comprehensive guide to settings, problems, and treatment approaches* (Vol. 1, pp. 424–443). New York: Jossey-Bass.

Linehan, M. M. (1993a). *Cognitive-behavioral treatment of borderline personality disorder.* New York: Guilford Press.

——— (1993b). *Skills training manual for treating borderline personality disorder.* New York: Guilford Press.

Linehan, M. M., Armstrong, H. E., Suarez, A., Allmon, D., & Heard, H. L. (1991). Cognitive behavioral treatment of chronically parasuicidal borderline patients. *Archives of General Psychiatry, 48,* 1060–1064.

Linehan, M., Kanter, J. W., & Comtois, K. (1999). Dialectical behavior therapy for borderline personality disorder: Efficacy, specificity, and cost. In D. S. Janowsky (Ed.), *Psychotherapy indications and outcomes* (pp. 93–118). Washington, DC: American Psychiatric Press.

Linehan, M. M., Schmidt, H., Dimeff, L. A., Craft, J. C., Kanter, J., & Comtois, K. A. (1999). Dialectical behavior therapy for patients with borderline personality and drug dependence. *American Journal on Addictions, 8,* 279–292.

Marlatt, G. A., Witkiewitz, K., Dillworth, T. M., Bowen, S. W., Parks, G. A., Macpherson, L. M., *et al.* (2004). Vipassana meditation as a treatment for alcohol and drug use disorders. In S. C. Hayes, V. M. Follette, & M. M. Linehan (Eds.), *Mindfulness and acceptance: Expanding the cognitive-behavioral tradition* (pp. 261–287). New York: Guilford Press.

Mederos, F. (1999). Batterer intervention programs: The past, and future prospects. In M. Shepard and E. Pence (Eds.), *Coordinating community responses to domestic violence* (pp. 127–150). Thousand Oaks, CA: Sage.

O'Leary, K. D. (2001a). Psychological abuse: A variable deserving critical attention in domestic violence. In K. O'Leary & R. Maiuro (Eds.), *Psychological abuse in violent domestic relations* (pp. 3–28). New York: Springer Publishing.

——— (2001b). Conjoint therapy for partners who engage in physically aggressive behavior: Rationale and research. In R. Geffner & A. Rosenbaum (Eds.), *Domestic violence offenders: Current interventions, research, and implications for policies and standards* (pp. 145–163). New York: The Haworth Maltreatment and Trauma Press.

O'Leary, K. D., Heyman, R. E., & Neidig, P. H. (1999). Treatment of wife abuse: A comparison of gender-specific and conjoint approaches. *Behavior Therapy, 30,* 475–505.

Pence, E., & Paymar, M. (1993). *Education groups for men who batter: The Duluth model.* New York: Springer.

Rathus, J. H., & Miller, A. L. (2002). Dialectical behavior therapy adapted for suicidal adolescents. *Suicide and Life-Threatening Behavior, 32,* 146–157.

Renzetti, C. M. (1997). Violence and abuse among same-sex couples. In A. P. Cardarelli (Ed.), *Violence between intimate partners.* Boston: Allyn & Bacon.

Rondeau, G., Brodeur, N., Brochu, S., & Lemire, G. (2001). Dropout and completion of treatment among spouse abusers. *Violence and Victims, 16,* 127–143.

Rosenbaum, A., & Leisring, P. (2003). Beyond power and control: Towards an understanding of partner-abusive men. *Journal of Comparative Family Studies, 34,* 7–28.

Rosenfeld, B. D. (1992). Court-ordered treatment of spouse abuse. *Clinical Psychology Review, 12,* 205–226.

Scott, K. L. (2004). Predictors of change among male batterers: Application of theories and review of empirical findings. *Trauma, Violence, and Abuse, 5,* 260–284.

Segal, Z., Williams, J. M. G., & Teasdale, J. D. (2001). *Mindfulness-based cognitive therapy for depression: A new approach to preventing relapse.* New York: Guilford Press.

Sonkin, D., Martin, D., & Walker, L. (1985). *The male batterer.* New York: Springer.

Straus, M. A., Hamby, S. L., Boney-McCoy, S., & Sugarman, D. V. (1996). The revised Conflict Tactics Scales (CTS2): Development and preliminary psychometric data. *Journal of Family Issues, 17,* 283–316.

Taft, C., Murphy, C., Elliott, J., & Morrel, T. (2001). Attendance enhancing procedures in group counseling for domestic abusers. *Journal of Counseling Psychology, 48,* 51–60.

Teasdale, J. D., Segal, Z. V., Williams, J. M. G., Ridgeway, V. A., Soulsby, J. M., & Lau, M. A. (2000). Prevention of relapse/recurrence in major depression by mindfulness-based cognitive therapy. *Journal of Consulting and Clinical Psychology, 68,* 615–623.

Tolman, R. M. (1999). The validation of the Psychological Maltreatment of Women Inventory. *Violence and Victims, 14,* 25–35.

Tolman, R. M., & Bennett, L. W. (1990). A review of quantitative research on men who batter. *Journal of Interpersonal Violence, 5,* 87–118.

Tweed, R. G., & Dutton, D. G. (1998). A comparison of impulsive and instrumental subgroups of batterers. *Violence and Victims, 13,* 217–230.

Wilson, G. T. (2004). Acceptance and change in the treatment of eating disorders: The evolution of manual-based cognitive therapy. In S. C. Hayes, V. M. Follette, & M. M. Linehan (Eds.), *Mindfulness and acceptance: Expanding the cognitive-behavioral tradition* (pp. 243–260). New York: Guilford Press.

PART VI

APPLICATIONS FOR STRESS REDUCTION IN THE WORKPLACE

16

MINDFULNESS-BASED STRESS REDUCTION (MBSR) IN A WORKSITE WELLNESS PROGRAM

KIMBERLY WILLIAMS

Department of Community Medicine, West Virginia University, Morgantown, West Virginia

THEORETICAL AND CONCEPTUAL RATIONALE

HEALTH AND WELLNESS

In the 21st century, the burden of illness is due primarily to chronic degenerative diseases such as heart disease, diabetes, and cancer. These diseases are related to modifiable risk factors, including hypertension, high cholesterol, obesity, smoking, and lack of physical activity (Chenoweth, 1998). The rising cost of health care for employees has motivated organizations and businesses to fund worksite wellness programs. The business portion of the health care bill has increased from 18% to 30% during the 32-year period from 1965 to 1997, and it is estimated that 50% of profits are spent on employee health care (Chenowith, 1998). Since health care cost inflation increases twice as fast as general inflation, it is predicted that soon health care spending in the United States will consume 20% of the nation's gross national product (Chenowith, 1998). In an attempt to contain health care expenditures due to modifiable risk factors, worksite wellness/health promotion programs have aimed to provide employees with the awareness, education, and skills to adopt healthy lifestyles.

The majority of studies examining medical claims and modifiable risk factors in large organizations have focused on behavioral risk factors such as smoking, being overweight, inadequate seat belt use, excessive alcohol use, lack of exercise, elevated cholesterol, and high blood pressure, rather than psychological risk factors (Bertera, 1991). However, approximately 40 million working-age Americans suffer from psychological disorders, and according to the National Institute for Occupational Safety and Health, stress-related disorders are fast becoming the most prevalent reason for worker disability (Sauter, Murphy, & Hurrell, 1990). There is a growing body of evidence now indicating that psychosocial factors including depression, anxiety, hostility, social isolation, and stress increase the risk of coronary heart disease when behavioral and biological factors are controlled for (Rosanski, Blumental, & Kaplan, 1999). In a sample of 46,026 employed persons, medical care costs were 70% higher for those who reported being depressed and 46% higher for those who reported being stressed. Only 2.2% of the sample reported being depressed, but 18% reported being stressed (Goetzel et al., 1998). In addition to its own contribution to the pathogenesis of coronary artery disease, stress increases the tendency to adopt unhealthy behaviors that also contribute to it (Breese, Overstreet, & Knapp, 2004; Erblich, Lerman, Self, Diaz, & Bovbjerg, 2004; Greeno & Wing, 1994; La Rosa, Consoli, Le Clesiau, Soufi, & Lagrue, 2004; Morley, Levine, & Rowland, 1983; Rozanski et al., 1999; Tagliacozzo & Vaughn, 1982).

RATIONALE FOR APPLYING MBSR TO WORKSITE WELLNESS

In West Virginia, where the program described in this chapter was conducted, the prevalence of risk factors for chronic disease, such as hypertension, high cholesterol, obesity, smoking, and lack of exercise, is higher than the national average. Not surprisingly, heart disease, diabetes, and cancer also are more prevalent in West Virginia. The program we developed used mindfulness-based stress reduction (MBSR) within a wellness program at West Virginia University (WVU). We wanted to determine whether the MBSR program could be successful in a wellness context with self-referral rather than physician referral into the program. Wellness is an approach to health that emphasizes self-responsibility (Edlin, Golanty, & Brown, 1997). *Health* is defined not just as the absence of disease but the harmonious functioning of the many dimensions of wellness, including the physiological, mental, emotional, social, spiritual, and environmental aspects of individuals and their communities. Its target is optimal health and well-being and prevention of disease and injury through healthy lifestyle choices. With the emphasis of the MBSR program on self-responsibility and healthy lifestyle practices that impact all the dimensions of wellness, the MBSR program was a perfect fit for the vision and goals of wellness.

The format and content of the MBSR program (described in more detail in Chapter 1 of this volume) is consistent with social cognitive theory, which has been used by health educators and worksite wellness programs to develop interventions geared toward changing behavior (Bandura, 1997). This theory contains a number of constructs that are important for understanding human behavior and how it can be changed. These include reciprocal determinism (in which there is a dynamic interplay between the environment and the person's cognitions and behaviors), the importance of the person's perception of the environment, behavioral capability (an index of the person's knowledge and skill to perform a given behavior), anticipated outcomes of behavior and the value a person places on the outcome, self-control, observational learning, reinforcement, self-efficacy, and emotional coping responses.

In the MBSR program, participants are given the opportunity to develop the skills to increase their behavioral capability for self-control as well as their self-efficacy. The premise is that individuals can learn to improve self-regulation and draw on inner resources for health and wholeness through detached observation of their internal states. These skills are taught through didactic instruction as well as experiential and observational group learning. Participants learn about how their cognitive appraisal of a situation affects their behavior and their social environment. They also develop outcome expectations as a result of their experiences with the practices of mindfulness and their application to daily life. For example, participants may find that they are more relaxed after practicing the body scan and thus do it whenever they feel tension or irritation developing. As participants experience improved ability to manage their stress-related symptoms as a result of practicing the body scan, they may choose to do this exercise for stress-related symptoms rather than escaping from their discomfort through drugs or maladaptive coping strategies. Participants' social environments also may be positively influenced when they have found more constructive ways to deal with negative emotions in response to stress.

The positive internal and external effects of practicing mindfulness may reinforce participants' desires to practice regularly rather than waiting for adverse events to arrive. A large part of mindfulness training is geared toward changing a stress reaction into a stress response, in which emotional arousal is effectively managed. Emotional arousal decreases present-moment awareness and inhibits the ability to see the whole context of the situation and the options available. Under such conditions, individuals become victims of their conditioning and do not have the presence of mind to switch to more conscious and creative responses. Although the MBSR program was not guided by social cognitive theory, it is consistent with it in many ways.

Most wellness programs conduct health risk appraisals and screenings, educate their population about healthy lifestyle, and offer low-intensity, short-duration programming in exercise and nutrition. At the time that this project began, the wellness program at WVU gave lectures and handouts on stress management. No skill-building or behavioral-change program was in place. It seemed clear that this approach to stress management at the worksite was not comprehensive enough to address deeply ingrained emotional and behavioral reactions to stress. This view is consistent with the findings of Heaney and Goetzel (1997), who reviewed 36 articles examining health-related outcomes of multicomponent worksite health promotion programs, and of Murphy (1996), who reviewed 64 published studies of preventative stress management programs. Heaney and Goetzel (1997) concluded that "low intensity short duration programs aiming at increasing awareness of health issues for an entire employee population were not sufficient to achieve the desired outcome"; rather, programs of sufficient intensity, breadth, and duration with opportunities for individual counseling and skill building were found to be most effective in reducing health risk. Murphy's (1996) review examined the effectiveness of a variety of methods. He found that a combination of approaches, addressing the somatic and cognitive aspects of stress, as well as techniques for coping with stress, was the most effective. However, a criticism of the research on stress management programs containing a variety of techniques and approaches was that frequently there was no unifying theoretical framework guiding the programming.

The MBSR program addresses many of the concerns raised previously with regard to health promotion and preventative stress management programs. It is a comprehensive individualized program guided by an underlying theoretical framework addressing the cognitive and somatic dimensions of stress. Unlike many health promotion and cognitive behavioral approaches, mindfulness training focuses on cultivating inner resources rather than changing what is wrong with a person. Instead of trying to change problematic thinking, maladaptive coping responses, or physiological measures of risk directly, mindfulness training focuses on cultivating calmness of mind and a larger perspective on the difficulties of life. By decreasing emotional reactivity and enhancing cognitive appraisal, participants develop a wider range of options for responding to stressful situations. Thus, mindfulness training may reduce resistance to change and foster conditions conducive to the elimination of dysfunctional behavioral patterns.

CASE STUDY

This Case Study is taken from the first cohort who participated in the MBSR program offered by the Worksite Wellness Program at WVU in the fall of 1995. The cohort comprised 50 employees from the university. They were divided into 3 groups consisting of 15–18 people each. Each group meet for 2.5 hours per week for 8 weeks with the facilitator of the MBSR program. The facilitator was a health professional who worked for the Wellness Program as the research associate. She was an avid practitioner of yoga and meditation and had trained for a number of years in Iyengar yoga and insight meditation with senior teachers from Canada, the United States, and Europe. She had participated in the one-week health professional training for the MBSR program at the Omega Institute for Holistic Studies in Rhinebeck, New York. All groups came together on the Saturday of the sixth week to participate in the all-day silent retreat (see Chapter 1 in this volume for a more detailed discussion). Participants were each interviewed before and after the program to determine their specific needs for stress reduction, to share their experience of learning mindfulness and applying it to their daily lives, and to tell the facilitator what they got out of the program. They were also asked to complete questionnaires before and immediately after the program, 3 months later, and 1 year after completion of the program. These included the Medical Symptom Checklist (MSCL) (Travis, 1977) and the Daily Stress Inventory (DSI) (Brantley & Jones, 1989). The MSCL lists 115 symptoms. Respondents note whether they have been bothered by each symptom within the last month. The DSI measures frequency of daily hassles and the degree of stress associated with them over the preceding 7 days. Participants also were asked to complete the Stress Map (Orioli, 1991) during the fourth week of the program in order to help them become more aware of their external and internal sources of stress. This inventory includes 21 dimensions of stress, such as pressures, changes, and satisfactions at work and in personal life, and physical, behavioral, and emotional symptoms. Each dimension is classified as *optimal performance, balance, strain,* or *burnout,* based on the respondent's ratings.

Participants were also asked to redo the stress map at the end of the program to see whether any change had occurred in their performance in the 21 dimensions of stress. After completion of the program and 3 months and 1 year later, a follow-up questionnaire was distributed to participants asking about duration, frequency, and value of the mindfulness practices along with the MSCL and DSI. At the end of the program, support groups were set up at different locations on campus to create a community or *sangha* of mindfulness practitioners at WVU. The aim was to help participants adhere to mindful living and to deepen the sense of community amongst practitioners. Although the wellness office reserved the rooms, the participants were encouraged to provide leadership to the group and to spend time each meeting doing a mindfulness practice together. One of these support groups flourished and had weekly meetings for approximately one year, although the others were not sustained.

CLIENT BACKGROUND

John was a 45-year-old man who was married and worked full-time for WVU. He had a master's degree and a faculty-equivalent position. He had worked in the same job for 23 years and had been promoted as high as he could go. He indicated that his job was very stressful because of the heavy workload, the strain of working for two different departments and in four different physical locations, the need to mobilize people he supervised as well as those he did not, and differences of opinion and poor communication with his supervisor. He no longer found his job satisfying and was interested in beginning another career in a new field. However, he lacked confidence in his ability at his age to learn a whole new field, and thus he had not taken any steps toward making a career change. He had chronic pain in his right foot that prevented him from hiking, one of his favorite pastimes. He reported frequent stress headaches that required him to take large doses of extra-strength Tylenol, and difficulty getting a good night's sleep as a result of his wife's snoring. He was taking Prozac and had seen five mental health specialists over a number of years to deal with repressed anger, childhood abuse, shyness, and poor communication skills. At the preprogram interview, he indicated that the mental health specialists had helped him to some extent but that after a certain point he felt they were either not helping him anymore or they were taking him in the wrong direction. He was searching for something new to improve his health at the time the MBSR program began at WVU. He typically dealt with stress by escaping from problematic situations and burning off pent-up emotion by going for a walk, running up and down stairs, and, in the past, bashing pieces of lumber into the ground. He reported that he often left his house or workplace in a state of anger. This was very upsetting to those left behind who usually tried unsuccessfully to stop him. His goals for participating in the MBSR program were to improve his sleep, to increase his mental and physical energy, to become a calmer person, and to make changes in his career and personal life.

Prior to the start of the program, John checked off 45 medical symptoms on the MSCL, which was 2.6 times higher than the group average of 17.5 for this instrument. He reported a score of 3.31 on the DSI, placing him at high risk for stress-related health problems. Of the 21 scales of the stress map inventory, he obtained a performance rating of *burnout* on 13, of *strain* on 5, of *balance* on 2, and of *optimal performance* on 1. Areas of burnout included work changes, work pressures, personal changes, personal pressures, personal satisfactions, direct action and time management, personal power, connection, expression, physical symptoms, behavioral symptoms, and emotional symptoms. Areas of strain were work satisfaction, adaptability, self-esteem, positive outlook, and compassion. Areas of balance were support seeking and situation mastery. The area of optimal performance was self-care.

COURSE OF TREATMENT

John found the mindfulness practices of yoga and meditation to be very exciting and very rewarding. He reported "gradually coming to see them as tools that I could use to do a lot of what I was trying to do, just reduce stress, focus on things, eliminate a lot of old, outmoded, and outdated things from my life to make room for new things. This seems to be the route that has been most successful for me." John indicated that this had affected every area of his life. He reported realizing that it takes a lot of work to stay on track and could see why it is absolutely essential to keep practicing mindfulness on a daily basis. He reported trying to do something every day for 45 minutes, and alternated the yoga and body scan practices. Some of the challenges he reported with the practices included having difficulty staying awake during the body scan and the need to stop practicing yoga for a week when he injured his back pulling up the garage door. He also thought the body scan tape was too long. Near the end of the program he was able to stay awake through the whole body scan. Like others in the program, he found it difficult to make the time to do the practices at home with his current schedule. To create the time to practice he had to eliminate other things. Because mindfulness practice was a priority and he had a previous goal of wanting to direct his own activities rather than allow family plans, attendance at professional meetings, or established routines to dictate what he did, he was able to incorporate it. To find the time, he stopped going along on routine family expeditions and curtailed his attendance at professional meetings.

OUTCOMES OF TREATMENT

After the program, John attended the downtown campus support group and began yoga classes in the community. He indicated that he was able to focus on things more easily, even things that he did not like to do, and as a result was able to stay awake in meetings and be more assertive and expressive of his feelings with his supervisor. His wife and coworkers told him that they thought he had much calmer reactions to crises and daily annoyances. In response to his son's criticism, he is finding that he is now more amused than annoyed. A coworker shared with him, "Now instead of watching you to see how angry you're going to get, so I know how angry I have to get about something, I sit there in amazement and watch you say, 'Nah, no big problem, we can't do anything about it,' so it's been a great relief for me." Rather than leaving situations in a huff when he became angry, he reported making a conscious decision to relax his body and mind and tell himself that the matter was not worth getting upset about. He stated, "Now I can't escape it, I have to deal with it." John managed a large number of people and reported realizing that how he perceived and handled the hourly crises had a large impact on the employees who worked with him. To decrease the stress amongst the employees he supervised he began bringing the informal practices into the meetings he chaired and sharing what he had learned from the MBSR program. He reported that after voicing his concerns and desires with his supervisor and changing what was within his responsibility, he was able to let go of his expectations and attachment to desired outcomes and accept that his supervisor was not likely to change his ways. He made a deliberate effort to stop dwelling on the negative in his work and to put his efforts into more constructive things. Although he had not taken any action toward a new career, he felt more hopeful and confident about his ability to learn what was necessary. He stated that he was not where he wanted to be but was on his way. He also realized that "in my prior state of mind, it wouldn't matter where I was, I would feel that the workplace was frustrating and inflexible."

At the end of the 8-week program, John reported a 64% reduction in the number of medical symptoms that were bothersome in the last month and a 31% reduction in perceived stress on the DSI. He also reported sleeping more soundly. He noted that he had been up in the middle of the night only two or three times during the past 8 weeks, whereas this had occurred nightly before the MBSR program. He was no longer taking medication for his headaches. Rather than automatically heading for the medicine cabinet when he felt a headache coming on, he reported doing a body scan or a sitting meditation for 10–15 minutes. He described this as "meditating instead of medicating" and noted that it helped him avoid the long-lasting episodes so typical of the drug-treated headaches he used to have. John also reported in the follow-up questionnaire that the frequency and severity of his foot pain was much less by the 1-year assessment. His number of doctor visits was also reduced at the end of the program and at the 1-year assessment.

At the follow-up assessments, 3 months and 1 year later, John maintained his reduction in medical symptoms. His perceived stress still remained below the threshold for high risk of stress-related health problems, although his stress levels increased somewhat. John's scores on the stress map also moved in a positive direction by the end of the program. Improvements were seen in 9 of the 13 scales on which his performance had been rated as *burnout* at baseline. These included work changes, work pressures, personal changes, personal pressures, personal satisfaction, direct action, time management, expression, and emotional symptoms. Three of the five areas rated at baseline as *strain* also improved, including work satis-faction, adaptability, and self-esteem. The two scales rated at baseline as in *balance* (support seeking and situation mastery) got worse and fell under *strain*.

In a telephone interview with John 10 years after his enrollment in the MBSR program, he reported the following after reflecting on his experience in the program and how it impacted his life. He no longer had pain in his foot. After completing the MBSR program, he attended yoga classes for 4 years. Along with physical therapy, the yoga helped him to strengthen and gain flexibility in his foot and gave him pain relief. He also indicated that he used meditation to alleviate his headaches and he now rarely has headaches. John felt empowered by these two experiences. Through his own efforts with mindfulness, he was able to decrease his dependence on painkilling drugs. He stayed in the same job, which he had hoped to leave 10 years ago, and had taken on additional responsibilities. However, he reported enjoying his work and feeling content with his decision to stay on. He attributed his change in attitude to his ability to prioritize what needed to be done and putting in the appropriate amount of effort to bring the project to completion. Previously, he would try to do too much and get overwhelmed when he wasn't able to meet unrealistic deadlines. He reported that now he typically doesn't get stressed out by deadlines or others' expectations. He doesn't worry or get upset as much and if he does, he can calm himself down and redirect his energy within a couple of days instead of staying angry for a long time. He also indicated that his previous boss was replaced by a supervisor he works well with and that he has been able to replace problem employees with new employees who have a wonderful attitude. In fact, one person he hired serves as the wellness coordinator for his department and encourages him to be involved in all the programs she is running for the employees. Lastly, John reported a greater enjoyment of life. He got divorced in 1998 and has lived alone ever since. This is the first time he has lived alone and it has required him to be more self-reliant and take full responsibility for all that needs to be done.

Although John reported taking much greater responsibility in both his personal and professional life, he was enjoying the opportunities and challenges that life was giving him. When John was asked whether he continues to practice mindfulness, he reported that he does not do the formal practices on a regular basis. Rather, he does them occasionally as needed. He attributed his sustained benefits to the general lessons that he learned from Jon Kabat-Zinn's book *Full Catastrophe Living,* which were reinforced by participation in the MBSR program and by the community yoga classes. He reported stopping yoga classes because of a shoulder injury, and then never got back to it, and that he now goes to the gym regularly for a cardiorespiratory workout.

DISCUSSION

John's success in the program seemed to be due to a number of factors. First, he was highly challenged by a large number of stress-related medical symptoms. He was looking for ways to reduce his stress and improve his health and was ready to make changes in his life to achieve those goals. He was at the action stage of Prochaska's stages-of-change scale (Prochaska, Norcross, & DiClemente, 1994). Even though he had rated at *burnout* on 13 of the 21 scales of the stress map at baseline, he was functioning optimally in self-care, and thus probably found it easier than most to do the things recommended in the MBSR program to take care of himself. He indicated that the program affected all aspects of his life, so it is likely that he made a heroic effort to embody the principles of mindfulness and apply them to his daily life. He indicated that he created time for 45 minutes of daily practice by eliminating activities that were less of a priority to him, and at the end of the program participated in weekly support groups and community yoga classes. As he gained success in one area, it appeared that it gave him confidence and trust that it would be useful in other areas. By the end of the program, he had found ways to take care of his headaches and insomnia without outside intervention and he dealt with annoyances and anger in more constructive ways. Because he was in a position of influence and authority, he was also able to have an impact on those he worked with and supervised by creating a work environment for his coworkers that was less stressful. John had become empowered to take care of his mental and physical health and was now empowering those around him to do the same. Since not all participants are as successful as John, it will be important to determine what factors predict success and failure in wellness-based MBSR programs. It is interesting that he continued to manage and thrive from his growing responsibilities at home and at work in the absence of a regular mindfulness practice. It appears that as a result of his exposure to mindfulness practice and philosophy, he developed an approach to life that helped him to keep the stressors in life in perspective.

EMPIRICAL SUPPORT FOR MBSR IN WORKSITE PROGRAMS

RANDOMIZED CONTROLLED TRIAL

The West Virginia University Wellness Program evaluated the impact of the MBSR program with community volunteers with high perceived stress. The purpose of the study was to (1) determine whether these subjects, many of whom were WVU employees, would complete and benefit from the intensive MBSR program at a time when the community was familiar with more conventional and less-intensive risk-reduction programs, and

(2) compare the outcomes of community volunteers with those of patient-based MBSR programs. A total of 103 adults participated in the study, with 59 randomized into the intervention group and 44 into the control group. The intervention consisted of an 8-week MBSR program tailored to the needs of individuals rather than patients. The control group received educational materials on stress management and was encouraged to use community resources. Most participants were married (62%), older than 30 years (93%), female (72%), attended college or university (95%), and were employed in professional occupations (78%). The mean age was 42.9 ± 2.2. Eighty-five percent of the subjects completed the study. The level of compliance was slightly higher than that reported with outpatients at the Stress Reduction Clinic (76%) (Kabat-Zinn & Chapman-Waldrop, 1988) and at an inner-city community health center (60%) (Roth and Creaser, 1997). Intervention subjects reported significant decreases from baseline in the effect of daily hassles (24%), psychological distress (44%), and medical symptoms (46%) compared with the control subjects (Williams, Kolar, Reger, & Pearson, 2001). These improvements were maintained at the 3-month follow-up. Upon completion of the MBSR program, 88% of the subjects were still meditating, 69% were practicing yoga, and 64% were using awareness of breathing. The reductions in medical symptoms and psychological distress were similar to those reported by primary care patients attending an MBSR program at an inner-city community health center (Roth & Creaser, 1997) but were greater than the improvements reported by chronic pain patients (Kabat-Zinn, 1982). This study indicates that community volunteers with high perceived stress can be compliant to the high demands of the wellness-based MBSR program. Since significant health and stress reduction benefits were obtained that are comparable to patient populations, the potential exists to reduce the incidence of stress-related conditions and their associated health care costs by offering the MBSR program to people before they get sick.

PROGRAM EVALUATION OF MBSR AS A WORKSITE WELLNESS INITIATIVE

A total of 141 WVU employees participated in the 8-week MBSR program offered at the worksite by the WVU Wellness Program over a 2-year period from 1994 to 1996 (unpublished data). Participants had the following demographic characteristics: Average age was 45.31 ± 1.13 years, two-thirds were female, and the majority were married, had university degrees, and held technical, administrative, or faculty positions. Most participants were nonsmokers, drank modestly, and were physically active. Participants presented with a variety of medical conditions, including insomnia, fatigue, allergies, back pain, and anxiety. Prescribed medications were taken by 62% of the participants. Upon entry into the program, 44%

perceived themselves to be in a constant state of high stress (DSI ≥ 3.17). Eighty-two percent of the participants completed the program. At the end of the program, participants reported a 31% decrease in the mean number of medical symptoms ($p < .05$), a 17% decrease in the mean impact of daily hassles ($p < .05$), and a 30.7% decrease in psychological distress ($p < 0.05$). The improvements were greater at the 3-month follow-up. All 21 categories on the stress map inventory were significantly improved by the end of the program, and a number of positive changes in attitudes and behaviors were reported as a direct result of participating in the MBSR program. At the end of the program, 92% were still meditating, 75% were practicing yoga, and 90% were using awareness of breathing.

OTHER STUDIES

An additional study of a worksite MBSR program with healthy individuals was a randomized controlled trial conducted by Davidson *et al.* (2003) with employees of a biotechnology company in Madison, Wisconsin. Of the 48 employees enrolled in the study, 41 completed the MBSR program and at least two of the three assessments. The program was 8 weeks in duration, and subjects were evaluated for brain (electrical activity) and immune function (antibody titer to influenza vaccine). The former was measured at baseline, immediately after completion of the program, and 4 months later, and the latter at 3–5 weeks and 8-9 weeks after completion of the program. The intervention group consisted of 25 employees, 19 of whom were female. The wait-list control group had 16 subjects, 10 of whom were female. The average age was 36 years, and the majority of subjects were white. At the end of the program, subjects in the MBSR intervention group had greater left-side activation in the brain, (a measure of emotion-related brain activity that is thought to reflect more adaptive responses to stress) and a greater antibody response to influenza vaccine compared with controls. Furthermore, the magnitude of left-side activation was positively associated with the rise in antibody titer to the vaccine. This is the first study to show positive effects of meditation on brain and immune function in healthy volunteers. Although the employee population was compliant and responsive to the intervention, the authors indicated that the highly demanding work environment was not the ideal place to conduct the intervention.

PRACTICAL ISSUES IN IMPLEMENTING
MBSR IN WORKPLACE SETTINGS

The worksite is a unique setting for conducting the MBSR program. There are many factors that make the worksite ideal for implementing

MBSR, but it also presents a number of barriers to overcome. The worksite is likely to provide use of a room at no charge, easy access, and a reduction in travel time for employees who want to attend wellness programs. There is also flexibility as to when the program can be offered, either during the workday or immediately before or after work. There are existing channels of communication that can be utilized to aid recruitment (e-mail, internal newsletters and university or hospital newspapers, staff and "town hall" meetings) and a mandate to implement wellness education and activities for employees at a growing number of worksites. There are advantages and disadvantages to offering the program to a community of people who have been working together. On the positive side, they can support each other and create a work environment more conducive to being mindful. It is likely that their group effort to practice mindfulness will impact their decision making in the workplace and make it a less stressful and more inspiring place to work. It could also help decrease existing tensions and disagreements amongst coworkers and give them a positive approach to resolving conflict. On the other hand, employees may be less inclined to share their inner life openly with their coworkers than they are with strangers. This could make the weekly discussions of personal experience more challenging to facilitate. It may also widen the gap between those who participate and those who do not because of the changes that occur in an individual's values and behavior as a result of practicing mindfulness. It has also been reported (Davidson *et al.*, 2003) that the demanding workplace environment is not ideal for delivery of MBSR.

For the delivery to be successful, the support of upper-level administrators is needed, as well as that of the staff of the wellness program or initiative at the organization. It can be helpful to have the instructor already on staff, but it is not essential if there is enough support for MBSR from upper-level administrators to create an independent budget for the program. It can be challenging to find a room with open, carpeted floor space that can be used on a consistent basis. In addition, finding the right person for the job may prove challenging if there are no funds for hiring an MBSR program instructor. Mindfulness must play a central role in the life of the instructor, who if hired from within, faces the same stressors as the employees. This can be an advantage if the instructor has learned to respond to those stressors with mindfulness. It may be possible to train an employee to become an MBSR instructor, as in the health professions, if time can be freed up from his or her existing responsibilities to deliver the program.

The greatest challenge for worksite MBSR is financial. Businesses are already faced with paying a large percentage of their employees' rising health care costs. To pay for disease prevention is risky business. Generally, there are few third-party payers who will pay for employees to participate in wellness programs. However, this may be changing. In West Virginia, the

Public Employees Insurance Agency (PEIA), for state workers, has funded a program called *Pathways to Wellness,* which pays for participating schools and businesses to offer wellness education and programs to employees (see the Wellness Councils of America website at www.welcoa.org). This program is being evaluated to determine whether risk factors for cardiovascular disease can be reduced as a way to decrease employee health care costs. However, the types of wellness programs being offered deal with large populations and are much less intensive than MBSR. In addition, many individuals are willing to pay out of pocket for complementary and alternative medicine (Eisenberg *et al.,*1993, 1998), and wellness programming has been found to be most successful if individuals contribute to the cost of the programs they participate in (see the PEIA *Pathways to Wellness* website at www.peiapathways.com). The way of the future for worksite MBSR may be a combination of business sponsorship, private contribution, and insurance coverage.

After the organizational constraints have been addressed, several other factors must be considered concerning the individuals who participate in the program. For example, who is eligible for the program? If there is a third-party payer, there may be a requirement for the individual to have a certain number of modifiable risk factors to be eligible. If there is a need to demonstrate effectiveness, a measurable and modifiable outcome such as perceived stress and/or risk of disease, lowered productivity, or absenteeism will be required to detect differences before and after the program. If the organization is sponsoring the program, the greatest determinant of eligibility may be the employee's motivation and willingness to commit to the requirements of the program. To track the impact of the program, it is important to measure attendance and completion rates in addition to changes in outcomes. Keeping track of participants and following up with them when they have been absent can improve attendance and completion of the program. It can also be helpful to have a buddy or mentoring system in place to help participants who are struggling to keep up and remain motivated. A major challenge that intensive wellness programs like MBSR face is to motivate participants to make the time to practice and implement what they are learning, especially when it involves nondoing. In addition to pointing out the benefits of engaging in mindfulness, it is important to discuss barriers and possible solutions, and to have strong community resources in place to support the practice.

REFERENCES

Bandura, A. (1997). *Self-efficacy: The exercise of control.* New York: W. H. Freeman.
Bertera, R. L. (1991). The effects of behavioral risks on absenteeism and health-care costs in the workplace. *Journal of Occupational Medicine, 33,* 1119–1124.

Brantley, P. J., & Jones, G. N. (1989). *Daily stress inventory professional manual.* Odessa, FL: Psychological Assessment Resources.

Breese, G. R., Overstreet, D. H., & Knapp, D. J. (2004). Conceptual framework for the etiology of alcoholism: A "kindling"/stress hypothesis. *Psychopharmacology, 178,* 367–380.

Chenoweth, D. H. (1998). *Worksite health promotion.* Champaign, IL: Human Kinetics.

Davidson, R. J., Kabat-Zinn, J., Schumacher, J., Rosenkranz, M., Muller, D., Santorelli, S. F., *et al.* (2003). Alterations in brain and immune function produced by mindfulness meditation. *Psychosomatic Medicine, 65,* 564–570.

Edlin, G., Golanty, E., & Brown, K. M. (1997). *Essentials for health and wellness.* Sudbury, MA: Jones & Bartlett.

Eisenberg, D. M., Davis, R. B., Ettner, S. L., Appel, S., Wilkey, S., Van Rompay, M., & Kessler, R. C. (1998). Trends in alternative medicine use in the United States, 1990–1997: Results of a follow-up national survey. *Journal of the American Medical Association, 280,* 1569–1575.

Eisenberg, D. M., Kessler, R. C., Foster, C., Norlock, F. E., Calkins, D. R., & Delbanco, T. L. (1993). Unconventional medicine in the United States: Prevalence, costs, and patterns of use. *New England Journal of Medicine, 328,* 246–252.

Erblich, J., Lerman, S., Self, D. W., Diaz, G. A., & Bovbjerg, D. H. (2004). Stress-induced cigarette craving: Effects of the DRD2 Taql RFLP and SLC6A3 VNTR polymorphisms. *Pharmacogenomics Journal, 4,* 102–109.

Greeno, C. G., & Wing, R. R. (1994). Stress-induced eating. *Psychological Bulletin, 115,* 444–464.

Goetzel, R. Z., Anderson, D. R., Whitmer, R. W., Ozminkowski, R. J., Dunn, R. L., & Wasserman, J. (1998). The relationship between modifiable health risks and health care expenditures: An analysis of the multi-employer HERO health risk and cost data base. *Journal of Occupational and Environmental Medicine, 40,* 843–854.

Heaney, C. A., & Goetzel, R. Z. (1997). A review of health-related outcomes of multi-component worksite health promotion programs. *American Journal of Health Promotion, 11,* 290–307.

Kabat-Zinn, J. (1982). An outpatient program in behavioral medicine for chronic pain patients based on the practice of mindfulness meditation: Theoretical considerations and preliminary results. *General Hospital Psychiatry, 4,* 33–47.

Kabat-Zinn, J., & Chapman-Waldrop, A. (1998). Compliance with an outpatient stress reduction program: Rates and predictors of program completion. *Journal of Behavioral Medicine, 11,* 333–352.

La Rosa, E., Consoli, S. M., Le Cleisiau, H., Soufi, K., & Lagrue, G. (2004). Psychosocial distress and stressful life antecedents associated with smoking: A survey of subjects consulting a preventive health center. *Presse Medicine, 33,* 919–926.

Morley, J. E., Levine, A. S., & Rowland, N. E. (1983). Minireview: Stress-induced eating. *Life Sciences, 32,* 169–182.

Murphy, L. R. (1996). Stress management in work settings: A critical review of the health effects. *American Journal of Health Promotion, 11,* 112–135.

Orioli, E. M. (1991). *The stress map (corporate edition): A comprehensive self-scoring stress assessment and action planning guide.* San Francisco: Essi Systems Inc.

Prochaska, J. O., Norcross, J. C., & DiClemente, C. C. (1994). *Changing for good: The revolutionary program that explains the six stages of change and teaches you how to free yourself from bad habits.* New York: W. Morrow.

Roth, B., & Creaser, T. (1997). Mindfulness meditation-based stress reduction: Experience with a bilingual inner-city program. *The Nurse Practitioner, 22,* 150–176.

Rozanski, A., Blumental, J. A., & Kaplan, J. (1999). Impact of psychological factors on the pathogenesis of cardiovascular disease and implications for therapy. *Circulation, 99,* 192–217.

Sauter, S. L., Murphy, L. R., & Hurrell, J. J. (1990). Prevention of work related psychological disorders: A national strategy proposed by the National Institute for Occupational Safety and Health (NIOSH). *American Psychologist, 45,* 1146–1148.

Tagliacozzo, R., & Vaughn, S. (1982). Stress and smoking in hospital nurses. *American Journal of Public Health, 72,* 441–448.

Travis, J. W. (1977). *Wellness workbook for health professionals.* Mill Valley, CA: Wellness Resource Center.

Williams, K. A., Kolar, M. M., Reger, B. E., & Pearson, J. C. (2001). Evaluation of a wellness-based mindfulness stress reduction intervention: A controlled trial. *American Journal of Health Promotion, 15,* 422–432.

17

ACCEPTANCE AND COMMITMENT THERAPY (ACT) IN THE WORKPLACE

PAUL E. FLAXMAN AND FRANK W. BOND

Goldsmiths College, University of London, New Cross, London, UK

INTRODUCTION

The estimated costs of occupational ill-health to employees, organizations, and societies are substantial. For example, in the United Kingdom, approximately half a million employees report experiencing occupational stress at a level that is making them ill, with one in five working individuals describing their job as "very" or "extremely" stressful (Health and Safety Executive [HSE], 2004). Similarly, in recent surveys of British health care workers, more than 25% of respondents reported a sufficient level of distress to make them probable cases of various minor psychiatric disorders (typically anxiety and/or depression) (Hardy, Woods, & Wall, 2003; Wall et al., 1997). Moreover, these high rates of mental ill-health amongst the working population are associated with increased absenteeism, with current estimates indicating that work-related stress, anxiety, and depression result in 13 million lost working days per year in Britain alone (Hardy *et al.*, 2003; HSE, 2004; Kessler & Frank, 1997).

In view of the apparent scale and impact of occupational ill-health, it is not surprising that some authors have described the enhancement of well-being at work one of the most important issues of modern times (Puryear & Hurrell, 1994; Reynolds, 1997). The aim of this chapter is to describe how this issue can be addressed, at least in part, by implementing worksite interventions based upon acceptance and commitment therapy (ACT).

THEORETICAL AND CONCEPTUAL BACKGROUND

OCCUPATIONAL STRESS: ORGANIZATION- AND INDIVIDUAL-FOCUSED APPROACHES

Although there has historically been a great deal of "hoopla and ballyhoo" surrounding the concept of occupational stress (Woolfolk & Lehrer, 1993, p. 3), most occupational health psychologists now subscribe to a *transactional* view of the stress process (Lazarus & Folkman, 1984; Matheny, Aycock, Pugh, Curlette, & Cannella, 1986). According to this perspective, stress occurs when people believe that a particular event threatens their well-being, because they evaluate it as taxing or exceeding their coping resources (Lazarus & Folkman, 1984; Meichenbaum, 1993). Importantly, this transactional model has provided the rationale for two general approaches to worksite stress prevention and reduction. The first is directed at the organization, and it seeks to reduce work-related stressors (or "threatening" events); the second targets the individual's appraisals (or evaluations) of threat, and his or her repertoire of coping skills (Bond, 2004).

Organization-Focused Interventions

Organization-focused interventions typically involve the redesign of work and management processes in order to reduce workers' exposure to sources of stress. Outcome research examining such interventions has provided empirical support for work redesign initiatives that target unfavorable work characteristics such as a lack of worker control, poor workplace support, inadequate workplace communication, role conflict and ambiguity, and work overload (Bond & Bunce, 2001; Wall & Clegg, 1981). While the focus of this chapter is on an individual-oriented worksite intervention (i.e., ACT), we do not wish to underestimate the importance of organization-focused approaches to work stress. Indeed, recent European Union legislation imposes a legal duty on organizations to ensure that steps are taken to reduce workplace stressors at their source (Cox *et al.,* 2000). As we have discussed elsewhere (Bond, 2004), we believe that targeting both work design characteristics *and* individuals' psychological coping styles provides a comprehensive worksite intervention strategy.

Individual-Focused Interventions: Cognitive-Behavioral Stress Management

There are a number of features of the stress process that support the use of individual-focused worksite interventions. First, some work-related stressors, such as seasonal deadlines and difficult customers, cannot easily be removed or reduced. Second, there is a plethora of extraorganizational sources of stress, such as family discord, that can have a detrimental impact on an employee's well-being and yet remain immune to organization-focused interventions. Finally, as we mentioned previously, the transactional model of stress emphasizes the importance of an individual's coping resources. This model suggests that inappropriate coping efforts, such as avoidance, have the potential to exacerbate sources of stress at work and to prolong or increase mental ill-health (Lazarus & Folkman, 1984; Matheny et al., 1986). Consistent with this line of thought, researchers have found that undesirable psychological coping styles—for instance, avoidance coping and type A behavior pattern—are reliable predictors of stress in the workplace (Jex, 1998; Jex, Bliese, Buzzell, & Primeau, 2001; Quick, Quick, Nelson, & Hurrell, 1997).

Accordingly, individual-focused worksite interventions are generally designed to enhance workers' personal resources for coping with potential stressors and to reduce unwanted cognitive and emotional correlates such as worry and anxiety. This type of intervention, which usually takes the form of *stress management training* (SMT), has received a great deal of empirical attention. Reviews of the stress management literature suggest that the most common and most effective of these interventions are coping-skills training programs that are based on traditional cognitive-behavioral therapy (CBT) techniques such as cognitive restructuring and muscular relaxation (Murphy, 1984, 1996; Saunders, Driskell, Johnston, & Salas, 1996; van der Klink, Blonk, Schene, & van Dijk, 2001). For example, in a recent meta-analysis, van der Klink et al. (2001) reviewed 43 worksite SMT outcome studies. They found a medium effect size for both cognitive-behavioral interventions and multimodal programs (usually a mixture of cognitive therapy and relaxation techniques), and a small effect for relaxation training, across various measures of psychological health and coping. These findings, along with those from qualitative reviews (DeFrank & Cooper, 1987; Murphy, 1996), suggest that CBT-based training programs can have a beneficial impact on employees' well-being.

When examining worksite SMT programs over the last 30 years, it is readily apparent that their changes in content and intervention strategies have mirrored the evolution of the behavior and cognitive therapies. For example, during the 1970s, worksite interventions began to incorporate relaxation techniques that stemmed from systematic desensitization (e.g., Goldfried, 1971; Wolpe, 1958), one of the first generations of behavior therapies (Newman & Beehr, 1979; Peters, Benson, & Porter, 1977). A second generation of behavior therapies emerged with the development of the cognitive-based approaches of Beck (1976) and Ellis (1962); and since the 1980s, the principles and procedures from these cognitive therapies have become a central feature of SMT programs (Meichenbaum, 1985; 1993;

Saunders *et al.*, 1996; White, 2000). The model of change that underpins these approaches suggests that individuals can alleviate psychological distress through first-order change; that is, by altering the *content* of dysfunctional thoughts (e.g., through cognitive restructuring or guided self-dialogue) and by *reducing* unpleasant arousal (e.g., through relaxation training). More recently, a new generation of "third wave" CBTs has emerged, having in common an emphasis not on the second-wave goal of changing the form and frequency of people's psychological events, but on changing the way people relate to their thoughts, feelings, memories, and physiological sensations (Hayes, Strosahl, & Wilson, 1999; Linehan, 1993; Segal, Williams, & Teasdale, 2002; Wells, 2000). In view of the synchronous relationship that has existed between CBTs and stress management, it would seem that these third-wave developments have important implications for the design of individual-focused worksite interventions.

At the forefront of this new generation of CBTs is acceptance and commitment therapy (ACT) (Hayes *et al.*, 1999). We have been particularly interested in developing and testing ACT as a worksite intervention, as the model on which it is based is applicable to most (if not all) forms of psychological distress. In the following sections, we discuss the general ACT approach, before describing how we have implemented it in a worksite training context.

THE ACT MODEL OF PSYCHOPATHOLOGY: COGNITIVE FUSION AND EXPERIENTIAL AVOIDANCE

Rather than directly targeting the content of psychological phenomena for therapeutic change, which has been the traditional CBT approach, ACT attempts to alter the potentially stultifying function of unwanted thoughts and feelings by modifying the psychological contexts in which they are experienced (Hayes & Wilson, 1994). This emphasis on function and context in ACT stems from its behavior-analytic philosophy of functional contextualism (Biglan & Hayes, 1996), which is also reflected in relational frame theory (RFT), which underlies ACT. RFT is a detailed account and empirical research program that focuses on the fundamental nature of human language and cognition (see Hayes, Barnes-Holmes, & Roche, 2001; Hayes *et al.*, 1999).

From an ACT/RFT perspective, most forms of psychopathology are the result of two contexts that are built into the very fabric of human language: *cognitive fusion* and *experiential avoidance*. Cognitive fusion occurs when a person becomes entangled (or *fused*) with the literal content of his thoughts, so that those thoughts (and related emotions) are taken to be true interpretations of experience; for instance, when worrisome thoughts are taken to be accurate prophecies about the future, rather than mere *thoughts* about the future (Hayes, Strosahl, Bunting, Twohig, & Wilson, 2004).

In a context of fusion, people are generally unaware of the process of thinking and are less in contact with present-moment experiences, and their actions are largely determined by the psychological content that they have become fused with (even when that content leads to ineffective or harmful behaviors) (Hayes, 1989; 2004). Experiential avoidance occurs when people are unwilling to remain in contact with unwanted psychological events (e.g., thoughts, emotions, somatic sensations) and instead attempt to change the content or reduce the frequency of those undesirable experiences, even when doing so is counterproductive, as in thought suppression; harmful, as in drug and alcohol misuse; and life restricting, as in situational avoidance (Hayes *et al.,* 1996; 1999; Marlatt *et al.,* 2004; Wegner, Schneider, Carter, & White, 1987).

As can be seen, ACT, like other third-wave behavior therapies, does not view negative psychological content as inherently toxic to an individual's well-being. Rather, it is seen as a problem only to the extent to which it is taken literally (fusion) and is construed as something to be removed or avoided (experiential avoidance). Ironically, the contexts of fusion and experiential avoidance, used to make people feel better, may actually increase the intensity and frequency of unwanted internal states, as a person "plunges inward" to struggle (usually futilely) with difficult psychological content (Blackledge & Hayes, 2001; Wegner & Zanakos, 1994). In addition to this unintended effect of the contexts of literality and experiential avoidance, there is perhaps an even more pernicious one: As people continue to attempt (again futilely) to control their unwanted thoughts and feelings, their strategies for doing so (e.g., avoiding certain people and situations) become life-constricting barriers to pursuing goals and values like being an attentive spouse or an effective worker.

Interestingly, the contexts of fusion and avoidance are supported by our own language community, where negatively evaluated private events tend to be regarded as valid reasons for dysfunctional behavior (e.g., "I wanted to go out, but I was too depressed"). Such language conventions promote the unhelpful assumption that in order to obtain valued outcomes, we must first minimize (and thus control) unwanted internal events (Block, 2002; Hayes *et al.,* 1999). This assumption of experiential *control* (and hence, avoidance) undermines the goals of ACT; thus, as we will describe, attempts to control unwanted internal events are seen as the problem, not the solution.

ACT INTERVENTIONS: CULTIVATING MINDFULNESS TO PROMOTE VALUED LIVING

In general terms, ACT interventions aim to break down the contexts of fusion and avoidance, and do not, therefore, focus on the removal of unpleasant thoughts and emotions. Thus, consistent with other mindfulness-based approaches (e.g., Segal, Williams, & Teasdale, 2002), ACT alters the way people relate to their internal events, with the aim of helping them move toward the goals and values to which they aspire. To these ends, ACT has six core therapeutic strategies that:

1. highlight the costs and ineffectiveness of experiential avoidance strategies;

2. establish psychological *acceptance* and cognitive *defusion* (or mindfulness) skills, in order to break down the literal content of thoughts and to encourage full contact with difficult psychological content;

3. identify a sense of self that is distinct from, and therefore not threatened by, psychological content (self-as-context);

4. promote contact with present-moment experience;

5. help to clarify *values* as chosen life directions, and distinguish values from goals and actions; and

6. build patterns of *committed action* linked to chosen values (Hayes, 2004).

In the ACT model of therapeutic change, acceptance, defusion, self-as-context, and contact with the present moment form a larger set of mindfulness/acceptance skills, while contact with the present moment, self-as-context, values, and committed action together delineate values-based action skills (Hayes, 2004).

ACT's emphasis on mindfulness/acceptance skills is consistent with other third-wave behavior therapies (e.g., Linehan, 1993; Segal *et al.*, 2002). They have in common an emphasis on changing the function of psychological content, so that such internal events are experienced as a flow of ever-changing thoughts and feelings and not as representations of reality or of one's "self." As just noted, though, ACT also emphasizes values-based action skills; this is a construct that other third-wave behavior therapies do not emphasize to the extent that ACT does. Indeed, for ACT, acceptance/mindfulness is very much viewed as a *means* to an end—goal-directed action—whilst other third-wave therapies appear to promote this state more as an end in itself.

In ACT, this key integration of mindfulness and values-based, committed action produces *psychological flexibility*: the propensity to persist with behaviors that are consistent with one's chosen values and to desist from those that are not (Hayes, 2004; Hayes, Strosahl, *et al.*, 2004). The promotion of psychological flexibility appears to have considerable therapeutic utility, with a growing body of research finding ACT to be an effective treatment for a range of clinical problems, including polysubstance abuse, psychosis, evaluation anxiety, chronic pain, depression, and eating disorders (for a recent review of this research, see Hayes, Masuda, Bissett, Luoma, & Guerrero, 2004).

In the remainder of this chapter, we describe how we have applied ACT, and the mindfulness/acceptance skills at the core of it, to the problem of work-related stress. We suggest, however, that this protocol could also be used in training programs for other populations that have to cope with demanding situations—test-anxious students, caregivers, etc. The content of the protocol (described later) includes many techniques that have become core components of most ACT interventions, and as a result, they have been described in detail elsewhere (see Bond, 2004; Bond & Hayes, 2002; Hayes *et al.*, 1999). We do not, therefore, provide a full description of every core ACT technique that is applied to stress; instead, our primary aim here is to illustrate how the link between mindfulness and values-based action is continually played out across the training program.

ACT IN THE WORKPLACE: IMPLEMENTATION AND CASE STUDY

The first study to evaluate the efficacy of ACT as a worksite stress management intervention was published by Bond and Bunce (2000). Over the past 5 years, we have continued to evaluate our ACT training protocol in various organizations (as described later), and more than 300 people have now attended our workshops. Comprehensive descriptions of the manual that was empirically validated by Bond and Bunce can be found in Bond and Hayes (2002), with an updated version in Bond (2004). While the basic structure of the training protocol has remained the same, as has its aim—to promote psychological flexibility—the technical content is continually being refined in response to feedback from our participants and innovations in ACT techniques and strategies. As a result, the following account of our ACT training sessions describes some material that was not included in our previous manuals. For example, we discuss some ACT techniques that we have recently, and successfully, incorporated into our training program; in addition, we focus more on the language that we use when introducing and explaining ACT principles in a group training context: an innovation that we have found particularly important. We hope that this additional material, based upon our "lessons learned," proves useful to other clinicians and trainers who are preparing to deliver ACT-based stress programs.

Despite these changes to our ACT SMT, we continue to adopt the "2 + 1" method of delivery (Barkham & Shapiro, 1990) that Bond and Hayes (2002) described and that was shown to be effective by Bond and Bunce (2000). This format involves three training sessions: two on consecutive weeks and a third 3 months later, with each session lasting for approximately 3 hours. We have found that this structure is not only therapeutically beneficial (see Bond & Hayes, 2002), but it also serves to reduce the disruption to our participants' working schedules. The content of each of these three sessions is described in the following sections.

In the following description of our intervention, we have included the experiences of Margaret, a fictional participant who is 43 years of age, has two teenage children, and works in the welfare department of a local government organization. Margaret's experiences represent some of the typical responses and issues that may arise when delivering ACT in the workplace.

SESSION 1 (WEEK 1)

The aims of session 1 are: (1) to undermine the effectiveness of experiential avoidance strategies; (2) to show that in the realm of thoughts and emotions, control is the problem, not the solution; and (3) to introduce *psychological acceptance*, or mindfulness, as the alternative to experiential avoidance.

At the beginning of the first session, the ground rules for the training are set out. Participants are told that any personal information that is discussed in the three training sessions is confidential and should not be shared with anyone outside the room (including family members). Participants are also informed that they are free to leave any of the sessions at any time they wish, and the fact that they left would not be reported to anyone in the organization. We have begun our recent ACT interventions by writing the general aim of the training on a white board, as follows: "To teach you how to deal with psychological barriers to effective and enjoyable living." We have found it useful to provide this description at the outset, as it sets the scene for the two central components of ACT: mindfulness and values-based action. Participants are asked to provide their own definitions of "effective and enjoyable living," and these responses are noted on the board. They are then asked to describe examples of "psychological barriers" that can interfere with effective and enjoyable living. In response to this second question, participants usually report a range of undesirable internal states such as anxiety, worry, stress, negative thinking, low self-confidence, and so on. Following this, the trainer elicits from participants (a) examples of the (avoidance) strategies that they have used to change or remove this undesirable psychological content, and (b) their experiences of the effectiveness of these strategies.

> Trainer: Could anyone explain how these things interfere with effective and enjoyable living?
>
> Participant 1: When I've had a stressful day at work, they tend to take over a bit.
>
> T: They take over?
>
> P1: Well, I often get home from work feeling uptight and on edge, and all I want to do is hide upstairs away from my family—I don't think that's very "effective!" I also can't help being snappy with my husband, and he doesn't deserve that. I can't stop thinking about work even when I'm at home. It's like it takes a while to get it out of my system.

T: What do you do to stop thinking about it?

P1: I just try to block it out.

T: Does that work?

P1: Not really. It might do for a bit, but then work or something just pops back in again and drags me down, and makes me snappy.

Participant 2: I do a lot of cleaning when I feel like that.

T: How does that work? Does it get rid of the undesirable internal stuff?

P2: Well my house is really clean! But then my family think I'm nuts because I clean when I get home like a madwoman. I sometimes get up in the small hours to clean if there's something on my mind.

T: So, does the cleaning get rid of the psychological barriers that you described?

P2: I suppose while I'm cleaning it's okay because I really throw myself into it. But even when I'm cleaning, I can quite easily start worrying about something else.

T: (lightheartedly) I notice that you didn't include "cleaning" in your description of "effective living." Shall I add it to the list?

P2: No! (laughs) I mean it's effective in a way because I like the place to be clean. But I wouldn't call it effective living—it's just the way I cope with stress.

(Similar conversations are conducted with a few more members of the group.)

T: So, what we have is a list of some things that we humans do to try to remove or reduce this undesirable internal stuff that can interfere in our lives. We have: blocking it out; hiding; not thinking about it; cleaning; and trying to get it in perspective. When I asked you about the effectiveness of these strategies, I got the general picture that they may work for awhile, but over the long haul they don't really stop the undesirable thoughts, worries, etc., from showing up. Does that seem accurate?

Through conversations such as these, the trainer begins to undermine the perceived workability of experiential avoidance strategies. The goal is not to persuade participants that these strategies are ineffective, but to encourage them to look to their own experience and be guided by that. In the following section, the trainer continues to undermine experiential avoidance, by highlighting the "unworkability" and costs of internal control attempts:

So, it's odd isn't it? We employ all these elaborate strategies to avoid feeling bad or thinking negative thoughts, and yet, in the long term, they don't really seem to work. As some of you have noted, the strategies themselves can make the situation worse. Why is this the case? Well, human language and rationality have given us a tremendous advantage as a species: We are able to solve complex problems, plan for the future, and so on. In ninety-five percent of our existence, *in the world outside the skin*, our minds have worked wonders for us. Just look at what we have: computers, complex organizations, mobile phones, beautifully designed buildings, supermarkets full of ready-to-eat meals, etc. Throughout our evolutionary history we have been extraordinarily successful because we have been working to a rule that goes something like this: "If we don't like something, figure out how to change it or get rid of it, and do it!" Our primitive ancestors didn't like being cold, and so they worked out how to keep warm. They didn't like going hungry, so they worked out how to store food, etc. In the world outside the skin, this rule is still working for us today. What we are talking about here is CONTROL. We humans have been very successful at controlling the environment around us. So, control works great in the world outside of the skin.

However, there is another aspect to our experience. There's the other five percent which is *inside the skin*. This is an important world, but it is also quite a strange world. It's not a world that's full of solid things like chairs, tables, and computers. It's a "virtual" world of thoughts, emotions, moods, and physical sensations. It often *seems* like the real world, but it's *not* the real world. Despite our considerable success outside the skin, we humans tend to get into difficulties from the way we deal with events that occur inside the skin. We often try to apply the control rule that works so well in the *real* world, outside the skin, to the *virtual* world inside the skin. Thus, we try to change, remove, or avoid the thoughts, memories, and feelings that we don't like. Unfortunately, as we have been discussing, control attempts do not really work inside the skin. It's not easy to just stop thinking about something we don't want to think about. In fact, isn't it true that trying not to think about something makes us think about it even more? Consider this and see if it applies to your own experience: The problem is that when we try to control thoughts and feelings, etc., we embark on a "no-win struggle" with whole aspects of our own experience. This internal struggle is costly. The stuff we struggle with is likely to become more, not less, important. And the struggle will continually draw us away from the present moment, from the here and now. Also, the struggle may involve us avoiding situations, and this can reduce our ability to achieve our goals in life. Because of these costs, in the world *inside the skin*, our efforts at control actually become the problem, not the solution. I'm not asking you to just take my word for this. I'm asking you to look to your own experience to see if this is the case for you.

We also introduce the *polygraph metaphor* at this stage (see Bond & Hayes, 2002; Hayes *et al.*, 1999, pp. 123–124) to further illustrate the distinction between using control inside and outside the skin (e.g., "Keep calm or I'll shoot you" versus "Clean my house or I'll shoot you"). (Parenthetically, when we introduce ACT metaphors, we present them in pictorial as well as verbal form.) A thought suppression exercise can also be introduced here to demonstrate the paradoxical effects of cognitive avoidance attempts (e.g., "Don't think about ... warm chocolate cake!").

This first phase of ACT is designed to induce a state of readiness amongst participants for learning alternative coping strategies. In ACT, this psychological state of readiness is referred to as *creative hopelessness* (although this term would not normally be used with participants), because people are beginning to make experiential contact with the unworkability of their avoidance-type coping methods. We have found that this state is often expressed by participants at this stage generally in the form of, "Okay, so trying to control thoughts and feelings doesn't work. What should we do instead?" Participants may also discuss reasons why everyone "expects" to be able to control internal states. The trainer can help out here by pointing out the language conventions that seemingly support experiential avoidance. For example when we say to a child, "don't be angry with your sister," we may be giving them the impression that they should be able to turn off their anger at will. Also, when teenagers goad each other with "you're not scared are you?", "being scared" is likely to be construed as something that needs to be, and even can be, eliminated.

The Alternative: Psychological Acceptance

> So, we've seen how trying to control our thoughts, feelings, and emotions is not a reliable, nor helpful, strategy for reducing stress, worry etc. The alternative to these unhelpful control attempts is *acceptance*. That is, if we are willing to experience an emotion or a thought for what it is, without struggling with it, then we can escape all the inevitable problems that come with internal struggles, such as more stress, avoidance, and a reduced capacity to be aware of the here and now. (Therapist)

It is not uncommon at this stage of the training for participants to express concerns about the idea of acceptance (e.g., "I'm being asked to do two people's jobs. I don't see how accepting that is going to help"). We usually respond to these concerns by reiterating the distinction between the world inside the skin and the "real world" outside the skin. We explain that when we use the term *acceptance*, we are referring to the acceptance of internal events—thoughts, feelings, and sensations—and that, in the next session, we will be discussing how accepting internal events can help us to deal more effectively with the real world. We explain that "acceptance can be developed through repeated practice of mindfulness techniques, which basically involve us looking at our thoughts and feelings in a different way, from a different perspective. By using these techniques, we can begin to catch a glimpse of thoughts *as* thoughts, and emotions *as* emotions. When thoughts and emotions are observed mindfully, and accepted for what they are (i.e., thoughts and feelings instead of the content of those thoughts and feelings), we are much less likely to engage in unhelpful struggles with them, and they are much less likely to interfere with effective living. Let's practice our first mindfulness technique. It's called 'leaves on the stream.'"

At this point, participants are asked to sit comfortably, close their eyes, and imagine that they are sitting in a theater watching a film that their minds and bodies project onto the screen. They are asked to spend a few minutes noticing their breath as they inhale and exhale, and then to become aware of bodily sensations and to observe these without trying to change them. If they notice their minds wandering away, they are asked to return their attention gently to the present moment. Next they are asked to imagine themselves sitting next to a gentle stream in a beautiful valley, with leaves floating gently down the stream. They are instructed to notice when thoughts or images come into their awareness and to imagine placing each one on a leaf and watching it float down the stream.

Following the exercise, the trainer asks, "How did you find this exercise?" and, if it has not come up during the discussion, "How does this exercise relate to what we have been discussing?" Margaret noted that

life satisfaction can be obtained by consistently engaging in actions that move us in valued directions. We also try to get participants to see that a life dedicated to controlling unwanted internal events is unlikely to be infused with vitality, because living a valued (and hence, vital) life will inevitably, and often, expose people to undesirable psychological events (e.g., anxiety and even guilt).

To help participants get in touch with their values in various life domains, we begin with a "eulogy" exercise (see Bond, 2004), in which participants are asked to imagine that they have miraculously been able to show up, in spirit form, at their own funeral. Participants are asked to write down the sorts of things they would like their family, friends, colleagues, etc., to say about them. That is, what would they like to be remembered for? During this exercise, Margaret wrote that she wanted to be remembered for being a "great mum." Following this, participants are provided with a *values assessment* form that encourages them to record values in different areas of their lives, such as personal and work, along with any specific goals or actions that would move them in those directions. We recommend providing some examples to ensure that participants understand the distinction among values, goals, and actions. We give participants between 15 and 30 minutes (in session) to work on identifying 3 or 4 of their most important life values. The general theme is, "What do you want your life to stand for?" Margaret indicated that her most important value was to be a patient and supportive parent for her two teenage boys, and she generated a number of goals that would move her in this valued direction, including spending more time with her family at the end of the working day and taking more time to listen patiently to her boys without nagging them about various issues.

Self-as-Context

When experienced within a context of fusion, difficult thoughts and emotions can appear to threaten a person's sense of self, as when anxiety threatens the self-conceptualization of being a "calm" or "rational" human being. And, in doing so, they are likely to lead to the use of unhelpful experiential avoidance strategies. One of the core aims of ACT is therefore to help clients establish a sense of self that is distinct from their difficult psychological content. The goal is to encourage a person to make experiential contact with themselves as the "conscious vessel" that contains, but is not threatened by, difficult internal events (self-as-context) (Hayes *et al.*, 1999, p. 188). In ACT, this transcendent sense of self-as-context is referred to as the "observing self" and is accessed through various defusion and mindfulness exercises (Hayes, 2004; Hayes *et al.*, 1999).

In our ACT workshops, we introduce the idea of the observing self by using the *cloud and sky* metaphor (from Hayes *et al.*, 1999, p. 187), where the clouds are the "verbal chatter" of the mind, behind which lies blue sky. The theme here is that we do not have to remove the clouds to know that there is blue sky; if we learn to look, we will see that it is always there. This metaphor leads into the *observer* exercise (Bond & Hayes, 2002; Dahl & Lundgren, this volume). In this, participants are encouraged to make contact with the observing self (or the blue sky that lies behind the clouds of mind chatter)—a sense of self that is not the content of their mind (e.g., their fears or unhappiness), but, rather, the context in which that content occurs; a place that they can get to by being in the present moment, through acceptance/mindfulness. The observer exercise can also be accompanied by the *chessboard* metaphor (Hayes *et al.,* 1999, pp. 190–192). In this metaphor (which we would introduce in the session with a real chessboard and pieces), the board can be thought of as the observing self, and the pieces on the board as all the different thoughts and emotions that we experience. The trainer can make the distinction between being at "piece level" (or wrapped up in a cloud), as when we have been pulled into a struggle with particular psychological content, and being at "board level," which equates to a sense of the observing self, or the "sky" (i.e., defused and mindfully observing the pieces).

Passengers on the Bus

Toward the end of session 2, we have found it useful to introduce the *passengers on the bus* metaphor (Hayes *et al.,* 1999, pp. 157–158) to draw the mindfulness and values components together. This metaphor is accompanied by a cartoon-like drawing of "scary" passengers on a bus. Participants are asked to imagine that they are the driver of a bus that is full of passengers (some of whom are scary looking). These passengers represent the driver's thoughts, emotions, memories, urges, etc. The idea is that the scary-looking passengers will often try to commandeer the bus and demand that the driver take the bus in directions that may not serve the driver's valued directions. Our attempts to struggle with, or placate, these passengers tend to be counterproductive, in that to do so, we must either hand over control of the bus to the passengers or stop the bus to struggle with them. Participants are encouraged to view the direction of the bus as representing their chosen values and the "unhelpful" passengers as the psychological barriers that may be encountered along the way.

Following this metaphor, the trainer asks, "Can anyone see how this relates to what we have discussed in the training so far?" The goal here is for participants to see that the mindfulness skills are in the service of keeping the bus moving in valued directions.

We have previously included other ACT techniques in this second session, such as *getting off our buts* and the *tin can monster* exercise. These are not detailed here, as they are presented in Bond and Hayes (2002).

We have found that the number of techniques that can be used in a 3-hour session varies from group to group. Some groups generate a lot of discussion, while others seem to prefer to try out a wide variety of techniques. We do not see these technical variations as a particular problem, so long as the mindfulness and values components have both received sufficient attention.

At the end of the second session, we remind participants that the third, and final, session does not occur for 3 months, and they are encouraged to use that time to continue developing their mindfulness skills (we provide audiotapes containing two or three exercises). We particularly encourage the daily use of short mindfulness techniques such as the "white screen." They are also strongly encouraged to finish the values assessment exercise at home and, over the next 3 months, to begin taking steps, however small, that are consistent with their chosen life directions.

SESSION 3 (3 MONTHS LATER)

The aims of session 3 are (1) to provide a booster session for mindfulness skills; (2) to discuss any barriers to valued action; and (3) to further highlight the link between mindfulness and valued action. The trainer begins the session with a short mindfulness exercise (e.g., leaves on the stream) and a discussion of any issues related to the training that have arisen over the last 3 months. Margaret reported that once she got the "gist" of the mindfulness exercises on our tape, she was increasingly able to untangle herself from her psychological content throughout the day. She had found these exercises particularly useful and was frequently amused to notice the "automatic" (and at times strange) whims and vagaries of her mind. Margaret also felt that her relationship with her two teenage boys had improved since the last session (in line with her most important value). In particular, she had reduced the frequency with which she expressed her impatience with her sons (even though she reported that they still regularly provided her with impatient thoughts and feelings!).

Following this discussion, the trainer makes the link between mindfulness/acceptance and values, using the following *bubble in the road* metaphor (from Hayes *et al.*, 1999, p. 230). Participants are reminded that large soap bubbles can simply absorb smaller bubbles when they touch. They are asked to imagine being a soap bubble floating along a chosen path and encountering a smaller bubble that blocks the way. At this point, they can choose to stop and change direction, or they can make contact with the smaller bubble, absorb it, and continue along the chosen path. In this metaphor, the smaller bubbles represent thoughts, feelings, and memories that appear as obstacles blocking our chosen directions. "Willingness" refers to continuing to move in these directions even when unhelpful thoughts, such as "you shouldn't go this way!" pop up. Willingness means choosing a valued direction and sticking to it, even with such apparent obstacles inside.

The trainer then discusses with participants the nature of the barriers (or "bubbles") that interfere with movement in valued directions. Examples of values, goals, actions, and barriers are listed on a white board, and the trainer particularly discusses those barriers (worry, low self-confidence, doubts, etc.) that are internal events. The general theme of this dialogue is that when these internal events are observed mindfully (i.e., seen for what they are, not for what they say they are), their potential to be barriers is greatly reduced. This discussion of psychological barriers to valued action is then related to the passengers-on-the-bus metaphor introduced in the previous section.

Weather permitting (in London!), we may also employ the *taking your mind for a walk* exercise (Hayes *et al.,* 1999, pp. 162–163) in order to promote the idea that it is possible to keep moving in chosen directions even when the mind is "chattering on" unhelpfully. Participants are instructed to walk in pairs for a few minutes. One participant is designated the Person and the other is that person's Mind. The Person chooses where to go, the Mind must follow. The Mind chatters almost constantly: describing, analyzing, encouraging, predicting, worrying, criticizing, warning, and so on. The Person does not communicate with the Mind but goes wherever he or she pleases, regardless of the content of the Mind's chatter, which is likened to having a radio on in the background. After 5 minutes, roles are switched. For the final 5 minutes, participants walk separately, now noticing the chatter of their own minds, while continuing to move in the directions they choose.

In this final session, we would also try to provide participants with further opportunities to practice ACT techniques that were introduced in previous sessions (such as the observer exercise and/or the tin can monster exercise). Then, toward the end of the session, we ask participants to make a public commitment to one particular life value: "I would like to go around the room and have each of you, if you are willing, tell us one of your valued directions and an action that you will take to move in that direction. If there is no value and action that you are prepared to state here, try stating one to your partner, or to a close friend, or even to yourself in the mirror. The goal is to make as public a commitment as possible: a statement of purpose in relation to a value that you have." Margaret shared with the group her value of being a supportive mum, and stated that she would spend more time engaged in activities with her sons that they wanted to do, as well as listen to them more and talk a little less.

PRACTICAL ISSUES

We have found that the successful implementation of ACT in the workplace is contingent upon a number of core issues. These include the marketing of the intervention and recruitment of participants, the need to address the organizational factors that can impact upon the success of this type of intervention, taking steps to reduce participant attrition, and managing in-session difficulties.

MARKETING AND RECRUITMENT

The marketing of ACT (and other interventions) to organizations generally occurs in two stages. The first concerns the initial approach to an organization, which is designed to spark the interest of relevant stakeholders and decision makers. To this end, we usually contact the occupational health and/or human resource (HR) departments within an organization, outlining the key aims of the training and the outcomes from our previous ACT research. Recently, we have moved away from marketing our ACT worksite intervention as "stress management," which, in our view, has become an overused term that even well-meaning organizations are trying to avoid; instead, we call it "work and life effectiveness training" and explain in our initial marketing material that it is designed to improve both well-being and performance.

More often than not, we implement ACT as part of a funded research program and are therefore able to offer the training to organizations free of charge. In circumstances in which we request payment for delivering our ACT intervention, we "sell" it to the organization by referring to research that has demonstrated a link between psychological acceptance and key organizational outcomes, such as job performance and absenteeism (Bond & Bunce, 2000; 2003; Bond, Flaxman, & Bunce, in prep). Not surprisingly, organizations are often very interested in training that has the potential to improve these work-related outcomes.

Once we have gained access to an organization, a second stage of marketing begins, and this is aimed at recruiting participants for the ACT intervention. We base the information in our recruitment material on the values and mindfulness components of ACT, advertising the training as an intervention that is designed to (1) help people move toward their work and life goals, and (2) teach strategies for dealing with the "psychological barriers" (e.g., anxiety, low self-confidence) that can interfere with effective working and living. Recruitment of participants should ideally be conducted in consultation with an occupational health or HR representative within the organization. In our experience, this "in-house" contact performs a crucial role, by providing information about the organizational culture and climate, as well as managing the logistics involved in the implementation of ACT in the workplace (distributing recruitment information, allocating people to sessions, booking rooms, etc.). We really cannot overstate the importance of an in-house contact in ensuring the success of ACT training.

This recruitment approach usually attracts a range of volunteers with varying levels of mental ill-health. We do not employ any screening procedures when recruiting participants, as we believe (and our data suggest) that ACT can be beneficial for employees with "normal" levels of mental ill-health, as well as for those who are reporting moderate to high levels of psychological distress. However, we usually find that volunteers for our ACT training have higher levels of mental ill-health than the general working population; for example, in our recent ACT studies, approximately 50% of participants were reporting baseline levels of distress that would make them probable cases of a minor psychiatric disorder (as based upon the General Health Questionnaire).

ORGANIZATIONAL ISSUES

In order to maximize the effectiveness of individual-focused worksite interventions, such as ACT, it is desirable that the organization also implement organization-directed initiatives (e.g., work redesign) aimed at reducing peoples' exposure to sources of stress at work. If ACT is employed in isolation, an undesirable (and unethical) situation may be created, in which employees are taught strategies, like mindfulness, for coping with stressors, only to be sent back into a "toxic" work environment that management is not trying to rectify (e.g., by increasing people's control over how they do their work). A likely outcome of such a one-sided approach to stress is that participants will be less motivated to engage in ACT. This has frequently been evident to us during ACT sessions, when participants (quite understandably) question why their organization is trying only to "fix" them (i.e., by teaching them coping strategies), when they face difficulties from organizational problems, such as a lack of staff, poor communication from management, and conflicting roles. We have found that the best way to address these concerns, which are usually expressed by participants at the beginning of the training, is to ensure that ACT is one component of a more comprehensive intervention approach that also includes stressor-reduction activities. At the very least, it is important to acknowledge fully participants' concerns about work-related stressors and find a way to feedback these concerns to senior management at the organization. By adopting this approach, we have found that the work-related information that is discussed in ACT sessions can be used to inform the design of concurrent, or subsequent, organization-focused interventions.

MANAGING ATTRITION

In our recent ACT worksite interventions, participant attrition has ranged between 29% and 47% across the three training sessions, with most dropping out between sessions 2 and 3 (which occur 3 months apart). We have been unable to identify any demographic differences between those who drop out of ACT and those who attend all three sessions; for example, in two recent ACT interventions, those who dropped out had slightly lower levels of general mental health at baseline than those who remained, but this pattern was reversed in a third study (conducted at a similar organization). Although we have not formally collected data regarding peoples' reasons for failing to attend all three sessions, our informal enquiries have revealed a wide range of reasons, including work scheduling, absenteeism, turnover, program content, annual vacations, and forgetting to attend. Regardless of the reasons, we have found that the single most important factor in managing attrition is to have an organizational representative, such as an occupational health officer, who is able to contact participants with reminders to attend the training. In our experience, this in-house project management can reduce attrition by approximately 20%.

Finally, it is important to remember that in work-based ACT groups, participants are often closely linked, if not known directly, to other members of the group. This can raise a number of issues relating to privacy, confidentiality, and fear of evaluation by coworkers, which may influence peoples' decisions about engaging in the intervention. It is therefore particularly important in this context to ensure that all participants adhere to confidentiality rules, which should be reiterated by the trainer in each session. Where possible, we have also found it useful to allow ACT participants to change groups if they have been allocated to the same group as a manager or coworker with whom they have a difficult relationship. In addition, Bond (2004) describes how certain values-related exercises have been altered so that they minimize the need for people, in worksite training groups, to share their values and goals with group members (i.e., work colleagues).

IN-SESSION DIFFICULTIES

While ACT can undoubtedly be an emotionally challenging intervention, we have found that it is rare for participants in our worksite interventions to get into serious emotional difficulties as a result of ACT techniques. We would suggest that this is a key difference between delivering ACT in the workplace and facilitating ACT therapy groups, which are likely to involve clients with higher levels of distress (see Walser & Pistorello, 2004, for an interesting discussion of delivering ACT in a group format). However, such difficulties do sometimes arise and, in this worksite context, can pose a particular challenge for the trainer. On the few occasions when we have sensed that the level of distress being experienced by a participant was beyond the remit of the worksite training context, such as in the case of a recent bereavement, we have called for a brief break and have discussed with the distressed individual the pros and cons of continuing with the training at this time. We always ensure that we are in possession of information relating to the organization's employee assistance (e.g., counseling) services, and we will refer the participant on to those services if we feel it is appropriate. In addition, we remind such participants of other resources available to them, such as their general practitioner (who, in the United Kingdom, can refer people to state-sponsored mental health professionals). To some, such referrals may seem like a "rescuing" move that is not necessarily consistent with ACT principles (Walser & Pistorello, 2004); however, in worksite ACT interventions, where it is often not possible to have individual therapy sessions, we believe that this approach may sometimes be a practical and therapeutic necessity.

RESEARCH ON ACT IN THE WORKPLACE

Bond and Bunce (2000) published the first study into the effectiveness of ACT as a worksite training program. These researchers conducted a randomized controlled trial (RCT) in a large UK media organization, comparing ACT with a wait-list control group, and they also conducted a training program that taught workers how to reduce work-related stressors at their source (this latter intervention is not discussed further here, but see Bond & Bunce, 2000, for details). Using the 2 + 1 method of delivery (described previously), Bond and Bunce found that ACT significantly improved employees' general mental health, depression, and innovation potential. Furthermore, their mediation analyses revealed that ACT produced these beneficial outcomes because it increased participants' *psychological acceptance,* as measured by the Acceptance and Action Questionnaire (AAQ) (Hayes *et al.,* 2004), and not because it changed their dysfunctional cognitive content, as measured by the Dysfunctional Attitude Scale (DAS) (Beck, Brown, Steer, & Weissman, 1991).

Since the publication of that first study, we have conducted two further RCTs in large UK local government organizations (Flaxman & Bond, in prep). In the first of these studies, ACT was compared with a traditional CBT stress management program (based on stress inoculation training), and a wait-list control group. Both intervention groups reported large improvements in mental health between baseline and our two follow-ups, which occurred 3 months after the first two training sessions, and again 3 months after the final training session. Tests for mediation revealed that each intervention produced these beneficial effects for the reasons posited by their respective models. Specifically, 3 months after the first two sessions of training, increases in psychological acceptance accounted for, or mediated, the mental health improvements shown in the ACT group; in contrast, reductions in dysfunctional cognitions served as the mechanism, or mediator, by which mental health improvements occurred in the second-wave CBT group.

In our most recent study, we compared our ACT training intervention with a control group in order to gain further insight into the impact of ACT on the content of dysfunctional cognitions. The results of this study were generally consistent with the findings from the two studies just mentioned. That is, the ACT intervention produced a large improvement in employees' general mental health, as well as significant reductions in the reported frequency of dysfunctional cognitions (particularly between baseline and 6-month follow-up). However, these reductions in dysfunctional cognitions were not the mechanism by which ACT improved employees' mental health; rather, in replication of our previous findings, results suggested that the benefits of the ACT training resulted primarily from increases in psychological acceptance.

In sum, the results of these three studies suggest that the ACT intervention, described in this chapter, can significantly improve mental health in the workplace and that such improvements are mediated principally by increases in psychological acceptance. In these studies, we also found evidence that, over time, ACT reduces the frequency of dysfunctional cognitions. However, in general, these frequency changes did not function as a meaningful mechanism of change. Taken together, these results are consistent with the ACT model of therapeutic change, which targets the function (via acceptance/mindfulness) rather than the form (or frequency) of difficult psychological content.

CONCLUSION

While these empirical data are promising, they are not the only source of information that drives our advocacy of ACT as a worksite training intervention. In particular, our own experiences of conducting, and participating in, ACT workshops have shown us that this approach has a number of features that make it particularly amenable to the worksite. First, ACT encourages the healthy acceptance of undesirable internal states that may stem from unalterable work demands, such as difficult customers, and that might otherwise interfere with effective work-related behaviors—in this case, providing good customer service. Second, we have found that the values component of ACT can readily be used to help individuals (and even work groups) identify work-related goals and actions that are likely to enhance their work motivation and performance (if enhancing motivation and performance is something that they value). Also, as others have noted (e.g., Orsillo & Batten, 2002), the mindfulness techniques that are central to ACT can be practiced with "neutral" thoughts, as well as with more difficult psychological content; thus, participants do not have to be in "stress mode" to develop, and indeed practice, mindfulness skills. This technical feature is particularly useful for *preventive* worksite interventions, which are generally offered to all workers, irrespective of their current level of distress.

While we promote the use of ACT as an effective workplace intervention, we do not suggest that organizations use it (or any other individual-focused approach) as their sole strategy for tackling work-related stress. Instead, we view ACT as an important adjunct to organization-focused (e.g., work redesign) initiatives, which attempt to reduce employees' exposure to sources of stress that reside in the design and management of work, including such factors as low job control and excessive work demands (Bond & Bunce, 2001; Cox *et al.*, 2000). Based on our recent research, we predict that this combination of ACT and work redesign will provide the most comprehensive and effective strategy for reducing the considerable costs of occupational ill-health.

REFERENCES

Barkham, M., & Shapiro, D. A. (1990). Brief psychotherapeutic interventions for job-related distress: A pilot study of prescriptive and exploratory therapy. *Counselling Psychology Quarterly, 3*, 133–147.

Beck, A. T. (1976). *Cognitive therapy and the emotional disorders.* New York: International Universities Press.

Beck, A. T., Brown, G., Steer, R. A., & Weissman, A. N. (1991). Factor analysis of the Dysfunctional Attitude Scale in a clinical population. *Psychological Assessment, 3*, 478–483.

Biglan, A., & Hayes, S. C. (1996). Should the behavioral sciences become more pragmatic? The case for functional contextualism in research on human behavior. *Applied and Preventive Psychology: Current Scientific Perspectives, 5*, 47–57.

Blackledge, J. T., & Hayes, S. C. (2001). Emotion regulation in acceptance and commitment therapy. *JCLP/In Session: Psychotherapy in Practice, 57*, 243–255.

Block, J. A. (2002). *Acceptance or change of private experiences: A comparative analysis in college students with public speaking anxiety.* Unpublished doctoral dissertation, University at Albany, State University of New York.

Bond, F. W. (2004). ACT and stress management. In S. C. Hayes & K. D. Strosahl (Eds.), *A practical guide to acceptance and commitment therapy.* New York: Springer.

Bond, F. W., & Bunce, D. (2000). Mediators of change in emotion-focused and problem-focused worksite stress management interventions. *Journal of Occupational Health Psychology, 5*, 156–163.

———— (2001). Job control mediates change in a work reorganization intervention for stress reduction. *Journal of Occupational Health Psychology, 6*, 290–302.

———— (2003). The role of acceptance and job control in mental health, job satisfaction, and work performance. *Journal of Applied Psychology, 88*, 1057–1067.

Bond, F. W., Flaxman, P. E., & Bunce, D. (in preparation). Mediators and moderators of a work reorganization intervention: The effect of an individual characteristic on the success of work redesign.

Bond, F. W., & Hayes, S. C. (2002). ACT at work. In F. W. Bond & W. Dryden (Eds.), *Handbook of brief cognitive behaviour therapy*. Chichester, UK: John Wiley & Sons.

Cox, T., Griffiths, A., Barlowe, C., Randall, R., Thomson, L., & Rial-Gonzalez, E. (2000). *Organisational interventions for work stress: A risk management approach*. Norwich, UK: Health and Safety Executive/Her Majesty's Stationery Office.

DeFrank, R. S., & Cooper, C. L. (1987). Worksite stress management interventions: Their effectiveness and conceptualisation. *Journal of Managerial Psychology, 2*, 4–10.

Ellis, A. (1962). *Reason and emotion in psychotherapy*. Secaucus, NJ: Lyle Stuart.

Flaxman, P. E., & Bond, F. W. (in preparation). Investigating the mechanisms of change in acceptance-based and control-oriented stress management interventions.

Goldfried, M. R. (1971). Systematic desensitisation as training in self-control. *Journal of Consulting and Clinical Psychology, 37*, 228–234.

Hardy, G. E., Woods, D., & Wall, T. D. (2003). The impact of psychological distress on absence from work. *Journal of Applied Psychology, 88*, 306–314.

Hayes, S. C. (Ed.), (1989). *Rule-governed behavior: Cognition, contingencies, and instructional control*. New York: Plenum Press.

———— (2004). Acceptance and commitment therapy and the new behavior therapies: Mindfulness, acceptance, and relationship. In S. C. Hayes, V. M. Follette, & M. M. Linehan (Eds.), *Mindfulness and acceptance: Expanding the cognitive-behavioral tradition*. New York: Guilford Press.

Hayes, S. C., Barnes-Holmes, D., & Roche, B. (2001). *Relational frame theory: A post-Skinnerian account of human language and cognition*. New York: Kluwer Academic/Plenum Publishers.

Hayes, S. C., Masuda, A., Bissett, R., Luoma, J., & Guerrero, L. F. (2004). DBT, FAP, and ACT: How empirically oriented are the new behavior therapy technologies? *Behavior Therapy, 35*, 35–54.

Hayes, S. C., Strosahl, K. D., Bunting, K., Twohig, M., & Wilson, K. (2004). What is acceptance and commitment therapy? In S. C. Hayes & K. D. Strosahl (Eds.), *A practical guide to acceptance and commitment therapy*. New York: Springer.

Hayes, S. C., Strosahl, K., & Wilson, K. G. (1999). *Acceptance and commitment therapy: An experiential approach to behavior change*. New York: Guilford Press.

Hayes, S. C., Strosahl, K., Wilson, K. G., Bissett, R. T., Pistorello, J., Taormino, D., et al. (2004). Measuring experiential avoidance: A preliminary test of a working model. *Psychological Record, 54*, 553–578.

Hayes, S. C., & Wilson, K. G. (1994). Acceptance and commitment therapy: Altering the verbal support for experiential avoidance. *Behavior Analyst, 17*, 289–303.

Health and Safety Executive. (2004). *SWI03/04 survey of self-reported work-related illness*. Available from http://www.hse.gov.uk/index.htm

Jex, S. M. (1998). *Stress and job performance*. London: Sage.

Jex, S. M., Bliese, P. D., Buzzell, S., & Primeau, J. (2001). The impact of self-efficacy on stressor-strain relations: Coping style as an explanatory mechanism. *Journal of Applied Psychology, 86*, 401–409.

Kessler, R. C., & Frank, R. G. (1997). The impact of psychiatric disorders on work loss days. *Psychological Medicine, 27*, 861–873.

Lazarus, R. S., & Folkman, S. (1984). *Stress, appraisal and coping*. New York: Springer.

Linehan, M. M. (1993). *Cognitive-behavioral treatment of borderline personality disorder.* New York: Guilford Press.

Marlatt, G. A., Witkiewitz, K., Dillworth, T. M., Bowen, S. W., Parks, G. A., Macpherson, L. M., *et al.* (2004). Vipassana meditation as a treatment for alcohol and drug use disorders. In S. C. Hayes, V. M. Follette, & M. M. Linehan (Eds.), *Mindfulness and acceptance: Expanding the cognitive-behavioral tradition.* New York: Guilford Press.

Matheny, K. B., Aycock, D. W., Pugh, J. L., Curlette, W. L., & Cannella, K. A. S. (1986). Stress coping: A qualitative and quantitative synthesis with implications for treatment. *Counseling Psychologist, 14*, 499–549.

Meichenbaum, D. (1985). *Stress inoculation training.* New York: Pergamon.

―――― (1993). Stress inoculation training: A 20-year update. In P. M. Lehrer & R. L. Woolfolk (Eds.), *Principles and practice of stress management* (2nd ed.). New York: Guilford Press.

Murphy, L. R. (1984). Occupational stress management: A review and appraisal. *Journal of Occupational Psychology, 57*, 1–15.

―――― (1996). Stress management in work settings: A critical review. *American Journal of Health Promotion, 11*, 112–135.

Newman, J. E., & Beehr, T. A. (1979). Personal and organizational strategies for handling job stress: A review of research and opinion. *Personnel Psychology, 32*, 1–43.

Orsillo, S. M., & Batten, S. V. (2002). ACT as treatment of a disorder of excessive control: Anorexia. *Cognitive and Behavioral Practice, 9*, 253–259.

Peters, R. K., Benson, H., & Porter, D. (1977). Daily relaxation response breaks in a working population: I. Effects on self-reported measures of health, performance, and well-being: *American Journal of Public Health, 67*, 954–959.

Puryear, K. G., & Hurrell, J. J. (1994). Introduction, *Job stress in a changing workforce.* Washington, DC: American Psychological Association.

Quick, J. C., Quick, J. D., Nelson, D. L., & Hurrell, J. J. (1997). *Preventive stress management in organizations.* Washington, DC: American Psychological Association.

Reynolds, S. (1997). Psychological well-being at work: Is prevention better than cure? *Journal of Psychosomatic Research, 43*, 93–102.

Saunders, T., Driskell, J. E., Johnston, J. H., & Salas, E. (1996). The effect of stress inoculation training on anxiety and performance. *Journal of Occupational Health Psychology, 1*, 170–186.

Segal, Z., Williams, J. M. G., & Teasdale, J. D. (2002). *Mindfulness-based cognitive therapy for depression.* New York: Guilford Press.

van der Klink, J. J. L., Blonk, R. W. B., Schene, A. H., & van Dijk, F. J. H. (2001). The benefits of interventions for work-related stress. *American Journal of Public Health, 91*, 270–276.

Wall, T. D., Bolden, R. I., Borrill, C. S., Carter, A. J., Golya, D. A., Hardy, G. E., *et al.* (1997). Stress in NHS Trust staff: Occupational and gender differences. *British Journal of Psychiatry, 171*, 519–523.

Wall, T. D., & Clegg, C. W. (1981). A longitudinal study of group work redesign. *Journal of Occupational Behavior, 2*, 31–49.

Walser, R. D., & Pistorello, J. (2004). ACT in group format. In S. C. Hayes & K. D. Strosahl (Eds.), *A practical guide to acceptance and commitment therapy.* New York: Springer.

Wegner, D. M., Schneider, D. J., Carter, S. R., & White, T. L. (1987). Paradoxical effects of thought suppression. *Journal of Personality and Social Psychology, 53*, 5–13.

Wegner, D. M., & Zanakos, S. I. (1994). Chronic thought suppression. *Journal of Personality, 62*, 615–640.

Wells, A. (2000). *Emotional disorders and metacognition: Innovative cognitive therapy.* Chichester, UK: Wiley & Sons.

White, J. (2000). *Treating anxiety and stress: A group psycho-educational approach using brief CBT*. Chichester, UK: John Wiley & Sons.

Wolpe, J. (1958). *Psychotherapy by reciprocal inhibition*. Stanford, CA: Stanford University Press.

Woolfolk, R. L., & Lehrer, P. M. (1993). The context of stress management. In authors (Eds.), *Principles and practice of stress management* (2nd ed.). New York: Guilford Press.

AUTHOR INDEX

References in *italics* denote main citation(s).

A

Achenbach, T. M., 150, *165*
Adams, D., 337, 341, *354*
Adcock, A., 169, *187*
Addis, M. E., 68, *73*
Agha, Z., 193, *212*
Agras, W. S., 76, 77, 82, 83, *89, 90, 91, 236*
Ahern, D. K., 197, *212*
Alcaine, O. M., 53, *73*
Alferi, S. M., 242, *257, 258, 259*
Allen, B. P., 193, *212*
Allen, H. N., 79, *89*
Allman, C., 169, *187*
Allmon, D., 184, *188,* 230, *235,* 334, *357*
American Psychiatric Association, 31, *49,* 52, *73,* 75, *89,* 94, *114,* 240, *257*
Andersen, B., 244, *257,* 362
Anderson, D. R., 362, 364, *375*
Anderson, N. D., 224, *233,* 336–338, *355*
Anderson, R. N., 168, *187*
Andrews, J. A., 168, 169, *187*
Andrykowski, M. A., 242, *258*
Angen, M., 254, *258, 260,* 310, *330*
Anglin, K., 339, 348, 351, *355, 356*
Anthony, W. A., 97, *116*
Antoni, M. H., 242, 244, 245, *257, 258, 259, 260*
Antonuccio, D. O., 111, *115*
Appel, S., 374, *375*
Apple, R. A., 77, *89*

A (continued)

Armstrong, H. E., 184, *188,* 230, *235,* 334, *357*
Arndt, L. A., 244, *258*
Arnow, B., 76, *89*
Aro, H. M., 169, *188*
Aron, A., 311, 315, *329*
Aron, E. N., 311, 315, *329*
Aronoff, M., 169, *188*
Astin, J. A., 310, *329*
Averill, P. M., 192, *212*
Aycock, D. W., 378, 379, *401*

B

Babcock, J. C., 334, 337, 339, 341, 342, 352, 354, *355*
Bach, P., 27, 97, 102–106, 109, 111, 286, *305,* 334, *355*
Baer, R. A., 78, 83, *89,* 106, 111, *114, 165,* 218, *233,* 276, *284*
Bagley, H., 194, *212*
Baker, C. A., 106, *116*
Ball, E. M., 184, *189*
Balneaves, L. G., 251, *257*
Baltes, P. B., 220, *234*
Bandura, A., 363, *374*
Barber, J. P., 33, *49*
Barkham, M., 383, *399*
Barksy, A. J., 197, *212*
Barlow, D. H., 52, 60, 67, 72, *73,* 221, 223, *233, 234,* 287, *306*
Barlowe, C., 378, 399, *400*

403

Danoff-Burg, S., 242, *260*
Daston, S., 83, *89*
Daughters, S. D., 224, *234*
Davidson, L. A., 222, *234*
Davidson, R. J., *138,* 276, *284,* 372, 373, *375*
Davis, R. B., 374, *375*
DeBernardo, M., 76, *91*
DeFrank, R. S., 379, *400*
de Graff, R., 193, *213*
Deikman, A. J., 148, *165*
Delbanco, T. L., 374, *375*
DelliCarpini, L. A., 249, *260*
DeMichele, A., 240, *260*
Denton, N., 275, *284*
Depp, C. A., 206, *214*
de Ridder, M. A. J., 184, *189, 236*
Derogatis, L. R., 240, *258, 330*
DeRubeis, R. J., 33, *49*
Detweiler, M., 79, 83, *90*
Devlin, M. J., 76, *91*
De Wilde, E., 168, *188*
Deyo, R., 286, *305*
Diaz, G. A., 362, *375*
DiClemente, C. C., 370, *375*
Dieksta, R., 168, *188*
Dillworth, T. M., 334, *357,* 381, *401*
Dimeff, L. A., 111, *115,* 117, *139,* 184,
    188, 235, *235, 357*
Dimidjian, S., 106, *114*
DiNardo, P. A., 60, *73*
Dohm, F. A., 76, *91*
Drake, R. E., 109, *114*
Driskell, J. E., 379, 380, *401*
DuCette, J., 242, *259*
Dugas, M. J., 67, *73*
DuHamel, K. N., 242, *260*
Dukoff, R., 192, *214*
Dunbar, G. L., 209, *214*
Dunford, F. W., 341, 354, *355*
Dunn, R. L., 362, *375*
Dury, V., 107, *114*
Duthie, E. J. Jr., 193, *212*
Dutton, D. G., 337, 339, *355, 358*
Dyck, M. J., 32, *49*
Dyer, J., 94, *114*

E
Eaton, W. W., 52, *74*
Eccleston, C., 194, *214,* 286, 287, 303, *306*
Eckhardt, C. I., 234, 337, 339, *355*
Edlin, G., 362, *375*
Edwards, C., 275, *284*
Ehrenreich, J. T., 148, *165*

Eifert, G. H., 79, 83, *90*
Eisenberg, D. M., 374, *375*
Eiser, M. P., 239, *260*
Eldredge, K. L., 76, *89*
Elkin, I., 32, *50*
Ellenbogen, M. A., 224, *234*
Elliott, J., 334, 353, *358*
Ellis, A., 379, *400*
Emery, R. E., 334, *355*
Epperson, D. L., 339, *355*
Epsein, M., 270, 272, *284*
Epstein, R. M., 123, *138*
Erber, R., 111, *116*
Erblich, J., 362, *375*
Erikson, E. H., 170, *188,* 195, *213*
Ernst, D., 32, *49*
Ettner, S. L., 374, *375*
Eunson, K. M., 32, *49*
Evans, M. D., 32, *49*

F
Fairburn, C. G., 76, 77, 86, *89, 91*
Fawzy, F. I., 244, 245, *258*
Fawzy, N. W., 244, 245, *258*
Feldman, G., 336, 337, *356*
Fergusson, D. M., 169, *188*
Fetting, J., 240, *258*
Fiebert, M. S., 150, *165*
Figueredo, A. J., 255, *260*
Fillingim, R., 275, *284*
Fincham, F. D., 329, *329*
Fink, B. C., 287, *305*
Fiore, L. B., 151, *165*
Fischer, L. R., 194, *213*
Fischer, S., 78, 83, 169, *189*
Fish, M. C., 151, *165*
Fisher, G., 108, *115*
Fisher, P., 169, *189*
Flasher, L., 242, *259*
Flaxman, P. E., 394, 397, *400*
Fletcher, A. E., 192, *214*
Fletcher, K. E., *194, 213, 214,* 334, *357*
Flint, A. J., 194, 206, *213*
Floyd, F. J., 310, 311, 313, *330*
Foa, E. B., 149, *165*
Fobair, P., 244, 249, *259*
Folkman, S., 378, 379, *400*
Follette, V. M., 24, *27,* 53, 67, *73,* 79, *90,*
    289, *305, 356*
Fonagy, P., 77, *91*
Fontana, D., 151, 161, *165*
Foster, C., 374, *375*
Foster, R., 339, *356*

102–106, 109, 111, 112, *114–116,*
218, 223, *234,* 286, 287, 289, 299,
303, *305,* 333, 334, *355, 356,*
380–383, 386, 390, 392, 393,
397, *399, 400*
Hayhurst, H., 125, *139*
Heagerty, P., 184, *188,* 234, *235*
Health and Safety Executive, 377, *400*
Heaney, C. A., 364, *375*
Heard, H. L., 184, *188,* 230, *235,* 334, *357*
Heatherton, T. F., 78, 81, 82, *90*
Heavey, C. L., 310, 316, 328, *330*
Hebert, J. R., 246, 251–255, *259, 260*
Heckert, D. A., 342, 350, 351, *356*
Heffner, M., 79, 83, *90*
Heimberg, R. G., 54, *74*
Henggeler, S. W., 169, *188*
Henriksson, M. M., 169, *188*
Herbert, J. D., 102, 105–108, *114, 116*
Herman, C., 81, *90*
Hernández, B., 304, *306*
Herron, K., 334, 339, *356*
Herzog, D. B., 76, *90*
Hetherington, M., 78, 81, *90*
Heun, R., 205, *213*
Heyman, R. E., 340, *357*
Hiday, V. A., 109, *116*
Hiebert, B., 151, *165*
Himmelfarb, S., 192, *214*
Hollon, S. D., 16, *27,* 32, 34, *49,* 225, 230,
234, 235
Holtzworth-Munroe, A., 334, 338, 339,
348, 351, 354, *355–357*
Hooker, C., 240, *261*
Hopkins, J., 76, *90*
Houts, P. S., 249, *260*
Howland, R. H., 225, *236*
Hu, S., 53, *73*
Huey, S. J., 169, *188*
Hugo, M., 108, *115*
Humphrey, J. H., 151, *165*
Huppert, J. D., 125, *139,* 185, *189*
Hurrell, J. J., 362, *375,* 377, 379, *401*
Hurt, S. W., 169, *188*
Huss, D. B., 83, *89*
Hutchinson, G., 338, *356*

I
Iacovino, V., 244, *259*
Imber, S. D., 32, *50*
Ingram, R. E., 33, 34, *49, 50*
Ironson, G., 244, 245, *260*
Isometsa, E. T., 169, *188*

Ivanoff, A., 184, *189*
Iverson, K. M., 338, *356*

J
Jackson, J., 194, *213*
Jacobsen, B. S., 242, *259*
Jacobson, N. S., 68, *73,* 95, *115,* 310, *330,*
339, *355*
Jarzobski, D., 255, *260*
Jeffrey, R., 76, *91*
Jersild, A. T., 224, *234*
Jewell, A., 195, *213*
Jex, S. M., 379, *400*
Jha, A., 151
John, O. P., 122, 124, *138*
Johnson, B. A., 169, *187*
Johnson, M. P., 334, *357*
Johnston, J. H., 379, 380, *401*
Jones, A. S., 352, *357*
Jones, G. N., 365, *375*
Jones, R., 192, *214*
Jorm, A. F., 108, *114*
Judd, L. J., 32, *49,* 192, 193, *213, 214*
Juipers, E., 110, *116*

K
Kabat-Zinn, J., 3–6, *27,* 41, 57, 63, *73,* 123,
138, 154, 161, *165,* 191, *194,* 196, 197,
200, 203, 207, *213, 214,* 218, 230, 231,
234, 246, 247, 249, 251–254, 255, *259,*
260, 270, 272, 275, 276, 282, *284,*
310–312, 322, 327, *330,* 334, *357,* 369,
371–373, *375*
Kagee, A., 240, *260*
Kane, R. L., 339, *355*
Kanter, J. W., 111, *115,* 184, *188,*
235, 352, *357*
Kaplan, J., 362, *375*
Karney, B. R., 309, *330*
Kaslow, N. J., 144, *165*
Kass, J. D., 315, *330*
Katona, C., 194, *213*
Katz, L. Y., *139,* 185, *188*
Katz, R. C., 242, *259*
Katzman, R., 207, *213*
Kazdin, A. E., 349, *357*
Keefe, P., 76, *90*
Keefer, F. J., 275, *284,* 287, 306
Keller, M. B., 76, *90*
Kendall, P. C., 16, *27,* 147, *165*
Kessler, R. C., 52, *74,* 374, *375,* 377, *400*
Kienhorst, C., 168, *188*
Kilbourn, K. M., 242, *257, 258*

SUBJECT INDEX